ECONOMICS
A CRITICAL APPROACH

ECONOMICS
A
CRITICAL APPROACH

M. A. G. VAN MEERHAEGHE
Professor of Economics
at the University of Ghent

WEIDENFELD AND NICOLSON
5 Winsley Street London W1

ISBN 0 297 00361 5 Casebound
ISBN 0 297 00497 2 Paperback

Printed in Great Britain by
Cox and Wyman Ltd
London, Fakenham and Reading

Il est plus aisé de dire des choses nouvelles que de concilier celles qui ont été dites.

Vauvenargues

Contents

PART 2 HOUSEHOLDS AND FIRMS

CONTENTS

CONTENTS

APPENDIX: ECONOMIC DOCTRINES

CONTENTS

List of Abbreviations

AER	The American Economic Review
BSUN	United Nations Monthly Bulletin of Statistics
Ec	Economica
Em	Econometrica
EI	Economia Internazionale
EJ	The Economic Journal
JPE	The Journal of Political Economy
Ky	Kyklos
OEP	Oxford Economic Papers
PE	Problems of Economics
QJE	The Quarterly Journal of Economics
REP	Revue d'Economie Politique
RES	The Review of Economics and Statistics
RESt	The Review of Economic Studies
RISEC	Rivista Internazionale di Scienze Economiche e Commerciali
SP	International Monetary Fund Staff Papers
WA	Weltwirtschaftliches Archiv
ZN	Zeitschrift für Nationalökonomie
ZS	Zeitschrift für die Gesamte Staatswissenschaft
BIS	Bank for International Settlements
EAEC	European Atomic Energy Community
ECSC	European Coal and Steel Community
EEC	European Economic Community
EFTA	European Free Trade Association
EIB	European Investment Bank
EMA	European Monetary Agreement
EPU	European Payments Union
GATT	General Agreement on Tariffs and Trade
IBRD	International Bank for Reconstruction and Development
IMF	International Monetary Fund
OECD	Organization for Economic Cooperation and Development
OEEC	Organization for European Economic Cooperation
UNCTAD	United Nations Conference on Trade and Development

List of Symbols

We have normally used the universally acceptable symbols. Where this has not been done, the reason is to avoid using the same symbol for different meanings. Capitals denote variables in money terms and lower-case letters denote coefficients. Where it seemed preferable to use the same letter for two different notions, it is followed by an asterisk in one of the two cases. In a few instances, this was not necessary because mathematical context ruled out any possibility of confusion (e.g. $i = 1, \ldots, m; t = 1, \ldots, t$). Capitals with an accent denote variables in real terms, while a bar over the letter denotes an arithmetic mean. Use of the same letter with more than one connotation has also been avoided in the subscripts. The letters used for subscripts are in no way related to those which are not. The following list does not include conventional mathematical notations (e.g. d: differentiation operator; ∂: partial differentiation operator; Δ: first difference operator; Σ: summation operator; f: function).

C Consumption
$\quad C_h$ household consumption
$\qquad C_{he}$ household consumption purchased from enterprises
$\qquad C_{hg}$ household consumption purchased from government
$\quad C_g$ government consumption
$\qquad C_{ge}$ government consumption purchased from enterprises
$\quad C_z$ constant part of consumption
$\quad C_l$ consumption in the long term
D Depreciation
$\quad D_e$ depreciation of enterprises
$\quad D_g$ depreciation of government
D^* Demand
$\quad D_{\lambda i}^*$ final demand of industry i
E Exports (broad sense)
$\quad E_a$ exports of goods and services
$\quad E_b$ compensation to residents by the rest of the world

E_{bg} compensation to government

E_{bh} compensation to households

E $E_a + E_b\,(+\,V_f)$

F Factor services

G Government

G_o government expenditure

G_t government receipts

H Cost (total)

H_e total fixed cost

H_v total variable cost

H_d differential (or incremental) cost (per unit)

H_μ marginal cost

H^* Hoarding

I Investment

I_α net investment

$I_{\alpha e}$ net investment of enterprises

$I_{\alpha g}$ net investment of government

I_β gross investment

$I_{\beta e}$ gross investment of enterprises

$I_{\beta g}$ gross investment of government

I^t induced investment

I_ρ replacement investment

I_z constant part of investment

J Purchases by enterprises

J_{eg} purchases by enterprises from government

K Capital

L Labour

M Imports (broad sense)

M_a imports of goods and services ($M_a = M_{ae} + M_{ah}$)

M_{ae} imports of goods and services by enterprises

M_{ah} imports of goods and services by households

M_b compensation to foreigners

M $M_a + M_b\,(+\,V_f)$

M_z constant part of imports

M^* Money supply

M_1^* notes and coin

M_2^* deposit money

N Terms of trade

P Price

P_L price of labour

P_K price of capital
P_E average export price
P_M average import price
P_S exchange rate
P^* General price level
Q Quantity
R Revenue (total)
R_μ marginal revenue
R_d differential (or incremental) revenue
R^* Interest payments
R_g^* interest payments by government
S Saving
S_α net saving
$S_{\alpha e}$ net saving of enterprises
$S_{\alpha g}$ net saving of government
$S_{\alpha h}$ net saving of households
S_β gross saving
S^* Supply
T Taxes
T_i indirect taxes
T_j direct taxes
T_{je} direct taxes paid by enterprises
T_{jh} direct taxes paid by households
T^* Quantities traded
U Utility
U_μ marginal utility
V Transfer payments
V_f transfer payments from and to the rest of the world
V_{hf} transfer payments to households from the rest of the world
V_{hg} transfer payments to households from government
V^* Velocity of circulation of money
V_1^* velocity of circulation of notes and coin
V_2^* velocity of circulation of deposit money
W Subsidy
X Production
X_α net national product (at factor cost)
X_α^d net domestic product (at factor cost)
$X_{\alpha m}$ net national product (at market prices)
$X_{\alpha m}^d$ net domestic product (at market prices)

LIST OF SYMBOLS

	X_β	gross national product (at factor cost)
	$X_{\beta m}$	gross national product (at market prices)
	X_L	production with labour
	X_K	production with capital
Y	Income	

$Y_\eta = X_\alpha$ earned national income

Y_h household income from productive activities

Y_{he} compensation of factor services by enterprises

Y_{hf} compensation of factor services by the rest of the world (E_{bh})

Y_{hg} compensation of factor services by government

$Y_{h\delta}$ disposable income of households

Y_{gf} government income from the rest of the world (E_{bg})

$Y_m = X_{\alpha m}$ (national income at market prices)

Y_π personal income

Y_ψ received national income

Z Constant value (quantity) or term

b Average resting time of money

c Propensity to consume

c_μ marginal propensity to consume

e Elasticity

$e_{Q_i P_i}$ direct price elasticity of demand

$e_{Q_i P_j}$ cross elasticity

$e_{Q_i Y_i}$ income elasticity

e_E elasticity of external demand for own exports

e_M elasticity of domestic demand for imports

f Productivity

f_L average labour productivity

$f_{L\mu}$ marginal labour productivity

f_K average capital productivity

$f_{K\mu}$ marginal capital productivity

g Growth rate of national income

g^* Growth rate of average national income

h Cost (sequences): $h_1, h_2 \ldots h_n$

i Propensity to invest

i_μ marginal propensity to invest

k Capital coefficient

k_d differential capital coefficient

l Labour coefficient

l_a	differential labour-output ratio
$l*$	Percentage change in labour supply
m	Propensity to import
m_μ	marginal propensity to import
o	Technological or input coefficient
p	Prices (sequences): $p_1, p_2, \ldots p_n$
q	Quantities (sequences): $q_1, q_2, \ldots q_n$
r	Market interest
$r*$	Target rate of interest
$r**$	Internal interest
s	Propensity to save
s_μ	marginal propensity to save
t	Tax rate
v	Accelerator
w	Multiplier
w_E	export multiplier

Preface

This is a translation of *Economie: Een kritisch handboek* (Stenfert Kroese, Leiden 1970), which is basically the sixth edition of my *Handboek van de economie* (A Manual of Economics), published in 1966. The new title is intended to reflect the more systematically critical approach I have adopted to accepted theory.

Writing an introduction to economics is a thankless task. The author is obliged to keep up to the best of his ability with the literature of all branches of the subject – an arduous enough undertaking – but the end product is still regarded as 'merely' an introduction. Since there are already plenty of introductory texts in this field, some justification is required for producing yet another. In this book I have tried to take a more critical – my colleagues would say 'sceptical' or even 'cynical' – view of traditional theory. Conventional textbooks give the student too much the impression that economics is an exact science: the graphs, the algebra and the formulas enable him to work out precise solutions to economic problems. Before long, however, he realizes that much of the theory he has been taught is of little or no practical use to him. He knows nothing, for example, of the fundamental problems of the firm, though he is very well versed in drawing the most complicated graphs which have little bearing on reality.

Most economists live almost in a dream-world. They are a kind of sect engaging in mental gymnastics – impressive on occasion – in their own cabalistic language. They lose sight of the fact that what is important is the analysis and interpretation of the real world. Should some spoil-sport point out that their theories do not fit the facts, then they are inclined, like Zeno, to retort: 'So much the worse for the facts!'

If there were no 'conventional wisdom' I should have written this book differently, devoting more attention, for instance, to the economics of the firm. But I had to bear in mind that the student is constantly coming up against the conventional theory in the literature and that his examiners expect him to be familiar with it.

I have endeavoured to be concise. The criticism will perhaps be levelled against me that because of this there are parts of the text that will be immediately intelligible only to the better students. This I do not consider a valid objection: a course in economics is not intended as light reading matter, after all. Furthermore, without some attempt to be succinct a book such as this may turn out to be excessively long, and the attendant risk is that the reader will find it difficult to follow the author's line of argument – as in certain American manuals. In the bibliographies too I have generally mentioned only the most recent works. To cater for English and American readers, on the whole unfamiliar with foreign languages, I have left out – with a few exceptions – the literature in languages other than English.

Some words may be useful about the structure of the book. Following an introduction (Chapter 1), Chapter 2 sets out to give an overall picture of the relations between the principal groups of economic units. This is not easy and requires unremitting attention; in order to define a wide variety of major concepts, distinctions have to be drawn between a great many types of transactions.

Thus the way is opened up for an analysis of the separate groups of economic units. On account of its major significance in exchange, however, money must have priority of treatment. This it is given in Chapter 3.

Part 2 deals with households (Chapter 4) and firms (Chapters 5 and 6), and in particular examines the factors influencing these two groups' decisions. From here we can go on to study price and income determination (Part 3). The first step is to ascertain how the different prices and incomes find their respective levels (Chapters 7 and 8). The principles underlying price determination have to be known in order to account for the level of the national product and of the *overall* price level (Chapter 9). Attention is also devoted to the factors determining the growth of the national product (Chapter 10).

Up to this point, discussion is in the context of a 'closed economy'. In Part 4, an investigation is conducted into the repercussions of external economic relations (Chapters 11 and 12). This brings us finally to a chapter on the forms of action open to the government (Chapter 13).

In an appendix, a concise survey is given of the most important lines of economic thought, this being intended particularly for students not studying the various doctrines individually and yet possibly requiring an understanding of the leading economic schools. We think it is pointless for the study of economics to begin with the various schools of economic thought because the student is not yet in a position to grasp the judgments arrived at by these schools. After all, the study of mathematics does not start with the history of the subject.

These details on the content of the book show that I am not enthusiastic about dividing the subject matter into macroeconomics and microeconomics – a distinction which is very difficult to maintain in practice.

Since we know that the Dutch edition of this book is also used for reference purposes we have included sections on linear programming (Chapter 5.11), input-output analysis (Chapter 13.2a), etc., which can be omitted without impairing the understanding of the text as a whole.

My thanks are due to those persons who were kind enough to read and comment on the manuscript – Dr J. Koolschijn and my assistant Mr J. de Buck for the Dutch version, Dr G. Denton, Reader in Economics at the University of Reading, for the English version.

I am indebted to the team who produced the English translation in a relatively short space of time. Mr John Cairns, FIL, translated Chapters 1–3, 11 and 12 and the Appendix, Mr Dudley Cobb, MA, Chapter 7, Mr Robert Leslie, BA, Chapter 5, Mr Leonard Scott, MA, Chapters 4, 6, 10 and 13 and the Concluding Remarks, and Mr Frank Winter, MA, Chapters 8 and 9. Mr Scott also read the whole text for the purposes of uniformity of style; in addition to the linguistic observations he made, there were also a number of points at which he supplemented the text with specifically British material.

Finally, I am grateful to my assistants for their cooperation in the production of this book. Mr F. Dernicourt, Mr A. Eggermont and Mr F. Willockx helped the translators in tracking down economic terms. Mr P. Visser undertook to compile the indexes and Mr A. Eggermont checked many bibliographical details; both came up with a large number of suggestions from which the text has benefited.

My thanks are also due to my wife who gave useful assistance at every stage in this project.

PART 1

Introduction

1 Basic concepts

In the social sciences it all too frequently happens that the same terms are used to cover different concepts. It is accordingly advisable to start by closely defining the basic concepts involved.

We begin, therefore, by defining the term 'economics', although a really satisfactory definition of a science can only be given after the relevant subject-matter has been duly analysed.

Since the bulk of this chapter, then, is given over to definition, this will perhaps make for rather dull reading; this procedure, however, will relieve us of the need to break up the flow of the ensuing chapters by introducing these definitions.

1 A definition of economics

Economics is the science which studies human efforts to satisfy wants with scarce resources.

a. Wants and scarce resources

Wants, or the desire for certain things, are legion. Those of a physiological nature are all-important, as non-satisfaction endangers human life. Cultural wants, however, must not be underrated: they have increased considerably, although food requirements, being more diversified, have also undergone an expansion. Non-biological needs in particular are conditioned by the customs and habits of the society in which we live.

The means of satisfying our numerous wants, namely goods and services, are only available in a limited degree. The fertility of the soil and accessible minerals are not inexhaustible; nor is the time available for producing the desired goods and services unlimited. The fact that human endeavours to satisfy wants are performed with the aid of scarce resources is a distinctive feature of economic science. Scarce

3

resources may be defined as resources the desired quantity of which would exceed the available quantity if they were freely available.

O. Lange's definition of economics ('. . . the science of administration of scarce resources in human society') also serves to remind us that the economic problem (the restriction imposed by the scarcity of resources) must be examined in the context of society. In a certain sense this is self-evident: the satisfaction of individual wants cannot be studied as something quite apart from human society, which is based so largely on specialization (the production of a particular good or a particular type of good), and consequently on exchange. The Robinson Crusoe household is of little interest to economic science.

From what has been said above it follows that we are obliged to establish a system of priorities in our attempts to satisfy our wants. This is necessary even in countries where such choices are made by government.

That resources can be put to alternative uses is underlined in the definitions by L. Robbins ('. . . the science which studies human behaviour as a relationship between ends and scarce means which have alternative uses') and P. Hennipman ('. . . the science which studies a specific category of options, namely the employment of scarce goods for which there are alternative uses').

b. Are resources scarce?

It is sometimes claimed that all human wants could be satisfied if, say, the population increase were kept within certain limits, wants were not stimulated artificially (e.g. by advertising), there were no wastage (unemployment) or unprofitable use of resources (e.g. for the armed forces), compulsory labour service were introduced, and goods and services were equally distributed. This may be true, as regards biological needs at least, but it would involve organizing society in such a way that individual freedom would be drastically curtailed, and in particular that there would be too little scope for choice (no variety in production).

c. The difficulty of formulating a definition

A great many definitions of economics have been advanced during the past two centuries. In the USSR a definition is accepted in which Karl Marx's historical materialism (Appendix 6) finds expression, namely 'the science which studies the laws concerning the production

4

and distribution of goods during the successive stages in the development of society'.

Without subscribing to W. Eucken's characterization of the war of words among the champions of the multifarious definitions as a '*nutzloser Streit*' (futile struggle), one is forced to admit that all these reflections, some of which have a highly philosophical flavour, have brought little grist to the mill.

d. Economics and the other sciences

Economic phenomena form part of a larger complex of phenomena. Of this complex as such, history sets out to portray a coherent picture. The other social sciences, such as economics, investigate specific aspects of it. Sociology, for instance, 'studies the general and abiding aspects of the reciprocal relations between the activities of men in their dealings with their fellow-men' (J. P. Haesaert).

Hence it is that the explanation of economic phenomena nearly always necessitates recourse to other sciences (especially sociology, history and psychology).

e. Economy

Economics must not be confused with 'economy', the satisfaction of the wants in a given country or area (e.g. the economy of the United Kingdom). Political economy was the common name for economics until recent years. Nowadays it is used to indicate the study of the interrelationship of political and economic processes.

f. The subject matter of this book

This book concerns the study of general economics, with the exception of special areas such as public finance, agricultural economics, transport economics and business economics. The last-named field deals with the firm's economic activity (Chapter 5.1). Social economics is sometimes defined as relating to the social aspects of economic activity, but this makes it difficult to distinguish from general economics.

Also dealt with are the principles of theoretical economics, while concrete, descriptive data are regularly furnished on the economies of specific countries (descriptive economics).

From time to time we will dwell on a particular form of economic policy, but no systematic outline of this is given until the end of the book (Chapter 13). Economic policy covers the economic aspects of general or government policy, by which is meant the line of action followed by the government in order to achieve specific aims.

2 Wants and welfare

a. Wants

A person's desire to possess a certain thing (Section 1) derives from his realization that he lacks that thing and is therefore of a subjective nature. In some of the less-developed countries there is no actual want for goods conducive to hygiene. Wants sometimes have to be fostered. Economics does not ascertain whether such wants are or are not detrimental. It takes them for granted – in contrast with psychology, which concerns itself with the 'why' and the 'wherefore'.

Foremost among the salient features is satiability. Even though wants, viewed as a whole, constantly increase, they are individually limited in volume and satiable. (The fact that the craving for money is unlimited does not constitute an exception, as money provides the means of satisfying all wants.) This applies particularly to essential but also to luxury goods.

Experience has shown that most wants are susceptible of substitution: if it becomes difficult or impossible to satisfy a given want with a particular commodity, efforts are made to find a substitute. This happens when the first commodity is unavailable or too expensive (e.g. coffee and chicory, natural and synthetic rubber). Some of these substitutes continue to be felt as wants even after the circumstances which gave rise to substitution have ceased to operate (chicory). Substitutability is slight in the case of physiological needs (bread) but greater in the case of less essential wants (theatre and cinema).

b. Welfare (*standard of living*)

A distinction is sometimes made between the level of living (actual living conditions), the standard of living (anticipated living conditions), and the norm of living (desirable living conditions), though 'standard of living' is commonly used to signify any or all of these.

The definition of welfare or the standard of living may be conceived in broad or in narrow terms. In the narrow or strictly economic sense, what is meant is the extent to which wants are satisfied. Both the material and the immaterial aspects have to be taken into consideration. Indicators are, for example, health (expectation of life at birth), education (number of children attending school), working conditions (length of work week) and employment (number of unemployed). In the wider sense, 'welfare' is more subjective: greater satisfaction of wants does not necessarily bring more happiness. Moreover, the term becomes relative, since a wage increase which enables more wants to be satisfied or produces more leisure is often not regarded by the beneficiaries as an increase in welfare if it is equivalent to or less than that enjoyed by other wage earners.

3 Goods

Goods are all things by means of which wants can be directly or indirectly satisfied.

a. Utility

The ability to satisfy a want directly or indirectly is called the utility of a good. In other words, a good *has* utility. But utility can also be defined as what results from the use of a good, in which case a good *provides* utility.

This is subjective (or economic) utility. Alcohol, cigarettes and other harmful commodities are useful from an economic standpoint. (Hence V. Pareto introduced a new designation for utility, namely 'ophelimity'.) Objective utility is the capacity of a good to enable a specific objective result to be achieved (1 lb of coal yields x calories). Sometimes goods which have no objective utility are nevertheless desired (certain drugs and cosmetics).

b. Types of goods

Goods can be subdivided according to various criteria: free and economic, durable and non-durable, divisible and indivisible, consumer and capital, private and public goods. Sometimes a distinction is made between goods which are arbitrarily multipliable and those which are not (paintings).

1. Free goods are goods available in abundance for the satisfaction of wants (air). They are not objects of exchange. Economic goods are not available to an unlimited extent: an effort is needed to acquire them. Scarce articles are not, of course, goods if they are not felt to satisfy wants (meteorites). Depending on circumstances, a good may be free or economic (water in the desert). Hereinafter the word 'good' is used in the sense of an economic good.

2. Services performed by persons and institutions may be

7

considered immaterial goods. When we refer to 'goods' in this text, the term usually embraces services.

3. Durable goods can be used many times over (clothing, factories); non-durable goods can only be used once (bread, iron ore, slaughter cattle).

4. Divisible goods can be divided into small quantities without suffering any impairment of their utility (water, raw materials). Indivisible goods (a machine, a bicycle) cannot.

5. Consumer goods satisfy human desires directly (bread, foot-wear, clothing). Capital goods are used to produce other goods, whether consumer or other capital goods (fuel, railways, factories). The need for them is not directly felt by the consumer (though it is by the enterprise: Section 7). Hence the phrase 'directly *or indirectly*' in the definition of 'goods'. By convention, all stocks – including those of consumer goods which have not yet been delivered to households (cf. Section 7) – are deemed to be capital goods.

Capital goods may be durable or non-durable. If they are durable, they can be used in various production processes – machines, fac-tories, railways. They are supposed to have a working life of at least one year. If they are non-durable, they are either used up or destroyed during the first production processes. Direct (raw) materials (cotton, ores) are used up, or processed; that is to say, they are to be found in the end product. Indirect materials (oil, coal), on the other hand, are consumed (used and destroyed during production). Accessory materials are raw materials only small quantities of which are required for production purposes (e.g. thread in the clothing industry).

In practice, classification into capital and consumer goods is not always an easy matter. Dwellings – durable consumer goods – can be leased, the owner acting in the capacity of head of an enterprise or production unit (Section 7); he supplies utilities or 'residential ser-vices'. Dwellings are accordingly deemed to be capital goods even if occupied by their owners, who are themselves assumed to pay the rent and collect the proceeds. Similar difficulties arise in the case of motor vehicles. (Only vehicles used in industry are regarded as being capital goods.) Roads, hospitals and schools are likewise classed as capital goods, since they are also used to provide services.

6. Private and public goods satisfy individual and social wants respectively. As a rule the latter are not felt directly as wants by the individual (administrative buildings, hospitals). Sometimes the term 'collective wants' is used as a synonym for social wants, though it is

also used to signify the needs of institutions (excluding government agencies), such as trade unions.

4 Value and price

By reason of its utility, a good has a use value. Here, as in the case of utility, a distinction must be made between an objective and a subjective use value: whereas the former is the same for everyone (a certain objective result is achieved), the latter differs from person to person on account of the varying importance attached to the good in question (cf. the cosmetics example quoted above).

The exchange value of a good is the power of that good to make possible the acquisition of other goods by means of exchange transactions. Since there can be no exchange value without a use value, the former is influenced by the latter.

In contradistinction to the subjective use value (intensity of feeling), the exchange value of a good is measurable, being expressed by the value of the goods for which the good in question can be exchanged. For this purpose it is customary to use money, which is a generally accepted means of exchange (Chapter 3.4).

The usual or generally accepted (objective) exchange relationship does not necessarily reflect the views of all the parties concerned in the transaction; some of them may consider it favourable and others unfavourable (subjective as opposed to objective exchange value).

The objective exchange value expressed in terms of money is called the price of a good. Prices can either be determined by the free play of supply and demand or else fixed by the entrepreneurs or the authorities. Through the existence of money and prices, exchange, and consequently the allocation of resources among wants, is facilitated.

Just as the objective exchange value of the unit of a good or group of goods is indicated by the number of money units (price) that have to be paid for it, so is the objective exchange value of the money unit expressed by the quantity of goods that can be obtained for it. Comparison with a single good achieves no purpose, as the purchasing power of money may fall in relation to one good and rise in relation to another. The purchasing power of a money unit must therefore be determined with respect to all goods.

The more goods that can be purchased with this money unit, the greater is the value of the money. The higher the prices, the smaller is the number of goods that can be bought with a money unit. The value

9

of money is consequently the reciprocal of the overall price level (which reflects the various prices in a given country), the trend of which is gauged by means of index numbers.

Price indices

Index numbers facilitate comparison of a specific series of figures; one of these numbers is assigned the value 100 and the others are calculated proportionately (Table 1).

TABLE 1: Wholesale price of electrolytic copper in absolute figures and index numbers 1963–9 (1963 = 100)

Year	United Kingdom[a]		United States[b]	
	£ per long ton	Index numbers	Cents per kg	Index numbers
1963	234	100	67·4	100
1964	351	150	70·5	104
1965	468	200	77·1	114
1966	555	237	79·7	118
1967	418	178	84·1	124
1968	526	224	92·4	137
1969	621	264	105·0	156

[a] Domestic import price, standard electrolytic wirebars, spot price ex-warehouse, London
[b] Domestic price f.o.b., ex-works, wirebars and ingots
Source: Calculated on the basis of BSUN, November 1970, p. 173

A great many questions arise in the determination of price indices. As it is impossible to take account of every single price, it is necessary to be selective. The importance of the various commodities varies from person to person, from country to country, and from period to period. This can be remedied by weighting the various prices, which means assigning a 'weight' to each of them. Instead of determining straight away the average (11) of, for instance, 9, 11 and 13, these prices are first multiplied by their weights, $9 \times 3 = 27$; $11 \times 5 = 55$; $13 \times 2 = 26$; $27 + 55 + 26 = 108$; 108: 10 (the sum of the weights) $= 10·8$.

It is further necessary to ascertain whether the quality of the products remains the same. The base period must not be too far back and must be a 'normal' one; in order to eliminate the influence of residual factors, the mean value for several years is frequently adopted. Furthermore, the mean value selected is important: the arithmetic mean is invariably greater than the geometric mean.

On account of the heterogeneity of the goods to be incorporated, however, index numbers relating to the 'overall' price level are omitted in favour of those for the principal groups (raw materials, wholesale and retail commodities).

5 Production and the factors of production

By production is meant the creation of utilities – in other words, the creation of goods (and services). It follows that the storage and transport of goods are also productive activities. Utility ceases to exist with the final satisfaction of the relevant wants, or upon consumption of the relevant goods or services. (The 'quasi-consumption' or 'technical consumption' of capital goods in the production process is not identified with economic consumption.) In the communist countries, most services (government, trade) are not considered to be productive, so transfer incomes (Chapter 2.3) are paid to the workers concerned.

In order to define production and consumption as accurately as possible, productive performances within households (see Section 7) are left out of account (e.g. ironing of linen, preparation of meals). There are certain exceptions to this principle (paid staff). For the same reason, consumption is deemed to correspond to consumption expenditures (i.e. the goods purchased do not need to be consumed immediately).

Traders buy and sell goods without using them up or processing them themselves. They can be divided into distributive and collecting traders. Whereas the latter buy primary products (e.g. vegetables and milk) and deliver them to industry, the former's function is distribution to the final consumer. This is done by the wholesaler (distributive wholesale trade) and the retailer (retail trade). By intermediate trade is meant any trade situated between the producer and the consumer. It is not a synonym for distribution because it embraces, for instance, imports and exports.

Production requires in particular the cooperation of what are called the factors of production, namely labour, land and capital (see Chapter 5.1 and 6.1 on the role of the entrepreneur). In communist literature, only labour is mentioned in this connection, together with

11

subjects of labour (natural resources, raw materials) and instruments of labour (buildings, roads).

a. Land
In order not to depart from normal usage the term 'land' will be used, even when the reference is to all natural resources.

By making its resources available free of charge, nature plays a part in the production process. Rain, wind and sun are not always regarded as components of this production factor, because man cannot exercise any control over them. They must, however, be viewed as an integrated part of nature.

One of the salient features of land is the fact that it cannot be increased or reduced (although reclamation, for example, can be instanced as an exception to this statement). The reference here is not, of course, to the fertility of the soil. Fertile regions have sometimes degenerated into deserts, and arid regions have been made to flourish.

While the contribution of land to production – unlike that of the other factors – does not as a general rule involve costs, it should be added that this applies only to natural advantages. Natural fertility can be increased by artificial means, and this does incur costs.

b. Labour
Labour as a factor of production is human activity employed in the production process. Games or sport are *ipso facto* ruled out – except where they are pursued professionally. Labour is the active and the principal factor, without which nothing can be accomplished.

The distinction between manual labour and brainwork is based on the preponderance of the one or the other. In manual labour, a distinction is made between skilled and unskilled work (whether or not training is required). In point of fact, the mental aspect of work is the dominant one, since sheer muscular strength and simple control operations can be replaced by machines. Precisely because of the intellectual character of work, 'organization' must, in our view, be rejected as a fourth factor of production. In the organizer and the entrepreneur the intellectual aspect finds more expression, but no fundamental difference compared with other types of labour can be demonstrated.

c. Capital
In primitive society, efforts were already being made at a very early

stage to step up production by indirect means, i.e. by producing durable instruments such as arrows, axes and fishing nets. Such instruments have already been listed above as capital goods. As capital is formed by the combined action of land and labour (the original factors) it is called the derived factor of production. In contrast with the original factors, however, this one is reproducible.

At the present time, practically all goods are produced with capital, which is thus considered to be a third, equivalent, factor of production. There is an ever-increasing trend towards classifying land itself under the head of capital. No fundamental difference exists between land, which was believed to be free and permanent, and capital, which is produced and non-permanent. Cultivation changes the soil into capital, and in consequence it is no longer possible to make any distinction between the original benefits of land and the properties resulting from improvements effected by human agency. Moreover, natural resources are not always permanent (erosion). Sometimes even labour is regarded as capital (because education is invested in skilled labour, and labour is becoming more and more a matter of skills).

Replacement and net (extension) investment
Since capital has a limited life, it has to be replaced after a given period. The gradual wear and tear should be accompanied by the accumulation of the necessary funds (depreciation allowances) for the purchase of new capital goods (replacement investment) superseding the existing capital goods. When we speak of a country's gross and net product, we mean its output including and excluding replacement investment.

Depreciation allowances, which make replacement investment possible, are conditioned by the working life of the relevant capital goods. If a machine costing £50,000 is in the normal course worn out after five years, this means that £10,000 must be kept in reserve each year. If after three years a new invention is put on the market and the existing machine thus ceases to be competitive, the depreciation period may be reduced from five to three years corresponding to the technical as distinct from the economic working life. Because the economic working life is difficult to estimate, the required annual amount of depreciation allowances cannot be accurately determined.

Net investment has the effect of increasing the existing stock of capital goods. In most cases, replacement investment also gives rise to some net investment – for example, a new machine usually has a greater production capacity – so that the difference between the two types of investment is not always easy to determine.

In a *stationary economy*, i.e. an economy in which the population, technological knowledge and production do not change, the means of production are replaced, when the depreciation process has been completed, by comparable means having the same value.

In a *growing economy*, where production *per capita* is (continuously) increasing, the usual tendency is to purchase means of production which yield higher or better results (intensive investment as against extensive investment). Depreciation can then be used to finance net investment in whole or in part. In such a case, production rises at a faster rate than the population through the application of improved technology. The economy can also be expanded while technological knowledge remains unchanged – that is, where the rise in production exceeds that of the population (through the introduction of unused factors of production) or where the population decreases while production remains at the same level.

d. Three factors of production?

It must not be forgotten that production is not determined by the three 'classical' factors alone. Stable political and social conditions, initiative of the people, social and economic mobility, for example, are equally necessary (cf. Chapter 10.7*d*). Such 'non-economic' factors are as important as the purely 'economic' factors.

Furthermore, to restrict the factors of production to three or two is a bold simplification. Both skilled and unskilled labour have countless subdivisions (what are called the 'non-competing groups'). Capital goods also assume many differing forms. (Only in the case of money capital can there be said to be more homogeneity.) Natural resources (e.g. ores, woods, hydroelectric facilities) are of varying types, which are very unevenly distributed. Agricultural land is to be found everywhere, but it too can be classified into thousands of categories.

e. The production function

Production X' may be considered a function of – that is, to be determined by – the quantity and the quality of the factors of production. If we assume that there are only two factors, labour L' and capital K', then the production function, which represents the technical relation

14

between the quantity of the good produced and the quantity of the factors employed, is expressed as follows:

$$X' = f(L', K').$$

The function may relate to a firm, an industry or an economy. It can thus be expressed in both micro and macroeconomic terms (see Chapter 5.4b).

Whereas microeconomic data and problems relate solely to individual enterprises or commodities (e.g. determination of the price of a product), macroeconomic data, which are derived from the combination of microeconomic data (aggregation: Chapter 4.6), relate to the entire economy (e.g. total production, total consumption). The term 'macroeconomics' was introduced in 1933 by R. Frisch.

6 Capital: other meanings

'Capital' is used in other senses still. In order to avoid misunderstanding, it is variously referred to as social (the capital goods produced), lucrative, legal, business and paid-up capital. As with many other economic concepts, however, terminological confusion abounds. Thus when some economists speak of social capital, what they have in mind is the means of production in the public sector. It is therefore always necessary to ascertain which definition is preferred, or adopted, by the writer.

a. Lucrative capital

Lucrative capital consists in goods which are a source of income to the owner (in other words, which yield him a specific sum of money or the equivalent over a certain period). Ownership of capital goods can provide an income as remuneration for the contribution made to the production process (interest: Chapter 8.6) in countries where possession of capital goods by private persons is allowed. Partial ownership (shares; Chapter 5.2) affords the same advantages (dividend: Chapter 5.2). The making available of money (claims) – money capital or loan capital – gives entitlement to income.

In most cases, the terms social and lucrative capital overlap. The leasing of machinery provides the owner with an income; the machinery in question is also social capital. Shares in a limited company (Chapter 5.2) usually represent social capital. Certainly the proceeds of a debenture loan (Chapter 5.2) can be used to acquire social

15

capital, but this is not necessarily the case (consumer credit: Chapter 3.6). Consumer goods may also be a source of income.

b. Legal capital

Lucrative capital must not be confused with legal capital, the latter simply evidencing the possession of a right of ownership of certain goods but not connoting the idea of income. Thus an unoccupied house is legal capital without being lucrative capital. Generally speaking, however, legal capital and lucrative capital coincide. Both are covered by the designation 'private capital' (provided they are not publicly owned).

c. Business and paid-up capital

By business capital is meant the whole of the assets or instruments of activity. Paid-up (or committed) capital, on the other hand, in principle signifies the contribution of the owners of an enterprise to financial means. Understanding of either term requires a knowledge of the concept 'balance sheet'.

A balance sheet is a statement of a firm's financial position on a given date, showing on the left the property and rights it owns – its current and fixed assets, how it has used the funds available to it (buildings, goods, claims) – and on the right the debts it owes – consisting of liabilities and owners' equities, its sources of funds. It should be added that it is the accountancy practice in the United Kingdom to put the assets on the right-hand side, whereas in the United States the assets and the liabilities plus owners' equities (net worth) are often set one below the other. Since both expressions relate to the use of funds and their sources respectively, the assets and the liabilities plus owners' equities are equal; hence the designation 'balance sheet'.

A distinction is made between a firm's borrowed capital and its own capital. In general parlance, however, capital is always held to signify the firm's own financial means or owners' equities – in other words the goods at its disposal (at a given time) plus claims on and less debts to other units. As will be shown below, the owners' equities not only include the paid-up capital, but also the reserves created. Whereas income is a flow, financial assets are a stock.

A firm's owners' equities may change as a result of its operations (profit or loss; Chapter 8). In most countries a balance sheet has to be drawn up at least once a year; in actual practice, this is done more

16

frequently. Between times, transactions are entered on other records from which the income statement or profit and loss account and the changes in assets and liabilities are periodically calculated.

In the case of a proprietorship, the net profit (or loss) is transferred to the capital at the end of the accounting period. But this is not the normal practice in a corporation or company (partly because a company has legal personality). The undistributed profits generally go to the reserve fund. Thus the capital is not adjusted annually, but kept constant. After one year's operations therefore, Balance Sheet 1 may have been superseded by Balance Sheet 2. On a given date, the reserves may be wholly or partly incorporated in the capital.

BALANCE SHEET 1 – at 31 December 1970

(£m.)

Assets (current and fixed)	6·0	Liabilities (current and long-term)	1·5
		Paid-up capital (net worth or owners' equities)	4·5
	6·0		6·0

BALANCE SHEET 2 – at 31 December 1971

(£m.)

Assets (current and fixed)	6·5	Liabilities (current and long-term)	1·7
		Paid-up capital (net worth or owners' equities)	4·5
		Reserves	0·3
	6·5		6·5

7 Economic units

Depending on the objects at which they aim or the functions which they fulfil, economic units can be divided into three types – households, enterprises and government.

Households are economic units with mainly consumption aims. They include not only families but also non-profit institutions (except when they work for enterprises) and individual persons not living in families.

17

Enterprises are economic units in which the factors of production are combined to produce goods and services for sale at a price intended at least to cover the cost. Firms may be either private or public enterprises. Most persons simultaneously belong to a household and an enterprise.

Government comprises central or local government agencies which do not come within the category of enterprises. These institutions are financed largely from taxation (Chapter 2.2). They organize services for the community which enterprises cannot or are not properly equipped to provide and which are not sold on the market. Official institutions which do work for the market (public enterprises) are classed with enterprises.

Economic units are all faced with the economic problem and they all make their plans or programmes, though not necessarily in any formal manner.

Transactions between the various economic units assume the following forms:

a. The purchase and sale of goods and services (against payment or the creation of a debt in the case of a purchase, and against a receipt or the acquisition of a claim in the case of a sale);

b. the exchange of goods, services or financial assets (which are available in the form of or can be quickly converted into money; Chapter 3.1);

c. the acquisition or transfer of goods, services or financial assets without any apparent *quid pro quo* (e.g. taxes, gifts).

8 Structure of the economy

Economic activity takes place within a framework of natural, technological and social circumstances (data) some of which may be said to be constant and others variable. The data which may be called constant or quasi-constant – at least in the short term – determine the structure or the basis of an economy. The most important structural elements are physical environment, population, wants, capital stock, technological knowledge (see, however, Chapter 10.3*b*) and the economic system.

a. The physical environment
That human wants can be satisfied is due to the physical environment. Natural conditions are in many cases the decisive factor in the type of

18

economic activity pursued (influence of geographical situation, climate, condition of the soil).

Although it is considerable, the importance of the physical environment must not be exaggerated, since man can to an appreciable extent remedy the imperfections of nature; for instance, raw materials can be transported to all parts of the world, and such items as artificial fertilizer exert a major influence.

The countries of Western Europe are deficient in raw materials and thus depend heavily on external sources, so that they have a typically open economy.

b. Population

The size and the composition of the population also have a marked effect on a country's production and consumption. The preponderance of either sex, or of specific age or ethnological groups, plays a significant role in the dynamics of economic activity.

Of the countries in the European Economic Community (EEC), the Netherlands (Table 2) has the highest birth rate (number of live births per thousand inhabitants). Other high figures are those for the United States (17·7), Canada (17·6) and particularly the less-developed countries (Chapter 2·4), such as Jamaica (34.2), El Salvador (41·9) and Mexico (42·2). The Netherlands has one of the lowest death rates (number of deaths per thousand inhabitants), so that the natural increase (difference between birth and death rates) is greatest in that country; persons under 15 years of age account for 27·6 per cent of the total population (as compared with 23·9 per cent in Belgium, 23·3 per cent in Western Germany, 25·1 per cent in France and 24·4 per cent in Italy). The Netherlands is, indeed, the most densely populated country in the EEC (375 inhabitants per square kilometre at mid-1967), being followed immediately by Belgium (314). In certain districts of the other EEC countries there is also a high population density, cases in point being North Rhine-Westphalia and Campania (483 and 372 respectively, or more than double the national averages). France displays the lowest density, only the Paris region having a high figure (765) – as, of course do all major conurbations (e.g. Hamburg, with 2453, and Bremen, with 1866).

For the EEC area as a whole, there are about 150 inhabitants per square kilometre – far more than in the United States (21) or the USSR (11)

19

TABLE 2: Birth and death rates in the EEC countries, United Kingdom and United States (1969)

Country	Birth rate	Death rate
West Germany[a]	15·0	12·0
Italy	17·6	10·1
France	16·7	11·3
Netherlands	19·2	8·3
Belgium	14·6	12·4
Luxembourg	13·5	12·5
United Kingdom	16·6	11·9
United States	17·7	9·5

[a] Excluding West Berlin   Source: BSUN, November 1970, pp. 6–9

The distribution of occupations among the various sectors of acivity gives an indication of the degree of economic development. The higher the degree of economic development, the greater usually is the proportion of the total manpower in industry and mining (the secondary sector) and in services (the tertiary sector); employment in agriculture and forestry (the primary sector) is correspondingly lower.

In the EEC, the percentage of the working population engaged in agriculture (1969 figures) is still relatively high for Italy (23), France (15) and West Germany (9). It is lowest in Belgium (6) and the Netherlands (8). In the United Kingdom it is under 4 per cent (cf. also Chapter 10.1b). The percentages for the USA, Canada and Japan are respectively 5, 9 and 23.

c. The stock of capital goods

The extent of the stock of capital goods, like technological knowledge, is another factor which exercises an appreciable influence on the level of production. Only rough estimates are available, scarcely lending themselves to comparison. More and better data are to be found on the increase in the stock of capital goods (the volume of investment each year less depreciation).

There are no fundamental differences among the western countries as regards the degree of industrialization.

The term 'economic infrastructure' is sometimes used to denote the modes of transport, public institutions, schools, etc., necessary for the operation of all sectors of industry.

d. The economic system
As regards the organization of economic activity or the economic system, we may start by ascertaining how the decisions of the various economic units are coordinated. This is done either by a central organization or by the price system. More particularly, resources have to be allocated: society has to decide what has to be produced, how, where, how much and for whom.

In a centrally planned economy, all important decisions are taken by the government. (In practice, this can also be done by a private institution, e.g. a holding company – Chapter 6.7 – which has acquired considerable power in the economy.) In particular, the government determines what goods are to be produced (not necessarily taking account of the consumers' desiderata) and in most cases also fixes the relevant prices. Such centralized control requires large administrative bodies and accurate information.

In a market economy, buyers' and sellers' dealings are brought into line by prices, which are determined without government intervention.

These two methods are not mutually exclusive; each can be applied to different sectors of the economy. In practice, one or the other normally predominates. The USSR has a centrally planned economy, the western countries' economies are based rather on the market system.

On much the same lines, economic systems can also be classified according to their aims.

When firms as a general rule aim at maximizing profits, the economy is said to be a private-enterprise economy. The means of production are privately owned. (If they are not, the system is called 'state capitalism'.) The government does not participate directly in economic activity, its role being of an indirect and comprehensive nature. In principle, then, reliance is placed on the machinery of the market. In the event of preparation for war or of actual hostilities, however, the system is forced to accept central controls.

The drawbacks of capitalism (inequality in the distribution of income – accentuated by the right of inheritance and the influence of economic on political power – poor social conditions, unemployment) have called forth a reaction in certain countries, leading to a higher degree of government intervention. It has even gone as far as nationalization of some industries (see below, and also Chapter 5.1*b*), though the public sector has not become dominant in the process. Non-capitalistic forms of organization – for instance, the

c

cooperatives (Chapter 5.3) – have been introduced or extended. There are no longer any purely capitalist economies.

When the interests of the community as a whole have priority over profit-seeking, with particular attention paid to the provision of full employment, the raising of production and living standards and equitable distribution of income and property, the economy is termed 'socialist' (cf. Appendix 6).

Such an economic system calls for judicious organization of production. Collectivistic measures (nationalization) may be desirable, the means of production being placed in the hands of the government. But the extension of official intervention is not an end in itself: as far as possible, economic power is decentralized. This is brought out in the Socialist International's 'Frankfurt Declaration' (1951):

The structure of the country concerned must decide the extent of public ownership and the forms of planning to apply. Public ownership can take the form of the nationalization of existing private enterprises or the creation of new public concerns, municipal or regional enterprises, consumers' or producers' cooperatives. These various forms of public ownership should be regarded not as ends in themselves but as means of controlling basic industries and services on which the economic life and welfare of the community depend, of rationalizing inefficient industries or of preventing private monopolies and cartels from exploiting the public. Socialist planning does not presuppose public ownership of all the means of production. It is compatible with the existence of private ownership in important fields, for instance in agriculture, handicraft, retail trade and small and middle-sized industries.

The transfer of the means of production to the government must be aimed at eliminating the disadvantages of a private enterprise economy. The spirit in which the firm is operated must change; otherwise it is a case not of nationalization but of state capitalism.

The theory of economic systems describes the various types of economic system, with particular reference to their influence on economic activity.

9 Rationality in economics

Economics does not express any opinion concerning priorities for the various categories of wants. For instance, non-commodities (such as leisure time) may be ranked higher by some people than commodities. A tea-break is judged by E. J. Mishan to be just as commendable as the additional satisfaction of other wants (by producing more goods).

Economics normally concerns itself only with wants which make claims on goods. Wants such as the desire for love, friendship and social standing generally fall outside its scope, though these wants sometimes influence economic activity to a great extent. Of particular significance are man's efforts to mark himself out from his fellow-men, the struggle to secure social prestige – calling to mind J. Huizinga's *homo ludens*. Certain products are bought not because they are necessary as such but because they are regarded as status symbols. The classical *homo œconomicus*, on the other hand, aims solely at acquiring as much money (command over goods) as he can.

According to most authors, rational economic activity implies that the consumer seeks as much utility as possible, the entrepreneur as much profit as possible and the government maximization of social welfare (for this concept, see Chapter 13.1). The 'economic principle' must be applied: with the given means, as many aims as possible are achieved, or existing wants satisfied as far as possible. Here grading of wants is necessary, and the most urgent of them must be satisfied first.

Moreover, for each individual objective, account is taken of the 'technical principle' (i.e. the economic principle embraces the technical principle): a minimum amount of resources is used to fulfil a certain purpose or, to put it another way, an attempt is made to achieve a maximum result with the given means. To obtain a certain temperature with the minimum of fuel is a technical problem (a single aim); if other aims are *also* taken into consideration, the problem is an economic one (several objectives). The position is the same when, out of a number of production processes, the most advantageous is chosen on the basis of the respective costs.

Somebody acting on the economic principle does not necessarily do so infallibly; he *believes* he is acting rationally. If the consumer's actual choice is also assumed to be the rational one, the term 'rational' loses its significance and the economic principle becomes 'a completely neutral and empty proposition, such a harmless one . . . that it is certainly inadequate as a psychological premise' (P. Hennipman). On this assumption, man always acts rationally and rational action could be viewed as modal action (from 'mode', a statistical term meaning the most frequently occurring phenomenon or the most frequently made observation).

23

The economic principle must not be confused with 'economic motive'. Whereas motive relates to the objective (for the consumer the satisfaction of wants), the principle relates to efficiency.

10 Methods of investigation

The function of economic theory is to describe and explain economic phenomena. Like every science, economics endeavours to trace the causal connections between the phenomena it studies. The relations or 'laws' established may be causal or functional. (In the USSR, economic laws are seen to represent actual aims; the 'fundamental economic law', for instance, consists in constantly stepping up and improving production.)

Investigation of the connection between economic phenomena may be performed either deductively or inductively. The first of these methods is based on certain hypotheses (e.g. the economic principle), the second on close examination of individual facts.

As it is not possible to study all economic phenomena simultaneously, a large number of them (notably those relating to the economic system) are assumed to remain unchanged (the *ceteris paribus* assumption). Oversimplification, however, produces a theory which is inconsistent with the facts. On the other hand if account is taken of all the data of that complex field which is economic activity, it becomes more difficult to build up a theory. In order to be of any use in economic policy, theoretical economics, which forms the basis of such policy, must accord as closely as possible with the realities.

Statistics constitutes a useful aid for the assessment of the mass of individual economic phenomena. This is a scientific method the object of which is the observation and grouping of phenomena which are susceptible of mass observation, and consequently facilitate their interpretation.

Statistics are of fundamental importance to economics, but they must be used and interpreted carefully. Many economic phenomena are difficult to study owing to lack of statistical data.

Whereas mathematical economics consists in the formulation of economic theory by mathematical methods, econometrics sets out to verify statistically the conclusions arrived at in theoretical economics; it is mathematical economics using concrete data. Although there is also a tendency to go too far in the other direction, the most commonly observed propensity is to over-refine the mathematical

24

machinery and employ complicated mathematical formulae where simpler calculations will usually prove adequate.

Statics and dynamics

Economic dynamics is the study of the changes in economic phenomena between successive dates; while static analysis deals with the relationships between them at one and the same time. The former process deals with continuing changes, the latter with a single change.

We shall use, then, dynamics as a synonym for sequence analysis. In practice only dynamic analysis is relevant.

11 Bibliography

Especially for theoretical economics: K. E. Boulding, *Economic Analysis*, two volumes *Microeconomics, Macroeconomics* (4th ed. New York 1966). Not as complete, but more exhaustive on specific matters: E. Schneider, *Pricing and Equilibrium* (2nd ed. London 1962) and *Money, Income and Employment* (London 1968), translations of the tenth German edition.

For an excellent synthesis on the state of economic science during the period 1948–52: *A Survey of Contemporary Economics*, Vol. 1 (ed. H. S. Ellis, Philadelphia 1948); Vol. 2 (ed. B. F. Haley, Homewood, Ill. 1952). A less systematic view is to be found in *Surveys of Economic Theory* (Part 1: *Money, Interest and Welfare*; Part 2: *Growth and Development*; Part 3: *Resource Allocation*), published in 1965–6 by the American Economic Association and the Royal Economic Society. For criticism of current economic theory: A. Lowe, *On Economic Knowledge* (New York 1965).

Political Economy: A textbook (London 1957) is the translation of the 2nd edition (Moscow) of the Soviet official textbook on economics. Half of it is devoted to the criticism of pre-capitalist and capitalist economic systems; it is mainly based on the work of K. Marx, F. Engels and V. Lenin.

In a not very systematic and one-sided, but much-discussed work – *The Affluent Society* (Cambridge, Mass. 1958) – J. K. Galbraith believes that in the western hemisphere economic behaviour is still too much affected by ideas which date from an age of poverty and a greater inequality in income distribution. Production can no longer be considered the central theme. Closely related: E. J. Mishan, *The Costs of Economic Growth* (London 1967).

a. The definition of economics

Apart from L. Robbins, *An Essay on the Nature and the Significance of Economic Science* (2nd ed. London 1935), the more voluminous study of P. Hennipman, *Economisch motief en economisch principe* (Amsterdam 1945) should be cited, as well as O. Lange, 'The Scope and Method of Economics', *RESt*, 1945–6, No. 33; H. Guitton, *L'objet de l'économie politique* (Paris 1951), gives a survey of the different views advanced during the period 1900–50 (this study appeared in the series *Bilans de la connaissance économique* and includes an analytical and critical bibliography).

b. The definition of certain economic concepts

F. Machlup, *Essays on Economic Semantics* (ed. M. H. Miller, Englewood Cliffs, N. J. 1963), illustrates with a lot of examples the evident confusion in this field (e.g. the notion 'dynamics'). On the standard of living: *International Definition and Measurement of Levels of Living. An Interim Guide* (UN, New York 1961). On the economic units: *A Standardized System of National Accounts* (OEEC, Paris 1959).

c. Economics and the other sciences

T. Parsons and N. Smelser, *Economy and Society* (London 1957), deal with the integration of economics and social theory. The standard work of J. P. Haesaert, *Sociologie générale* (Brussels 1956), pp. 344–59, gives a lucid exposition of the consequences of economic activity on the life of the community.

G. Katona, *Psychological Studies of the American Economy* (New York 1960), thinks economics does not pay due regard to psychological data and examines the motives and behaviour of economic units; in the same spirit: P. Reynaud, *La Psychologie économique* (Paris 1954), with annotated bibliography.

d. The structure of the economy

A detailed consideration of the various definitions is found in A. Marchal, *Systèmes et structures économiques* (Paris 1959).

The notions primary, secondary and tertiary production were introduced by A. G. B. Fisher, 'Economic Implications of Material Progress', *International Labour Review*, July 1935; *id.*, 'Primary, Secondary and Tertiary Production', *Economic Record*, June 1939. The statistical verification was performed by C. Clark, *The Conditions of Economic Progress* (1st ed. 1940, 3rd ed. London 1957), Chapter 9.

On economic systems: W. Eucken, *Die Grundlagen der National-ökonomie* (6th ed., Berlin 1950); G. N. Halm, *Economic Systems: A Comparative Analysis* (rev. ed., New York 1960), both of whom favour a free-enterprise economy. C. Landauer, *Contemporary Economic Systems* (Philadelphia 1964), on the contrary, shows preference for socialism. More concrete: A. G. Gruchy, *Comparative Economic Systems* (New York 1966), concentrates on how the economies he deals with operate (the United States, West Germany, and France under capitalism; the Scandinavian countries and the United Kingdom under socialism; the USSR, the East-European countries and China under communism).

See also the bibliography on planned economies and socialism in Chapter 13.8*b* and on the cooperative movement in Chapter 5.13*c*.

e. Methods of investigation
B. Nogaro, *La Méthode dans l'économie politique* (2nd ed., Paris 1950), points to the dangers to which an unwary use of deductive methods is open; A. Marchal, *Méthode scientifique et science économique*, Part 1: *Le conflit traditionnel des méthodes et son renouvellement* (Paris 1952), Part 2: *Problèmes actuels de l'analyse économique: ses 'approches' fondamentales* (Paris 1955), is less convenient for a first insight into the matter; Part 2 in particular requires a preliminary knowledge of the basic economic concepts. The same holds true for the last two papers in T. C. Koopmans, *Three Essays on the State of Economic Science* (New York 1957).

For Marxian views on economic laws and method: Chapters 3 and 4 of O. Lange, *Political Economy*, Vol. 1: *General Problems* (New York 1963 – translation of the second Polish edition).

On the accordance of the hypotheses underlying theory with actual facts: J. Melitz, 'M. Friedman and F. Machlup on the significance of testing economic assumptions', *JPE*, February 1965, and the bibliography set out in this article.

Finally, see also *The Structure of Economic Science: Essays on Methodology* (ed. S. R. Krupp, Englewood Cliffs, N. J. 1966) – a series of papers including M. Bronfenbrenner, 'A "Middlebrow" Introduction to Economic Methodology'.

f. Statistics
See F. E. Croxton and D. J. Cowden, *Applied General Statistics* (2nd ed., Englewood Cliffs, N. J. 1955); G. U. Yule and M. G. Kendall, *An*

Introduction to the Theory of Statistics (14th ed., London 1950); see also W. R. Buckland and K. A. Fox, *Bibliography of Basic Texts and Monographs on Statistical Methods 1945–1960* (London 1963), which contains a supplementary list for 1960–2; K. A. Fox, *Intermediate Economic Statistics* (New York 1968).

From 1919 onwards, a *Monthly Bulletin of Statistics* has been published, first by the League of Nations and subsequently by the United Nations; figures on separate countries, however, are more conveniently available in national publications.

g. *Econometrics*

In our view, the best works are L. R. Klein, *An Introduction to Econometrics* (Englewood Cliffs, N. J. 1962); more elaborate: J. Johnston, *Econometric Methods* (New York 1963) and E. Malinvaud, *Statistical Methods of Econometrics* (Amsterdam 1970).

h. *The most important periodicals*

Articles from the leading journals are classified by subject in the following publications of the American Economic Association (Homewood, Ill.): in 1961: *Index of Economic Journals*, Vol. 1: 1886–1924; Vol. 2: 1925–39; Vol. 3: 1940–9; in 1962: Vol. 4: 1950–4; Vol. 5: 1954–9; in 1965: Vol. 6: 1960–3; in 1969: *Index of Economic Articles in Journals*, Vol. 7: 1964–5; *Index of Economic Articles in Collective Volumes*, Vol. 7A: 1964–5; *Index of Economic Articles in Journals and Collective Volumes*, Vol. 8: 1966.

Since 1963 brief summaries of some articles from the most important economic journals have been published by the American Economic Association in *The Journal of Economic Abstracts*; the name of this journal was changed on 1 January 1969 to *The Journal of Economic Literature*.

Hereafter, the most important journals are listed in order of foundation.

1. *Zeitschrift für die gesamte Staatswissenschaft*, 1844, quarterly (West Germany).
2. *De Economist*, 1855, bimonthly (Netherlands).
3. *Jahrbücher für Nationalökonomie und Statistik*, 1863, irregular (West Germany).
4. *Schweizerische Zeitschrift für Volkswirtschaft und Statistik*, 1865, bimonthly (Switzerland).

5. *The Quarterly Journal of Economics* (Harvard), 1866, quarterly (United States).
6. *Giornale degli Economisti e Annali di Economia*, 1886, bimonthly (Italy).
7. *Revue d'Economie Politique*, 1887, bimonthly (France).
8. *The Economic Journal*, 1891, quarterly (United Kingdom).
9. *The Journal of Political Economy* (Chicago), 1892, bimonthly (United States).
10. *Zeitschrift für Nationalökonomie* (Vienna), 1929, irregular. Previously (1892–1917 and 1923–7) *Zeitschrift für Volkswirtschaft, Sozialpolitik und Verwaltung* (Austria).
11. *The American Economic Review*, 1911, quarterly (United States).
12. *Weltwirtschaftliches Archiv*, 1913, quarterly (West Germany).
13. *The Review of Economics and Statistics* (Harvard), 1948, bimonthly, succeeding (1918–47) *The Review of Economic Statistics* (United States).
14. *Economica*, 1921, quarterly (United Kingdom).
15. *Recherches Economiques de Louvain*, 1961, eight numbers a year. This was the successor to the *Bulletin de l'Institut de Recherches Economiques et Sociales* (1946, eight numbers a year), which itself superseded the *Bulletin de l'Institut des Recherches Economiques* (1937, quarterly) and the *Bulletin de l'Institut des Sciences Economiques* (1929, quarterly) (Belgium).
16. *The Review of Economic Studies*, 1933, irregular (United Kingdom).
17. *Econometrica*, 1933, quarterly (United States).
18. *Oxford Economic Papers*, 1938, irregular; since 1948 every four months (United Kingdom).
19. *Kyklos*, 1947, quarterly (Switzerland).
20. *Economie appliquée*, 1948, quarterly (France).
21. *Economia Internazionale*, 1948, quarterly (Italy).
22. *Revue Economique*, 1950, six times a year (France).
23. *International Monetary Fund Staff Papers*, 1950, six times a year (IMF).

2 The circular flow of economic activity

*Even the fragmentary outline of a synthesis is
better than no synthesis at all.*

Aldous Huxley

In order to obtain a clear idea of the relations between the numerous
economic units in a country, it is best to reduce them to homogeneous
groups. For example, all households may be considered as one whole,
since their economic activities are more or less of the same type.
Enterprises and government agencies too can each be grouped apart.
Through economic activity (production, consumption, capital formation etc.), these groups are linked up not only with each other but also
with other economies – the rest of the world – by flows of goods and
money. All these currents make up the circular flow of economic
activity.

The present chapter starts with a simple example and then gradually
amplifies it so as to bring it more into line with the real world. This is
done in three distinct stages. The instruments – such as the national
accounts and input-output tables – which enable a comprehensive
view to be obtained of the various flows in the economy are also
described and discussed.

1 Households and enterprises

The assumption is adopted that the only economic units are households and enterprises. It is postulated first that only consumer goods
are produced (not for the accumulation of stocks, however, since they
would then be deemed to be investment; Chapter 1.3b) and subsequently that capital goods – originally only for replacement investment, but eventually also for extension investment – are also produced. However, no account is taken of technological advance.

a. Consumer goods
Through the factor services F' of households, enterprises produce a
quantity of consumer goods X'_α; the value of these goods in money

30

terms is expressed by X_α. For their contribution to the production process, households receive an income Y, all of which they spend on the purchase of goods for consumption C. The value of the factor services is then equal to Y and that of X_α' to C. The net final result of economic activity in a given country during a specific period, or net national product (at factor cost; see below) X_α is equal to the goods produced. As these goods are sold to households, they coincide with consumption. X_α is also equivalent to the national income Y, or the sum of the payments to the factors of production for their contribution to the production process:

$$X_\alpha = Y = C. \tag{1}$$

These relations are represented diagrammatically in Figure 1, in which the movements of money are denoted by dotted lines and the movements of goods by solid lines. While the money flow may be considered a genuine cycle – the money remains *in* the economy – the goods flow invariably consists of newly produced goods, so that here the cycle has to be interpreted figuratively.

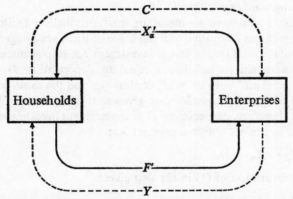

Figure 1: The circular flow of economic activity (A)

Movements of money can also be expressed in accounts. In Example 1 the first item, 'purchases from enterprises' corresponds with the fourth item 'sales to households', and the second to the third. The first figure indicates the sequence of the various items for each account – first the expenditure, then the income), the second the corresponding item (each transaction appearing twice – as an

31

expenditure on the one account and as an income on the other), and
finally comes the symbol for the relevant item.

EXAMPLE 1

	Households			
Expenditure				*Income*
(1·4) C	Purchases from enterprises	300	(2·3) Y	Remuneration of factor services	300

	Enterprises			
Expenditure				*Income*
(3·2) Y	Remuneration of factor services	300	(4·1) C	Sales to households	300
X_α	Net national product (at factor cost)	300	X_α	Net national product (at factor cost)	300

b. Consumer and capital goods

Since enterprises have to maintain their production facilities and
replace machines from time to time, some of them are obliged to produce capital goods (replacement investment I_ρ). Replacement investment is assumed to be always equal to depreciation D (but see
Chapter 1.5c) and both to be effected in one and the same period. In
order to obtain the complete, or gross national product (at factor
cost) X_β, therefore, depreciation D or replacement investment I_ρ must
be added to the net national product X_α:

$$X_\beta = X_\alpha + D. \tag{2}$$

Substitution of (1) in (2) also gives:

$$X_\beta = Y + D \tag{3}$$
$$X_\beta = C + I_\rho. \tag{4}$$

In Example 2, a 'capital transactions' account is now introduced.
It is assumed that the enterprises' depreciation allowances flow to this
account and that replacement investment constitutes the corresponding item. The effect of this convention is that the capital goods appear
as an income on the 'enterprises' account, despite the fact that they
are sold to the enterprises themselves and thus do not represent actual

income for the sector as a whole. The depreciation allowances are included under the head of expenditure; they are indeed production costs (Chapter 5.7) but not remuneration for factor services rendered.

EXAMPLE 2

Households

Expenditure					Income
(1·5) C	Purchases from enterprises	300	(2·3) Y	Remuneration of factor services	300

Enterprises

Expenditure					Income
(3·2) Y	Remuneration of factor services	300	(5·1) C	Sales to households	300
(4·8) D	Depreciation	20	(6·7) I_ρ	Replacement investment	20
X_β	Gross national product (at factor cost)	—— 320	X_β	Gross national product (at factor cost)	—— 320

Capital transactions

Expenditure					Income
(7·6) I_ρ	Replacement investment	20	(8·4) D	Depreciation	20

c. Savings and extension investment

In point of fact households do not spend their entire income on consumption. The unspent portion is called (net) saving $S_{\alpha h}$. Since

$$Y = C + S_{\alpha h} \tag{5}$$

then

$$S_{\alpha h} = Y - C. \tag{6}$$

Enterprises, for their part, use some of their production capacity, not only to make replacement investment possible, but also to increase the volume of capital goods. This extension investment, plus the growth or minus the decline in stocks, is equal to the difference between gross investment and depreciation, or net investment:

$$I_\alpha = I_\beta - D. \tag{7}$$

33

This net investment must be taken into account in the calculation of the net national product:

$$X_\alpha = C + I_\alpha. \tag{8}$$

As X_α is equal to Y – equation (1), it follows from equations (5) and (8) that

$$C + I_\alpha = C + S_{\alpha h} \tag{9}$$

or

$$I_\alpha = S_{\alpha h} \tag{10}$$

Enterprises often refrain from distributing part of their income to households, allocating it to the reserves (Chapter 1.6c). This constitutes saving by enterprises $S_{\alpha e}$, which must be added to $S_{\alpha h}$ in order to obtain the total net savings:

$$S_\alpha = S_{\alpha h} + S_{\alpha e}. \tag{11}$$

From the foregoing it follows that the national income now breaks down into two components (since enterprises do not distribute the whole of their income to households):

$$Y = Y_{he} + S_{\alpha e}. \tag{12}$$

In addition, equations (2), (3) and (4) must be adjusted on the basis of the new assumptions – cf. equations (8) and (12):

$$X_\beta = C + I_\alpha + D \tag{13}$$
$$X_\beta = Y_{he} + S_{\alpha e} + D \tag{14}$$
$$X_\beta = C + I_\alpha + I_\rho. \tag{15}$$

Depreciation and net savings now together make up gross saving, which equals gross investment:

$$S_\beta = S_\alpha + D = I_\alpha + I_\rho = I_\beta. \tag{16}$$

EXAMPLE 3

Expenditure			Households		Income
(1·7) C	Purchases from enterprises	260	(3·4) Y_{he}	Remuneration of factor services	300
(2·12) $S_{\alpha h}$	Saving	40			
		300			300

Enterprises					
Expenditure					*Income*
(4·3) Y_{he}	Remuneration of factor services	300	(7·1) C	Sales to households	260
(5·14) D	Depreciation	20	(8·10) I_ρ	Replacement investment	20
(6·13) $S_{\alpha e}$	Saving	10	(9·11) I_α	Net investment	50
X_β	Gross national product (at factor cost)	330	X_β	Gross national product (at factor cost)	330

Capital transactions					
Expenditure					*Income*
(10·8) I_ρ	Replacement investment	20	(12·2) $S_{\alpha h}$	Saving by households	40
(11·9) I_α	Net investment	50	(13·6) $S_{\alpha e}$	Saving by enterprises	10
			(14·5) D	Depreciation	20
I_β	Gross investment	70	S_β	Gross saving	70

2 Government

Because of the major part central and local government agencies play in the economic process, they also form a separate element in the circular flow (Example 4).

a. Influence on prices

The government influences prices of goods by imposing indirect (or cost-increasing) taxes T_i and by granting subsidies W (gifts to producers). The effect of the former (e.g. excise duties on beer) is normally to bring about an increase (or counteract a fall) in prices; the effect of the latter is to reduce them (or neutralize price rises caused by other factors; e.g. subsidies to keep bread or milk prices steady).

Thus a difference arises between the value of production at factor cost X_α (the remuneration value of services rendered by the factors of production) or Y and the value at prices ruling on the market (see Chapter 7.1), or in other words at market prices $X_{\alpha m}$. In order to arrive at the second from the first the indirect taxes must be added and the subsidies deducted:

$$X_{\alpha m} = X_\alpha + T_i - W \tag{17}$$
$$X_{\alpha m} = Y + T_i - W \tag{18}$$

$X_{\alpha m}$ remains equal to consumption plus net saving – cf. equation (5) – or consumption plus net investment – cf. equation (8) – but the last-named item naturally has to be expressed in terms of market prices:

$$X_{\alpha m} = C + S_\alpha = C + I_\alpha. \tag{19}$$

In Example 4, these data are in fact expressed in market prices, as they are in the two subsequent examples.

b. Influence on incomes

The government's influence on incomes finds expression particularly in transfer payments and direct taxes (apart from the payment of Y_{hg} to households).

By transfer payments is meant transfers of money without any equivalent service in return from the beneficiary (e.g. social assistance from the government, gifts to and from households abroad – see Section 3; subsidies are a special case). They are not identifiable with productive activity on the part of the beneficiaries but have an effect on the latter's consumption or saving.

In order to determine the total income of households or personal income Y_π, these transfer payments V_{hg} must be added to the incomes from productive activities Y_{he} and Y_{hg} which are paid respectively by the enterprises and by the government:

$$Y_\pi = Y_{he} + Y_{hg} + V_{hg}. \tag{20}$$

The disposable personal income $Y_{h\delta}$ is smaller as a result of the payment of direct taxes T_{jh}. These are regular levies on the income and/or property of households (and enterprises). Owing to the direct taxes T_{je} (not shown in the example) on the profits of the enterprises, the amount left for reserves and profit-distribution is smaller. Sources of government income other than taxes include the rendering of services to households (school fees) and enterprises and its contribution to production (as a provider of capital). Transfer payments from households to other sectors (these are not shown in Example 4) also have to be deducted; those transferred to households have to be added. Such income may be applied either to consumption or to saving:

$$Y_{h\delta} = Y_\pi - T_{jh} = C_h + S_{\alpha h}. \tag{21}$$

The disposable private income comprises disposable personal income and the undistributed profits (before taxation):

$$Y_{h\delta} + S_{\alpha e} + T_{je}.$$

c. Government investment and consumption

Now enterprises also produce capital goods for the public sector (government). This public investment, like private investment, is entered on the capital transactions account. Public sector expenditure also includes an item designated 'depreciation'.

The portion of the disposable resources appropriated by government for the purpose of making its services available to other economic units is called government consumption. This is accordingly equal to the value of government services less any revenue from that source ($C_{hg} + J_{eg}$: sales to households and enterprises).

The value in question is, however, difficult to calculate because government services are usually provided free of charge or below the normal price. It is therefore assumed that their value is equal to the cost price (see Chapter 5.7b) or to associated expenditure (payment of factor services Y_{hg}, purchases from enterprises C_{ge}, depreciation D_g):

$$C_g = Y_{hg} + C_{ge} + D_g - C_{hg} - J_{eg}. \tag{22}$$

d. Interest on the public debt

To cover its expenditure, the government is as a general rule constrained to issue loans, and interest is paid to the households and enterprises which have subscribed to the loan. In Example 4 it is assumed for the sake of simplicity that only enterprises receive interest on the public debt. This investment (in securities) increases income of enterprises (and consequently their savings, $S_{\alpha e}$).

It is generally accepted that money borrowed by government is not used for production purposes (e.g. to cover a deficit on the ordinary budget, which relates to current income and expenditure). Incomes deriving from holdings of government bonds (R_g^*) are therefore considered to be transfer incomes. This must be taken

37

into account in the calculation of the national income: since R_g^* is included in $S_{\alpha e}$, it must be deducted therefrom in order to determine the net national income. To put it in another way, equation (12) becomes

$$Y = Y_{he} + Y_{hg} + S_{\alpha e} + T_{je} - R_g^*. \tag{23}$$

The incorporation of government in the circular flow entails the adjustment of several equations. Thus (19) and (10) become respectively:

$$X_{\alpha m} = C_h + C_g + I_{\alpha e} + I_{\alpha g} \tag{24}$$

$$I_\alpha = S_{\alpha h} + S_{\alpha e} + S_{\alpha g}. \tag{25}$$

EXAMPLE 4

Households

Expenditure			Income		
(1·13) C_{he}	Purchases from enterprises	280	(5·11) Y_{he}	Remuneration by enterprises	300
(2·26) C_{hg}	Purchases from government	6	(6·19) Y_{hg}	Remuneration by government	24
(3·28) T_{jh}	Direct taxes on households	36	(7·22) V_{hg}	Transfer payments by government	37
(4·32) $S_{\alpha h}$	Saving	39			
		361			361

Enterprises

Expenditure			Income		
(8·27) J_{eg}	Purchases from government	8	(13·1) C_{he}	Sales to households	280
(9·29) T_i	Indirect taxes	40	(14·20) C_{ge}	Sales to government	9
(10·35) D_e	Depreciation	20	(15·30) $I_{\beta e}$	Sales to enterprises	75
(11·5) Y_{he}	Remuneration to households	300	(16·31) $I_{\beta g}$	Sales to government	12
(12·33) $S_{\alpha e}$	Saving	29	(17·23) W	Subsidies	15
			(18·24) R_g^*	Interest on the public debt	6
		397			397

Government

Expenditure			Income		
(19·6) Y_{hg}	Remuneration to households	24	(26·2) C_{hg}	Sales to households	6
(20·14) C_{ge}	Purchases from enterprises	9	(27·8) J_{eg}	Sales to enterprises	8
(21·36) D_g	Depreciation	5	(28·3) T_{jh}	Direct taxes on households	36
(22·7) V_{hg}	Transfer payments to households	37	(29·9) T_i	Indirect taxes	40
(23·17) W	Subsidies	15			
(24·18) R_g^*	Interest on the public debt	6			
(25·34) $S_{\alpha g}$	Saving	−6			
		90			90

Capital transactions

Expenditure			Income		
(30·15) $I_{\beta e}$	Gross investment by enterprises	75	(32·4) $S_{\alpha h}$	Savings by households	39
(31·16) $I_{\beta g}$	Gross investment by government	12	(33·12) $S_{\alpha e}$	Saving by enterprises	29
			(34·25) $S_{\alpha g}$	Saving by government	−6
			(35·10) D_e	Depreciation of enterprises	20
			(36·21) D_g	Depreciation of government	5
I_β		87	S_β		87

3 The rest of the world

The maintenance of external relations makes it necessary to distinguish the domestic product from the national product. In the foregoing examples, the two terms have been considered as identical and designated 'national product'. Definitions of 'national resources' and 'national expenditure' are given below. In the 'rest of the world' account, income and expenditure are viewed from the standpoint of other countries. That is to say, the expenditure is expenditure *by* other countries and the income is likewise income *of* other countries.

39

a. Domestic product

Enterprises, and to a lesser extent households, procure goods (and services) from other countries. The respective values are here represented by M_{ae} and M_{ah} and their sum by M_a. Enterprises deliver goods (and services) E_a to the rest of the world. Money flows take place in the opposite direction. (For convenience, only these movements are illustrated in Figure 2.)

E_a and M_a have to be taken into account in determining the volume of production. E_a is also produced by the enterprises; M_a, on the other hand, is supplied from abroad.

This gives us the domestic product at market prices $X_{\alpha m}^d$. It is generated by the activities of the persons who are normally resident in the country concerned (both nationals and foreigners). Equation (24) then becomes:

$$X_{\alpha m}^d = C + I_\alpha + E_a - M_a. \tag{26}$$

In Example 5:

365 = 289 (items 1 + 2 + 3) + 24 (items 24 + 25 + 26 − 31 − 32) + 55 (items 19 − 14) + 7 (items 20 − 26) + 60 (item 36) − 70 (items 41 + 42).

EXAMPLE 5

			Households			
Expenditure						*Income*
(1·17) C_{he}	Purchases from enterprises	280		(6·15) Y_{he}	Remuneration by enterprises	300
(2·31) C_{hg}	Purchases from government	6		(7·24) Y_{hg}	Remuneration by government	24
(3·41) M_{ah}	Purchases from the rest of the world	3		(8·37) Y_{hf} $= E_{bh}$	Remuneration by the rest of the world	2
(4·33) T_{jh}	Direct taxes on households	36		(9·27) V_{hg}	Transfer payments by government	37
(5·45) $S_{\alpha h}$	Saving	41		(10·39) V_{hf}	Transfer payments by the rest of the world	3
		366				366

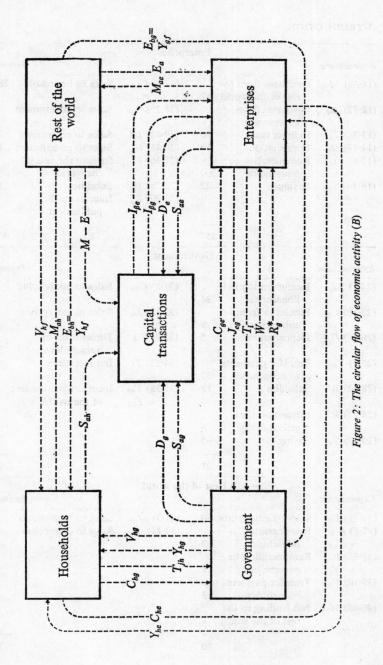

Figure 2: The circular flow of economic activity (B)

Enterprises

Expenditure			Income		
(11·42) M_{ae}	Purchases from the rest of the world	67	(17·1) C_{he}	Sales to households	280
(12·32) J_{eg}	Purchases from government	8	(18·25) C_{ge}	Sales to government	9
(13·34) T_i	Indirect taxes	40	(19·43) $I_{\beta e}$	Sales to enterprises	75
(14·49) D_e	Depreciation	20	(20·44) $I_{\beta g}$	Sales to government	12
(15·6) Y_{he}	Remuneration to households	300	(21·36) E_a	Sales to the rest of the world	60
(16·46) $S_{\alpha e}$	Saving	22	(22·28) W	Subsidies	15
			(23·29) R_g^*	Interest on the public debt	6
		457			457

Government

Expenditure			Income		
(24·7) Y_{hg}	Remuneration to households	24	(31·2) C_{hg}	Sales to households	6
(25·18) C_{ge}	Purchases from enterprises	9	(32·12) J_{eg}	Sales to enterprises	8
(26·50) D_g	Depreciation	5	(33·4) T_{jh}	Direct taxes on households	36
(27·9) V_{hg}	Transfer payments to households	37	(34·13) T_i	Indirect taxes	40
(28·22) W	Subsidies	15	(35·38) Y_{gf} $= E_{bg}$	Income from the rest of the world	1
(29·23) R^*	Interest on the public debt	6			
(30·47) $S_{\alpha g}$	Saving	−5			
		91			91

Rest of the world

Expenditure			Income		
(36·21) E_a	Sales by enterprises	60	(41·3) M_{ah}	Sales to households	3
(37·8) E_{bh} $= Y_{hf}$	Remuneration to households	2	(42·11) M_{ae}	Sales to enterprises	67
(38·35) E_{bg} $= Y_{gf}$	Remuneration to government	1			
(39·10) V_{hf}	Transfer payments to households	3			
(40·48) $M-E$	Net lending to the rest of the world	4			
		70			70

Expenditure				Income	
			Capital transactions		
(43·19) $I_{\beta e}$	Gross investment by enterprises	75	(45·5) $S_{\alpha h}$	Saving by households	41
(44·20) $I_{\beta g}$	Gross investment by government	12	(46·16) $S_{\alpha e}$	Saving by enterprises	22
			(47·30) $S_{\alpha g}$	Saving by general government	−5
			(48·40) $M\text{-}E$	Net borrowing from abroad	4
			(49·14) D_e	Depreciation of enterprises	20
			(50·26) D_g	Depreciation of government	5
I_β	Gross investment	87	S_β	Gross saving	87

b. National product

In order to calculate the net national product at market prices, we must add to the domestic product $X^d_{\alpha m}$ the payments made to a given country's own nationals for contributions to production abroad (E_b), and deduct that country's corresponding payments to foreign factors of production (M_b):

$$X_{\alpha m} = X^d_{\alpha m} + E_b - M_b. \tag{27}$$

In Example 5 (in which M_b does not appear):
$$368 = 365 + 3.$$

c. National resources and expenditure

The balance on transfer payments from and to other countries V_f affects the disposable national resources. If it is a surplus, then it may be added to the net national product in order to calculate the net disposable national resources. A deficit, on the other hand, has to be deducted.

In Example 5, in which only V_{hf} occurs (in surplus), $368 + 3 = 371$.

The net disposable national resources make possible the net national expenditure, namely consumption C, net domestic investment I_α and expenditure abroad (the difference between, on the one hand, claims resulting from exports and contributions to foreign production plus any surplus on transfer payments from and to other

43

countries and, on the other hand, debts arising through imports and foreigners' contributions to domestic production plus any deficit on transfer payments from and to other countries).

If there is assumed to be a surplus on transfer payments (as in Example 5), then:

$$X_{\alpha m} + V_f = C + I_\alpha + (E_a + E_b + V_f) - (M_a + M_b) \quad (28)$$

or, if $E_a + E_b + V_f$ are represented by E and $M_a + M_b$ by M (a deficit V_f needing to be added to the imports figure):

$$X_{\alpha m} + V_f = C + I_\alpha + E - M. \quad (29)$$

In Example 5, $371 = 313 + 62 - 4$.

Since $X_{\alpha m} + V_f$ or the net disposable resources, are used for consumption or saving:

$$X_{\alpha m} + V_f = C + S_\alpha. \quad (30)$$

From (29) and (30) it follows that:

$$C + I_\alpha + E - M = C + S_\alpha \quad (31)$$

or

$$I_\alpha = S_\alpha + M - E. \quad (32)$$

This equation applies if $M > E$ or $M - E > 0$; then $I_\alpha > S_\alpha$. In order to maintain the equality of S and I – cf. equations (10) and (25) – $M - E$ is equated with a foreign saving (loan or gift to the home country). By this means domestic investment can be increased.

In Example 5, $62 = 58 + (67 + 3 + 0) - (60 + 3 + 3)$.

If $E > M$, then $E - M > 0$ and S_α would be greater than I_α. Now $E - M$ is deemed to correspond to a foreign investment: $I_\alpha + E - M = S_\alpha$.

Furthermore, equations (20) and (23) now have to be adjusted as follows:

$$Y_\pi = Y_{he} + Y_{hg} + Y_{hf} + V_{hg} + V_{hf} \quad (33)$$

and

$$Y = Y_{he} + Y_{hg} + Y_{hf} + S_{\alpha e} + T_{je} + Y_{gf} - R_g^*. \quad (34)$$

4 National product, national income and national expenditure

Following what we have just set out, we should give a systematic definition of the national product and the corresponding data such

44

as national income and national expenditure, at the same time clarifying the interrelationship between them.

a. National product
With the exception of households (although domestic servants, for instance, may also perform productive work), every sector contributes to the gross national product.

In calculating the value of production by enterprises, we must take care to avoid double counting; raw materials or semi-finished products delivered by certain firms are further processed by other firms. Only the value added must be taken into account, i.e. the value of the goods and services produced (including the provision of domestic capital) after the value of purchases from other firms has been deducted. If this method is employed, the danger of such duplication is ruled out, as inter-firm transactions are not included.

Calculation of the value added by government activity occasions difficulties, as government services are not made available at market prices. It is accordingly assumed that the value of the actual production is equal to the cost price (see Section 2c). Components of the latter are payments made to factors, depreciation allowances, and purchases of goods and services. As in the case of firms, however, such purchases must be deducted so as not to count in the same production twice.

The contribution from the rest of the world is equal to the payment received from other countries for the contribution of resident nationals of the home country (not foreign residents) to production abroad. The corresponding income paid to foreigners, however, is deducted. In the domestic product, no account is taken of this distinction, as the relevant production is due to the activity of both nationals and foreigners. Remuneration to nationals resident abroad is thus disregarded.

A country's gross national product can therefore be defined as the sum of the values added during a given period in all branches of the economy, plus income from abroad and less income accruing to foreigners for their contribution to production (see also Example 6).

The net national product is calculated by deducting from the gross national product the expenditure required for maintaining the capital stock.

In both the net and the gross national product at market prices, account is taken of cost-increasing taxes and of subsidies.

b. National income

The national product yields an income to the factors of production which contribute to it. By 'national income' is meant income paid during a given period to a country's normal residents by enterprises, government and other countries.

In the case of households, such income consists in payment for their productive activity; in the case of enterprises, it is undistributed income (reserves before direct taxation); and in the case of the government, it takes the form of income from the government's own property less the interest which it pays on the national debt (Example 6).

National income is obtained at the value of the payments made to the factors of production (factor cost), while the national product is expressed in terms of market prices. In order to convert national income into national product, therefore, account has to be taken of the items which influence market price, namely indirect taxes and subsidies.

The earned national income Y_η, which is equal to X_α, must not be confused with the received national income Y_ψ to which is added the balance on transfer payments from and to other countries. Personal income Y_π is that part of the received national income which flows to households plus the transfer payments received from government. If taxes T_{jh} are deducted from personal income, this gives the disposable personal income $Y_{h\delta}$ which is applied to consumption or saving.

'National income' is frequently used as a synonym for net national product at market prices (also referred to as national income at market prices Y_m), so that both concepts may be represented either by $X_{\alpha m}$ or by Y_m. (Henceforth, whenever the two concepts are not expressly contrasted, the symbol Y_m will be used, as has become the usual practice, or – where there can be no possible confusion with the national income in the restricted sense – the symbol Y is used.)

In conformity with the production concept used in the USSR (Chapter 1.5), the Soviet system takes no account of certain services (public sector, trade) in the calculation of the national income.

c. National expenditure

The resources which can be used for expenditure are furnished by the gross national product $X_{\beta m}$ and the balance on transfer payments to and from other countries V_f. The expenditure itself consists of consumption and investment.

d. Macroeconomic relationships

The most important relations find expression in the equations on page 48 and in Figure 3. The figures are those employed in Example 5, and the bars in Figure 3 are drawn to scale, the crosshatched portions representing negative amounts. In equation (34), to round off the picture, allowance is made for direct taxes T_{je} paid by enterprises (which are not shown in the example). The same applies to M_b of equation (27).

Appraisal

The national product affords an idea of a country's economic importance (Figure 4). It must nevertheless be remembered that the national product includes many services which have no, or no direct, influence on a country's welfare, e.g. defence expenditure. An increase in such expenditure even causes, when there is full employment, a fall in the production of other goods and services. The drawbacks inherent in many types of production (air pollution, water contamination) are disregarded. If output of motorcars is stepped up, expenditure rises as a consequence of the increased traffic (hospitals, police), the relevant incomes being incorporated in the national product in this case too.

In point of fact, the only welfare indicator is *per capita* consumption, but if account is to be taken of the possibilities of increased consumption in the future, allowance must also be made for investment and accordingly calculations must be based on the *per capita* national product.

The national product is used a great deal as a yardstick in international studies. If, for instance, gross investment is seen to account for 24 per cent of the gross national product at market prices in Western Germany (1967) and only 17 per cent in the United Kingdom, the first impression from these figures is that Germany's welfare will in the future grow at a faster rate than the UK's.

Care must be exercised when it comes to making international comparisons, not only on account of the divergent relative importance of incomes of, for example, members of the armed forces and useless intermediaries in the distribution process, but also because the

and from other countries by the expenditure of the economics of consumption and investment.

Equation (26)
at factor cost:

$$X_\alpha^d = C + I_\alpha + E_a - M_a$$
$$340 = 350 + 60 - 70$$

Equation (27)
at factor cost:

$$X_\alpha = X_\alpha^d + E_b - M_b$$
$$343 = 340 + 3 - 0$$

Equation (17):

$$X_{\alpha m} = X_\alpha + T_i - W$$
$$368 = 343 + 40 - 15$$

Equation (2)
at market prices:

$$X_{\beta m} = X_{\alpha m} + D$$
$$393 = 368 + 25$$

Equation (29)
gross:

$$X_{\beta m} + V_{hf} = C + I_\beta + E - M$$
$$393 + 3 = (289 + 24) + 87 - 4$$

Equation (1):

$$X_\alpha = Y$$
$$343 = 343$$

The received national
income:

$$X_\psi = Y + V_{hf}$$
$$346 = 343 + 3$$

Equation (34):

$$Y_h + S_{\alpha e} + T_{je} + Y_{gf} - R_g^* = Y$$
$$326 + 22 + 0 + 1 - 6 = 343$$

Equation (33):

$$Y_\pi = Y_h + V_{hg} + V_{hf}$$
$$366 = 326 + 37 + 3$$

Equation (21):

$$Y_{h\delta} + T_{jh} = Y_\pi$$
$$330 + 36 = 366$$

Equation (21):

$$C_h + S_{\alpha h} = Y_{h\delta}$$
$$289 + 41 = 330$$

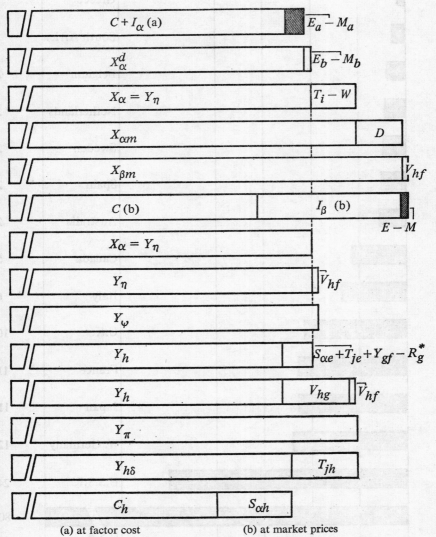

(a) at factor cost   (b) at market prices

Figure 3: The relationship between selected macroeconomic data

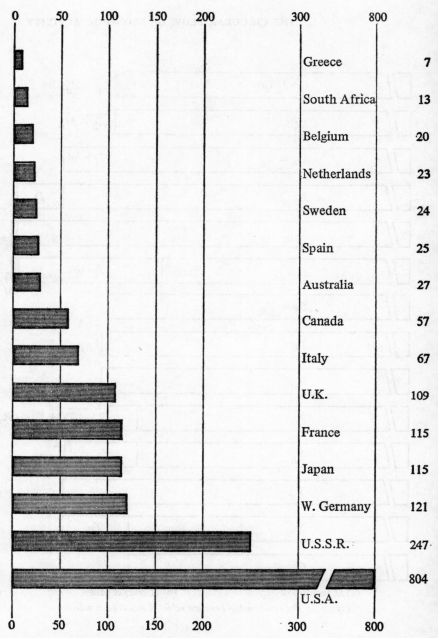

Figure 4: Gross national product at market prices of selected countries ($000 m. 1967)

accuracy with which the national product is calculated varies considerably from country to country (and exchange rates do not accord with purchasing-power parities; Chapter 12.5).

Fluctuations in economic activity (business cycles; Chapter 9.1) and economic growth are illustrated by the changes in the national product. The best basis to adopt is the real (and not the nominal) national product, in which price movements are eliminated. Should the (nominal) national product amount to £5,000 million in 1971, as compared with £4,000 million in 1970, this is not a 25 per cent rise if prices have risen by an average of 10 per cent in the course of the year. The real national product is then £4,545 million – (£5,000 million ÷ 110) 100 – and the real increase only 14 per cent. The movements of the national product are therefore often calculated in terms of constant prices of a base year and not in terms of current prices.

The *per capita* national product or income is a criterion for assessing the degree of development of different countries (see Chapter 10.6). That it is a relative and approximate measure is a point that must not be overlooked. Not infrequently, countries are labelled 'underdeveloped' when their *per capita* national product is less than a quarter of that of the United States. This is somewhat misleading because in some areas the growth potential is slight. Nor is the euphemistic term 'developing country' wholly correct, because many economies have achieved no progress for several decades. The best way would be to speak of poor and rich countries, but this is avoided for psychological reasons. In our view, the designation 'less-developed countries' is to be preferred.

Overall welfare indicators, such as the *per capita* national product, take no account of the distribution of the national income over the various regions (southern and northern Italy), social classes (Western Europe and Latin America) or ethnic groups (United States, South Africa) in a country.

To base calculations on the net real *per capita* national income is to ignore the changes in hours worked and in the ratio of the working population (those involved in the production process) to the total population. It would accordingly be better to examine the trend of production per man-hour, but exact calculation of this trend gives rise to further difficulties.

There is not necessarily a direct connection between the national capital stock and the national product: the (social) capital of a country represents part of its production capacity, which is either used or unused.

5 The national accounts

The description of the circular flow of economic activity has been supplemented by accounts for illustrative purposes. All such accounts (Example 5) may be regarded as a system of national accounts or of national accounting. More accounts can be created where statistically possible.

As a general rule, transactions are entered on the date at which the resultant debts and claims arise. (This also applies, for instance, to taxes.) For practical reasons, goods transactions with the rest of the world are recorded on the dates when the relevant consignment crosses the frontier.

In certain circumstances, transactions are not accompanied by payments or detailed valuation, which therefore has to be estimated (imputation). Instances which come to mind are food and clothing for conscripts, agricultural output consumed on the farm ('captive consumption'), and owner-occupied housing.

In Example 5 a method of institutional accounting is adopted. The economic units are grouped in sectors, for which separate accounts have been drawn up in each case. Thus the national product is not directly calculated. It can, however, be deduced from the various accounts.

In actual practice, the general procedure is to base calculations directly on a 'national product and national expenditure' account and on a 'national income' account. One reason for this is that in the case of many transactions by firms it is not possible to determine accurately the sectors with which they have been concluded. These two accounts are thus substituted for the 'enterprises' account. Apart from these, accounts in respect of households, government, the rest of the world and capital transactions are maintained. In Example 6, therefore, only the 'national product and national expenditure' account and the 'national' income account are shown (in which a number of items have been combined). On the national income account, however, the interest on the public debt has been deducted from government income from the rest of the world. (This was not done in Example 5, so that in a complete Example 6 the relevant interest must be shown as a negative item upon the income side in the government account.)

EXAMPLE 6

National product and national expenditure account

Y	National income	343	C_h	Household consumption ($C_{he} + C_{hg} + M_{ah}$)	289
D	Depreciation	25	C_g	Government consumption	24
T_i	Indirect taxes	40	$I\beta$	Gross investment ($I\beta_e + I\beta_g$)	87
W	*Less:* Subsidies	−15	E	Sales to the rest of the world and factor remuneration by the rest of the world ($E_a + E_{bh} + E_{bg}$)	63
			M	*Less:* Purchases from the rest of the world and factor remuneration to the rest of the world ($M_{ah} + M_{ae}$)	−70
X_m	Gross national product at market prices	393	$X\beta m$	Gross national expenditure at market prices	393

National income account

Y_h	Household income ($Y_{he} + Y_{hg} + Y_{hf}$)	326	Y	National income	343
$S_{\alpha e}$	Saving by enterprises	22			
Y_{gf}	Government income from the rest of the world	1			
R_g^*	*Less:* Interest on national debt	−6			
		343			343

Appraisal

The national accounts system affords a comprehensive picture of the whole economy, since it brings all the individual economic units together in groups and shows the relation between these groups.

The national accounts provide a clearer idea of the influence of economic policy. Relevant problems '. . . can be analysed adequately only within the framework of the national income accounts. Only a complete system of accounts is capable of making explicit the economic relations involved' (R. and N. D. Ruggles). Estimates of future national accounts make it easier to draw up the government budget. In some countries, therefore, such accounts (estimated national accounts for the following year, which are called the national budget) are published at the same time as the government budget.

Needless to say, not all data fundamental to knowledge of a country's economic situation are to be found in the national accounts, but the latter can, if appropriate, be supplemented with the desired information (notably an input-output table: Section 6).

The 'capital transactions' account in the foregoing examples contains only those transactions which have taken place in the real sector (saving, investment, depreciation). It would be preferable to record all capital transactions (including loans and issues), but this is usually precluded by lack of statistics. Several countries publish flow-of-funds accounts (Chapter 3.11), which show changes in the amount of credits, foreign reserves (Chapter 3.5a), bank notes, shares and bonds (Chapter 5.2). Knowledge of such a statement makes it easier to judge a country's financial situation.

A 'national balance sheet' account is difficult to draw up – only changes are shown – because it is hard to estimate the national assets or national wealth with any real degree of accuracy. By 'national wealth' is meant the sum of the assets of all economic units (including claims on other countries) or the national assets less debts to other countries (cf. Chapter 1.6c). Here again we find divergent definitions. Some writers consider national resources and national capital synonymous with national wealth. Depending mainly on whether paid-up, social, lucrative or legal capital is meant, various definitions of the national capital are given. We shall not dwell on the problems of calculation involved, because the relevant data have very little significance if at the same time no indications are available as to the distribution, composition and quality of the national capital – and it is precisely on these points that information is scarce.

6 Input-output table

In the national accounts shown above, transactions between individual industries have been disregarded. To include them it would have been necessary to extend the accounts system by preparing an account for every form of activity. An alternative method is to compile a double-entry square table in which the horizontal rows indicate how, over a given period (in most cases one year), each industry's output is divided among the other industries, and the vertical columns show how the inputs to each industry are provided by the other industries.

In the example at Table 3 the industries have, for the sake of simplicity, been grouped in four sectors. The intra-sector transactions are also incorporated: for instance, the interrelationships in the energy sector (including coalmining and electricity generation) total £1·3 million. Internal transactions (in each sector) can be omitted from the table, which would then display a blank main diagonal.

Manufacturing industry supplies goods (horizontal figures, in millions of pounds in each case) valued at 2·1 to agriculture, fishing and forestry; 0·5 to the energy sector; 12·1 to itself; and 2·1 to trade, transport and services; total deliveries to what is known as 'intermediate demand' equal 16·8. Final demand (42·0) embraces exports, capital formation and private and government consumption.

The transactions are entered at the prices received by the producers; trade margins, transport costs and indirect taxes are recorded separately (rows 4 and 7).

Column (c) shows the value of the purchases made by manufacturing industry from the other sectors: 9·4 from agriculture, fishing and forestry; 2·4 from the energy sector; 12·1 from itself; and 3·6 from trade, transport and services. This gives a total of 27·5. The manufacturing sector has also had to expend 3·6 to the rest of the world (for imports of goods not produced at home; competitive imports are assumed to be in transit over the sectors concerned, from where they are delivered) and 1·6 to the government (indirect taxes). The difference between all these payments and total output (58·8) is the value added to the gross domestic product (26·1). For the four sectors combined, this contribution amounts to 60·8 (the difference between 109·6 and 48·8).

Value added by all sectors: 109·6 − (36·4 + 8·6 + 3·8)	60·8
Value added by the rest of the world and government	6·6
Gross national product at factor cost	67·4
Indirect taxes, subsidies	9·4
Gross national product at market prices	76·8

TABLE 3: Example of an input-output table

Producing sectors	Purchasing sectors						
	Agriculture, fishing, forestry (a)	Energy (b)	Manufacturing industry (c)	Trade, transport, services (d)	Intermediate demand (e) = (a) + (b) + (c) + (d)	Final demand (f)	Total output (g) = (e) + (f)
1. Agriculture, fishing, forestry	—		9·4	—	9·4	5·0	14·4
2. Energy	0·1	1·3	2·4	1·0	4·8	2·2	7·0
3. Manufacturing industry	2·1	0·5	12·1	2·1	16·8	42·0	58·8
4. Trade, transport, services	0·9	0·5	3·6	0·4	5·4	24·0	29·4
5. Total purchases from other sectors (1 + 2 + 3 + 4)	3·1	2·3	27·5	3·5	36·4	73·2	109·6
6. Imports	2·2	0·7	3·6	2·1	8·6	—	8·6
7. Indirect taxes less subsidies	-0·2	0·2	1·6	2·2	3·8	5·6	9·4
8. Value added	9·3	3·8	26·1	21·6	60·8	6·6	67·4
9. Total input	14·4	7·0	58·8	29·4	109·6	85·4	195·0

Dividing the value of each input to a particular industry by the value of that industry's total input (and, if appropriate, multiplying this amount by 10, 100 or 1,000) gives us the technological, or input, coefficients (Table 4) – that is to say, the proportions in which each means of production must contribute to produce a unit of a given good (cf. the capital-output ratio; Chapter 10.4). Production of £1,000 worth of energy, for example, requires £186 worth of consumption of energy, £71 worth of products of manufacturing industry, £71 worth of trade and transport services and £100 worth of imported products.

TABLE 4: The technological coefficients (derived from Table 3)

Producing sectors	Purchasing sectors			
	Agriculture, fishing, forestry	Energy	Manufacturing industry	Trade, transport, services
1. Agriculture, fishing, forestry	—	—	160	—
2. Energy	7	186	41	34
3. Manufacturing industry	146	71	206	71
4. Trade, transport, services	62	71	61	14
5. Total purchases from other sectors	215	328	468	119
6. Imports	153	100	61	71
7. Indirect taxes less subsidies	−14	29	27	75
8. Value added	646	543	444	735
Total	1,000	1,000	1,000	1,000

Appraisal

The input-output table is a worthwhile extension of the national accounts. It gives an idea of the cost structure and useful indicators concerning the supply and demand factors on certain markets. The necessary statistics are hard to obtain, however: we have to make do with rough estimates. Moreover, breaking the figures down into sectors which are assumed to produce homogeneous goods engenders a number of intractable problems (as with industries engaged in different types of production). Again, there is assumed to be a proportional relation between the inputs and the outputs (technological

57

knowledge remaining the same); this is scarcely a realistic hypothesis and deprives the input-output table of some of its significance as a forecasting instrument. That no influence is exerted by prices on the technological coefficients (as is implicitly assumed) is also improbable.

7 Bibliography

a. The national accounts and national income

By way of introduction: H. Edey and A. Peacock, *National Income and Social Accounting* (London 1954); W. I. Abraham, *National Income and Economic Accounting* (Englewood Cliffs, N. J. 1969). For a more thoroughgoing discussion: R. and N. D. Ruggles, *National Income Accounts and Income Analysis* (2nd ed., New York, 1956); A. and D. Vandermeulen, *National Income: Analysis by Sector Accounts* (Englewood Cliffs, N. J. 1956).

In order to promote international comparison, the Organization for European Economic Co-operation (OEEC) has published *A Standardized System of National Accounts* (OEEC, Paris 1959). Comparable publications have been issued by the EEC: *European System of Integrated National Accounts* (Brussels 1968), and the United Nations: *A System of National Accounts and Supporting Tables* (3rd rev. ed. New York 1969). See also *Problems in the International Comparison of Economic Accounts* (*Studies in Income and Wealth*, Vol. 20, Princeton 1957).

P. Studenski, *The Income of Nations: Theory, Measurement and Analysis. Past and Present: A Study in Applied Economics and Statistics* (New York 1958), gives a survey of the history, method and working-out of national income calculations in all countries, to be consulted for its historical review. On the method to be adopted for the calculation of the real national product: D. Usher, *Rich and Poor Countries: A Study in Problems of Comparisons of Real Income* (London 1966).

In communist countries, the definition of national income is affected by the prevailing views on the concept of 'production'. See 'A Note on some Aspects of National Accounting Methodology in Eastern Europe and the Soviet Union', *Economic Bulletin for Europe*, 1959, No. 3; M. Kaser, 'A Survey of the National Accounts of Eastern Europe', in *Studies in Social and Financial Accounting* (ed. P. Deane, London 1961).

An extensive and annotated bibliography can be found in *Biblio-*

graphy on Income and Wealth, Vol. 1, 1937–47 (ed. D. Creamer, Cambridge 1952); Vol. 2, 1948–9 (ed. P. Deane, Cambridge 1953); the subsequent volumes were also edited by P. Deane.

On financial accounts: see Chapter 3.12*e.*

b. The national wealth

See *Studies in Income and Wealth*, Vol. 2 (Princeton 1938), Vol. 12 (New York 1950) and Vol. 14 (New York 1951). The last two volumes are devoted to national wealth; Vol. 12 includes several papers on the concept as such and estimates concerning agriculture, industry and government. The seven articles contained in Vol. 14 consider the problem in the national context and in the light of economic theory. *The Measurement of National Wealth* (ed. R. W. Goldsmith and C. Saunders, Chicago 1959) comprises contributions on national wealth in several countries.

For the United States: R. W. Goldsmith, *The National Wealth of the United States in the Postwar Period* (Princeton 1962); see also Vol. 29 of the above mentioned *Studies in Income and Wealth* (New York 1964).

c. Input-output tables

The theory is developed in W. W. Leontief, *The Structure of the American Economy, 1919–1939: An Empirical Application of Equilibrium Analysis* (2nd ed., New York 1951); *id. et al., Studies in the Structure of the American Economy* (New York 1953). See also W. W. Leontief, *Input-Output Economics* (New York 1966), a collection of eleven articles published from 1947 to 1965.

Commentary on the theory can be found in *Input-Output Relations* (Leiden 1953); *The Structural Interdependence of the Economy* (ed. T. Barna, New York 1954). These two works are collections of conference papers, including some by W. W. Leontief. *Input-Output Analysis: An Appraisal* (Vol. 18 of *Studies in Income and Wealth*, Princeton 1955), is another series of papers contributed to a conference on this subject (see especially the contribution of C. Christ); see also R. Dorfman, 'The Nature and the Significance of Input-Output', *RES*, May 1954.

A systematic exposition is given by H. B. Chenery and P. G. Clark, *Interindustry Economics* (New York 1959).

For the USSR: M. Eidelman, 'Inter-Branch Balance of the Social Product and its Economic Content', and L. Berri, F. Klotsvog and

S. Shatalin, 'The Inter-Branch Balance and its Use in Planning', *PE*, August 1962; M. Eidelman, 'The Input-Output Table in the Soviet Union', in *Input-Output Tables: Their Compilation and Use* (ed. O. Lukács, Budapest 1962); this is a translation of the Hungarian edition; it also deals with Hungary and Poland.

d. Statistical data

Information concerning the pre-war period can be found in P. Studenski, *The Income of Nations*. For the Belgian national accounts, see *Bulletin de Statistique*; for the Netherlands, *Nationale rekeningen 19–*; West Germany, *Wirtschaft und Statistik*; France, *Etudes et Conjoncture*; Italy, *Bollettino mensile di Statistica*; Luxembourg, *Cahiers Economiques*; the United Kingdom, *National Income and Expenditure 19–*; the United States, *Survey of Current Business*. A description of the national accounts of the United Kingdom is given in R. Maurice, *National Accounts Statistics: Sources and Methods* (London 1968).

Input-output tables on a uniform basis have been published for the EEC countries: *Tableaux entrées – sorties pour les pays de la Communauté Economique Européenne*, December 1965; see also the *General Statistical Bulletin* (EEC) 1966, No. 9.

3 Money

> ... *ce roi est un grand magicien* ..., *S'il n'a*
> *qu'un million d'écus dans son trésor et qu'il en ait*
> *besoin de deux, il n'a qu'à leur persuader qu'un*
> *écu en vaut deux, et ils le croient. S'il a une*
> *guerre difficile à soutenir et qu'il n'ait point*
> *d'argent, il n'a qu'à leur mettre dans la tête qu'un*
> *morceau de papier est de l'argent, et ils en sont*
> *aussitôt convaincus.*
>
> Montesquieu

A definition of money has already been given in Chapter 1.4. Attention is now directed to the composition of the circular flow of money in an economy and to the financial accounts, which supplement the national accounts dealt with in the previous chapter. Here too, for the sake of convenience, concepts which in fact are difficult to distinguish from one another (e.g. paper money, credit, banking) are discussed separately.

1 The functions of money

Division of labour (Chapter 6.4*a*), upon which the modern economy is based, implies the necessity for exchange. The greater the scope for exchange, the further the division of labour can be carried. The bartering of goods for goods caused innumerable difficulties, and it was not long before an indirect form of transaction was initiated, a third good being introduced between the goods to be exchanged. In the early stages, precious metals were used for this purpose and, in primitive societies, shells, salt and cattle were employed. Thus money was originally defined as any good that is generally accepted as an instrument of payment for goods and services. When the most recent forms of money have been studied, it will be seen that the term 'any good' must be construed in a very broad sense.

The principal function of money is that of a medium of exchange. It simplifies transactions and saves a great deal of time. As a medium of exchange, money must express the value of the goods being traded.

This second function – standard of value (means of expressing prices) – helps in arriving at rapid economic valuations, which in turn enable the price mechanism to function. What are known as units of account are used solely as a standard of value and have no function as exchange media. Thus it was that the countries in the European Payments Union (EPU) adopted a unit of account with a gold value of 0·88867088 fine grams ('Epunit'). The actual payments were effected in gold, dollars, or other generally accepted national currencies (a currency being the unit upon which a nation's monetary system is based).

In order to be a good standard of value, money must have a fixed value. Sometimes, when the value of money is subject to heavy fluctuations, calculations are made in terms of more stable foreign currency units.

Another function of money is to act as a standard of deferred payments, a reserve of purchasing power. The less the preference for current rather than future consumption, the less is the volume of spending and the greater that of saving. Hence the term 'time preference'. If anybody wishes to have immediate disposal over his savings at all times, he keeps them in the form of financial assets, mainly money or securities or deposits readily convertible into money (see below Sections 3 and 4). 'Securities' is the collective name for various titles such as shares and bonds (Chapter 5.2). Bills of exchange, promissory notes (see Section 6) and cheques (see Section 4), which like money are instruments of payment, are not regarded as securities. The preference for liquid assets (i.e. media which are immediately negotiable) is called 'liquidity preference'. In other words, the higher the proportion of savings maintained in this form, the greater is the liquidity preference.

The motives for holding cash balances are:

a. the transactions motive: to make payments for consumption (income being received at regular intervals) and investment;

b. the precautionary motive: to deal with unexpected or possible contingencies;

c. the speculative motive: investment in securities (Chapter 5.2) and spending are deferred in anticipation of more favourable terms (lower prices); conversely, they are advanced in a period of rising prices.

When saving is prompted by motives b and c, it is called hoarding;

62

this is also the case when funds which were intended to be used for transactions are assigned a more passive role (for reasons of precaution and speculation). To transfer liquid funds from the passive or non-active sphere (precaution and speculation) to the active sphere (transactions), on the other hand, is dishoarding. Hoarding is markedly influenced by custom and tradition (as in the Middle East and Asia). Classification into the three motives is rather arbitrary; sometimes it is difficult to distinguish one from another.

The various functions of money are closely interlinked.

2 Coin

Money is subdivided into coin, paper money and deposit money. The first category can be discussed in terms of standard and token coin, small coin and trade coin. Of these, only small coin is still a factor, albeit a not very important one, in the quantity of money.

a. Standard coin

Standard coin is a precious metal currency which is unlimited legal tender and may also be coined without restriction. This means that everyone has the right to make coins from gold or silver himself (or to have this done by a specialized institution, against payment of costs) and that such coins must be accepted by everybody up to an unlimited amount. In practice, coin is issued mainly by the government.

Precious metals, especially gold and silver, were accepted as a medium of exchange at a very early stage. Compared with other goods, they offered numerous advantages, including the following:

1. they are homogeneous and durable;
2. they represent a high value in relation to their size;
3. they can easily be divided up into small quantities without loss (striking coins was eventually adopted in order to obviate the need for weighing);
4. they are fairly stable in value; considering the vastness of stocks, the annual increase is quite small, although the discovery of new mines has been known to cause disruption.

In monetary systems a distinction is made, according to the number of precious metals from which the coins are minted, between monometallism, or single standard, and bimetallism, or double standard.

In the latter case, the ratio between the two standard coins is usually laid down by law.

Bimetallism was the practice in several countries in the eighteenth century (in France from 1726, in the United States from 1792), the value ratio between silver and gold being usually 1:15·5.

The United Kingdom was the first country to declare gold the sole standard of value (in 1816). Up to that time, silver had frequently been overabundant compared with gold (after the discovery of the silver mines at Potosí in 1544), so that the nominal value (that shown on the coin itself) was sometimes higher than the metal, or intrinsic, value. This meant that it was worth while striking new silver coins, since they still had to be accepted at their nominal value for payment purposes.

b. Token coin

Token money is a metal currency which is unlimited legal tender but may not be freely coined. It is used in countries with a bimetallic system when the intrinsic metal value of one of the standard currencies is less than the nominal value. To ensure that there is no mass coining, the government has to reserve the right to issue such money.

After a short period during which the ratio of value between gold and silver changed in favour of the latter – as a consequence of the discovery of gold in California (1848) and Australia (1851) – and some countries even introduced silver monometallism (Belgium from 1850 to 1861, the Netherlands from 1847 to 1873, eighteen German states from 1838 to 1871), the working of the Nevada silver mines in 1870 led to a fresh reduction in the value of silver. Even the discovery of the gold mines in Transvaal (1889) and the Klondike (1896) brought no change in this situation. Countries with a bimetallic or silver currency system were compelled to switch to the gold standard and thus prohibit the coining of silver (Germany in 1871, Belgium in 1873, the Netherlands in 1875, France and Italy in 1878).

This state of affairs gave rise to the limping standard, a system in which a gold standard money and a silver token money are in circulation at the same time.

There is still a token money in Belgium today (the silver hundred-franc piece).

Gresham's 'law'

With a bimetallic system where the *de facto* ratio between the two standard coins does not correspond to the *de jure* ratio, and with the limping standard, there is a preference for the currency with the stronger position. If, for instance, a standard and a token coin circulate together, people elect rather to spend the latter – the 'bad money', so-called because the value in metal is lower than the nominal value – and to hoard the former – the 'good money' (both values of which are equal) – especially for making payments to other countries, where only the intrinsic value counts. Bad money is said to drive out good (from circulation); this is called Gresham's 'law'.

This 'law', which had actually been formulated before Gresham's time (1519–79), holds good for all types of money. Thus in some countries of continental Europe, during the Second World War, pre-war bank notes were hoarded by some people because they were wrongly thought to have a higher value.

c. Small coin

Small coin may be legal tender to a limited extent only. That is to say, the law may not require it to be accepted in payment in excess of the stated amount. Coin may not be struck freely. It is issued by the government. From an economic standpoint, however, the difference between token and small coin is unimportant, because no one would think of refusing small coin above a specific amount. Nor, indeed, may government departments do so.

In theory, Belgian fifty franc silver coins are only legal tender up to one thousand francs. In West Germany the corresponding sums for mark and pfennig coins are twenty marks and five marks. In other countries, notably Italy and France, there are provisions to the same effect. In the United Kingdom they date right back to 1817 (copper being legal tender up to a shilling, silver up to two pounds). Under United States law, all coins are legal tender. Most modern writers consider all small coin token money, on the definition that token coin is coin whose intrinsic metal value is less than its nominal value.

d. Trade coin

Trade coins may be freely minted but are not legal tender. Austrian Maria Theresa thalers are still struck in Europe and are generally accepted in the Red Sea region.

3 Paper money

Paper money may be either representative, fiduciary or conventional.

a. Representative paper money

Representative paper money came into circulation through the depositing of precious metals with a money-changer or cashier (to avoid difficulties of transport and storage). In exchange, the depositor received a paper certificate or cashier's certificate having the same value as the metal he had surrendered, which it represented and for which it was encashable. Initially, certificates were issued for amounts which corresponded to the value of the gold or silver deposited. Later on, it was found to be easier to put certificates representing round sums into circulation.

The authorities too can issue such certificates. Prior to 1933, the United States Treasury brought out 'gold certificates', which were fully covered by gold. (The present 'silver certificates' are covered by silver but at the latter's nominal value; they thus represent silver token money.)

b. Fiduciary paper money

Fiduciary paper money evolved out of representative paper money. It was found by the money-changers or cashiers that not all the precious metal they held was demanded at the same time, and accordingly they were able to issue more paper than was covered by their stock precious metals. Cover was no longer sufficient to guarantee full and immediate exchangeability. Because of the confidence placed in banks, this uncovered paper could be put into circulation; hence the name 'fiduciary money'. The cashiers played a more active part: they became bankers (see Section 7).

c. Conventional paper money

In the case of conventional paper money, the authorities are no longer obliged to exchange on demand. This system is adopted when the bank of issue (whether a government institution or a private firm) finds itself unable to meet its commitments – when, for instance, there is a danger of war or economic difficulties arise and the general public try to convert all their notes into gold, or when, in exceptional circumstances, the government orders a large additional amount of paper money to be issued.

To take a few examples, exchangeability was suspended in France in 1720 (see Section 10*c*), from 1848 to 1850, from 1870 to 1878, from 1914 to 1928, and from 1936; in Belgium from 1914 to 1926 and from 1940; in Germany from 1914 to 1930 and from 1931 onwards; in Italy from 1914 to 1927 and from 1935; in the United Kingdom from 1931; in the United States from 1933; and in the Netherlands and Switzerland from 1936.

At the present time, conventional paper money is in circulation everywhere.

Nor is exchangeability obligatory in the case of what are known as 'currency notes'. These consist of paper money which is issued directly by the government (not through the agency of the Central Bank, even if the latter is in fact a public enterprise) in place of and alongside small coin which is also issued by the government itself. The *assignats* during the French revolution and the German *Reichskassenscheine* in the pre-1924 period were currency notes. At the time of writing, currency notes are still circulating in the United States, Belgium and the Netherlands. In Belgium, the government can issue notes of denominations up to fifty francs (together with coin) up to a ceiling of Fr 9,000 million, and in the Netherlands notes of denominations up to 2·50 guilders up to a ceiling of 2·5 million guilders.

4 Deposit money

In addition to 'fiat money' – the notes and coins the issue of which is based on legal provisions – there is bank or deposit money (*monnaie scripturale, Buchgeld*) – balances with a bank or giro institution which are payable on demand and without restrictions (see Section 7). As used to be the case with coins, notes are handed into these institutions for custody in order to prevent loss and facilitate payments. Transactions in such assets are effected by cheques and transfers (which themselves are not deposit money).

A cheque is a document in which a financial intermediary (in some countries this must be a bank) is given an order to pay on demand a specific amount of money.

If the payee of a cheque has a balance (an account) with the same bank as the person giving the order to pay, payment may be effected by means of a giro or transfer, the payee's balance being increased (his account at the bank credited) and the drawer's reduced (his

67

account debited) by the same amount, without any notes or coin being put into circulation. The money is transferred.

In other words, transactions between two persons who have accounts with the same institution can be settled, or cleared, by transfers without money changing hands at all: payment is a purely bookkeeping operation.

If the two persons in question have accounts with different banks, they can still make transfers. The major banks are continuously settling claims between themselves, the balance then being transferred. For this purpose, representatives of the banks come together in what are known as clearing houses.

In such cases, the money does not assume material form, and consequently our earlier definition of money is not wholly correct: money is not always a good, but can also be a symbol or token. Furthermore, it now has a personal character, and payment in round sums is no longer required.

Thus, money consists of freely disposable coins and bank and currency notes, and also of balances held by the general public (excluding money-creating institutions and central government).

Deposits which are not payable immediately but on a fixed date (e.g. after three or six months) or at two or more months' notice ('time deposits') are not counted as money proper but as 'near money'; that is to say, they are not classed with current or deposit accounts (demand deposits) unless the notice of withdrawal required is less than one month (see below).

If notes or coin are deposited with a bank in order to open or add to a deposit account, money substitution takes place. (Fiat money is converted into deposit money, the money in the possession of the bank not being deemed part of the country's total quantity of money, at least when the bank concerned is a money-creating institution.) Time deposits, however, lead to creation of money when they are changed into demand deposits. (The reverse occurs when demand deposits are converted into time deposits.) The creation of credit (see Section 6) also leads to the creation of money (destruction of money takes place on repayment), as does the sale of bills or bonds to the bank. (Here too, a money-destruction process takes place on the date of maturity.)

In the United States and the United Kingdom, deposit money accounts for over threequarters of the total quantity of money, in Italy for about 70 per cent, in Belgium, the Netherlands, West Germany and France for 50 to 65 per cent. In the United Kingdom, deposit money was introduced with the object of circumventing the stringent provisions concerning the issue of banknotes in the 1844 Bank Charter Act.

'Near money' is a concept which covers assets that cannot be used directly as a medium of exchange but which can be converted into money in the fairly short term – time deposits, bonds and treasury certificates (Chapter 5.2). When bonds and treasury certificates are sold on the stock exchange (Chapter 7.1), the amounts received vary on account of changes in stock-exchange quotations. Actual money, on the other hand, has a constant nominal value.

5 Metallism and nominalism

a. Metallism

In metallism, the exchange value of money is based on the value of the underlying metal (cover): under the gold standard, the value of a bank note is equal to the value of the gold for which it can be exchanged.

1. Gold specie standard and gold bullion standard

Within the gold standard there are two distinct systems – the gold specie and the gold bullion standard.

Under the gold specie standard, bank notes are exchangeable for gold coin (as in most countries prior to 1914).

Under the gold bullion standard, notes can be exchanged for a specified minimum quantity of gold. This was the system in Belgium from 1926 to 1940, in Germany from 1930 to 1931, in France from 1928 to 1936, in the United Kingdom from 1925 to 1931, in Italy from 1927 to 1936, and in the Netherlands from 1926 to 1936. In the United Kingdom prior to 1931, for instance, the minimum that could be tendered in notes was the equivalent of a gold ingot of 400 ounces (£1,699).

Sometimes all or part of the gold cover is replaced by foreign exchange. The latter includes foreign coin and paper money and other external claims (mainly on the United States) which are convertible into gold in the countries concerned. Thus by foreign exchange is meant all internationally accepted instruments of payment (e.g. foreign bank notes, foreign bank demand deposits, securities readily exchangeable for money). Gold currencies are currencies which are exchangeable for gold. This system is known as the gold exchange standard; it had its heyday in the period from 1925 to 1931.

Foreign gold covers not only foreign currency but also the national currency. It was thus easier for countries lacking in gold to adhere to the gold standard. Unlike gold, foreign exchange frequently yields a return (foreign bank deposits). Holders are, however, at the mercy of conditions abroad; devaluation (Chapter 12.6) of a foreign currency sometimes occasions heavy losses. This was the experience of the West European countries in 1931 after the depreciation of the pound sterling.

2. *Gold cover*

The extent of the gold cover is governed by either of two distinct principles – the banking principle and the currency principle. Under the first, there is no limit to the volume of notes and coin and deposit money, provided exchangeability is maintained. Under the currency principle, the note issue is subject to strict regulation (gold or gold currency cover) – directly, by imposition of a ceiling on the volume of unbacked notes issued, or indirectly, by taxation of notes in excess of a certain amount.

The most widely adopted formula is proportional cover, in which notes (and possibly demand deposits with the central bank) must always be backed to a minimum proportional extent.

At present, it is applied by the three countries (Belgium, the Netherlands and Switzerland) where there is still a statutory gold cover. In Belgium this was 40 per cent from 1926 to 1940, including at least 30 per cent in gold; since 1957 one third in gold (since 1969 including also claims in gold on international financial institutions and drawing rights on the International Monetary Fund). In the Netherlands, it was 40 per cent in gold from 1864 to 1914 and from 1929 to 1945 and since 1956 has been 50 per cent in gold and convertible foreign exchange. In Switzerland, it has been 40 per cent in gold since 1905.

The system in Germany from 1875 to 1914 and from 1924 to 1931 was 40 per cent in gold or gold currency but at least 30 per cent in gold; a lower cover ratio was then allowed, and in 1939 the compulsory cover rule was abolished. From 1928 to 1939, the French authorities required a 35 per cent gold cover. From 1927 to 1935, the Italian authorities prescribed 40 per cent in gold or gold currency. The corresponding cover ratio in the United States was 40 per cent in gold from 1913 to 1945, after which it was 25 per cent until 1968.

In the United Kingdom, the amount of unbacked bank notes has been fixed by Parliament since 1844 (in September 1939 the compulsory-cover system was abolished). A comparable system was introduced in Germany in 1875; in this case a tax had to be paid on uncovered notes, and this was not abolished until 1933.

It is noteworthy that in the communist literature a traditional view is championed: the quantity of money is based on gold and the rouble is defined in terms of gold (although this has not much significance since they are not exchangeable).

b. Nominalism

The theory of nominalism rightly points out that the value of money is independent of the metal from which it has been made or for which it is exchangeable (paper standard). People accept money not because they know it can be exchanged for precious metal but because they can exchange it for goods or services. The exchange value of money has therefore nothing to do with the cover. Various countries have a stable currency without having substantial gold reserves.

Since complete cover is scarcely ever to be found, the gold reserve is of little use in this respect. In normal circumstances, when there is confidence in the currency, no money is exchanged for gold; if war threatens, or if the economic situation deteriorates, the reserves are insufficient to satisfy public demand to the full.

If there is fractional cover, but exchangeability is not obligatory, as in Belgium, the Netherlands and Switzerland, this cannot be called a gold standard system. The purpose here is to counteract the issue of too much money, for any addition to the volume of bank notes necessitates an increase in the gold reserve. Economic policy, however, must be directed to preventing money from being created needlessly even when there are theoretically no limits to its issue (on account of its influence on the overall level of prices: Chapter 9.12). Regulations concerning the gold cover can even be harmful where they stand in the way of a necessary increase in the quantity of money.

So far, however, gold has continued to play an important role in international payments (Chapter 11.6d).

6 Credit

Demand deposits are practically never withdrawn in full. This is a form of liquidity preference on the part of depositors. Thus the banks have an unused amount of money at their disposal. Quite early on, they were induced, because of the return due on such deposits (interest), to make this reserve or part of it available to persons who needed money. They put the money deposits in earning assets and kept only partial cash reserves against the deposits (cf. the issue of fiduciary paper money: Section 3*b*).

Before a bank will lend money, it needs to have confidence in the borrower, as it will if he has already deposited a certain amount of money. But the bank can make money available even where the person requesting it has made no deposit at all, provided it believes (the Latin verb is *credere*) that the sum advanced (plus the interest) will be repaid. The bank is then said to have granted 'credit' (or opened a credit).

Goods too can be supplied prior to payment. By credit, therefore, we mean the provision of goods or sums of money without payment or repayment until some future date. (A credit is also the name used for authorization given by Parliament to the government to make expenditure.)

The theory of credit is closely bound up with the theory of interest (Chapter 8.6).

According to whether the relevant period is less than one or two years, up to 7 to 10 years or more than 7 to 10 years, a credit is described as short-, medium- or long-term; where it is for less than three or four months, it is called a very short-term credit. The classification differs from country to country (a short-term credit in Belgium and France being up to one year and in the Netherlands and Italy up to two years). To purchase bonds is to grant long-term credit. Treasury certificates and bills of exchange are short-term credit.

A bill of exchange is commercial paper, drawn up in accordance with statutory provisions, by which somebody (the drawer) gives another person (the drawee) an order to pay a specific sum at a given time (the due date) and at a designated place to the holder of the bill (the taker: a third party or the drawer himself). In a promissory note, the signatory undertakes to pay a certain sum on the due date to the taker, or beneficiary.

The markets in short- and long-term credit are called the money market and the capital market respectively. These two together form the credit market or market in loanable funds.

Depending on the use for which the credit is intended, it is either commercial or consumer credit. Commercial credit is used in productive operations (so the designation 'productive' credit would be preferable). Subclasses of commercial credit include mercantile, industrial and agricultural credit.

If the instalment capacity is not exceeded, consumer credit can have the effect of promoting savings. The immediate money-increasing effect is offset when instalments become due. While this is liable to operate to the detriment of commercial credit, it must not be forgotten that the increase in consumption may stimulate investment. In most countries, there are laws to protect the consumer (minimum deposit, maximum repayment terms – both of which can be reviewed in the light of the economic situation – and maximum rates for the interest charged).

Credit is either private or public credit, depending on the kind of borrower. A distinction is made between personal and collateral credit, this hinging on the guarantee: the first type is based on the personal standing of the borrower, while the second is covered by certain assets, either movable (e.g. shares) or immovable (dwellings). Mortgage credit is hampered by the high costs and the formalities involved. Cooperative credit has developed to a particularly marked extent in agriculture. In most cases, the underlying principles are still those set out by F. Raiffeisen (1818–88), who successfully introduced agricultural cooperatives in Germany around 1850 for the first time in history: one bank for each locality (so as to be better informed about borrowers), an unpaid management, and an overall coordinating body.

7 Banks and other financial institutions

A bank is an institution whose activity consists mainly in granting credit. For this purpose, it uses its own or borrowed funds, or else it creates money. Its name is derived from the old Italian *banca*, the bench or table employed by the former money-changers. Lending operations, however, are not a feature of banks alone: other financial institutions such as life insurance companies and investment companies grant credit. Nor can the capacity of money created be used as a criterion: if it were, only commercial and central banks and the central government (in issuing currency notes: Section 3c) would be banks. In fact, the word 'bank' does not lend itself to a precise definition, since, 'a great variety of financial institutions participate in providing one or more of the services generally regarded as banking functions'. The classification of financial institutions 'offers as many difficulties as does the wording of their definitions' (R. P. Kent). A single organization may be simultaneously engaged in a variety of operations. Moreover, the usual classification of financial institutions differs from country to country, the same designation often being used with different meanings.

a. Commercial banks

The commercial bank grants mainly commercial credit. What would otherwise be unused savings are thus incorporated into the economic process.

The bank's profit results from charging borrowers a higher rate of interest than is paid to lenders.

A commercial bank performs many other operations too. It acts as cashier for many enterprises (collecting bills of exchange and promissory notes, making payments) and administers the funds of a number of firms and private persons; it also provides such items as foreign exchange and travellers' cheques, and rents safes.

More than in any other business, care must be taken in banking to ensure that there is a sufficient degree of solvency and liquidity. Solvency is expressed as the ratio of total assets to total liabilities. Liquidity is a particular aspect of solvency – the proportion between liquid assets and total current liabilities. (Solvency does not imply liquidity since assets cannot necessarily be converted into liquid funds immediately.) The solvency ratio should generally be equal to unity; this is not required in the case of the liquidity ratio. As we have seen only a portion of the demand deposits is normally drawn out. If a bank finds that on average it needs to have about 20 per cent of its total deposits available in liquid form in order to meet customers' requirements, there is no point in maintaining a liquidity ratio of, say, 75 per cent. Allowance must, however, be made for any short-lived upsurge in the volume of drawings.

Since the extent of deposits is the basis for determining the total amount of credit to be granted (so as to maintain a minimum degree of liquidity), every new deposit increases the banks' lending potential. The credits themselves produce the same effect. A customer who has been granted a credit avails himself of it to make payments, which involve an increase in his creditors' bank deposits. This can be used by the banks concerned as backing for the issue of further credit (see Section 8).

74

b. Central banks

Originally there was no difference between a central bank and a commercial bank (cf. Section 3*b*). Gradually, as a consequence of its monopoly position, the central bank developed into a banker's bank. When other banks require liquid funds, they can apply to the central bank; for instance, bills of exchange which they have purchased or discounted before the due date can in turn be rediscounted by the central bank. By changing its discount or rediscount rate ('bank rate' in the United Kingdom) the central bank can either counteract or stimulate such operations (Chapter 13.4*a*). The central bank has major responsibility for controlling the quantity of money. It also grants credit to the government (Chapter 13.3*d*).

Although the central bank is in most cases an official institution, the usual practice is to ensure that it enjoys a certain degree of independence in relation to the government.

c. Other financial institutions

1. Savings banks

In the nature of things, all banks are savings banks, but what is meant here is banks where the small saver's money is deposited and which are sometimes subject to special obligations by law.

2. Investment banks

In the United States investment banks purchase from corporations and governments security issues and resell them to their customers at higher prices. While most issues are entirely underwritten in this way in the United States, firms and governments in West European countries generally offer part of their issues direct to the public.

3. Consumer credit institutions

Like commercial banks, consumer credit institutions grant loans to individuals. Some of them, such as finance houses and industrial banks, specialize in financing hire purchase.

4. Mortgage credit institutions

Mortgage credit institutions (building societies) grant loans for the purchase and construction of real property upon which they require mortgage liens as security.

5. Post office giro services

Not to be confused with the banks are the government-operated giro services (in the US the expression 'credit transfer system' is used). In

75

view of the fact that a large section of the population has or may be obliged to have accounts with such institutions, they do much to facilitate payments traffic. In most cases, the government pays its staff through the giro; it is, indeed, in the government's interest to encourage use of the giro, as it finds employment for the service's idle funds.

Little or no interest is paid on giro accounts, which means that they do not compete with the banks; the majority of these accounts are maintained exclusively for current transactions and minor contingency payments.

Following the success of the first experiment in Austria (1883), institutions of this type have been established in most countries (though still not in the United States), especially since the First World War. Examples are the *Service des Cheques Postaux* in Belgium and in France, the twelve *Postcheckämter* in Western Germany, and the *Postcheque- en Girodienst* in the Netherlands, where there is also a municipal giro service (Amsterdam). A National Giro, operated by the Post Office, was opened in the United Kingdom on 18 October 1968.

8 Credit ceilings

As was pointed out above, every credit granted enables fresh credits to be opened. There is, however, a limit to this snowball process, partly from liquidity considerations. This is made clear by Table 5.

Where the minimum liquidity ratio is 20 per cent, deposits with all banks amounting to £10 million can initially produce £8 million worth of credit. This makes it possible for demand deposits to be increased by up to £8 million, as a result of which new credits can be granted up to a ceiling of £6·40 million (80 per cent of £8 million). In the ensuing period, credit can be issued up to £5·12 million (80 per cent of £6·40 million).

The amount of credits opened finally totals (remembering that

$$1 + n + n^2 + n^3 \ldots = \frac{1}{1 - n}):$$

£10m. $\times$ 0·8 + £10m. $\times$ (0·8)² + £10m. $\times$ (0·8)³ + ...
£8m. + £8m. $\times$ 0·8 + £8m. $\times$ (0·8)² + ...
£8m. [1 + 0·8 + (0·8)² + (0·8)³ + ...]
£8m. $\times$ $\dfrac{1}{1 - 0·8}$ = £ $\dfrac{8m.}{0·2}$ = £40m.

With a 50 per cent liquidity ratio, the corresponding ceiling is only £10 million. The higher the liquidity ratio, the lower the ceiling for the amount of deposit money that the banks can lend.

The coefficient by which the original deposit in notes and coin is multiplied in order to obtain the maximum amount of additional deposit money for a given liquidity ratio is called the credit multiplier. For liquidity ratios of 20 and 50 per cent the credit multiplier is 4 and 1 respectively. In general, it is equal to the reciprocal of the liquidity ratio minus one.

In point of fact, the expansion in the quantity of money is smaller, for the following reasons:

a. The banks do not always receive sufficiently reliable applications for credit;

b. Part of the newly created deposit money is used for payments to abroad and thus cannot be employed as a basis for deposit formation at home. This may be offset, however, by a rise in exports (as a result of which deposits increase). Another portion of the new deposit money goes to persons who have no bank account; this does not give rise to any new deposits either.

TABLE 5: Credit ceilings of private banks, with liquidity ratios of 20 and 50 per cent (£m.)

Period	Liquidity ratio: 20 per cent			Liquidity ratio: 50 per cent		
	Deposits	Credits	Liquid assets	Deposits	Credits	Liquid assets
1	10·00	8·00	2·00	10·00	5·00	5·00
2	8·00	6·40	1·60	5·00	2·50	2·50
3	6·40	5·12	1·28	2·50	1·25	1·25
4	5·12	4·10	1·02	1·25	0·63	0·62
5	4·10	3·28	0·82	0·63	0·31	0·32
6	3·28	2·62	0·66	0·31	0·15	0·16
7	2·62	2·10	0·52	0·15	0·08	0·07
8	2·10	1·68	0·42	0·08	0·04	0·04
9	1·68	1·34	0·34	0·04	0·02	0·02
10	1·34	1·07	0·27	0·02	0·01	0·01
..	....	....	....	....	....	....
Total	50·00	40·00	10·00	20·00	10·00	10·00

c. Any one bank can only grant substantially more credit if the other banks do the same; in other words, the banks have to keep in step. Let us assume, for example, that a bank A holds 30 per cent of all demand deposits in a particular country (£10 million). Of these it maintains 25 per cent in the form of liquid funds, the rest being used for lending; by contrast, the other banks apply a liquidity ratio of 40 per cent. On the basis of its deposits of £3 million, bank A grants credit up to £2·25 million, and the other banks grant £4·2 million of credit against deposits of £7 million. On the assumption that its share in the total deposits remains the same, bank A receives 30 per cent of £6·45 million (£2·25 million + £4·2 million) or £1·93 million. Had the other banks adopted the same liquidity ratio as bank A, the latter would again have received £2·25 million, namely 30 per cent of £7·5 million (£2·25 million + £5·25 million). The greater circumspection shown by the other banks in the country restricts bank A's lending capacity.

Some writers maintain that credit operations are hampered because banks have only a limited supply of bank notes: 'No longer, therefore, is there a multiplier mechanism operating (any deposit entailing the formation of new deposits), but rather a limitative mechanism (the creation of any deposit money being obstructed by the diversion of bank note flows, which makes commercial banks dependent on the central bank)' (P. Berger).

9 The influence of money on the circular flow of economic activity

Despite these limiting factors, the government too exercises control over bank lending – not only to protect depositors but also in order to keep track of the trend of the quantity of money (Chapter 13.4c).

The fact is that the creation of money stimulates overall demand, whereas destruction of money does the contrary. So money is not neutral (as was implicitly assumed in Chapter 2).

The quantity of money has an impact on consumption, investment, exports and government spending. The effect differs with circumstances: it may be non-existent or of vital importance.

10 Banking in selected countries

This section gives some details on the origins of modern banking in the United States, the United Kingdom, the USSR, China and the

EEC countries. It is not a historical survey, which is something that should date from the earliest times.

a. United Kingdom

The Bank of England was established as long ago as 1694; in 1844 it was accorded a virtual monopoly of note issue. A similar privilege which had been granted to the Bank of Scotland in 1695 was not renewed in 1717. The first English commercial bank was incorporated in 1833.

The commercial banks (also called joint-stock banks) include the 'Big Four' (Barclays Bank, Midland Bank, Lloyds Bank and National Westminster Bank), together accounting for about 75 per cent of all deposits. 'Discount houses' receive and lend money on a short-term basis, e.g. by negotiating Treasury bills. (This designation is also used, especially in the United States, for business firms which sell mainly consumer durables at reduced prices.)

The 'merchant banks' – mostly private companies – undertake the financing of foreign trade, and to a lesser extent industry (e.g. Hambros, Baring, Lazard, Rothschild); some of them also play a major role in the issue of shares and bonds.

In 1946 the Bank of England, hitherto a joint-stock company, was nationalized.

b. United States

After attempts to organize a central bank (from 1791 to 1811 and from 1816 to 1836), and to institute a certain degree of control over the issue of bank notes had proved abortive, the foundations for the present Federal Reserve System (FRS) were finally laid in 1913.

A distinction is made in the United States according to whether a bank is chartered to operate by one of the states (state banks) or by the federal government (national banks). The national banks are obliged to be members of the FRS; the state banks are not.

The FRS comprises twelve Federal Reserve banks under the general supervision of the Federal Reserve Board in Washington. The twelve regional banks, located in Atlanta, Boston, Chicago, Cleveland, Dallas, Kansas City, New York, Minneapolis, Philadelphia, Richmond, San Francisco and St Louis, are independent, private, but non-profit-making institutions. Their capital is provided by about 6,700 member banks.

TABLE 6: Classification of the forty leading banks, by size of deposits ($'000m.; end 1969)

1. Bank of America (US)	22·2	21. Mitsubishi Bank (Japan)	6·8
2. First National City Bank (US)	19·1	22. Sanwa Bank (Japan)	6·6
3. Chase Manhattan Bank (US)	19·0	23. Société Générale (France)	6·6
4. Barclays Bank (UK)	12·5	24. Banca Commerciale Italiana (Italy)	6·4
5. Manufacturers Hanover Trust (US)	10·4	25. Continental Illinois National (US)	6·3
6. National Westminster Bank (UK)	9·7	26. Industrial Bank of Japan (Japan)	6·1
7. Royal Bank of Canada (Canada)	9·1	27. Lloyds Bank (UK)	6·0
8. Morgan Guaranty Trust (US)	9·0	28. Credito Italiano (Italy)	5·8
9. Banca Nazionale del Lavoro (Italy)	8·8	29. First National Bank of Chicago (US)	5·8
10. Westdeutsche Landesbank (Western Germany)	8·8	30. Dresdner Bank (Western Germany)	5·8
11. Banque Nationale de Paris (France)	8·7	31. Banco di Roma (Italy)	5·8
12. Canadian Imperial Bank of Commerce (Canada)	8·1	32. Security Pacific National Bank (US)	5·8
13. Chemical Bank (US)	7·9	33. Union Bank of Switzerland (Switzerland)	5·1
14. Bankers Trust (US)	7·8	34. Bank of Nova Scotia (Canada)	5·1
15. Crédit Lyonnais (France)	7·6	35. Commonwealth Banking Corporation (Australia)	5·0
16. Deutsche Bank (Western Germany)	7·5	36. Irving Trust (US)	5·0
17. Bank of Montreal (Canada)	7·2	37. Tokai Bank (Japan)	4·8
18. Midland Bank (UK)	7·2	38. Barclays Bank DCO (UK)	4·8
19. Sumitoma Bank (Japan)	7·2	39. Long-term Credit Bank of Japan (Japan)	4·7
20. Fuji Bank (Japan)	7·1	40. Commerzbank AG (Western Germany)	4·7

Source: American Banker, 31 July 1969, p. 73

In the United States banks were given the option of specializing in short- or long-term transactions in 1933.

The main function of the investment banks, unlike the commercial banks (national or state) is to finance new ventures, either with their own capital or by issuing shares or bonds.

The leading commercial banks are Bank of America (1904), Chase Manhatten Bank (1799), First National City Bank (1812), Manufacturers Hanover Trust Company (1831), Morgan Guaranty Trust Company (1861) and Chemical Bank New York Trust Company (1824). The first three are also the largest in the western world (Table 6). They account for 11·5 per cent of deposits in the United States.

c. France

The first experiment in note-issuing in France was not a success. The Banque Générale founded in 1716 (the name was changed to Banque Royale in 1718) by John Law (Appendix 2b) was obliged to close down in 1720. This was due to the bank's imprudent and speculative policy. Cover consisted partly of the future profits of recently incorporated trading companies; there was no issue ceiling, so that the volume of paper money was soon three times that of gold and silver coins, and the notes were soon worthless. The unsavoury memories associated with the word *banque* caused most private banks to eschew this word for many years when selecting their name.

In 1800 the Banque de France was established as the central bank. Large private banks came into being fifty to sixty years later – in 1848 the Comptoir National d'Escompte de la Ville de Paris (which later became Comptoir National d'Escompte de Paris); in 1852 the Crédit Mobilier; in 1863 the Crédit Lyonnais; and in 1864 the Société Générale pour favoriser le développement du Commerce et de l'Industrie en France. These institutions gradually developed into commercial banks. On the other hand, several investment banks were incorporated (notably the Banque de Paris et des Pays-Bas in 1872).

In 1945 this situation was sanctioned by law when the statutory distinction between *banques de dépôts* (commercial banks) and *banques d'affaires* (investment banks) was introduced. At the same time the Banque de France and the four major commercial banks – Crédit Lyonnais, Société Générale, Banque Nationale pour le Commerce et l'Industrie and Comptoir National d'Escompte de Paris – were nationalized. In 1966 the two last-named merged to form the Banque

Nationale de Paris (20 per cent of all deposits). The three nationalized banks account for more than half the country's deposits.

The investment banks have as their main object the acquisition and administration of security holdings. They comprise *sociétés par actions* (e.g. the aforementioned Banque de Paris et des Pays-Bas) and the *haute banque*, which consists of family concerns (e.g. Rothschild, Lazard, Mallet). In contrast with the commercial banks, the investment banks are not subject to any special government control.

d. Germany

From the middle of the nineteenth century a great many credit cooperatives (Chapter 5.3*b*) – called *Raiffeisenkassen* in the agricultural sector – and mortgage banks were set up. On the French model (Crédit Mobilier), investment banks for trade and industry were also created, including Deutsche Bank (1870), Commerzbank (1870) and Dresdner Bank (1872). Gradually these developed into mixed-type banks, engaging in investment as well as commercial banking. They are now the 'Big Three' in West Germany (17 per cent of deposits).

The central bank, the Deutsche Reichsbank, came into being in 1875, as the successor to numerous small banks of issue. Up to 1935 private banks continued to issue notes.

Pursuant to directives issued by the Allies, the private banks and also the central bank were decentralized after the Second World War. In 1945 the Bank Deutscher Länder was established to coordinate nine Landesbanken. In 1957, this federal organization was discontinued and the Deutsche Bundesbank was set up.

e. Netherlands

After a central bank, the Nederlandse Bank, had been established in 1814, a large number of mixed-type banks were founded in the course of the nineteenth century, notably Nederlandse Handel Maatschappij (1824), Twentse Bank (1861), Rotterdamse Bank (1863) and Amsterdamse Bank (1871).

Having pursued a prudent policy, the Dutch banks suffered relatively little during the depression in the 1930s. This accounts for the less stringent government control over the banks, and also for the absence of any provisions concerning short- or long-term transactions.

After the Second World War, the Nederlandse Bank too was nationalized (1948).

In 1964 mergers took place among the four leading banks listed above. This resulted in the formation of two banks, namely Amsterdam-Rotterdam Bank and Algemene Bank Nederland (which together held threequarters of the country's deposits).

f. Belgium

In 1850, only twenty years after Belgium became independent, the central bank, the Banque Nationale de Belgique, was established. (The State now owns half the capital of this limited company.) Previously (from 1837 onwards), bank notes had been issued by four private banks, including the Société Générale, which was incorporated in 1822. In 1871 another large bank, the Banque de Bruxelles, entered the field.

The drawbacks of the mixed type banks were felt keenly in Belgium during the thirties. As a consequence, this kind of bank has been banned since January 1936. Only commercial banks (*banques de dépôt*) may use the designation 'bank'; shares other than those of banks cannot be held permanently in their portfolios.

The most important banks today are the Société Générale de Banque (40 per cent of total deposits), the Banque de Bruxelles (24 per cent) and the Kredietbank (17 per cent).

As the investment banks (*banques de financement*) for the most part confine themselves to the administration of their holdings, they are frequently referred to as holding companies. The leading institution of this kind is the Société Générale; also prominent are the Compagnie Financière et Industrielle (Cofinindus) and the Société de Bruxelles pour la Finance et l'Industrie (Brufina), which together form the de Launoit financial group. Along with smaller groups, they exercise a preponderant influence on the various sectors of industry.

g. Italy

Here, more than in Germany, the fact that political unification took place fairly late had its repercussions on the creation of an efficient monetary system and central bank. The Banca d'Italia was not established until 1893, having originated from the Banca Nazionale Sarda, set up in 1861. It was, however, only in 1926 that it acquired a monopoly of issue.

The largest banks still operating came into being at the end of the nineteenth century, partly with financial aid from Germany – the

83

Banco di Roma (1880), the Banca Commerziale Italiana (1894) and the Credito Italiano (1895).

In 1936 the Italian authorities too laid down that transactions must be divided into short-term (up to one year) and long-term operations.

The three last-named banks together with the Banca Nazionale del Lavoro account for about 40 per cent of all deposits. The Banca Nazionale del Lavoro was set up in 1913 by the central government (which now holds approximately 88 per cent of the shares) to issue loans to cooperatives. The other three banks are, in fact, also nationalized, an official holding company, the Istituto per la Ricostruzione Industriale, IRI (1933) possessing at least 80 per cent of their stock. This has not, however, inhibited the growing rivalry between the banks.

Long-term and medium-term credit is provided mainly by semi-public or government bodies, including the Istituto Mobiliare Italiano, the Mediocredito (medium-term credit to small business) and the Cassa per il Mezzogiorno (development of southern Italy).

h. USSR

In the USSR, the central bank, Gosudarstvenni Bank (or Gosbank), which was established in 1921, has a monopoly of short-term lending. Since, moreover, all firms have to maintain current accounts with the Gosbank, it is not surprising that it is the largest bank in the world (deposits valued at $800,000 million). It is the government's cashier and also exercises financial supervision over the implementation of economic planning – with the qualification that the enterprises' potential production is determined by the economic plan and not by the credit received from the Gosbank.

In addition to numerous savings and insurance institutions, there is the Stroibank, or investment bank, which finances government projects, and the Vnershtorgbank, or bank for foreign transactions.

i. China

In communist China too, the central bank, the People's Bank, which was set up in 1948, has control over the execution of the various plans. There are also the Agricultural Bank and the Investment Bank. The People's Bank has jurisdiction over the Bank of China (in existence before 1949 but now nationalized), most of whose transactions are abroad, and the Joint State Private Bank, which was formed by the merger of some sixty small and medium-sized private banks (the major private banks had been seized immediately after the communist takeover) with the object of gradually nationalizing them.

11 The flow-of-funds accounts

The national accounts (Chapter 2) do not reveal financial transactions, such as how savings are invested. Nor do they give particulars of financial assets or illustrate the role of the financial institutions (notably the banks).

To remedy this, flow-of-funds accounts are compiled, the purpose of which is to afford a clearer picture of the economic units' financial relations and their degree of liquidity. So that the various sectors shall comprise units which react in a similar manner to changes in assets and liabilities, a separate account is drawn up for those financial institutions which accept money, not in order to invest it themselves, but in order to make it available to other economic units. The business sector is therefore split up into 'non-financial business' and 'financial institutions'.

Here too, only inter-sector relations are examined. The accounts show the changes that have occurred in the course of a specific period, in most cases one year.

There are as yet no uniform rules for drawing up flow-of-funds accounts, so appreciable differences are observed from country to country. In the normal course, only the balances for each account are shown; the financial assets are divided by type and degree of liquidity. If the transactions are entered at the value at which they were concluded, the connection with the national accounts is brought out very clearly. This procedure, however, is liable to give a false picture of the liquidity position, since the latter is based on the market value. (The stock-market value of securities fluctuates.) For the most part, the differences are of little consequence. Although it is recommended that only completed transactions (cash basis) should be included (in contrast with the method adopted for the national accounts, in which debts and claims are entered as soon as they arise), this frequently proves impossible in practice.

In Example 7, which links up with Example 5 in Chapter 2, six different groups of financial assets are shown.

In the case of households, cash in hand (18·0), deposits with financial institutions (12·1) and purchases of government and corporate securities (21·9) are on the increase. Gold and foreign exchange

holdings (—1·6) and credits granted (—0·5) are decreasing. Further
loans (8·9) are being contracted.

The non-financial business sector's cash in hand and deposits also
show rises (1·6 and 1·4 respectively). New security issues (7·7) are
being made, and additional credits (17·1) and loans (31·5) are being
taken up.

EXAMPLE 7

Households			
Use of funds		*Source of funds*	
Notes and coin	18·0	Loans	8·9
Gold and foreign exchange	—1·6		
Deposits	12·1		
Securities	21·9		
Credits	—0·5	Balance	41·0
	49·9		49·9

Non-financial business			
Use of funds		*Source of funds*	
Notes and coin	1·6	Securities	7·7
Deposits	1·4	Credits	17·1
Balance	53·3	Loans	31·5
	56·3		56·3

Government			
Use of funds		*Source of funds*	
Gold and foreign exchange	—0·2	Notes and coin	11·0
Deposits	5·5	Securities	30·5
Loans	23·3	Credits	—0·9
Balance	12·0		
	40·6		40·6

Rest of the world			
Use of funds		*Source of funds*	
Notes and coin	1·6	Gold and foreign exchange	3·2
Deposits	—1·5	Loans	4·6
Securities	12·2	Balance	4·0
Credits	—0·5		
	11·8		11·8

Financial institutions			
Use of funds		Source of funds	
Gold and foreign exchange	5·0	Notes and coin	10·2
Securities	4·1	Deposits	17·5
Credits	17·2		
Loans	21·7	Balance	20·3
	48·0		48·0

The government's gold and foreign exchange holdings are shrinking (−0·2), but it is depositing more money with the banks (5·5) and granting more loans (23·3). Bond issues are expanding (30·5), but the volume of borrowings is decreasing (−0·9). The volume of notes and coin issued is increasing (11·0). The government's assets are down (12) (in contrast with those of households).

Foreign holdings of notes and coin are up (1·6), as also are foreign purchases of securities (12·2). Deposits with financial institutions (−1·5) and credits granted (−0·5) are, however, on the downgrade. So, too, are gold and foreign exchange reserves (3·2). The volume of loans has swelled (4·6).

The financial institutions have stepped up their gold and foreign exchange reserves (5·0), subscriptions to security issues (4·1), credits granted (17·2) and loans (21·7). Their deposits show an accretion (17·5), and the central bank is issuing additional bank notes (10·2).

The assets and liabilities relating to the various categories are in equilibrium (Example 8), as also are the balances of the various accounts. Thus borrowings by firms (53·3) and government (12·0) originate from households (41·0), financial institutions (20·3) and the rest of the world (4·0).

The households' balance (41·0) represents savings from current income; it is the counterpart of item 5 (or 45) in Example 5. The balance for the rest of the world corresponds to item 40 (or 48) in the same example. In relating this to the national accounts, we have to allow for gross investment by firms and government in order to determine their balances. If the funds required (saving and depreciation) prove inadequate, the financing shortfall has to be made good by the other sectors.

Since the government's saving (−5) and depreciation (5) cancel each other out, gross public investment (12) has to be financed in full. This item appears as the balance in the government flow-of-funds

account. The 'non-financial business' and 'financial institutions'
flow-of-funds accounts combined are comparable with the 'enterprises' national account. Here too, the available funds (22 + 20) are
insufficient, and there is consequently a financing deficit (75 − 42 =
33). The balances for 'non-financial business' and 'financial institutions' come to the same figure (53·3 − 20·3).

EXAMPLE 8

Notes and Coin

Use of funds		Source of funds	
Households	18·0	Financial institutions	10·2
Non-financial business	1·6	Government	11·0
Rest of the world	1·6		
	21·2		21·2

Gold and foreign exchange

Use of funds		Source of funds	
Households	−1·6	Rest of the world	3·2
Financial institutions	5·0		
Government	−0·2		
	3·2		3·2

Deposits

Use of funds		Source of funds	
Households	12·1	Financial institutions	17·5
Non-financial business	1·4		
Government	5·5		
Rest of the world	−1·5		
	17·5		17·5

Securities

Use of funds		Source of funds	
Households	21·9	Non-financial business	7·7
Financial institutions	4·1	Government	30·5
Rest of the world	12·2		
	38·2		38·2

Credits			
Use of funds		Source of funds	
Households	−0·5	Non-financial business	17·1
Financial institutions	17·2	Government	−0·9
Rest of the world	−0·5		
	16·2		16·2

Loans			
Use of funds		Source of funds	
Financial institutions	21·7	Households	8·9
Government	23·3	Non-financial business	31·5
		Rest of the world	4·6
	45·0		45·0

Balances			
Use of funds		Source of funds	
Non-financial business	53·3	Households	41·0
Government	12·0	Financial institutions	20·3
		Rest of the world	4·0
	65·3		65·3

12 Bibliography

The material in this chapter is usually discussed in textbooks on monetary theory. Among the older publications, the standard work is J. M. Keynes, *A Treatise on Money*, Part 1 (London 1930); among the more recent: G. N. Halm, *Economics of Money and Banking* (rev. ed., Homewood, Ill. 1961); A. C. L. Day, *The Economics of Money* (2nd ed., London 1968); R. Harrod, *Money* (London 1969). More concise: W. T. Newlyn, *Theory of Money* (Oxford 1962); P. Berger, *La monnaie et ses mécanismes* (Paris 1967). See also *Readings in Monetary Theory* (ed. F. A. Lutz and L. W. Mints, Philadelphia 1951), with a classified bibliography by H. M. Smith.

Other introductory texts are mentioned below.

a. The concept and classification of money

J. M. Keynes considers the different liquidity motives in *The General Theory of Employment, Interest and Money* (London 1936), Chapter

15. M. Friedman shows in a concise study that the precautionary motive is the most important: *The Demand for Money: Some Theoretical and Empirical Results* (New York 1959); on the finance motive: P. Davidson, 'Keynes' Finance Motive', *OEP*, March 1965.

On the concept of money: R. Mossé, *La monnaie* (Paris 1950), Chapter 2. This work, published in the series *Bilans de la connaissance économique*, contains further observations by L. Federici and R. Triffin and comment on some hundred publications.

b. The monetary systems
A broad exposition on the concept itself: W. E. Mason, *Clarification of the Monetary Standard: The Concept and its Relation to Monetary Policies and Objectives* (University Park, Pa. 1966).

On the gold standard: R. G. Hawtrey, *The Gold Standard in Theory and Practice* (5th ed., London 1947).

c. Credit and banking
Clear textbooks are F. Baudhuin, *Crédit et banque* (3rd ed., Paris 1962); A. Weber, *Geld und Kredit: Banken und Börsen* (6th ed., Heidelberg 1959); L. V. Chandler, *The Economics of Money and Banking* (5th ed., New York 1969); R. P. Kent, *Money and Banking* (4th ed., New York 1961).

For an abstract study of money creation and destruction: E. Schneider, *Money, Income, and Employment* (London 1968), Chapter 2.

d. The banking system in selected countries
Under the title *A Collection of Central Bank, Monetary and Banking Laws* (ed. H. Aufricht) the IMF published two volumes in 1961 and 1967 respectively, the second of which is devoted to Europe. See also *Comparative Banking in Australia, Austria, Belgium, Canada, Denmark, Finland, France, Germany, Greece, Hong Kong, India, Italy, Japan, Netherlands, Norway, Portugal, Spain, Sweden, Switzerland, Turkey, United Kingdom, USA, the USSR* (ed. H. W. Auburn, 3rd ed., London 1966).

On certain central banks: *Eight European Central Banks: Organization and Activities of Banque Nationale de Belgique, Deutsche Bundesbank, Bank of England, Banque de France, Banca d'Italia, Nederlandsche Bank, Banque Nationale Suisse, Sveriges Riksbank. A descriptive study published under the auspices of the Bank for International Settlements, Basle* (London 1963).

Data concerning the American monetary system can be found in most textbooks on money and banking, including C. R. Whittlesey, A. M. Freedman, E. S. Herman, *Money and Banking: Analysis and Policy* (2nd ed., New York 1968); for a readable survey: E. Groseclose, *Fifty Years of Managed Money: The Story of the Federal Reserve* (New York 1966).

On Eastern Europe, G. Garvy, *Money, Banking and Credit in Eastern Europe* (New York 1966), does not cover Yugoslavia and Albania.

e. The flow-of-funds accounts

M. Copeland, *A Study of Moneyflows in the United States* (New York 1952), is the first to introduce financial transactions into the national accounts of the United States for the period 1936–42. *Flows of Funds in the United States 1939–1953* (Washington 1955) is a standard work. See also E. Hicks, 'The Theory and Use of Financing Accounts', and G. S. Dorrance, 'Balance Sheets in a System of Economic Accounts', *SP*, October 1959; G. S. Dorrance, 'The Present Status of Financial Accounts: A Review of Recent Developments', in *Studies in Social and Financial Accounting* (London 1961).

The Flow-of-Funds Approach to Social Accounting: Appraisals, Analysis, and Applications (Princeton 1962) is a volume of papers on the integration of national and financial accounts (Part 1), analysis of financial accounts data (Part 2) and the sources of information and technical problems (Part 3). On the integration of national and financial accounts see also: F. B. Rampersad, 'An Integrated System of Real and Financial Accounts', *Social and Economic Studies*, June 1962.

PART 2

Households and Firms

4 Households

Qui dit ménage, dit calcul.
François Quesnay

This chapter discusses the explanation of the choices made by households, the factors that influence demand and the saving and consumption functions.

1 Marginal utility and Gossen's 'laws'

The marginal utility of a quantity of the same goods is the (subjective) utility of the last unit added or removed. If you have drunk five glasses of beer and then drink a sixth, the marginal utility of the beer is equal to the utility of the sixth glass, i.e. the last unit added. In discussing marginal utility we ought really to operate with infinitesimal units.

a. Gossen's first 'law'
Experience shows that marginal utility declines as more units are added. This is known as the 'law' of diminishing marginal utility or Gossen's first 'law' (Appendix 8). After drinking a seventh glass of beer, you may well find that you have had enough: marginal utility may even be negative.

Although utility cannot be measured, at least not in absolute terms, the decline of marginal utility can be shown in a graph by giving an imaginary scale to the vertical axis (Figure 5).

The 'law' of diminishing marginal utility does not conflict with the observed fact that desire for a given good often increases through consumption, because there is a certain lapse of time between two successive acts of consumption. The 'law' begins to apply again from the next time we consume the good in question.

b. Gossen's second 'law'
In order to obtain optimum satisfaction of wants with the money available, we have to ensure that the utility of the last unit of money

spent on a given good is equal to the utility of the last unit spent on another good. This is known as the 'law' of equal marginal utilities or Gossen's second 'law'. While the first of his 'laws' could be derived from experience, the second had to be worked out deductively.

A person (or institution) compares the marginal utilities of goods by means of the prices he is prepared to pay for them. Maximum satisfaction of wants is obtained when the marginal utilities of the

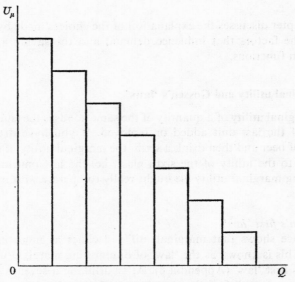

Figure 5: The 'law' of diminishing marginal utility

goods purchased are in the same proportion as the outlays needed to acquire them. In other words, the quotient of marginal utility and price must be equal for all goods. As long as prices are not in the same proportion as marginal utilities, total utility can be increased by replacing a good or part of a good by another or part of another (because its marginal utility is higher). That is to say, we need to aim at the following equations:

$$\frac{U^*_{\mu_1}}{P_1} = \frac{U^*_{\mu_2}}{P_2} = \dots \frac{U^*_{\mu}}{P_n}.$$

The equilibrium condition, the target of optimum satisfaction of wants, changes whenever the scale of our wants, prices and incomes change. Since each person's wants and income are different, the equilibrium condition is never the same.

Where we have two people with the same wants but different incomes, the one with the higher income can buy more of each good and obtain greater total utility; the marginal utility of each good is smaller, however – according to the 'law' of diminishing marginal utility – for the person with the higher income, even though the prices are the same.

In other words, marginal utilities are proportional to prices but vary with purchasing power or the marginal utility of the money available to each buyer. In view of the uneven distribution of purchasing power, therefore, the money spent by different people is no indicator of the utility actually obtained. Interpersonal utility comparisons are impossible.

Appraisal

These observations are unreal because the consumer does not know the amount of a good's marginal utility to him (since it is not measurable, quite apart from whether or not he is familiar with the concept). Exceptions to the first 'law' are not infrequent: for instance, a second glass of beer drunk immediately (cf. the end of Section *a* above) after the first one may provide greater utility than the first. The consumer has only imperfect knowledge of the prices of different goods. And in any case he makes no scholarly comparison of marginal utilities, though it is all too often assumed that he does. It would in fact be difficult to attain equality in the equations given above because of the limited divisibility or the indivisibility of most goods.

It may be doubted whether the consumer unconsciously aims at equality, as is frequently suggested. Much of the consumer's behaviour is a consequence of traditions and habits determined by his social environment. The consumer does not often deviate from his normal pattern of consumption, even when there are changes in prices or in income. When he does do so, the purchases he makes may be motivated by impulse or emotion (as when he buys goods that he happens to see without thinking it over). As J. Marchal has put it, the consumer is much more *'l'homme de Pavlov'* than *'l'homme de Descartes'*. He only takes time to buy a limited number of goods, and he also allows himself to be influenced by incidentals. Money may be spent liberally, for instance, on such commodities as make-up.

E. Wagemann was not exaggerating when he complained about

'how much ingenuity and trouble has been expended in speculating about marginal utilities.'

2 Indifference curves and the satisfaction of wants

To get round the difficulty that utility cannot be measured, 'indifference curves' are often used.

Let us assume that all five combinations of the two commodities shown in Table 7 provide the consumer with the same utility. He will as soon eat six pounds of bread and drink one pint of beer as eat one pound of bread and drink three pints of beer: it is a matter of indifference to him which combination he has.

TABLE 7 The bread/beer indifference schedule:

Combinations	Bread (lb)	Beer (pints)	Substitution ratio
1	10	0	—
2	6	1	4:1
3	3	2	3:1
4	1	3	2:1
5	0	4	1:1

In graph form this is represented by an indifference curve, also known as an equal-utility contour (Figure 6). The curve slopes down from left to right, as less of one and more of the other commodity is consumed. In the case of two commodities which are wholly substitutable, the curve is a straight line (the substitution ratio does not change); in the case of commodities which are wholly complementary (where substitution is impossible; see Chapter 5.5b), the indifference curve is parallel to the axes. Normally, it is convex to the point of origin because the consumer is less and less willing to give up bread in order to consume an extra unit of beer: the substitution ratio, or the way in which the substitution of commodities is effected at the margin, diminishes (successively, four, three, two and one pound of bread will be sacrificed for an extra pint of beer; theoretically, we should again be using infinitesimal quantities in order to speak about marginal ratios).

This marginal substitution ratio (bread to beer) shows what very small quantity of a given commodity (bread) we are prepared to give up (dQ_2) in order to obtain an additional infinitesimal unit of a second commodity (beer) (dQ_1) with no change in total utility. It is represented by $-dQ_2/dQ_1$ (the minus sign is needed because dQ_2 is a reduction). Each point along the indifference curve thus has its own substitution ratio. Mathematically, this is represented by the slope of the tangent to the curve at the appropriate point. For this is also

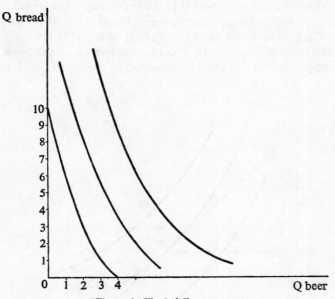

Figure 6: The indifference curves

equal to $-dQ_2/dQ_1$ (the substitution ratio is really the first derivative from the equation of the indifference curve).

The farther out the indifference curves lie from the point of origin, the more utility they provide: we are obtaining more and more, whether of a single good or of both goods. For the same reason, two curves cannot intersect: utility would be equal at the point of intersection, but different elsewhere.

Given that Z is the fixed sum that the consumer is prepared to spend on the two commodities together, we can solve his problem of choice diagrammatically. Where P_1 and P_2 are the prices of the two goods, and Q_{11} and Q_{21} the quantities purchased, then the equation $Z = P_1Q_{11} + P_2Q_{21}$ represents a straight line. It crosses the vertical axis ($Q_{11} = 0$) at Z/P_2 and the horizontal axis ($Q_{21} = 0$) at Z/P_1 (Figure 7). The slope is indicated by $-P_1/P_2$ (cf. Chapter 5.11) since the previous equation can be written

$$Q_{21} = - \frac{P_1}{P_2} Q_{11} + \frac{Z}{P_2}.$$

The greatest utility is obtained at the point where the straight line CD is tangential to an indifference curve, i.e. at point M on curve 2. Where CD crosses lower curves, the utility obtained is lower.

As the tangent at point M, CD also enables us to establish the substitution ratio at M: this is determined by means of the slope of

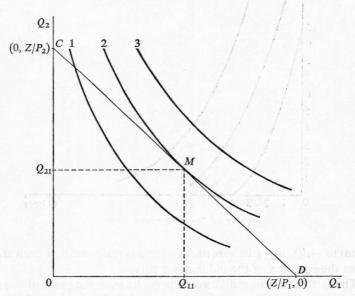

Figure 7: Determination of optimum consumption level by means of indifference curves

CD, i.e. $-P_1/P_2$. Once the substitution ratio is equal to this ratio, maximum utility is obtained. The consumer will then buy a quantity OQ_{21} of the one commodity and OQ_{11} of the other.

Whereas we saw in the last section that the prices of goods had to be in the same proportion as the marginal utilities, it is the price ratio and the substitution ratio that need to be equal here. In other words, the ratio of the marginal utilities, which cannot be measured, coincides with the substitution ratio, which can.

Appraisal

It is surely open to doubt whether the consumer can distinguish between a number of 'indifferent' situations. As we have said, the consumer buys the different goods in more or less constant ratios. There is in any case no point in assuming unlimited substitutability among the goods. The fact that this tool of analysis is not very realistic becomes clearer still when it is extended and used for more than two goods: how could the consumer possibly distinguish between the thousands of possible combinations?

In 1932 H. Mayer pointed out:

The more goods contained in a combination and the more heterogeneous those goods, the more grotesque the consequences that flow from the fiction that as we consume less bread or meat we will consume more salt, that every reduction in the amount of tea consumed is offset by an increase in the amount of sugar consumed in the equivalent (indifferent) daily combinations, the less furniture the more rooms, the less heating material the more aesthetic pleasure, the less clothing the more cigarettes, and so on. More clearly than any abstract argument, these absurd deductions expose the wholly unempirical nature of the supposedly empirical assumptions on which the construction of indifference curves is based.

As with marginal utility, we have to bear in mind the indivisibility of goods, especially of the expensive ones of which only one unit is normally purchased (car, refrigerator). Even if a second unit is purchased, the consumer goes for diversity and chooses a different model: the neighbours must be made to notice the second acquisition. In fact, not only different commodities are compared but also different qualities of the same commodity (each quality constituting as it were a different product).

Indifference curves are useful only in the analysis of problems of choice of a limited kind (e.g. between present and future consumption, between material possessions and leisure). However, they are not observable phenomena. To obviate this drawback, P. A. Samuelson has suggested basing analysis on consumer preferences as expressed in market conduct (see Chapter 7.1*b*), or actual purchases – the theory of revealed preferences. Even here it is very difficult to

101

draw the relevant curves or behaviour lines, since they would have to take account of large variations in income in order to reveal the associated preferences. Here again, it is often overlooked that the consumer's purchases are determined by habit and social environment and not by slight fluctuations in income – or only slightly (and even then not immediately).

We therefore agree with E. J. Mishan when he describes these theories of the consumer's behaviour as 'an unnecessary adornment on the apparatus of economic analysis'.

3 Demand and quantity demanded

How much of a given good is demanded depends first of all on consumers' wants: in theory, demand persists until the utility of the last unit obtained is zero (diminishing marginal utility). However, each consumer takes into account the level of his income – including his available cash and credit facilities. And, normally, the quantities demanded of different goods must also be such that the marginal utilities provided by each good are in the same proportion as the prices of those goods (Gossen's second 'law'). Other prices, then, mainly the price of substitute and complementary goods, influence demand for a given commodity.

a. The influence of price
If we assume that wants, prices of other goods, and incomes remain unchanged (the *ceteris paribus* assumption), we can investigate the impact of price changes on quantity demanded.

By demand we mean the series of quantities of a good that we are prepared to buy in the future at a given time or within a specified short period at various (hypothetical) prices. We distinguish between individual demand and aggregate demand, the latter being the sum of the former.

In the theory of demand it is assumed that a prospective purchaser does not yet know whether he will really make the purchase and that he makes a list, or schedule, of the quantities he wishes to buy at a number of possible prices (Table 8). This subjective (or imaginary) demand should not be confused with the objective quantities demanded – the quantity actually demanded and actually purchased at a given price; the expression 'demand' is used with this second meaning as well. When this demand schedule is represented in a

102

graph, it is called the demand curve (Figure 8). Following A. Marshall, and in contrast with mathematical custom, we show the independent variable on the vertical axis. Monetary demand is equal to ordinary physical demand multiplied by price (in Table 8, by a price of £4, i.e. £488).

A reduction in price normally results in an increase in the quantity demanded. Macroeconomically, the number of buyers may increase (people who previously considered the product too expensive). A price reduction provides supplementary income in a certain sense (real income goes up, though money income remains constant), and this is generally used to increase the quantity demanded of the cheaper good. This is known as an income effect.

TABLE 8: The demand schedule

Price	Quantity demanded	Price	Quantity demanded
1	190	6	90
2	164	7	76
3	142	8	64
4	122	9	54
5	106	10	44

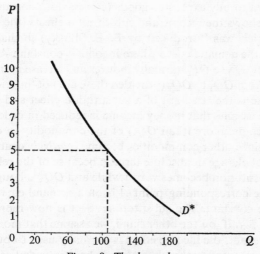

Figure 8: The demand curve

For certain commodities, however, the consequence of this phenomenon is that not more but less is bought – to the benefit of other
commodities considered better (wine instead of beer, butter instead
of margarine). A negative income effect of this kind appears only in
the case of goods regarded as inferior.

Another normal consequence of a reduction in price is that certain
quantities of other commodities are replaced by the commodity that
has become cheaper, even if real income has remained unchanged (if
the price reduction coincided with a compensatory reduction in
money income). The relative change in price produces a substitution
effect.

When prices go up, the opposite reactions can usually be expected;
the quantity demanded will vary inversely with price. A well-known
phenomenon, though it is not very common nowadays, at least in
developed countries, is the Giffen case. Sir Robert Giffen (1837–1910)
observed that for poor families an increase in the price of bread
resulted in an increase in the amount demanded: because their real
income had been reduced they had to cut down their spending, and
they did so by eating less of more expensive commodities such as
meat. For the Giffen effect to prevail, a considerable proportion of
the family's income must be spent on the commodity in question.

Similar consequences flow from the Veblen effect: demand increases because price goes up, since the consumer wishes to show that
he can afford to buy expensive goods (conspicuous consumption).

Figure 9 shows the income and substitution effects (the distinction
between which was introduced by E. E. Slutsky) in diagrammatic
form; D_1^* is the demand curve where income is constant. A reduction
in price from OP_1 to OP_2 normally induces an increase in the quantity
demanded from OQ_1 to OQ_2 (provided these are not 'inferior' goods).
This increase is the resultant of a substitution effect and an income
effect. If we assume that money income is reduced in order to maintain real income, more (than OQ_1) of the commodity in question is
demanded since other commodities become *relatively* dearer (though
prices do not change in absolute terms): because of the relative price
change, substitution becomes worth while and OQ_3 is bought instead
of OQ_1. The corresponding point A is on a demand curve D_2^*, with
real income constant. The substitution effect is now represented by
Q_1Q_3 or by BA. If, on the other hand, we assume that money income
remains constant, the income effect is normally used to buy more of
the cheaper commodity than had already been intended as a result of

the substitution effect. The quantity demanded goes up from OQ_3 to OQ_2 and the income effect is represented by Q_3Q_2 or AC.

We can now define the income effect and the substitution effect more accurately. The income effect is the result of a change in real income, which is itself caused by a change in price, provided money income and the prices of other commodities remain the same. The

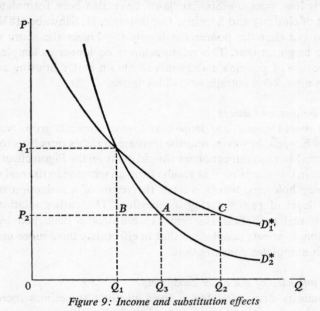

Figure 9: Income and substitution effects

substitution effect consists in the replacement of commodities that have become relatively dearer (because a price has changed) by commodities that are relatively cheaper, provided real income and the prices of other commodities remain the same.

b. The influence of income

We can also investigate the link between the quantity demanded and the level of income (where prices and wants remain unchanged); this brings us to the income-demand curve, a concept formulated by E. Engel (1821–96). The higher the income the greater the quantity demanded, provided the goods in question are not considered inferior. If they are inferior goods, the quantity demanded usually diminishes in favour of other goods.

105

Alongside Engel's curve we also have Engel's 'law': as income increases, expenditure on food may well go up too, but its share in total expenditure will fall. We first see to the basic necessities of life and only then think of other wants. This 'law' applies only after a certain degree of welfare has been attained; up to that point, the relative share of expenditure on food still goes up when income, which is low, goes up. Similar 'laws' have also been formulated in respect of clothing and housing. For instance, H. Schwabe (1830–74) pointed out that the poorer the family the bigger the share of its income to go on rent. This relationship is no longer as simple as it was because of people's endeavours to obtain better housing and to possess a weekend cottage or holiday home.

c. The influence of assets

As our assets increase, our propensity to save normally grows weaker. (It does happen, however, that the increase in riches impels us to own still more.) In this connection we should mention the Pigou effect – the increase in consumption that results from an increase in the real value of money holdings, which is itself the result of a reduction in the overall level of prices during a recession. The earlier relationship between real cash balances and expenditures is disturbed by the reduction in prices: people find that in effect they have more money, and this stimulates consumption.

d. The influence of the other consumers

The quantity demanded for a given product sometimes increases because people notice that it is being bought by other consumers, and people are always ready to imitate their fellows. In other cases the quantity demanded falls when we see other consumers buying a product, because we also like to be noticed and therefore buy a more expensive one (without necessarily spending more money). H. Leibenstein calls these phenomena the 'bandwagon effect' and the 'snob effect'.

They should not be confused with the 'demonstration effect': when we come into contact with more expensive products previously unknown to us, or with a greater variety of goods, we buy more and our consumption expenditure goes up even if our income has remained unchanged. In point of fact, the bandwagon effect and the demonstration effect usually coincide.

106

Appraisal

1. The construction of demand schedules and demand curves is very difficult. F. Machlup has called the operation a *tour de force*. Indeed, it requires us to establish the reactions of a consumer (or a group of consumers) to the different prices all obtaining at the same moment. As this is impossible, we are obliged to rely on assumptions or to study the amounts actually demanded at *different* times. The latter method is dangerous because the other circumstances that are assumed to remain the same change, in fact, even when the period of observation is relatively short. Even when we obtain satisfactory results, there is nothing to say that our demand curve will not be completely different the following day.

2. It seems hardly likely that the consumer considers what his reactions would be if other, hypothetical, prices were to obtain for the innumerable goods available on the market. If he does do so, he will still think in terms of the actual price and investigate fewer possibilities than are shown in Table 8. His price forecasts will cover a limited range (price fluctuations of, say, 10 per cent). It is sometimes assumed that the consumer has two limit prices in mind for a restricted number of commodities – a minimum price below which he refuses to believe that a reliable product could be supplied, and a maximum price above which he considers the product too expensive. The demand curve would consist in a few points only if this were the case.

3. Delayed reactions to price changes, which often occur in practice, are not taken into account. Moreover, the concept of demand is difficult to apply, at least microeconomically, to consumer durables. Price changes do influence purchases by new consumers, but not so much the purchases of consumers who already have the product in question. The further the price goes down the more readily will the latter replace durable goods they already possess (reducing the period of depreciation); at the same time they will be more likely to move over to a better-quality product. The stocks and durability of consumer durables have an important effect on the choice of other goods.

4. In the demand schedule it is assumed that each price is given. In other words, the buyer cannot influence the price by his purchase (because it represents a very small part of total purchases); this also implies that consumers' decisions are taken independently of each other (pure competition; see below). Some buyers, however, are in a

position to exert pressure on sellers (buyers such as department stores and other big firms).

5. As we have seen, price is only one of the factors that influence demand. Hence the distinction that is sometimes made, depending on the frequency and nature of purchases, between convenience goods, shopping goods and speciality goods. The first are bought regularly, promptly and almost automatically; in the case of the second category we first compare quality, model and price; while for the third category comparison is carried to even greater lengths because goods of this kind are bought only once or at fairly long intervals.

4 The elasticity of demand

a. The types of elasticity

Elasticity is a measure of the relative change in the relevant dependent variable associated with a relative infinitesimal change in one independent variable.

A distinction should be made between price elasticity, income elasticity and cross elasticity. We are usually concerned with physical demand in this context.

The price elasticity of demand for a good is the ratio between the relative change in the quantity demanded and an infinitesimal relative change in price causing the change in the quantity demanded. All other prices and income are assumed to remain unchanged.

Since A. Marshall, relative changes have been taken to obviate the need to compare different units (prices and quantities), though it is considered preferable in more advanced mathematical analysis – on which we need not dwell here – to compare absolute changes. If dQ and dP represent the infinitesimal changes in quantity Q and price P, elasticity at price P_i is represented by:

$$e_{Q_i P_i} = \frac{dQ_i}{Q_i} : \frac{dP_i}{P_i} .$$

The cross elasticity of demand is the analogous ratio between the quantity demanded of one good and the price of another good (again assuming that other prices and income are constant):

$$e_{Q_i P_j} = \frac{dQ_i}{Q_i} : \frac{dP_j}{P_j} .$$

Finally, income elasticity compares the change in the quantity demanded with the change in income (at constant prices):

$$e_{Q_i Y_i} = \frac{dQ_i}{Q_i} : \frac{dY_i}{Y_i} .$$

b. The degree of elasticity

Price elasticity is normally negative (movements in price and quantity are in opposite directions) and income elasticity positive (movements in income and quantity are in the same direction). Cross elasticity is usually positive in the case of substitute goods (butter and margarine), negative in the case of complementary goods (fountain pens and ink).

When the absolute measure of price elasticity is greater than unity, demand at the given price is called elastic: a price change of, say, 1 per cent elicits a change of 3 per cent in the quantity demanded. If price elasticity (again in absolute terms) is less than unity, demand is said to be inelastic: a price change of 1 per cent might result in a change of 0·5 per cent in the quantity demanded. If elasticity at each price is zero, then demand is perfectly inelastic; if it is infinity, then demand is perfectly elastic (Figure 10).

Elasticity can change at each point on a demand curve. If the demand curve is a straight line, the higher the price the greater the absolute measure of elasticity. In Table 8, for instance, at a price of £2 elasticity is −0·27 (−22/164 ÷ 1/2), at £7 it is −1·1 (−12/76 ÷ 1/7).

The quantity demanded in terms of money changes in the same direction as the quantity demanded as long as demand is elastic and in the opposite direction when demand is inelastic (Table 9). At a price of £5 the elasticity of commodity A (1/2 ÷ −1/5) is −2·5, and that of commodity B (1/10 ÷ −1/5) is −0·5. For commodity C (3/12 ÷ −1/5) we have −1·25; in fact the elasticity of this commodity is always equal to unity: if it is not, this is only because we are not working with infinitely small changes. If revenue remains the same when price undergoes a small change, this is expressed by the equation $dP.Q = dQ.P − dQ.dP$; in other words, the revenue lost by a price cut dP over Q units is equal to the revenue obtained by selling dQ units at a lower price $P − dP$. Elasticity is equal to unity when $dP.Q = dQ.P$ or when $dQ.dP$ can be discounted (or is infinitely small).

109

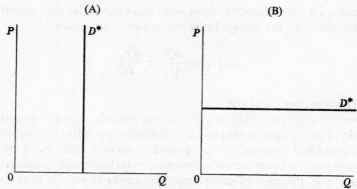

Figure 10: Perfectly inelastic (A) and perfectly elastic (B) demand

TABLE 9: Demand schedules for three commodities

Commodity A			Commodity B			Commodity C		
P	Q	PQ	P	Q	PQ	P	Q	PQ
5	2	10	5	10	50	5	12	60
4	3	12	4	11	44	4	15	60
3	5	15	3	12	36	3	20	60

c. Graphical representation of elasticity

Graphically, the elasticity at each point of the demand curve can be determined by drawing a tangent to that point; elasticity is then indicated by the formula P_1O/P_1A or MB/MA (Figure 11).

It is assumed that MM' is such a small part of the curve that it can be considered a straight line. MM' can therefore be plotted on AB, the tangent to point M. So the elasticity is:

$$\frac{dQ}{Q} : \frac{dP}{P} = \frac{dQ}{dP} \cdot \frac{P}{Q} = \frac{NM'}{MN} \cdot \frac{Q_1M}{OQ_1}. \qquad (1)$$

Since the triangles NMM' and Q_1MB are similar,

$$\frac{NM'}{MN} = \frac{Q_1B}{MQ_1}. \qquad (2)$$

Substitution of (2) in (1) gives:

$$\frac{Q_1B}{MQ_1} \cdot \frac{Q_1M}{OQ_1} = \frac{Q_1B}{Q_1O}.$$

Given the properties of similar triangles:

$$\frac{Q_1 B}{Q_1 O} = \frac{MB}{MA} = \frac{P_1 O}{P_1 A} \, .$$

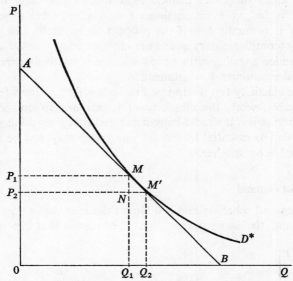

Figure 11: The geometrical determination of elasticity

Appraisal

Our appraisal of the demand curve shows that it is no easy task to establish the degree of elasticity. Accurate results are obtainable only if infinitely small price changes should occur. Moreover, the statistics are largely inadequate for providing reliable information. Finally, in attempting to measure elasticity we must again assume that other circumstances remain unchanged. Although this is very seldom the case, we are all too liable to lose sight of the fact that *ceteris paribus* is 'a very tricky assumption' (S. Schoeffler) and a 'slippery tool' (A. F. Burns).

With this reservation, the calculations made so far show, for instance, that demand for food, drink and tobacco, clothing and footwear is usually inelastic and demand for domestic appliances, furniture and luxury articles elastic. Demand for durables is normally more elastic than demand for food, because purchases can be post-

111

poned. Income also plays a part: the elasticity of demand for luxury articles may well be low for those in the higher-income brackets. Substitutability implies that demand for groups of like products such as spirits is less elastic than demand for individual items such as different kinds of strong drink. Other factors that may influence elasticity include the proportion of outlay to total expenditure (elasticity is normally low if the proportion is small) and complementarity (complementary goods are often relatively inelastic if they are demanded together with goods which are relatively expensive – petrol and motorcars, for instance).

Income elasticity too is supposed to be low for products felt to be indispensable, while the elasticity of goods not so considered is greater than unity. It should be remembered that something which is not regarded as essential by one income group may well be thought indispensable by another.

5 Shifts in demand

A new demand schedule and a different demand curve may appear for one and the same commodity. This means that the quantity

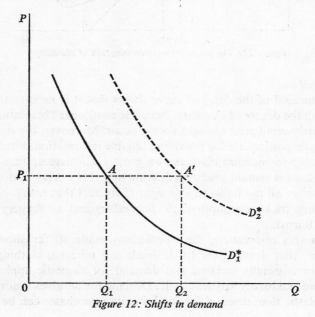

Figure 12: Shifts in demand

demanded changes without the price changing (Figure 12). The arrival of a new demand curve should not be confused – as was already stressed above – with a change in the quantity demanded on the same demand curve when prices change (though 'demand' is often used to mean the quantity demanded).

A change in demand may be the result of:

a. a change in tastes – resulting from technological advance (e.g. cassette tape recorders);

b. a general rise or fall in incomes (economic expansion or recession); when price increases are expected (as the economy revives), demand may go up even if price remains unchanged;

c. a change in the prices of other goods;

d. an increase or decline in the population.

6 Consumption and saving

a. Consumption

If we add up a household's contemplated monetary demand for all goods, this gives us the value of its planned consumption. Consumption can be regarded as a function of prices and the household's income:

$$C_i = f(p_1, p_2, p_3 \ldots p_n, Y_1).$$

Consumption is also affected by cash in hand, credit facilities, assets and expected income. The consumption of other households also has its repercussions: we often wish to buy products that other people have, for reasons of prestige (the demonstration effect). There is a certain interdependence of wants.

To establish the macroeconomic consumption function – the sum of microeconomic consumption functions – we must take all incomes into account. (We shall not dwell on the statistical problems that arise in the aggregation of microeconomic to macroeconomic data.)

$$C_1 = f(p_1 \ldots p_n, Y_1)$$
$$C_2 = f(p_1 \ldots p_n, Y_2)$$
$$\vdots$$
$$C_m = f(p_1 \ldots p_n, Y_m)$$
$$\text{or } C = f(P^*, Y)$$

On the assumption that prices remain constant, the consumption function expresses what consumption is expected by the household or

113

by households to coincide in the future at a given time or within a specified short period (planning period) with various (hypothetical) prices. This can be shown diagrammatically by the consumption curve (see below).

b. Saving

We agree with P. Hennipman's definition of saving as the conversion of part of one's income into wealth (the total net value of possessions). This can be done by refraining from consumption and transfers (in the form of gifts, for instance).

Savings can be calculated by deducting from disposable income over a certain period consumption in that period; but to define savings in this way is not very desirable: it attributes to saving a residual character which it does not always have. Saving is often the first item to be decided: a certain sum is set aside for an emergency. In many cases, however, particularly when incomes are high, savings do constitute a residue: wants are satisfied and what is left over is saved. This negative definition, however, is less applicable to firms and government. What is saved in firms (undistributed profits) is income that has not been transferred rather than what has not been consumed. Government savings constitute the difference between revenue and expenditure, the latter including transfer payments and investment.

Saving can be explained to some extent as the endeavour to obtain optimum allocation of consumption and wealth over time (P. Hennipman). In the case of savings for future consumption (or for more free time) no permanency is allotted to the creation of wealth: there is subsequent dissaving. Wealth is also valued in itself because of the satisfaction and social consideration that it brings. It is further used as a means of providing for one's relatives, and it is often intended to bring in revenue.

The factors that influence consumption also have repercussions on savings; as A. C. Pigou has pointed out, given equal incomes (and the same wants), different people may save different amounts because of a difference in wealth. The more wealth we have accumulated, the lower our propensity to save as a rule.

The savings function is defined, by analogy with the consumption function, as the function which shows the relation between various (hypothetical) incomes at a given time or over a given short period and the corresponding savings.

c. The propensity to consume and the propensity to save

The propensity to consume c is the relation of consumption to income C/Y; the propensity to save s is that of saving to income S/Y. Since $Y = C + S$, the propensity to consume and the propensity to save together equal unity; if £90 million is consumed and £30 million saved out of a national income of £120 million, the propensity to consume is 90/120 or 3/4 and the propensity to save 30/120 or 1/4.

The marginal propensity to consume c_μ is equal to the relation of a very small increase in consumption expenditure dC to an infinitesimal increase in income dY which occasioned the increase in consumption: dC/dY. The marginal propensity to save $s_\mu = 1 - dC/dY$. In fact we are calculating with very large sums. For instance, if the national income goes up by £10 million and £7 million of this goes to consumption, we say that the marginal propensity to consume, or that part of the extra income that is spent on consumption, is 0·7 (the marginal propensity to save being 0·3). The marginal propensity to consume is normally less than unity. Where we are not working with infinitesimal changes in income, it is better to speak of the differential propensity to consume. These definitions also apply microeconomically.

d. The consumption and savings functions

In Figure 13 BC represents a consumption curve. The savings curve ES can be derived from it. Even if no income is received, the basic necessities must be provided: a minimum level of consumption OB cannot be avoided, and the sum required must be raised by dissaving or by borrowing (OE). When income rises to OA, dissaving is no longer necessary: income and consumption are equal (in the triangle OAD, $OA = AD$; D is the point where the 45° line intersects the consumption curve). From this point on, saving is possible.

It is often asserted, following J. M. Keynes, that c_μ will gradually decline as income increases because saving can be stepped up (this is known as the 'absolute income hypothesis'). Consumption does go up as income rises, but not to the same extent. Particularly with high incomes, it seems hardly likely that consumption should always have the same relation to income. The consumption function, then, is represented by a rising curve gradually flattening out.

Particularly since the Second World War, growing interest has been shown in empirical inquiries into the factors that influence consumption and saving (D. H. Robertson having already shown before the war that it is not so much today's as yesterday's income

115

that is important). Special mention should be made here of J. S. Duesenberry, F. Modigliani and M. Friedman.

J. S. Duesenberry considers that because of the demonstration effect individual preferences cannot be regarded as given: they are

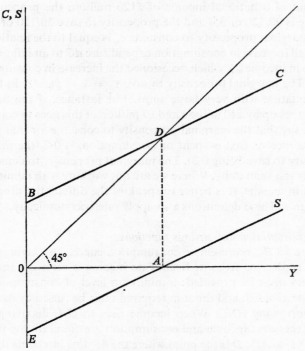

Figure 13: Consumption and saving curves

affected by the behaviour of other consumers ('keeping up with the Joneses'). Consumption increases in proportion to income; the saving ratio, too, is independent of the absolute level of income. This 'relative income hypothesis' is also maintained by F. Modigliani. In this case the consumption curve is a straight line (as in Figure 13): c_μ remains constant and the additional consumption always represents the same share of supplementary income (whatever the level income).

In the short term (the cyclical rather than the secular consumption function) the ratio varies more: consumption changes less readily

116

than income, particularly downwards. Demand is not easily reversed: if prices go up, consumption goes down much less than it goes up when there is a corresponding reduction in price (the ratchet effect). Once we have grown accustomed to a given level of consumption, we prefer to maintain it. So consumption (and hence saving too) is a function not only of current but also of previous (higher) income or – more likely – the previous level of consumption. The ratchet effect is weaker the longer ago the period of higher consumption.

The consumption function can then be written:

$$C_t = f(P^*, Y_0, Y_1 \ldots Y_{t-1}, Y_{t-2}).$$

The reason why delay is possible before the consumer reacts and adjusts his plans to changed circumstances is that durables (e.g. textiles) are bought only occasionally and their lifetime can be prolonged.

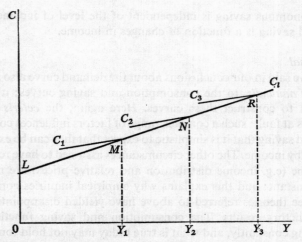

Figure 14: The short-term and long-term consumption curves

The relation between the short- and the long-term consumption curves can be shown as in Figure 14. At income OY_1, consumption equals Y_1M; when income falls, consumption does not follow along the ML line but along the short-term consumption curve MC_1. When income rises again, consumption rises along the straight line C_1M and then the straight line MC_l. Similar phenomena occur when income falls at higher levels (e.g. OY_2 and OY_3).

F

117

M. Friedman also maintains that saving always represents the same proportion of 'permanent' income and consumption (the 'permanent income hypothesis'), 'permanent' income including prospective income in succeeding periods. The proportion is determined by interest, wealth, the size and composition of consumption units, etc. F. Modigliani stresses 'permanent wealth' rather than 'permanent income'.

e. Kinds of saving

Saving may be involuntary (passive) or forced – as a delayed reaction to a change in income (a wage or salary increase not immediately followed by an increase in consumption) or as when consumer goods are rationed (at times of scarcity). Forced saving should not be confused with the monetary restriction of consumption (Chapter 6.2d), particularly as the latter is often called forced saving.

Autonomous saving is independent of the level of income, while induced saving is a function of changes in income.

Appraisal

What we said in our conclusions about the demand curve also applies, *mutatis mutandis*, to the consumption and saving curves: it is very difficult to construct these curves. Here again, the *ceteris paribus* clause is at fault: such a complex range of factors influences consumption and saving that it is simplistic to expect that they can be explained mainly by income. The other circumstances assumed to have remained the same (e.g. income distribution and relative prices) are never in fact constant; and this explains why empirical inquiries concerning the three theories referred to above have yielded disappointing and contradictory results. The consumption and saving functions are changing constantly, and what is true today may not hold tomorrow. Naturally, saving can be estimated *ex post*, as can its share in the national income or the family income. R. W. Goldsmith, for instance, estimates the share of private saving in disposable private income in the United States at 10·9 per cent in 1909–14, 12·2 per cent in 1922–9, 10 per cent in 1950–4, 11·3 per cent in 1955–9 and 11·4 per cent in 1960–4.

All of this bears out the statement of A. F. Burns that '. . . our ability to forecast what increment of consumer outlay will accompany a specified increment of income . . . is as yet very limited'.

TABLE 10: Average annual consumption per working-class household in some EEC countries (1963–4)

	Western Germany		France		Italy		Netherlands		Belgium	
	thousand DM	%	thousand FF	%	ten thousand lire	%	thousand fl.	%	thousand BF	%
Food, beverages and tobaccos[a]	3.9	42.6	6.4	45.4	65.8	49.1	3.2	37.2	53.5	39.2
Clothing and footwear	1.0	10.9	1.4	9.7	13.4	10.0	1.2	13.8	17.4	12.8
Rent etc., fuel and light	1.4	14.9	1.9	13.4	21.6	16.1	1.2	14.3	25.0	18.3
Furniture, household appliances and maintenance	0.9	9.4	1.1	7.8	7.7	5.8	0.9	10.5	11.3	8.2
Personal health and hygiene	0.3	2.7	0.6	4.5	2.8	2.1	0.2	2.6	4.4	3.2
Transport and communication	0.7	7.1	1.4	10.1	8.5	6.4	0.6	7.4	10.9	8.0
Education, entertainment and recreation	0.6	6.3	0.8	5.7	7.7	5.7	0.7	8.4	7.2	5.3
Other goods and services	0.6	6.1	0.5	3.3	6.6	4.9	0.5	5.8	6.8	5.0
		100.0		100.0		100.0		100.0		100.0
Total	9.2	83.5	14.1	94.7	134.0	92.5	8.7	83.3	136.6	90.1
Social security contributions and taxes	1.8	16.5	0.8	5.3	10.9	7.5	1.7	16.7	15.0	9.9
Total	11.1	100.0	14.8	100.0	144.9	100.0	10.4	100.0	151.6	100.0

[a] Less expenditure on servants and boarders

Source: Results of 1963–4 budget survey, Statistical Office of the European Communities, Annuaire de statistiques sociales 1968, pp. 226–9

7 Family budgets

Attempts are made to establish the consumption (and consumption schedules) of individual households by carrying out surveys (see Table 10). In surveys of this kind we must take care to distinguish between expenditure (cash outlay) and consumption (which does not necessarily involve payment); the latter includes families' consumption from their own kitchen gardens and livestock, wages in kind (the midday meal at the factory) and the rateable value of houses owned by the consumer.

Especially in international comparisons, these surveys must be based on consumption. For instance, in 1963-4 income spent by workers accounted for 97·3 per cent of consumption in the Netherlands and 93 per cent in Belgium.

One of the most variable items is the percentage accounted for by food – 49 per cent in Italy compared with 37 per cent in the Netherlands. This can be explained by Engel's law, but differences in the value attached to food may also play a role. The Italians and the French consume relatively expensive foodstuffs – meat and butter in France, cheese and fresh fruit and vegetables in Italy.

These surveys are used as a basis for cost-of-living indexes.

8 Bibliography

a. Marginal utility and the indifference method
The foundation of the marginal utility theory of value was laid by the Austrian school (see Appendix 8: W. S. Jevons, C. Menger and L. Walras). In 1927 the indifference concept was introduced by V. Pareto and afterwards used by, *inter alia*, J. R. Hicks, *Value and Capital* (2nd ed., Oxford 1946). The first three chapters of this work were later developed in J. R. Hicks, *A Revision of Demand Theory* (Oxford 1956).

T. Majumdar, *The Measurement of Utility* (London 1958) considers concisely the different positions taken up in this field (especially by J. R. Hicks and P. A. Samuelson).

The theory of revealed preferences was developed by P. A. Samuelson, *Foundations of Economic Analysis* (Cambridge, Mass. 1947); see H. Wagner, 'The Case for Revealed Preference', *RESt*, June 1959; B. B. Seligman, 'On the Question of Operationalism (A review article)', *AER*, March 1967.

For a brief and critical appraisal: E. J. Mishan, 'Theories of Consumer's Behaviour: A Cynical View', *Ec*, February 1961.

An elaborate annotated bibliography on these subjects is given by P. Newman, *The Theory of Exchange* (Englewood Cliffs, N. J. 1965). See also *Utility Theory: A Book of Readings* (ed. A. N. Page, New York 1968) and the good survey by R. Ferber, 'Research on Household Behaviour', in *Surveys of Economic Theory*: Vol. 3 *Resource Allocation* (American Economic Association and Royal Economic Society, 1965).

The quotations from J. Marchal and E. Wagemann come from an article in *ZN* (1949) and from *Berühmte Denkfehler der Nationalökonomie* (Berne 1951) respectively, that from H. Mayer is from 'Der Erkenntniswert der funktionellen Preistheorie', in *Die Wirtschaftstheorie der Gegenwart*, Part 2 (Vienna 1932).

b. Demand

H. Wold (assisted by L. Jureen), *Demand Analysis: A Study in Econometrics* (Stockholm 1952), establishes, on the basis of Swedish data, that demand is relatively stable: before and after the Second World War the structure of consumption remained approximately the same.

When the relation between price and quantity demanded is investigated, income is assumed to remain constant. On the question whether the basis should be a constant money or real income: M. Friedman, 'The Marshallian Demand Curve', *JPE*, December 1949; for further reading on this matter: L. B. Yeager, '*Methodenstreit* over demand curves', *JPE*, February 1960.

See also P. Newman, *The Theory of Exchange*. For a mathematical approach: I. F. Pearce, *A Contribution to Demand Analysis* (Oxford 1964).

The quotation from F. Machlup can be found in his contribution in *The Structure of Economic Science: Essays on Methodology* (ed. S. R. Krupp, Englewood Cliffs, N. J. 1966).

c. Income and substitution effects

Building on an article by E. E. Slutsky dating from 1915: R. G. D. Allen and J. R. Hicks, 'A Reconsideration of the Theory of Value', *Ec*, February and May 1934; J. R. Hicks, *Value and Capital*.

The infrequent Giffen case was mentioned by A. Marshall, *Principles of Economics: An Introductory Volume* (8th ed., London 1920).

121

d. Elasticity

Pioneering work in respect of elasticity was done by H. Schultz, *The Theory and Measurement of Demand* (Chicago 1938); however, we may wonder whether the rather poor results justify the use of such a complex mathematical apparatus. Better is R. Stone, *The Measurement of Consumer's Expenditure and Behaviour in the United Kingdom 1920–1938* (Cambridge 1954) and (connected with Stone) S. J. Prais and H. S. Houthakker, *The Analysis of Family Budgets with an Application to two British Surveys Conducted in 1937–1939 and Their Detailed Results* (Cambridge 1955); see also *The Demand for Durable Goods* (ed. A. C. Harberger, Chicago 1960).

The quotation from S. Schoeffler is drawn from *The Failure of Economics: A Diagnostic Study* (Cambridge, Mass. 1955), that from A. F. Burns from *The Frontiers of Economic Research* (Princeton 1954).

e. The propensity to consume and the propensity to save

The consumption curve was separately dealt with for the first time by J. M. Keynes, *General Theory of Employment, Interest and Money* (London 1936), Chapters 6 and 7. On the psychological foundations of consumption decisions: G. Katona, *Psychological Studies of the American Economy* (New York 1960), Part 1. On 'conspicuous consumption': T. Veblen, *The Theory of the Leisure Class* (New York 1934), Chapter 4. See also J. S. Duesenberry, *Income, Saving and the Theory of Consumer Behavior* (Cambridge, Mass. 1949) on the 'demonstration effect'; H. Leibenstein, 'Bandwagon, Snob and Veblen Effects in the Theory of Consumer's Demand', *QJE*, May 1950.

The relative-income and permanent-income hypotheses can be found in J. S. Duesenberry, *Income, Saving and the Theory of Consumer Behavior*; F. Modigliani, 'Fluctuations in the Savings-Income Ratio: A Problem in Economic Forecasting', in *Studies in Income and Wealth*, Vol. 11 (New York 1949); M. Friedman, *A Theory of the Consumption Function* (Princeton 1957).

Important literature on the subject: T. E. Davis, 'The Consumption Function as a Tool for Prediction', *RES*, August, 1952; I. Friend and I. B. Kravis, 'Consumption Patterns and Permanent Income', *AER*, May 1957; M. J. Farrell, 'The New Theories of the Consumption Function', *EJ*, December 1959; A. Zellner, 'Tests of Some Basic Propositions in the Theory of Consumption', *AER*, May 1960; *Proceedings of a Conference on Consumption and Saving* (ed.

M. Friedman and R. Jones, Philadelphia 1960), especially the paper by F. Modigliani and A. Ando, 'The "Permanent Income" and the "Life Cycle" Hypotheses of Saving Behaviour: Comparison and Tests'.

The quotation from A. F. Burns is from *Economic Research and the Keynesian Thinking of our Times* (New York 1946), the references to P. Hennipman from 'De economische problematiek van het sparen', in L. M. Koyck, P. Hennipman, C. W. Willinge Prins-Visser, *Verbruik en sparen in theorie en praktijk: Een overzicht van de problemen en resultaten van de economische theorie, het empirisch onderzoek en het streven naar een doelmatige inkomstenbesteding* (Haarlem 1957).

On aggregation: H. Theil, *Linear Aggregation of Economic Relations* (Amsterdam 1954); R. G. D. Allen, *Mathematical Economics* (2nd ed., London 1962), Chapter 20; H. A. J. Green, *Aggregation in Economic Analysis: An Introductory Survey* (Princeton 1964).

f. The Pigou effect
This is considered in A. C. Pigou, *Employment and Equilibrium* (London 1941); *id.*, 'The Classical Stationary State', *EJ*, December 1943. G. Haberler, *Prosperity and Depression: A Theoretical Analysis of Cyclical Movements* (3rd ed. Geneva 1941), also deals with this problem.

More recent: L. R. Klein, 'Assets, Debts and Economic Behavior', in *Studies in Income and Wealth*, Vol. 14 (New York 1951); G. Haberler, 'The Pigou Effect Once More', *JPE*, June 1952; see further the bibliography in M. Cohen, 'Liquid Assets and the Consumption Function', *RES*, May 1954.

5 Firms

*... l'entreprise, lieu géométrique des forces et des
faiblesses de l'économie capitaliste.*

François Perroux

It is the enterprise in an economy that produces goods and supplies services. In this chapter we explain various concepts, discuss the law of variable returns and show how the optimum combination of production factors is achieved.

1 The plant and the firm

a. The firm

In collectivist as well as in capitalist economies the combination of factors of production is effected in enterprises.

A distinction can be made between plant and firm. In thinking of the firm, we tend to be concerned with business objectives. In a capitalist economy the aim of the firm is normally considered to be the maximization of profit; the plant is more the means of achieving this aim. A firm can be made up of more than one plant. The plant, then, is a neutral concept as regards the economic system.

The entrepreneur decides to start the production of a commodity and proceeds to the organization of the production process. He generally entrusts some parts of the process to subordinates, but he retains overall control himself. He also assumes a risk: as a result of inaccurate estimates or other circumstances, it can happen that revenue does not cover costs and the firm makes a loss. If revenue exceeds cost, the entrepreneur makes a profit (Chapter 8.8*b*).

As the firm becomes more capital-intensive and the decision is taken to form a company (see Section 2), the entrepreneur is no longer able to supply all the capital required and has to call on investors. These become the true entrepreneurs once their interest is greater than that of the founder and promoter. The assumption of risk is a basic feature of the function of the entrepreneur.

If the manager of the firm does not run any financial risk and receives directives from the general meeting of shareholders and the

124

board of directors, his function is really that of a senior corporation executive. His role, like that of the entrepreneur-promoter, declines in importance with technological advance and increasing plant scale: if he is not to hold back production he has to allow more scope to subordinates; committees and groups take the place of the man acting on his own. This is true also of scientific research, in which teamwork is increasingly indispensable.

The share of the various investor-entrepreneurs in deciding management policy depends upon the strength of their position; antagonism is a factor that cannot be ruled out here. For instance, a group with a controlling interest can insist on having its own way – say, by pressing for profits to be ploughed back into the business against the wishes of the other shareholders, who want as much as possible paid out in dividend.

It is a feature of the capitalist system that decisions by entrepreneurs are the determinants of economic activity. In the USSR the sole entrepreneur is the government, which draws up an overall plan for the whole country.

b. The public enterprise
In the collectivist economy the role of the entrepreneur is taken over by the government. It is on the government's initiative that plants are set up, and the factory managers follow government directives.

In the USSR all the means of production are state-owned. In agriculture we find cooperative ownership: approximately 40 per cent of the cultivated land area (including small privately owned plots is exploited by cooperative ownership (*kolkhozes*), most of the rest directly by state farms (*sovkhozes*). Cooperatives (see Section 3) are also to be found in the craft trades and service industries. Consumer cooperatives account for some 30 per cent of consumer transactions. Private ownership of houses and cars is permitted (about 40 per cent of living accommodation is the property of private individuals); servants may also be employed. In China too they have state farms (4 per cent of the cultivated land) and cooperative farms. While in the USSR 4 per cent of the national income is produced by the private sector this proportion is about 25 per cent in Yugoslavia and Poland.

In some western countries nationalization schemes have been put into effect, but the nationalized industries are not sufficiently numerous or important to change the character of the economies in question.

In France, the United Kingdom and Italy the coal mines have been nationalized, as have the gas and electricity industries in most countries (though not in Belgium). Of the EEC countries, France and Italy have the greatest number of public enterprises (especially in the shipbuilding and motor industries; for banks, see Chapter 3.10). In West Germany some shipyards and coal mines and almost the entire aluminium industry are publicly owned. Unlike French and Italian nationalized concerns, West German public undertakings are not instruments of government economic policy; nor are they granted privileges as regards the provision of capital.

Moreover, some public enterprises came into being through considerations which had nothing to do with the ideological motivations which gave rise to the pursuit of nationalization:

1. to carry on an activity which private enterprise did not consider profitable (ports, railways);

2. to provide for the basic needs of all social groups (hospitals);

3. to operate services which would be very difficult to administer except by a state monopoly (postal services, the mint, railways, central banks);

4. for reasons of strategic policy (railways) or taxation (matches in France, tobacco in France and Italy).

At first, a great deal of criticism was levelled at public ownership: the rules proper to the administration of a government department could not be taken over as they stood (accounting, pay schemes), and the political influence that was brought to bear resulted in overstaffing. The suggestions made for overcoming these drawbacks included the establishment of state monopolies with financial independence and of mixed enterprises. In the latter, private interests and government jointly provide the capital and operate the business. Examples of the mixed enterprise are Sabena and Air France, the Belgian and French airline companies. But depending on which of the partners has more control, such an undertaking resolves itself in effect into either a public or a private operation.

In the absence of private enterprise, the government is frequently obliged to set up new plants itself. This is often the case in lessdeveloped countries (e.g. Turkey and India). Some government plants have subsequently been taken over by private owners; there are, however, not many people with enough capital to take over large state enterprises at their real value. Less-developed countries also extend the public sector as a means of keeping within reasonable bounds foreign influence on economic activity and the concomitant social and political problems (e.g. in Latin America).

Experience has shown that public enterprises can be run just as well as and sometimes better than firms in the private sector (e.g. the Régie Renault in France, the state-owned mines and farms in the Netherlands). However, they do often enjoy an important advantage over private business in the shape of more favourable terms in raising funds (the state either provides the capital itself or guarantees repayment). Another point is that cooperation between different public enterprises is normally easier.

c. Plants and government in the communist countries
In the USSR comprehensive economic plans are regularly drawn up for five-year periods and, within this framework, for each year. The individual plants are consulted: they put forward proposals to the offices of the Gosplan (the State Planning Committee). The Gosplan draws up the plan, and the plan must be adhered to (Chapter 13.2). The plants, then, receive their instructions from the central government; as has already been stressed (Chapter 1.8d), it is not necessarily the wishes of the consumers that determine what and how much is produced.

Up to now, Soviet planning has not worked faultlessly.

1. The plans themselves were, for the most part, drawn up too late, repeatedly modified and then communicated to the plants only after some delay. This caused, among other things, belated delivery of capital goods, which in turn had an adverse effect on production.

2. It was very much in the interest of the plant managers to attain the production targets laid down in the plans, even if it meant sacrificing quality. Whether or not there was a demand for the goods produced was of minor importance. The results of this policy could be seen in the fact that at the beginning of 1964 the country had more than 2,000 million roubles' worth of unsold goods (in excess of normal stocks) on hand, including such items as textiles and sewing machines. Nor was there any advantage in overfulfilling the norm, since the figures for each period are based on those of the preceding one.

3. The plant managers were not encouraged to bring out new products: this initially causes a drop in production, which would hinder attainment of the targets.

127

4. The scarcity (or the cost) of capital was not taken into account, so there was considerable wastage.

At the end of 1965 some reforms were introduced which represent a modest beginning in seeking to make the economy function more efficiently; these amounted to giving the plants greater independence.

1. The number of rules laid down was substantially reduced (those retained included stipulations on the size of the wage fund, profits, the ratio of profits to floating capital), and the figure for gross output in the plan was replaced by a sales target.

2. The interest on capital was to be at an average rate of 6 per cent (in some cases 3 per cent; in others, capital would be provided free of interest).

3. Interest was to be deducted from gross profit (sales less the cost of labour and materials). Part of the remaining net profit is divided among three funds – a social, cultural and housing fund, a workers' incentive bonus fund (representing at least 15 per cent of the wage fund) and a development fund. The rest of the net profit goes to the state. Previously, the profit was used mainly to set up new plants, which went against the interests of the existing enterprises.

In 1967 a start was made with reforming the agricultural sector along industrial lines. This process included elimination of the privileged position that the *sovkhozes* enjoyed over the *kolkhozes*.

In China, planning is of a more rudimentary nature. Since 1968 a greater measure of decentralization has been introduced. About 80 per cent of the state enterprises have been handed over to the provinces, autonomous regions or towns. Nevertheless, 80 per cent of their profit still has to go to central government, though the industrial plants which were already operated by regional or local authorities prior to this are not subject to this obligation.

Just as in the USSR, more importance began to be attached to profit as an indicator of efficient management in the early 1960s. But this approach seems to have been abandoned since the 'great cultural revolution' of 1966–7.

Jugoslavia was the first communist country (in the early 1950s) to move towards greater economic decentralization. Moreover, the changes were greatest in that country. Detailed planning came to an end and the price mechanism was assigned a greater role in the economy.

Our criticism of Soviet planning should not give the reader the impression that there are no disadvantages in the way western capitalism (and its price mechanism) works (Chapter 1.8*d*; Chapter 7).

2 The different types of business enterprise

The business enterprise is an organization in which factors of production are combined by two or more people for the purpose of making a profit.

In the partnership – and its continental European equivalents: *société en nom collectif, offene Handelsgesellschaft, società in nome collettivo, vennootschap onder een firma*, etc. – the partners are jointly liable to the full extent of their personal fortune for all the firm's obligations – a feature which has not been conducive to the widespread formation of partnerships. The limited partnership – *société en commandite, Kommanditgesellschaft, società in accomandita, commanditaire vennootschap* – is a partnership consisting of limited as well as general partners. Although the liability of the limited partners is confined to the capital they have invested in the firm, it is as a rule difficult to find such partners since they are not normally allowed to take part in the management of the business, and they are unwilling to surrender control of a large part of their capital without considerable safeguards.

In the private company under English law – roughly corresponding to the *société (de personnes) à responsabilité limitée, Gesellschaft mit beschränkter Haftung, società a responsabilità limitata, besloten vennootschap* – member's liability is limited to the nominal value of the shares he holds, but transfer of the shares is subject to certain restrictions. This type of company originated in fact in Britain but was first regulated by statute in Germany in 1892 (and not until 1907 in the United Kingdom, 1925 in France, 1935 in Belgium). The statutory distinction between private companies and public companies as understood in the United Kingdom is unknown in the United States, where the nearest equivalents to the private company are the 'close(d) corporation', whose charter limits the number of members and the transfer of stock, and in some states the joint-stock company, which can be regarded as lying midway between partnerships and corporations. (In English law, the joint-stock company covers companies set up by Royal Charter or by special Act of Parliament as well as the

129

public and private limited companies registered under the Companies Acts.)

The public company limited by shares in the United Kingdom, the corporation in the United States, and the *société anonyme, Aktiengesellschaft, società per azioni, naamloze vennootschap* in continental Europe are all forms of business organization in which the liability of the shareholders (as they are known in the UK) or stockholders (as they are known in the US) – a minimum of two in the Netherlands and Italy, five in West Germany and most states of the United States, seven in Belgium, France and the United Kingdom – are likewise limited to the capital they have invested. The principle of limited liability was given early recognition in the United Kingdom and France, most modern legislation dating from the second half of the nineteenth century.

A company's capital is divided into shares or stocks (ordinary shares in the UK; common stocks in the US). Preference shares (UK) or preferred stocks (US) entitle the holder to priority treatment of some kind; this varies from company to company but generally means that the holders are paid their dividend before the ordinary shareholders receive anything. Preference shares or preferred stocks are mainly offered in order to make a capital issue more attractive.

Shares or stocks are not to be confused with bonds (US) or debentures (UK), which are certificates issued as evidence of indebtedness to persons (bondholders, debenture holders) who have lent money to the company.

The share always represents a part of the owners' equities of the company, and so its real or market value is different from its face, nominal or par value. In the United States and Canada, unlike the United Kingdom and most other European countries (Belgium being an exception), stock need not have a specific value and is then designated no-par-value stock. When a business goes bankrupt the shareholder can lose the whole of his invested capital. The debenture holder, on the other hand, is a creditor just like any other, and when the business is wound up he may be repaid along with the other creditors before the shareholders. There may even be special guarantees in the form of debentures secured by mortgage on the company's assets. The debenture holder is not entitled to any say in the management of the company, though in some states of the United States a right of vote is granted in certain contingencies (if, for example, interest is not paid).

Governments too issue bonds. When these are repayable in the short term they are called Treasury Bills.

In Britain, deferred or founders' shares are sometimes issued to the founders or promoters of a company. In continental Europe, *actions de jouissance* (*Genußscheine, bewijzen van deelgerechtigdheid*) are types of profit-sharing certificate issued to holders of redeemed shares and entitling them to certain privileges which differ from country to country; these are unknown in Britain and America.

Since the liability of the members is limited to the extent of their share of the capital, it is easier for the limited company to attract capital, the more so since shares (which are usually 'bearer' shares and not 'registered' shares) can be freely traded on the stock exchange (Chapter 7.1). The fact that the capital of a limited company is divided into a large number of shares is a point that attracts the small investor. The system also ensures that risk is spread more widely.

Although the annual meeting of shareholders in principle exercises sovereign control, the major decisions of a company are in fact taken by the board of directors and the managing director(s).

One drawback of easy availability of capital has been the formation of companies lacking a sound economic foundation. The necessity for strict control over the founding and operation of the limited company was quickly recognized. The responsibility of the director is limited, and a frequent result of this is inadequate supervision of the company's management. Regular disclosure of many of the documents of the limited company is required by law.

The purchase of shares or debentures is a means of investment. Investment does not necessarily entail capital formation or investment in the strict sense. This only takes place when new securities are issued. Even then, the revenue from new capital issues can be put to non-productive purposes.

3 Cooperatives

a. The concept

The cooperative movement has its origin in the endeavours of working-class people to join together in defence of their interests – for instance, in the spheres of production and consumption. Profit as such is not an objective. The cooperative is, in other words, a non-capitalist organization which seeks to change the existing pattern of society. P. Lambert defines it as 'an enterprise formed and directed by

131

an association of users, applying within itself the rules of democracy and directly intended to serve both its own members and the community as a whole'.

It must fulfil the following conditions:

1. Participation must be personal. The cooperative is more an association by personal interest and liability rather than by contribution of capital or shares. The subordinate role played by capital can be seen in the voting arrangements (each member has an equal vote in the general meeting) and the remuneration (only limited interest paid). After sums have been set aside for the payment of interest, any surplus is distributed according to the members' share in the transactions of the cooperative or in services rendered.

2. Membership is voluntary (otherwise, they would be corporative in the political sense – associations of employees and employers in a basic industry of a corporative state – rather than cooperatives) and is normally open to anyone (provided there are no technical or economic obstacles: in a producer cooperative, for example, the labour force cannot be increased without good reason). A corollary of this is that the capital is variable; there is no objection to small shares.

In' most legislation these features of the cooperative are not stated in so many words (though French law on cooperatives was codified in 1947 in the *Statut général de la coopération*), so that many cooperatives are in fact disguised limited companies, the only difference being the variability of their capital.

In Belgium even large enterprises (e.g. in the electricity distribution industry) and cartels have assumed the form of cooperatives. Many writers are of the opinion that the cooperative must be considered quite separately from the economic system. The cooperative proper is extremely widespread in some countries, such as Finland. It has had most success as an association of consumers.

b. The different types

In the *producer* cooperative the members provide not only the requisite labour but also the capital, though the latter is often borrowed. It has long been the ideal of social reformers (including R. Owen and F. Lassalle).

Nowadays it is found only to a limited extent in, for instance, France and Britain. The first examples date from the mid-nineteenth century (in Britain the first producer cooperative was formed as long ago as 1760). Their major difficulties arose from shortage of capital: the founders were generally not very wealthy, and investors were not attracted to these cooperatives. There was even some boycotting by the business world. A lack of capable technicians and managers was often apparent: few were attracted by the relatively low wages. Eventually, the founder members departed from their original principles and recruited workers who did not become members of the cooperative.

Closely akin to the producer cooperative was the workers' limited company (*société anonyme ouvrière*), whose capital was provided by trade unions. The latter also appointed the directors. Companies of this kind were set up principally in Belgium early in the twentieth century at the instigation of the socialist statesman E. Anseele (1856–1938). In order to finance the first companies, the Belgian Workers' Bank was set up in 1913; by buying up shares, the Bank gained control of a number of firms, mainly in the textile industry. Like many other banks, the Workers' Bank went bankrupt during the critical years following the 1929 crash.

The first *consumer* cooperatives were also established in the middle of the nineteenth century (in Britain in 1827, in Germany and the Netherlands in 1860, in France in 1864, in Belgium in 1881). They made substantial contributions to the expansion of Western European socialist parties.

In some countries, consumer cooperatives account for a relatively large share of retail sales (34 per cent in Finland, 32 per cent in Iceland, 14·5 per cent in Norway, 13·5 per cent in Sweden, 11 per cent in the United Kingdom).

For the most part, the rules and principles of the Rochdale Society of Equitable Pioneers are still adhered to: sales at ruling prices with a dividend paid to members in proportion to their purchases; non-members can also buy goods from the cooperatives and this ensures a bigger turnover.

The purpose of the *credit* cooperative is to lend its members funds that they cannot borrow from banks – or not on such favourable terms. Its capital is raised mainly by floating loans. The guarantee offered to investors generally takes the form of a joint undertaking by all the members.

Finally, there are the cooperatives whose purpose is to purchase and sell raw materials or goods for the joint benefit of their members.

4 Productivity

There is a distinction to be drawn between average and marginal productivity.

a. Average productivity

By the (average) productivity of a combination of factors we understand the ratio of the output of this combination to the factors themselves:

$$\text{average productivity} = \frac{\text{output}}{\text{factors}}.$$

In calculating physical productivity (in physical units), we are faced with the difficulty that it is impossible to express not only the denominator but also, in the case of heterogeneous output, the numerator in the same unit.

Where output is homogeneous, the first difficulty can be solved by concentrating on partial productivity – the ratio of output to a single factor. For example, the average physical productivity of labour is determined by the formula:

$$f_{L'} = \frac{X'}{L'}$$

That is to say, we divide the output of a country, an industry or a plant over a certain period (year, month, day or hour) by the number of workers concerned. As the number of hours worked per day varies from country to country, it is often better to measure productivity per man-hour (Table 11). It is only in some industries (including coal

TABLE 11: Labour productivity

	Country A	Country B
Production per day	80,000 t	360,000 t
Number of workers	10,000	60,000
Hours worked per day	8	6
Productivity per day	8 t	6 t
Productivity per hour	1 t	1 t

mining) that physical productivity can easily be measured. In many branches of industry this is difficult since diverse and constantly

134

changing types of goods are manufactured. For this reason, productivity is also expressed in terms of money. Average labour productivity (f_L) is then equal to X/L, average capital productivity (f_K) to X/K. In calculating the value of the output, we should only take account of the value added by the production factors involved: raw materials purchased from other plants, for instance, are not to be taken into account; in other words, only the gross or net value added is of any importance. As with output, we can differentiate between gross and net productivity, depending on whether depreciation is taken into account. As depreciation allowances are often hard to estimate, it is usually gross productivity that we consider.

b. Marginal productivity

Starting from the production function, we can define the marginal productivity of a variable factor as the partial derivative of the production function with respect to this factor $f_{L'\mu} = \dfrac{\partial X'}{\partial L'}$ (marginal productivity of labour) and $f_{K'\mu} = \dfrac{\partial X'}{\partial K'}$ (marginal productivity of capital).

Where both factors change simultaneously, the change in total output represented by the total differential of the production function is called marginal product and is written:

$$dX' = \frac{\partial X'}{\partial L'}\, dL' + \frac{\partial X'}{\partial K'}\, dK'.$$

Where one factor remains constant, the marginal product of labour and capital respectively are represented by

$$dX'_{L'} = \frac{\partial X'}{\partial L'}\, dL' \quad \text{and} \quad dX'_{K'} = \frac{\partial X'}{\partial K'}\, dK'.$$

In other words, the marginal product of labour, $dX'_{L'}$ (the partial differential of the production function with respect to labour) is equal to the marginal productivity of labour, $f_{L'\mu}$, multiplied by an infinitesimal increase of L' or by dL' $dX'_{L'} = f_{L'\mu}\, dL'$. Although both are infinitely small, $\partial L'$ and dL' need not be equal.

In practice it is, generally speaking, impossible to calculate

135

marginal productivity and marginal product in this way, since the production function cannot be accurately determined and the factors and/or output are not wholly divisible. The marginal productivity of L' is therefore sometimes defined as the increase in X' where one extra unit is added to L'. Marginal product and marginal productivity should then be considered synonyms. Both concepts can be defined in another way – namely on the basis of a relative rather than an absolute change. Marginal productivity and marginal product of labour (when capital is supposed to be constant) are then represented

by $\dfrac{\partial X'}{X'} : \dfrac{\partial L'}{L'}$ and $\left(\dfrac{\partial X'}{X'} : \dfrac{\partial L'}{L'}\right) \dfrac{dL'}{L'}$ respectively. Once more, $\partial L'$ and

dL' are taken to be infinitesimal. In fact we start out from as small an increase as possible. If, for example, it is possible to increase the labour input by 1 per thousand and this brings about a 'measurable' increase in production of 2 per thousand, we say that $f_{L'\mu}$ is 2.

Appraisal

Since the concept of productivity is so often used, whether or not it is appropriate, it is perhaps a good thing to try to shed some light on its significance. As we have indicated, physical productivity is very difficult to establish. Interpretation of the relevant changes must nevertheless be made circumspectly because in each case the productivity of all factors is expressed: thus, gains in labour productivity often result solely from introducing new machinery.

When productivity is measured in terms of money, fewer difficulties seem to present themselves at first glance. However, there are other problems that come to the fore. For instance, the influence of inflation (see Chapter 9.10) and also of changes in demand for the commodities in question should be eliminated (for these cause prices to rise without any change in the production process). The repercussions of technological advance may also be lost from view: productivity can decline because technological advances bring prices down. Indeed, productivity in physical and money terms do not necessarily coincide (prices can drop, without a sufficient rise in output to compensate for this fall in prices).

There is little point in measuring total productivity in money terms: normally, this should always be equal to unity, the value of output equalling the value of the services provided by the production factors. If there is a discrepancy, this indicates a profit or a loss. In that case, however, we can as well work direct from profitability – the ratio of profits to the owners' equities (paid-up capital and reserves).

Partial productivity (in money terms), e.g. labour productivity, as a yardstick of economic efficiency is significant only if there has been no factor substitution or change in the factor combination. Even then it is doubtful whether the value of the different types of labour (which, moreover, do not remain unchanged) can be added up.

F. Schaller rightly observes that in the literature we can find the most varied formulas for measuring productivity, but that the real difficulty is to establish what productivity is, what is the object of our researches, and what precise significance we ought to attribute to the information found.

It would therefore be best to substitute the neutral expression 'production per unit of input of labour' for 'productivity' and 'labour productivity', and to avoid the expression 'marginal productivity'.

5 The isoquant and factor combination

If, in order to produce the same quantity of goods, the factors can be combined in a variety of ways, they are substitutable. If they cannot, then they are complementary.

a. Substitutability

Where factors are substitutable, less use of one factor is compensated by greater use of the others. The output of an outdated piece of machinery (little capital) together with many workers may be the same as that of a modern machine (much capital) with few employees.

The combination of a given quantity of labour OL'_3 with a certain quantity of capital OK'_1 will give an output corresponding to point M (Figure 15). A curve joining up all points which give the same output is called an isoquant; it shows the various possible combinations of capital and labour. For example, the same quantity will be produced by each of the following combinations:

OL'_1 units of labour and OK'_3 units of capital;
OL'_2 units of labour and OK'_2 units of capital; and
OL'_3 units of labour and OK'_1 units of capital.

If the factors are entirely substitutable, then production is a constant function of these factors. The Cobb-Douglas production function is a well-known means of expressing perfect substitutability:

$$X' = ZL'^{\alpha}K'^{1-\alpha},$$

where Z and α are positive constants, α is always less than unity; α and $1 - \alpha$ are the labour and capital elasticity of production respectively, i.e. the relative change in labour or capital which brought about the change in production. If the labour input is raised by 10

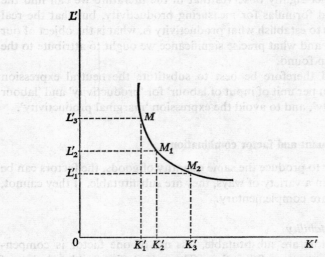

Figure 15: Output of the same quantity of a good (isoquant): possible combinations in the case of substitutability

per cent, while K' remains constant, and if $\alpha = 0.75$, then production increases by 7·5 per cent; an increase of 10 per cent in K' (with L' remaining constant) causes an increase of 2·5 per cent in production. If both rise by 10 per cent, production rises by the same percentage. If L' increases by 1 per cent and K' by 5 per cent, the rise in production will be 3/4 of 1 per cent plus 1/4 of 5 per cent, i.e. 2 per cent.

b. Complementarity
In the case of perfect complementarity, a given output can only be attained in an optimal way when the factors are combined in a precisely fixed ratio. The input coefficients (Chapter 2.6) are constant.
The combination of OK'_1 units with OL'_2 units (Figure 16, with

138

$M'MM''$ as isoquant) will by definition give the same output as the more efficient combination OK'_1 with OL'_1 (the number of units $L'_1L'_2$ are superfluous: they do nothing to raise production). This is equally true of the combination OL'_1 with OK'_2. The marginal productivity of each factor is zero. When each additional machine requires an input of the same number of extra workers, the two factors are complementary: the ratio between labour and capital remains unchanged (the slope of the straight line OB).

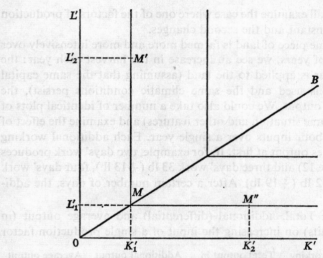

Figure 16: Output of the same quantity of a good (isoquant): possible combinations in the case of perfect complementarity

Appraisal

In reality, complete substitutability is nonexistent because factors are not entirely divisible. Machines have fixed capacities. In a plant with two machines capable of producing 2 cwt and 4 cwt respectively, part of the second machine's capacity will be idle if the plant produces 3 cwt. The same holds true of the labour input. In fact, only a limited number of combinations are possible.

Furthermore, we must not lose sight of the fact that there are no homogeneous production factors. The Cobb-Douglas function is static and takes no account of the numerous other factors which are of importance for economic growth. Mathematically, L' and K' are

139

two independent variables, but it is difficult to accept that they do not influence one another. F. Perroux has rightly called the two variables 'opaques'.

In fact we find neither complete substitutability nor a constant ratio between the factors of production. The law of variable returns makes this evident.

6 The 'law' of variable returns

Now we shall examine the case where one of the factors of production remains constant and the second changes.

If the same piece of land is farmed more and more intensively over a number of years, we see an increase in the harvest each year: the more labour is applied to the land (assuming that the same capital equipment is used and the same climatic conditions persist), the greater the output. We could also take a number of identical plots of land (the same situation and other features) and examine the effect of different labour inputs over a single year. Each additional working day increases output at first. If, for example, two days' work produces 20 lb (Table 12) and three days' work 33 lb (+13 lb), four days' work will yield 52 lb (+19 lb). After a certain number of days, the addi-

TABLE 12: Total, additional (differential) and average output (in physical units) on increasing the input of a single production factor

Number of working days (L')	Total output in lb (X')	Additional output in lb (X'_n − X'_{n-1})	Average output in lb (X'/L')
1	9	—	9
2	20	11	10
3	33	13	11
4	52	19	13
5	85	33	17
6	132	47	22
7	230	98	33
8	320	90	40
9	369	49	41
10	400	31	40
11	418	18	38
12	420	2	35
13	416	−4	32
14	406	−10	29

tional or differential output diminishes – even to the point of becoming negative if the workers are so numerous as to hinder each other. Production finally becomes impossible. This is to some extent self-explanatory; otherwise, it would be possible, by continually adding to the labour input on a piece of land, to grow all the produce we need on it.

From Table 12 we can plot the total, average and additional (or differential) product curves as in Figure 17. Since it is impossible to work with very small increments, we cannot speak of marginal product in this context: the more accurate designation is 'differential'.

One after another, the differential, average and total product curves reach their maximum. From being concave, the total product curve

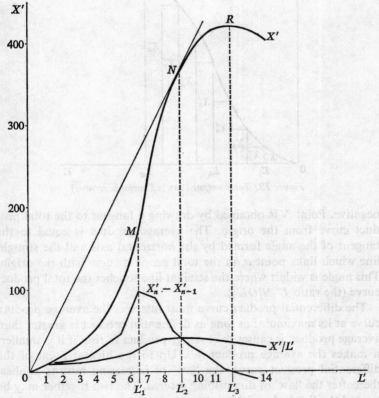

Figure 17: Total, average and differential output ('law' of variable returns)

141

becomes convex at M and the differential returns, which have been increasing, begin to diminish. In other words, the ratios $\frac{\Delta X'_{n+1}}{\Delta L'_{n+1}}$ are at first greater than $\frac{\Delta X'_n}{\Delta L'_n}$ then smaller (in Figure 18 from L'_4 onwards).

While the maximum differential return corresponds to output L'_1M (Figure 17), the highest average product is achieved at L'_2N. At output L'_3R the differential return is zero; beyond this point it is

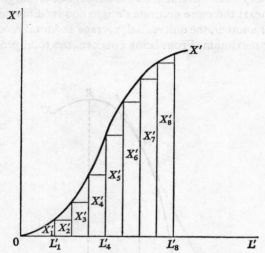

Figure 18: Total output ('law' of variable returns)

negative. Point N is obtained by drawing a tangent to the total product curve from the origin. The average product is equal to the tangent of the angle formed by the horizontal axis and the straight line which links point a on the total product curve with the origin. This angle is widest where the straight line touches the total product curve (the ratio L'_2N/OL'_2).

The differential product curve must intersect the average product curve at its maximum: as long as differential product is greater than average product, it causes the average product to rise; if it is smaller, it makes the average product fall. Up to the highest point of the differential product curve, the 'law' of increasing returns applies, thereafter the 'law' of diminishing returns. The two together may be termed the 'law' of variable returns.

142

The 'law' of variable returns, which is based upon experience, holds good only where all circumstances remain the same. If circumstances change (more rain, better organization of labour, new techniques), then total product may be different (as in Figure 19). Once the new data are taken as the basis, the 'law' will apply again.

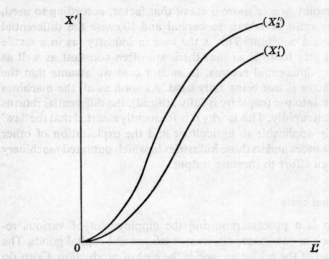

Figure 19: The shift of the total product curve (X_1') as a consequence of changes in circumstances (X_2') ('law' of variable returns)

The general formulation of the 'law' of variable returns runs as follows: *ceteris paribus*, successive additions of equal quantities of one factor of production to other fixed factors will result first in an increase and then in a decrease in the additional output.

Appraisal
This 'law' was first formulated with regard to the land: the economists spoke of diminishing returns from the land, though what was meant was the diminishing returns of labour, since labour is the variable factor.

Increasing returns are in a sense explained by the indivisibility of the constant factor: the proportion of one factor to another may not immediately be what is wanted; after the best combination has been achieved, the relationship will again become unsatisfactory. We can

143

also take the view that the 'law' simply expresses the fact 'that there is a limit to the extent to which one factor of production can be substituted for another' (J. Robinson). The validity of the 'law' depends upon the successively added units being homogeneous, and this is not always the case.

If the constant factor is at the same time divisible, then we can perhaps employ one or more units of that factor, according to need, so that the ratio of labour to capital and likewise the differential returns remain constant. This is the case in industry (as in a textile mill with thirty looms), so that there are often constant as well as diminishing differential returns. In such a case we assume that the constant factor is not being fully used. As soon as all the machines are brought into use (capacity is fully utilized), the differential returns will diminish rapidly. This is why it is frequently asserted that the 'law' is especially applicable to agriculture and the exploitation of other natural resources and to those industries in which outdated machinery is used in an effort to increase output.

7 Production costs

Production is a process requiring the employment of various resources, such as raw materials, human labour and capital goods. The money value of the resources used is the cost of production. Costs do not necessarily tally with expenditure (depreciation charges, for instance).

a. Types

1. The most important cost categories are those which relate to raw materials, labour, durable capital equipment, interest on owned and borrowed capital, and taxes. This last category includes not only indirect taxes but also direct taxes on the interest on owned capital and on 'quasi' profits (the difference between the historical cost – see below – and the [higher] replacement cost of stocks and capital goods).

2. Fixed and variable costs. Total fixed or constant costs (H_c) do not vary with the quantity of goods or services produced; they are independent of the capacity ratio (the ratio of actual to maximum possible output) but not of production capacity as such. The greater the number of goods produced, the lower the average fixed costs ($\overline{H}_c$), i.e. the fixed costs per unit of output (Figure 20).

144

The total variable costs (H_v) are those which vary with the quantity of goods produced and are thus dependent on the capacity ratio.

The sum of the total fixed and variable costs produces the total costs (H). Average variable costs ($\overline{H}_v$) are calculated by dividing total variable costs by the corresponding output. Average total costs ($\overline{H}$) are computed in the same way.

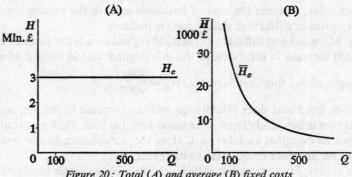

Figure 20: Total (A) and average (B) fixed costs

Total variable costs are generally degressive at first, then becoming proportional and finally – as the limit of capacity is approached – progressive (Figure 21; in Table 13 for the sake of simplicity a proportionally rising trend is assumed).

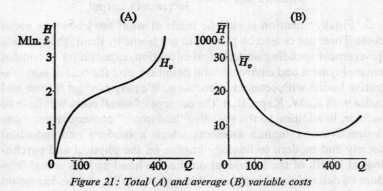

Figure 21: Total (A) and average (B) variable costs

Our knowledge of the trend of variable costs still leaves much to be desired. This is not surprising, because the figures have to be supplied by entrepreneurs, who generally regard them as confidential. For the

145

most part we have to be content with whatever figures are published.

3. Direct and indirect costs. Direct costs are those which can be directly identified with a particular product; indirect costs are those which cannot. This is important in plants producing a large number of goods. Classification into direct and indirect costs is quite separate from that into fixed and variable costs. Costs identifiable with machines which are used exclusively for one product (fixed costs) are direct costs, whereas the cost of buildings used in the production of many products (likewise fixed costs) is indirect.

4. Marginal and differential costs. Marginal cost is the ratio of the (small) increase in total cost to the infinitesimal rise in output which brought about this cost increase, $H_\mu = \dfrac{dH}{dX'}$.

Since fixed cost does not change with an increase in output, marginal cost arises solely from changes in variable cost. Hence, it is also known as marginal variable cost. Here too, calculation can be based either on absolute or on relative increases.

In reality, factors are not sufficiently divisible to cause production to increase by an infinitesimal amount. Even an increment of one unit is not always possible (except at abnormally high cost). In such a case, the increase is in groups of units; the corresponding costs may be termed differential costs (or incremental costs):

$$\text{Differential cost} = \frac{\text{increase in total cost}}{\text{increase in output}}.$$

5. Finally, mention should be made of what are known as social costs. These are caused by plants but not borne by them; they include government spending on technical education, expenditure to combat unemployment and environmental pollution, and the cost of administrative bodies with economic functions. We may even go further and claim with K. W. Kapp, that 'the concept of social costs will have to include, in addition to the so-called "economic" consequences, those destructive and human sacrifices which a modern and industrial society and modern technology impose on the physical and psychological health of the individual on the one hand and his actual freedom of determining his choices, his action, his life and his leisure on the other'.

6. Actual and cleared-in costs. Alongside historical or actual costs (i.e. costs actually incurred in the past – what the Germans call *Ist-Kosten*) we also distinguish cleared-in costs (*Soll-Kosten*), which do

not allow for waste. This is a distinction not normally employed in business (except in cost pricing), and there can be no objection to this provided wastage is not deliberate and is not very extensive.

7. Standard costs are future costs estimated on the basis of a certain standard (e.g. the normal capacity ratio, usually taken as 80 per cent). We speak of full standard costs when both fixed and variable costs are taken into account (absorption costing), and of variable standard costs when only variable costs are considered.

b. Cost price

Cost price relates to the unit cost of output and may be based either on historical or on standard costs (historical and standard cost price). If only variable costs are taken into account the expressions direct historical and variable standard cost price are used.

When a plant produces more than a single product – which is the general rule – the problem arises of the allocation of fixed (or of indirect) costs.

In order to establish total (fixed and variable) costs per product, we must allocate the fixed costs to the different commodities produced – e.g. by the surcharge method, in which it is assumed that the fixed cost incurred by a particular commodity is proportionate to the corresponding variable costs. If in the course of a given year a plant's variable costs amount to £40,000 (raw materials: 70,000 kg × 20 pence = £14,000; wages: 20,000 hours × £1·30 = £26,000) and its fixed costs amount to £20,000, then the surcharge percentage can be fixed at 50. The cost price of a product whose variable costs total £3·20 (3 kg × 20 pence + 2 hours × £1·30) would be £4·80 in such a case. There are many and more involved methods of cost allocation.

The universal tendency for prices to rise is causing firms to turn increasingly to standard costs. In pricing based on the (estimated) standard cost *of a particular product*, we take into account only the necessary inputs. These are arrived at by multiplying the standard quantities required (which are determined on the basis of precise inquiries and/or experience) by the standard prices. The latter are the average prices expected during the coming period (replacement prices).

By taking standard costs as a basis (costs when the plant is running at 'normal' capacity), we avoid the continual cost price changes which would arise from variations in output and hinder proper

147

calculation. In other words, the standard cost price is independent of the capacity ratio. Losses or profits resulting from the fact that output is lower or higher are transferred to the profit-and-loss account (see below).

c. The time span
In the matter of costs, the period under consideration is of great importance. The following, rather artificial, classification may be made:

1. The very short period: output remains unchanged. Fluctuations in demand need to be absorbed by stocks. When actual output (costs) is left out of account, we speak of the supply in the market period – as at the end of a potato or strawberry harvest, for instance (see Section 8).

2. The short run: output is variable, but capital equipment remains constant. Production is maintained with existing buildings and machinery.

3. The long run: all factors of production are variable. New machines are bought and factories are extended in order to increase output.

4. The very long or ultra-long run: at this stage even the institutional framework of production is considered variable. The population may increase or decrease. In other words, the structure of the economy takes on a different character.

Even within the short run, yet another time distinction is possible which is important for the allocation of fixed and variable costs. To begin with (over a few days), only raw materials and energy constitute variable costs; later, variable costs also include the wages of the workers who contribute directly to the production (within a month, for example, workers can be taken on or laid off). Changes in expenditure on staff in most technical and administrative departments will generally take even longer before the costs incurred can be considered variable. Changes in the cost of machinery and factory buildings come under the long run.

d. Variable returns and cost
From the 'law' of variable returns we can derive the shape of the cost curves. For differential output and differential cost (the increase in total cost, which equals the increase in the quantity of the variable

factor multiplied by its price) per unit are inversely proportional. This can be seen from Table 13, which links up with Table 12 and in which it is assumed that the variable costs (wages and social security charges) amount to £300 per working day and the total fixed costs £2,000. In Figure 22 (which reproduces some figures from Table 13) the differential cost (per unit) curve H_d intersects the average total and variable cost curves at their lowest point, because as long as differential costs per unit are less than the average total and variable costs, these must be falling. Immediately H_d becomes greater, $\overline{H}$ and $\overline{H}_v$ begin to rise.

The lowest point of the differential cost (per unit) curve coincides with the inflection point of the total cost curve. Thus, in Figure 23, which gives a second, more stylized example, this curve changes from convex to concave at output X'_{10}.

The analogy with the treatment of the variable returns is clear. The inverse proportion holds good only if the price of the variable factor remains the same (pure competition). The general shape of the curves is, however, maintained when the factor price increases: it is just that the curves climb more quickly.

Constant returns result in constant differential costs per unit. Total costs too show a linear shape in such a case. In industry, average total, variable and constant costs, and marginal costs, generally correspond approximately to the pattern illustrated in Figure 24.

8 Supply

The supply or supply schedule of a good is defined in the same way as demand or the demand schedule. It is the series of quantities of that good which sellers are prepared to offer for sale in the future, at a given time or within a specified short period, at various (hypothetical) prices. Again, a distinction is made between individual supply and aggregate supply, and between subjective (or hypothetical) supply and the objective (or actual) quantity supplied.

As regards supply in the market period, the whole of the available stocks will be offered for sale if the price is satisfactory to the producers. At a lower price many suppliers will hold back their products, especially if they think a price rise is imminent. If producers need liquid assets, or their goods are perishable (e.g. fish), they may have to sell at prices lower than they would like.

G

TABLE 13: Variable returns and costs

Number of working days L' a	Total output (cwt) X' b	Differential product (cwt) $X'_n - X'_{n-1}$ c	Total variable cost (£) H_v d	Total cost (£) H e	Differential cost (£) $H_n - H_{n-1}$ f	Average variable cost (£) $\frac{H_v}{\bar{H}}$ g = d/b	Average total cost (£) $\frac{H}{\bar{H}}$ h = e/b	Differential cost per unit (£) H_d i = f/c
1	9	—	300	2,300	—	33·33	255·55	—
2	20	11	600	2,600	300	30·00	130·00	27·27
3	33	13	900	2,900	300	27·27	87·87	23·07
4	52	19	1,200	3,200	300	23·07	61·53	15·79
5	85	33	1,500	3,500	300	17·65	41·18	9·09
6	132	47	1,800	3,800	300	13·63	28·79	6·38
7	230	98	2,100	4,100	300	9·13	17·83	3·06
8	320	90	2,400	4,400	300	7·50	13·75	3·33
9	369	49	2,700	4,700	300	7·32	12·74	6·12
10	400	31	3,000	5,000	300	7·50	12·50	9·68
11	418	18	3,300	5,300	300	7·89	12·68	16·67
12	420	2	3,600	5,600	300	8·57	13·33	150·00

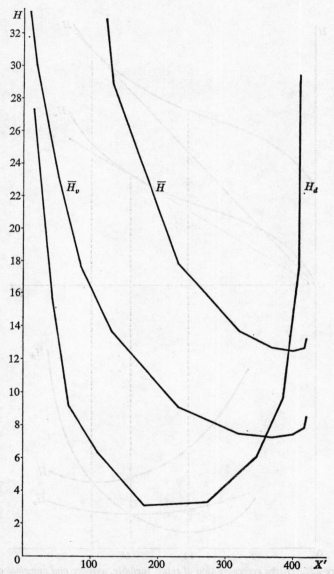

Figure 22: Diagrammatic representation of certain figures from Table 13

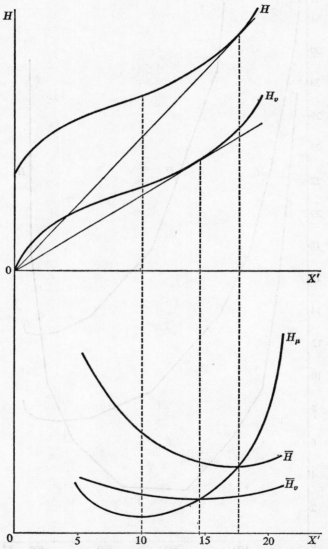

Figure 23: Stylized representation of total, variable, average and marginal costs

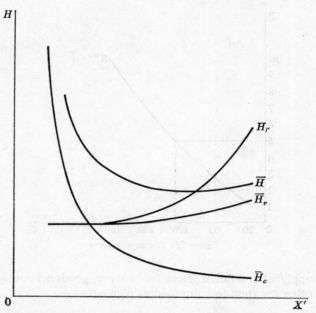

Figure 24: Stylized representation of most common pattern of cost curves in industry

TABLE 14: The supply schedule

Price	Quantity Supplied	Price	Quantity Supplied
1	16	6	124
2	42	7	142
3	66	8	156
4	86	9	170
5	106	10	184

In both the short run and the long run, the cost of production is the main determinant. Normally, the higher the price the greater the quantity supplied (Table 14 and Figure 25); quantity and price vary in the same direction. In the short run there may be a sharp rise in costs as the firm's capacity ratio reaches the maximum, giving a kinked supply curve.

It is usually the substitution effect that is observed in connection

153

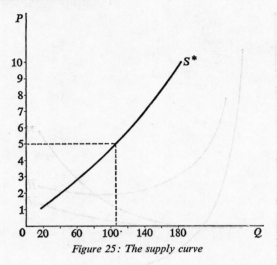

Figure 25: The supply curve

with supply: after a fall in prices, for instance, goods are consigned to some other use (potatoes are used as pigfeed).

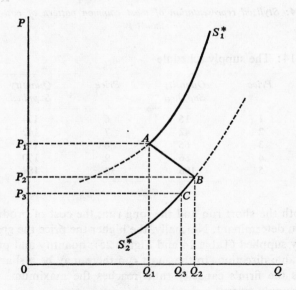

Figure 26: The supply curve (income effect)

Sometimes the income effect makes itself felt (Figure 26): after a fall in price (from OP_1 to OP_2), a seller who is in urgent need of liquid assets may be prepared to increase the quantity supplied (from OQ_1 to OQ_2) in order to command the same revenue ($OP_1 \times OQ_1 = OP_2 \times OQ_2$). This happens, for example, when the commodity supplied is the only source of income. If the price continues to fall (to OP_3), the supplier may be discouraged and the substitution effect will come into operation again: the quantity supplied will be reduced (to OQ_3).

Where two or more commodities are always offered together in a proportion which is difficult to modify (e.g. complementary goods), then a rise in the quantity supplied of one of them is naturally accompanied by an increase in the quantity supplied of the other or others.

A new supply curve can be formed by changes in circumstances, e.g. a change in production costs (wages, techniques, tax burden) or a reduction in the numbers of competitors.

Appraisal
Like the demand curve, the supply curve is extremely difficult to construct (partly because the other things assumed to be equal do not in fact remain equal). Here too, potential reactions will be examined over a limited price range only. Since prices are regarded as given, the supply schedule holds good only in the case of pure competition. Moreover, it is static (lags being ignored). The elasticity of supply is even more difficult to determine than that of demand – and it has not been studied as thoroughly. The level of costs, storage facilities, and factor availability and mobility are items of importance here.

9 The optimum combination of factors for a given level of output

Where factors are substitutable, the cheapest of the possible combinations for producing a given quantity must be selected. The price of factors is the decisive element in the process of selection.

The cheapest combination is that at which the marginal product of each additional unit of money spent on the factors is the same. If different additional sums are spent (and they are always assumed to be very small), then the respective marginal products should be proportional to them. If the price of one factor is higher than that of the

155

other(s), then the corresponding marginal product should be higher, i.e. the following equation should hold:

$$\frac{dX'_{L'}}{P_L} = \frac{dX'_{K'}}{P_K}.$$

If the proportions are not the same, it is in the entrepreneur's interest to change his factor combination. A rise in wages normally entails a changed factor combination: the quantity of labour demanded diminishes (the proportion of the marginal product of labour to the price of labour has become smaller), and the firm will turn to a more capital-intensive type of production.

When we are considering two factors alone, then theoretically the optimum combination can be sought by means of isoquants. The total costs H in such a case are equal to $L'P_L + K'P_K$, where L' and P_L represent the quantity and the price of labour and K' and P_K the quantity and price of capital. From this equation it follows that $L' = -K'P_K/P_L + H/P_L$.

With given costs (P_K and P_L are given), the labour utilized is, in other words, a downward-sloping linear function of capital; the slope is shown by the ratio $-P_K/P_L$. Each point on this line represents the combination of L' and K' that can be bought at the same cost (isocost line). For a different level of costs, we obtain another isocost line parallel with the first (Figure 27). The lines lying farthest from the origin represent those combinations which require the highest costs (see Chapter 4.2). In order to produce a specific quantity as economically as possible, taking into account the given factor prices P_L and P_K, the entrepreneur must take the point at which the lowest isocost line comes in contact with the desired isoquant. It is at the point of tangency that the marginal products of the factors are in proportion to factor prices.

Depending on factor prices, we have different factor combinations (Figure 28). A new price situation (wages show a relative rise) will give us a new isocost line and make the entrepreneur use more units of capital ($K'_1K'_1$) and fewer units of labour ($L'_1L'_1$).

If wages are low, then, the entrepreneur will choose a labour-intensive method of production: if wages are high, his production will be capital-intensive. The latter is also the case when labour remuneration is low but the marginal product of labour is less than the marginal product of capital. For example, production per unit of labour input may be low because the workers are underfed, live in an unhealthy environment and are not equal to factory work; absenteeism will be high in such circumstances. However, a high rate of capital input is often impossible because skilled manpower is not available.

For this reason the optimum combination varies from country to country and from period to period. In less-developed countries, where interest rates are high and wages low, it is usually more profitable to operate labour-intensive businesses such as building and

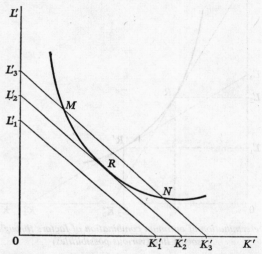

Figure 27: Determination of optimum combination of factors through isoquant and isocost line

fishing. In the fishing industry, for example, it was established in India in 1953 that there were two possible methods of increasing output by the same figure – motorizing thirteen or fourteen native boats with crews totalling 135 fishermen, or purchasing a trawler with a crew of twenty. The first method would cost $28,000 and the second $2,400,000.

In many circumstances, lack of capital should normally induce firms to buy machinery second-hand, and there is in fact a trade in used equipment – even in industrialized countries.

Appraisal

Since marginal products are difficult to calculate and isoquants even

157

more difficult to work out, these methods do not provide much of a basis on which to determine the optimum combination of factors. This is further hindered by the incomplete divisibility of factors.

Longer-term considerations can also play a part. When, for example, the speed with which a specified volume of production can

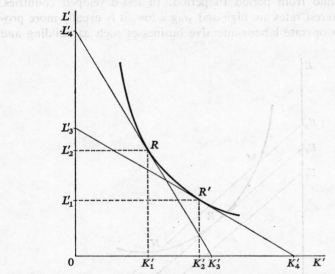

Figure 28: Determination of optimum combination of factors through isoquant and isocost line (various possibilities)

be reached is considered important, entrepreneurs in less-developed countries are sometimes obliged to have recourse to capital-intensive methods. This may also be warranted in these countries if the firm can count on a wide market.

In point of fact, firms generally go by trial and error – starting out from an existing set of circumstances and seeing what happens when they make a (small) change in the combination of factors – or else they rely on experience built up by other firms. In certain cases it is also possible to make use of linear programming (see Section 11).

10 Optimum production

At every level of production, observance of the principle that the marginal products must be proportional to the price of the corresponding factors will ensure that the firm is producing at the least possible cost. But what quantity should it be producing in order to make maximum profits? According to current economic theory we must go on to determine the additional revenue and additional cost of producing an additional infinitesimal quantity. As long as marginal revenue is greater than marginal cost, increasing output will increase profits. We therefore continue to produce up to the point where marginal cost equals marginal revenue. Marginal revenue is defined in the same way as marginal cost: the change in total revenue divided by an infinitesimal rise in the quantity sold. An extra unit of goods is sometimes used. The corresponding costs and revenue are then, in fact, differential costs and differential revenue. Table 13 also shows differential rather than marginal costs – arising from the production of groups of units rather than a single (small) unit. Likewise, marginal revenue cannot be deduced from the differential physical product of Table 13, even if we know the selling price of the products involved.

Marginal cost and marginal revenue are, however, difficult to calculate, and – what is more – the majority of entrepreneurs are not conversant with the concepts. So the entrepreneur would have to compare the total revenue and the total cost corresponding to each level of production. Where the difference is greatest, he no longer has any interest in expanding production. In practice, however, the optimum level of output sold is generally established from the variable costs per unit and the gross profits per unit (the difference between the selling price and the variable costs per unit; not to be confused with the concept 'gross profit' in the USSR; see Section 1c). The production level is then regarded as a function of sales. Methods of computing the optimum sales level include break-even point analysis and direct costing – the two not being mutually exclusive.

a. Break-even point analysis
A firm will be making neither a profit nor a loss when the gross profits per unit multiplied by the number of units sold cover the fixed costs for the period under consideration (usually a year). If the gross unit profit is 20 pence and the fixed costs £100,000 a year, the firm has to sell 500,000 units a year. If the firm wants to make a £20,000 profit, then it will have to sell 600,000 units. In this example, 500,000 units is the critical or break-even output.

This rather simplistic method works on the assumption that

159

production and sales follow the same pattern (no changes in stock) and that the variable costs per unit remain constant, which does not in fact happen. In the above example it was further assumed that the selling price remained unaltered. This too will not necessarily be the case: increased revenue may only be possible at a lower price per unit.

In Figure 29, R is the total revenue curve (as the entrepreneur sees it) and H and H_v the total cost and total variable cost curves (on the

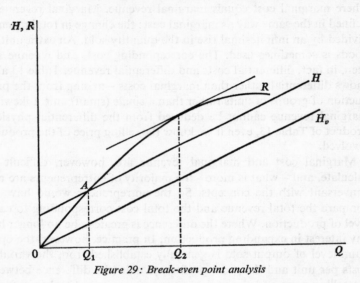

Figure 29: Break-even point analysis

assumption that the latter varies directly with output); OQ_1 is the break-even output. Profits are maximized where the difference between R and H (or between R and H_v) is greatest, i.e. where the output sold is OQ_2. Even then it is not certain that it would be in the firm's interest to sell at the corresponding price, since excessively high prices may bring new competitors into the market. Comparison with the standard cost price may provide the answer to this problem.

b. Direct (variable) costing
In direct costing we start out from the classification of costs into variable and fixed costs (or product costs and period costs) and *not* from the classification into direct and indirect costs, as the misleading term 'direct costing' might lead one to suppose. Fixed costs are not assigned to products manufactured but incorporated in the income

160

statement as they are. Direct costing can be based either on historical cost or on standard cost. The latter – direct standard costing – is the more usual. In the United Kingdom direct costing is often called marginal costing.

EXAMPLE 9

A plant manufactures three products A, B, and C (Table 15).

TABLE 15: Production data of a plant

	Product		
	A	B	C
Output (units)	1,200	1,000	700
Selling price per unit (in £)	65	50	45
Variable cost per unit (in £)	50	30	20

From Table 15 we can work out the total contribution for each product and net profit (with the additional data from Table 16).

TABLE 16: Contribution of each product (direct costing)

	Product			Total
	A	B	C	
Total revenue (in £)	78,000	50,000	31,500	159,500
Total variable cost (in £)	60,000	30,000	14,000	104,000
Total contribution per product (in £)	18,000	20,000	17,500	55,000
Total fixed cost (in £)				35,000
Net profit (in £)				20,500

Each of these products, then, makes a positive contribution towards covering the fixed costs, and so it qualifies for retention as part of the product range supplied by the firm. If the sales potential exceeds the production (when the plant is running at full capacity), the contributions can be used to decide which product it would be most profitable to sell (and therefore to produce). If, for example, to yield the total contributions of products A, B and C a given machine must be operated for 150, 100 and 50 hours respectively, then the corresponding hourly contribution will be £120 (£18,000 : 150), £200 (£20,000 : 100)

161

and £350 (£17,500 : 50). It is more profitable in this case to sell product *C* first, then *B*; there is no point in selling *A* unless the sales of *B* and *C* do not fully utilize production capacity. Obviously, the expected trend of sales of these products should also be taken into account.

EXAMPLE 10

Comparison with absorption costing may perhaps bring out the merits of direct costing. Once again, we take a plant that manufactures three products. Under absorption costing (Table 17) we might think at first glance that production of *B* and *C* should be abandoned. We must, however, remember that allocation of fixed costs is always to some extent arbitrary (allocation is on the basis of selling prices in Table 17).

TABLE 17: Absorption costing

	Product			Total
	A	*B*	*C*	
Variable cost (in £)	350	325	260	935
Allocated fixed cost (in £)	100	80	60	240
Total (in £)	450	405	320	1,175
Selling price (in £)	500	400	300	1,200
Net profit or loss (in £)	50	−5	−20	25

It is in fact doubtful whether shutting down the lines concerned will have any appreciable effect upon fixed costs.

Under direct costing (Table 18) *B* and *C* are shown to make a positive contribution towards covering fixed costs; it is not in the firm's interest to close down these departments.

TABLE 18: Direct costing

	Product			Total
	A	*B*	*C*	
Selling price (in £)	500	400	300	1,200
Variable cost (in £)	350	325	260	935
Contribution per product (in £)	150	75	40	265
Non-allocated fixed cost (in £)				240
Net profit (in £)				25

Appraisal

Break-even analysis mainly tells us the smallest amount the firm must sell in order to break even. And even then we must not lose sight of the fact that the total revenue curve in particular (which depends upon the market structure; Chapter 7.1a) is difficult to estimate. Finally, this method can only be applied with any ease where output is homogeneous. For heterogeneous production, direct costing is the method commonly employed.

The great advantage of direct costing lies in the fact that there is no allocation of fixed costs; this in itself represents a considerable saving of labour. Where it is not so important to know the cost price (because direct costing is only a partial cost-price calculation), i.e. in plants which have no need to worry about profits, this method is to be recommended.

Then too, we should not forget the difficulties involved in evaluating stocks: in direct costing stocks are undervalued (at variable cost), while this is not the case in absorption costing. Absorption costing therefore shows a higher profit when stocks increase (in direct costing, the fixed costs identifiable with these stocks go to the income statement). If, for example, stocks increase by 400 units and the total and variable unit costs are £20 and £15 respectively, then quite different results are obtained (Table 19), since the value of the stock increases amounts to £8,000 and £6,000 respectively.

TABLE 19: Calculation of profits under absorption costing and direct costing with a change in stocks

	Absorption costing	Direct costing
Total cost (£20 × 2,000)	40,000	40,000
Total revenue (£30 × 1,600)	48,000	48,000
Increase in stocks (£20 × 400)	8,000	
(£15 × 400)		6,000
Net profit (in £)	16,000	14,000

That is why direct costing is particularly suitable for those plants whose production and sales do not vary widely. Whenever an accurate knowledge of cost is wanted (custom work or unit production), then absorption costing is indicated. However, the two methods can be combined.

In practice it is not easy to determine the optimum level of production. If we apply break-even analysis, we have to estimate

163

future revenue, as we must with direct (standard) costing too. Pricing (see Chapter 7) is therefore of the greatest importance: normally, the aim should be to maximize profits. Profit-seeking, however, is not always the primary consideration in running a business (see Chapter 6.2 and 6.6; Chapter 7.7a). And many entrepreneurs' decisions (like those of the consumer) are questions of pure habit. This is especially true of frequently repeated purchases and those involving a small outlay. Personal feelings and reactions play their part, too.

11 Linear programming

An entrepreneur, with the inputs X'_j at his disposal, can produce a number of different outputs X'_i. Table 20 illustrates the quantity of each input he requires in order to produce one unit of X'_i; the o_{ji} are in other words, the technological or input coefficients (Chapter 2.6): they define the process concerned. Account must also be taken of the quantity of each input available (Z'_j).

TABLE 20: Quantities of input required to produce a unit of some products

Products Input	X'_1	$X'_2 \ldots X'_i \ldots X'_n$	Quantity available of each input
X'_1	o_{11}	$o_{12} \ldots o_{1i} \ldots o_{1n}$	Z'_1
X'_2	o_{21}	$o_{22} \ldots o_{2i} \ldots o_{2n}$	Z'_2
$\vdots$	$\vdots$	$\vdots \qquad \vdots \qquad \vdots$	
X'_j	o_{j1}	$o_{j2} \ldots o_{ji} \ldots o_{jn}$	Z'_j
$\vdots$	$\vdots$	$\vdots \qquad \vdots \qquad \vdots$	
X'_m	o_{m1}	$o_{m2} \ldots o_{mi} \ldots o_{mn}$	Z'_m

A product can be produced by means of various combinations of quantities or programmes. The techniques of activity analysis are used to find the optimum combination.

Linear programming is one of these techniques. The firm's activities are here considered to be linear in character: doubling the inputs has the effect of doubling output. Instead of a continuous production function we now have a series of independent linear activities (on a graph they are represented by straight lines). Here again, what is being looked for is the best programme.

For the entrepreneur this means obtaining the biggest profit he can at the given prices $p_1, p_2, p_3, ..., p_i, ..., p_n$ — in other words, the maximum excess of revenue over cost. If $h_1, h_2, h_3, ..., h_i, ..., h_n$ represent the production costs, then the linear profit function (the target function)

$R - H = (p_1 - h_1) X_1' + (p_2 - h_2) X_2' + ... + (p_i - h_i) X_i' + ... + (p_n - h_n) X_n'$

must be maximized, with the attendant condition that the constraints represented by the set of linear activities must be observed:

$$
\begin{aligned}
o_{11}X_1' &+ o_{12}X_2' + ... + o_{1i}X_i' + ... + o_{1n}X_n' &\leq Z_1' \\
o_{21}X_1' &+ o_{22}X_2' + ... + o_{2i}X_i' + ... + o_{2n}X_n' &\leq Z_2' \\
&\vdots \\
o_{j1}X_1' &+ o_{j2}X_2' + ... + o_{ji}X_i' + ... + o_{jn}X_n' &\leq Z_j' \\
&\vdots \\
o_{m1}X_1' &+ o_{m2}X_2' + ... + o_{mi}X_i' + ... + o_{mn}X_n' &\leq Z_m'.
\end{aligned}
$$

In order to maximize the objective function while at the same time satisfying the set of linear inequalities, various methods (including what is known as the 'simplex method') are used in linear programming. To enlarge on this subject would mean going beyond the scope of an introductory text.

However, like the satisfaction of wants (Chapter 4.2) and optimum factor combination (Section 9 above), a linear programming problem can be solved by means of a graph (and also algebraically, but we shall not go into that) if we assume only, say, two products and two production factors (X_1' and X_2': labour and capital). The possible factor combinations and availabilities are set out in Table 21.

TABLE 21: Combinations of input required to produce a unit of X'_1 and X'_2

Products Input	X'_1	X'_2	Quantity available of each input
Labour	1	5	100
Capital	2	1	110

If we assume a gross profit of £4 and £10 respectively per unit of output, then the linear programme will be

$$R - H = 4X'_1 + 10X'_2 \text{ (max.)} \tag{1}$$

$$X'_1 + 5X'_2 \leqslant 100 \tag{2}$$

$$2X'_1 + X'_2 \leqslant 110. \tag{3}$$

165

So it amounts to a question of determining how many units of each product must be produced in order to maximize total profits, subject to the possible factor combinations and availabilities.

After transforming inequalities (2) and (3) into equations, we can depict them graphically (Figure 30). Because of the scarcity of the inputs available, only those possibilities which correspond to the

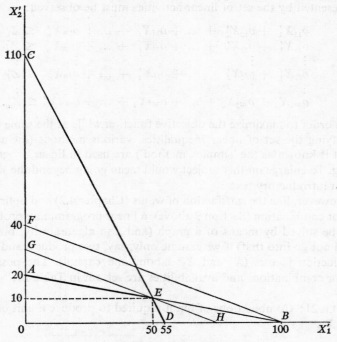

Figure 30: Linear programming

points on the broken line *AED* (or within *OAED*) are relevant (and only in the first quadrant are $X'_1 \geqslant O$ and $X'_2 \geqslant O$).

If the profits obtained by the production of one unit both of X'_1 and of X'_2 remain constant, then we can draw an isoprofit line. When, for example, total gross profits are 400, then the isoprofit line ($R - H = 4X'_1 + 10X'_2 = 400$) is represented by *FB*. Corresponding to different profit figures we have further, parallel, lines. The bigger the gross profits, the farther these are from the origin; however, the isoprofit line must come in contact with *AED*. Thus, the optimum

166

product range is at point E. What this represents can be found immediately by tracing the co-ordinates of the point of intersection of AB and CD ($X_1' = 50$; $X_2' = 10$). The usefulness of graphical representation is more clearly illustrated if there are more than two inputs. With three inputs, for example, the quadrilateral $OAED$ becomes a pentagon and the isoprofit line tells us which of the angular points offers the more economical solution.

Appraisal

Linear programming can be employed whenever there is a linear relationship between input and production – and in actual fact this is often the case. Whereas marginal theory attaches less importance to the technical aspects of production, activity analysis is concerned with just these questions of production. This technique is not based on costs; indeed, these cannot be ascertained until the product range has been decided by linear programming (which is why gross profits are needed as the criterion).

Linear programming can also be applied to an entire industry (e.g. in calculating the maximum production capacity of the steel industry, if certain factors are available in only limited quantities), to the relations between industries and plants (in determining the optimum distribution of a given demand for steel products among various firms, with an eye to minimizing transport costs) and to interindustry relationships in general.

In other words, the linear programming technique seeks one or more values for unknown data (e.g. products) a given function of which reaches a maximum or minimum value and which also satisfy a set of linear inequalities in which these data again appear as variables. It is especially useful if the production capacity is limited (no sales problems) and must therefore be used as judiciously as possible.

In the study of interindustry relations, linear programming provides an alternative to input-output analysis. The latter can be looked upon as a special form of linear programming, but it offers fewer possibilities. The production and demand aspects cannot be combined: either the final demand for the various goods is regarded as given and the production 'demanded' is calculated from this, or else the production capacity of the various industries is given and then we deduce from that what quantities of final goods are put on the market if all the factors are fully utilized. By linear programming, on the other hand, we can determine the production rates at which all available factors are used as efficiently as possible and yet there is no risk of overproduction in any industry.

12 Mobility of factors

Whether or not the optimum combination of factors can be achieved quickly depends on how readily we can call upon additional units. Mobility of factors is therefore very important in avoiding friction in the production process.

a. Labour

As regards labour, we differentiate between mobility from job to job and mobility from place to place. The latter is termed geographical mobility, although mobility between occupations may also entail mobility from place to place.

Job mobility is hindered by the requirement in most cases that the worker attend a training course. Except where the distance involved is small, geographical mobility is not easy to achieve, even if the workers know that wages paid elsewhere are higher. This is attributable to several factors:

1. the cost of moving and unemployment during the change-over;
2. attachment to one's own locality, language and customs;
3. years of service in a given firm, with correspondingly better prospects of promotion or pay rises and the difficulty of transferring pension rights;
4. emigration and immigration controls in certain countries.

Some of these difficulties can be overcome if workers are not required to move permanently but on a daily, weekly or seasonal basis only. However, these types of mobility have their drawbacks too.

The younger the worker, the more mobile he is likely to be. Better housing and recreation facilities in other areas can provide an incentive to move. Mobility may be spontaneous, or it may be systematically encouraged as a matter of policy.

Geographical mobility differs from country to country. It is fairly high in the United States, for instance, where change is sometimes regarded as an end in itself.

168

b. Capital

Capital is not a very mobile factor because capital goods are generally difficult to move from one place to another and can for the most part only be employed for manufacturing a given product. No doubt it is possible to convert an automobile plant into an armaments factory, but the cost of the operation ensures that it will be undertaken only in exceptional circumstances.

Some forms of lucrative capital such as money and shares, on the other hand, are highly mobile. The more saving takes place, the greater the mobility of savings, because the new capital can then be directed immediately to where demand is greatest. The same, indeed, is true of labour in the case of a sharp increase in population.

Land, of course, is spatially a totally immobile factor, though it is mobile in the sense that it can be transferred from one use to another (from crops to grass, for instance).

13 Bibliography

a. Plants and firms

J. Burnham, *The Managerial Revolution* (New York 1941), points to growing technocratic tendencies in industry; J. A. Schumpeter, *Capitalism, Socialism and Democracy* (London 1952), though not a socialist, states that capitalism smooths the path for socialism.

For the importance and structure of public enterprises in Europe: *The European Economy in 1966* (UN, New York 1967).

On the different objectives of the entrepreneur: G. Katona, *Psychological Studies of the American Economy* (New York 1960), Part 3; R. M. Cyert and J. G. March, *A Behavioral Theory of the Firm* (Englewood Cliffs, N.J. 1963); M. A. G. van Meerhaeghe, *Price Theory and Price Policy* (London 1969), Chapter 2.

E. Fels and R. Richter, 'Entrepreneurship as a Productive Factor', *WA*, 1957, Vol. 78, No. 2, stress that there is no point in considering entrepreneurship a distinct production factor.

On the present position of managers in the USSR: G. E. Schroeder, *Soviet Economic 'Reforms': A Study in Contradictions* (Soviet Studies, Washington, July 1968).

b. Co-operatives

P. Lambert, *Studies in the Social Philosophy of Co-operation* (Manchester 1963), which considers the problem within the framework of

169

the economic system. Practical information is given in *Co-operation: A Workers' Education Manual* (International Labour Office, Geneva 1956).

See L. Valko, *Essays on Modern Co-operation* (Washington 1964).

c. Productivity

On measurement see also: E. Ruist, 'Production Efficiency of the Industrial Firm: Some Methods of Measurement', *Productivity Measurement Review*, December 1961.

For a sceptical standpoint with reference to the measurability and meaning of productivity: F. Schaller, *Essai critique sur la notion de productivité* (Geneva 1966); *id.*, 'Qu'est-ce que la productivité', *RISEC*, May 1969.

On the United States: J. W. Kendrick, *Productivity Trends in the United States* (Princeton 1961), with a general introduction by S. Fabricant.

On the USSR: W. Galenson, *Labor Productivity in Soviet and American Industry* (New York 1955); *Labor Productivity* (ed. J. T. Dunlop and V. P. Diatchenko, New York 1964) – readings at a conference, held in 1961, by Soviet and western economists on the concept, its measurement, international comparison, its relationship with wages, influencing factors; A. Bergson, *Planning and Productivity under Soviet Socialism* (New York 1968) – three lectures dating from 1967.

d. Factor combination

The Nederlands Economisch Instituut, Rotterdam has published numerous concise papers on the optimum method of operation in less-developed areas: *The Economics of Mill versus Handloom-Weaving in India*, September 1956; *The Development of Offshore Fisheries and the Economics of Choice*, May 1958; *Second-hand Machines and Economic Development*, May 1958; see also the publication of a former member of this institute: G. K. Boon, *Economic Choice of Human and Physical Factors in Production: An Attempt to Measure the Micro-economic and Macro-economic Possibilities of Variation in Factor Proportions of Production* (Amsterdam 1964).

The advantages and disadvantages of labour- and capital-intensive methods are considered in 'Capital Intensity in Industries in Under-developed Countries', *Industrialisation and productivity*, April 1958 (bibliography on the degree of capitalization on p. 71). Writers who oppose the view that countries lacking capital normally have to use labour-intensive production methods include R. Nurkse, *Problems of Capital Formation in Underdeveloped Countries* (Oxford 1953); M. H. Dobb, *Economic Growth and Underdeveloped Countries* (London 1963).

e. The theory of production
Mathematical: S. Carlson, *A Study on the Pure Theory of Production* (New York 1956); R. Frisch, *Theory of Production* (Dordrecht 1965) (translation of the Norwegian edition of 1962); S. Danø, *Industrial Production Models: A Theoretical Study* (Vienna 1966).

See also introductory economics textbooks, including E. Schneider, *Pricing and Equilibrium* (2nd ed., London 1962), for a good (but not easy) analysis, and J. M. Henderson and R. E. Quandt, *Microeconomic Theory: A Mathematical Approach* (New York 1958), Chapter 3. See also the publications on price theory mentioned in Chapter 7.

See also the extensive bibliography in A. A. Walters, 'Production and Cost Functions: An Econometric Survey', *Em,* January–April 1963.

The Cobb-Douglas function was first mentioned in the paper by C. Cobb and P. Douglas, 'A Theory of Production', *AER,* March 1927. In P. Douglas, *The Theory of Wages* (New York 1934), Chapter 5, the main outline of this article is reproduced while the subsequent chapters demonstrate by means of examples that the formula for the United States appears to be $X' = 1 \cdot 01 \ L'\frac{3}{4} \ K'\frac{1}{4}$. See further P. Douglas, 'Are There Laws of Production?' *AER,* March 1948.

On the statistical application of the formula: E. H. Phelps Brown, 'The Meaning of the Fitted Cobb-Douglas Function', *QJE,* November 1957; more difficult: M. Nerlove, *Estimation and Identification of Cobb-Douglas Production Functions* (Amsterdam 1965).

The Cobb-Douglas function is a special case of the *CES* production function (constant elasticity of substitution). See B. S. Minhas, *An International Comparison of Factor Costs and Factor Use* (Amsterdam 1963) and the corresponding review article by W. W. Leontief in *AER,* June 1964. On the relationship between the function and technological advance: M. Brown, *On the Theory and Measurement of Technological Change* (Cambridge 1966).

The Theory and Empirical Analysis of Production (ed. M. Brown,

171

New York 1967) – volume of readings of a conference held in October 1965 (including P. H. Douglas, J. Tobin and M. Nerlove on recent research on production functions).

f. The 'law' of variable returns
In addition to the aforementioned works: K. Menger, 'The Choice of the Laws of Return: A Study in Meta-economics', in *Economic Activity Analysis* (ed. O. Morgenstern, New York 1954); this contains two articles published in *ZN* (March and August 1936) and considers the different forms of this 'law' and both the right and the wrong way of proving it. The 'law' is by no means certain and has to be verified time and again.

g. Production costs
See C. T. Horngren, *Cost Accounting: A Managerial Emphasis* (2nd ed., Englewood Cliffs, NJ 1967); *Accountants' Cost Handbook* (2nd ed., R. I. Dickey, New York 1967): 'presents practical information in the whole range of accounting for costs in a highly integrated and accessible form'. C. Gillespie, *Standard and Direct Costing* (Englewood Cliffs, NJ 1962). K. W. Kapp, 'On the Nature and Significance of Social Costs', *Ky*, 1969, No. 2.

h. Seller's surplus
Suppliers who would be willing to market their product at a price lower than the one they actually obtain are making a profit in a certain sense – the seller's surplus. The same observation applies to the consumer (consumer's or buyer's surplus). See A. Marshall, *Principles of Economics* (8th ed., London 1920), p. 124 and p. 140. For criticism of this concept: P. A. Samuelson, *Foundations of Economic Analysis* (Cambridge, Mass. 1947); E. J. Mishan, 'A Survey of Welfare Economics', *EJ*, June 1960.

i. Linear programming
The relevant theory was first elaborated by G. Dantzig in an unpublished study later incorporated in the volume *Activity Analysis of Production and Allocation* (ed. T. C. Koopmans, New York 1951); in this work the paper by T. C. Koopmans should also be consulted.

Good textbooks are D. Gale, *The Theory of Linear Economic Models* (New York 1960) and especially R. Dorfman, P. A. Samuelson and R. M. Solow, *Linear Programming and Economic*

Analysis (New York 1958), which also deals with input-output analysis and the theory of games. Especially for the firm: K. E. Boulding and W. A. Spivey, *Linear Programming and the Theory of the Firm* (New York 1960), with contributions by S. Cleland, H. H. Jenny, C. Kwang, C. M. White and Y. Wu.

For applications, see Part 2 of R. C. Geary and M. D. McCarthy, *Elements of Linear-Programming with Economic Applications* (London 1964).

J. R. Hicks, 'Linear Theory', *EJ*, December 1960, tries to indicate the points of importance for the economist who does not feel attracted to this technique.

Economic Activity Analysis is not a systematic outline but a series of articles (especially on input-output analysis and linear programming) related to the subject.

6 Firms (continued)

*Le grand phénomène de notre temps c'est, je crois,
que l'entreprise a cessé d'être de taille humaine.*
André Siegfried

The main theme of this chapter will be a discussion of some of the
following means of increasing production and/or of making production more efficient:

a. Intensifying the input of labour (without increasing the number
of hours worked). Production can also be raised by increasing the
labour input, but this may have the further result of lowering production per worker or per hour worked. By continually producing large
quantities of a specific good, workers can enhance their skill (learning
by doing). This, according to E. Lundberg, explained why a Swedish
factory's productivity had gone up by 2 per cent each year although
there had been no new investment for fifteen years (the Horndal
effect). It has also been found in the American aircraft industry that
whenever production doubles, average costs fall by 20 per cent.

b. Increasing the quantity of capital goods available.

c. Technological advance, which consists in invention and innovation (the introduction of newly invented or improved production
techniques or products). Improved methods of production which are
not a direct result of an invention (but rather of improved organization) are often classified under technological advance too (see Chapter
10.4*b*). A country's aggregate technological advance is the sum of
individual innovations.

d. Rationalizing management methods.

e. Improving the social climate in which production and selling
take place (hence the increasing importance of labour relations and
public relations).

1 Technological advance

It was J. A. Schumpeter who introduced the distinction between
invention, innovation and imitation. A relatively long time may

174

elapse between invention and innovation: penicillin, for instance, was discovered by A. Fleming in 1928, but it was fourteen years before his discovery could be applied; the gap between the two stages lasted from 1887 to 1922 in the case of radio and from 1948 to 1951 for transistors. Nowadays, the three stages are generally lumped together and called innovation. J. A. Schumpeter in fact regarded any improvement in quality or change in sources of supply and markets as an expression of innovation, emphasizing the major importance of the dynamic entrepreneur. E. Heuss has further elaborated the distinction made by Schumpeter between the entrepreneur (carrying out innovations) and the mere head or manager of a firm. Heuss distinguishes between the pioneering entrepreneur and the (spontaneously) imitative entrepreneur; he classifies both as 'initiating' entrepreneurs, as opposed to the 'conservative' entrepreneur (a class which he subdivides into entrepreneurs reacting to pressure and 'immobile' entrepreneurs).

Despite the important achievements of classical antiquity in other fields, their performance was relatively poor in technical matters. This cannot be said of the Middle Ages, however, when major innovations were introduced in agriculture (crop rotation), in energy (the water wheel and the windmill) and transport (better use of horses thanks to the stirrup, yoke, horseshoe and tandem harness; and improvements in the rigging of ships and the invention of the compass). During the Renaissance there were again comparatively few innovations, though the technique of navigation was further improved.

The invention of the steam engine by James Watt in 1769 ushered in the industrial era proper. Its application made mechanization possible (particularly in the English cotton industry). Technology has advanced at an unprecedented rate since then; all branches of human activity, but mainly transport, have benefited: one result of this has been considerable fluctuation in investment in transport (with a peak in 1855–75 for railways and in the 1920s for motorcars).

Although tools lighten the task of the worker, he still has to guide them and exert his strength on them. The machine, on the other hand, once it has been set in motion, is able to carry out tasks of some complexity itself. It does not normally need much effort to keep the machine going. Energy is supplied by a motor or by some other machine. Constant guidance is not normally required; supervision is enough.

a. The benefits of mechanization

A number of benefits flowing from mechanization and from consequent specialization should be mentioned:

1. An increase in productive capacity. Projects that would have been almost impossible can now be carried out (e.g. large canals).

2. Greater accuracy and homogeneity of production. In many cases the search for better quality is the cause of technological advance.

Standardization is the endeavour to reduce what is felt to be the excessive number of products or means of production in a given industry. The aim is not to eliminate variety as such, but to eliminate confusion and the disadvantages that result from an infinite number of superfluous kinds of product. The need to make products as uniform as possible internationally also encourages standardization (in railway gauges, building components, screws, razor blades, pipes). But there is still a great deal to be done. For instance, a Dutch radio has to be manufactured in twelve different models in order to satisfy the varying requirements (including safety requirements) of the countries to which it is exported. Standardization not only reduces cost but also facilitates the distribution of uniform parts: it is no longer necessary to stock a large variety of goods. In most countries agencies have been set up to promote standardization.

3. A reduction of the time spent at work; more hygienic and less tiring working conditions.

4. A reduction of cost as a result of increased production. The cost of acquiring machines is usually high but can be spread over more products. In this way what used to be luxury articles become ordinary consumer goods.

b. The drawbacks of mechanization

Certain drawbacks are also to be found in mechanization.

1. A reduction of the worker's enjoyment of his job. Workers are said to become like machines themselves and to see only a small part of the production process. However, the soul-destroying and tiring part of the work is what is often taken over by the machine. A man who used to be an operative may become a supervisor, and this may bring with it a certain satisfaction.

2. There may be greater sensitivity to business fluctuations – a consequence of any form of specialization – and overproduction;

these two dangers have nothing to do with the introduction of machines but are related to the organization of production.

3. Technological unemployment. This is a disadvantage that can hardly be avoided altogether: after all, it is precisely in order to save on labour that machines are purchased. On the other hand, mechanization does create new jobs too. The machines themselves have to be manufactured. The increase in demand for the goods they produce as prices go down means that additional factories have to be built, and these too provide employment. The English textile industry employed more workers after the Industrial Revolution than it had before. The use of machines generally increases corporate profits or brings down prices, or both. This makes more money available for new investment, and this in turn requires more labour. It should not be forgotten, however, that additional jobs are created only gradually and there will be unemployment in the meantime; moreover, the new jobs will not necessarily be the same as the old ones or even in the same district; workers have to be prepared to adjust to changed circumstances.

The major objection to mechanization is in fact the risk of unemployment. Where unemployment proves difficult to absorb and becomes a permanent feature, this indicates a lack of investment. Technological unemployment then becomes structural unemployment, meaning that the economic structure has not been properly adjusted. If new investment is considered economically unsound, the only way left to combat unemployment (apart from emigration) is to reduce the number of working hours (provided the level of welfare and the conditions of competition permit). Any such reduction will clearly give rise to complex problems.

In addition to technological and structural unemployment, we also have cyclical unemployment (relating to the business cycle), seasonal unemployment (caused by recurrent natural and other phenomena), institutional unemployment (arising from obstacles put in the way of labour mobility by public or private policy) and frictional unemployment (which occurs when a worker changes his job or his place of work – voluntarily or otherwise – and is generally of short duration). Frictional unemployment (at about 3 per cent of the total labour force) is unavoidable even in conditions of full employment – the situation in which all persons capable of working can find employment without much difficulty at normal rates of pay.

The term disguised unemployment refers to the situation in which those employed in a given industry are so numerous that production would not diminish (given unchanged working methods) if they moved over to another industry. This situation is found in agriculture and distribution in a number of countries.

This classification, however, is somewhat artificial: it is in fact difficult to distinguish between the different types of unemployment.

c. The computer and automation

Electronic computers emerged from cybernetics, the study of automatic communication mechanisms and controls in living organisms and machines. The first computer was completed in 1944, and commercial application began in 1952. Especially since 1964 they have had a growing success. The computer, a development of the calculating machine, is capable of making in a few seconds calculations that would previously have taken dozens of people weeks of work. One of its achievements has been to make space travel possible.

The computer processes information fed into it via an input unit according to instructions contained in a program that is recorded in the computer's central processing unit (the store or 'memory'). After processing, the information required is produced via the output unit. The information is recorded in code form (punched holes or magnetized material) on media such as punched cards, magnetic drums or tape. The codes are based on what is known as the binary notation, in which numbers are represented by only two digits – 0 and 1.

As the computer operates with two digits only, computation is considerably simplified (with the figure 1, electronic contact is obtained, with 0 none). As in decimal notation, there are rules which make it possible to carry out any calculation.

To save time and money, the codes are simplified as far as possible. Universal programming languages have been developed: ALGOL (Algorithmic Language) and FORTRAN (Formula Translation) are designed mainly for scientific calculation and COBOL (Common Business Oriented Language) for commercial uses.

It is the computer that has made automation possible. While the main purpose of the Industrial Revolution was to replace the physical effort of man and beast by machines, automation involves the introduction of mechanical equipment that operates automatically and regulates itself. In an automated process, machines are controlled by other machines: the control machinery verifies whether the finished product meets the required standard and if it does not action is taken to ensure that the necessary adjustments are made. Depending on the model, a computer costs from £6,000 to £100,000, so it can only be used by large firms (though there is the service known as time sharing where a number of firms are connected by telex to a single computer). In many plants the machines are directly linked to computers, which automatically process the information fed to them. Computers can be used to regulate the distribution of electricity or direct traffic in this way.

Automation is applied most successfully to continuous processes (e.g. chemical plants or oil refineries). It requires a radical change in production methods and can only be used if a substantial degree of standardization has been effected. This presupposes highly skilled labour and a large market.

Although maintenance staff has to be increased, automation can bring about an appreciable saving on manpower. For instance, typewriters and motorcar engines can be assembled with the help of machines. In automobile plants a rough casting can be transformed into a complete engine ready for use in fifteen minutes. This used to take nine hours. Large chemical plants can be operated by three men and large oil refineries by five.

The computer has proved most useful in the management of firms. As time goes on, computers are doing more and more of the calculations required for wages and salaries, inventory, invoicing and accounting. This means that the firm can be run with much fewer staff, but increased demands are made of the staff. There are matters, however, for which the computer cannot be substituted for man (e.g. investment and pricing decisions).

We can expect further developments in computers. It has been forecast that the cost of using a computer for an hour (which used to be several thousand dollars and is now about a hundred) will soon be only one dollar. There are even those who predict that in the future each family will have its own small computer for all kinds of domestic functions such as operating the central heating and household appliances.

2 The investment decision

Various criteria can be used in deciding whether an investment project is profitable or how it compares with other projects.

179

a. Interest
Entrepreneurs often rely on methods which amount to working out how much return an investment can be expected to yield.

1. Present value
Before an entrepreneur decides to invest a sum I, he should estimate the net return $R_1, R_2, R_3, \ldots R_n$ for the following n years. The investment is worth while if its cost I does not exceed the sum of the present values of the prospective returns. The present value of $R_1, R_2, \ldots R_n$ is represented by

$$\frac{R_1}{1+r^*}, \frac{R_2}{(l+r^*)_2}, \cdots \frac{R_n}{(l+r^*)^n}$$

It is calculated from r^*, the target rate of interest, which does not necessarily correspond to the market rate of interest r at the time when the investment is being contemplated. In other words, I must meet the following condition:

$$I \leqslant \frac{R_l}{1+r^*} + \frac{R_2}{(1+r^*)^2} + \cdots + \frac{R_n}{(1+r^*)^n}.$$

2. Internal rate of return
This second method is really the same as the first. We establish at what rate of interest r^{**} the invested sum I is equal to the sum of the present values of the estimated returns. We call r^{**} the internal rate of return – the interest we expect from the investment. If $r^{**} \geqslant r^*$, then the investment is profitable. If, for instance, the internal rate of return is 10 per cent and the target interest 8 per cent the investment is worth while.

Where the investment is an additional one J. M. Keynes calls this internal rate of return the 'marginal efficiency of capital' (I. Fisher had previously used the expression 'rate of return over cost'). Keynes introduced this term because the marginal productivity of capital relates only to the current (e.g. annual) additional return. The marginal efficiency of capital extends this concept to a longer period: all future returns are included.

3. The payoff method
A more rudimentary method – derived from the last, but with annual return assumed to be constant and interest not formally considered – is known as the payoff method. For instance, if a new machine costs

£80,000 and it is expected to yield a net return of £16,000 over five years, the payoff period is five years. If the entrepreneur considers that the payoff period should be four years at most (the common view in the United States), he will not make the investment.

Appraisal

In the present value and internal rate of return methods, the assessment of an investment project is determined mainly by the target rate of interest; this is governed by the market rate of interest and the ratio of owners' equities to borrowed capital. The payoff method also amounts to an estimate of the rate of interest, which is generally high.

Applied to one and the same investment project, the first two methods will produce the same result. Opinions differ as regards their application to the comparison of different investments. In general it is accepted that the best results are obtained from the present value method. The simple payoff method is nevertheless used a great deal.

The difficulty lies in estimating future returns – how long they will continue and what they will be each year. Estimates that are reliable or at all accurate are generally impossible to obtain. This explains the success of the relatively simple payoff method. If, however, the entrepreneur asks too much in respect of the payoff period, he runs the risk of lagging behind technological advance. The preference for a short payoff period springs from the fact that entrepreneurs say that they can anticipate the movement of certain factors for only a limited period.

Experience shows that the influence of the rate of interest in investment decisions, particularly the decisions of established concerns, is relatively slight (Figure 31; see also Chapter 13.4*a*). It appears to increase only when the rate is high (say, 8 per cent or more). The investment (and reserves) programmes of large firms run to a number of years and are not influenced by small interest-rate fluctuations.

b. The stock of capital goods

If the entrepreneur considers his stock of capital goods big enough, he will not invest, whatever the rate of interest. This might make us claim that there is a closer link between the desired stock of capital goods and investment than between investment and interest; to check the accuracy of such a claim is quite a problem because the appropriate size of capital goods stocks is difficult to establish.

H

c. Income

The link between investment and income is closer than that between investment and the stock of capital goods: as national income increases, entrepreneurs have bigger profits and can therefore invest more. Plans that could not be realized for lack of funds can now be put into effect. Investment that is affected by the level of national income is called induced investment. Many investments, however (autonomous investments), are in fact independent of national income. This is why fluctuations in investment are generally greater than fluctuations in national income and consumption.

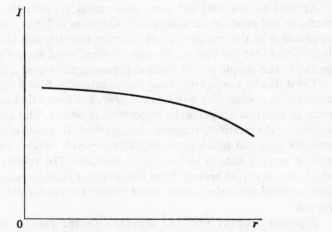

Figure 31: The relationship between investment and the interest rate

If we assume that the price of capital goods is constant, we can show the link – both macroeconomic (Figure 55) and microeconomic – between income and investment in a graph. The investment curve then shows what investments are expected to correspond to different incomes over a given planning period (cf. the consumption curve). Here, the same criticism can be made as was made of the construction of the consumption and savings curves. (See Chapter 4·6.)

d. The quantity of money

In a primitive economy saving and investment coincide. To make a fishing net or a bow, a man has to spend a certain amount of time, and the time spent is no longer available for supplying other wants:

182

he is abstaining from consumption, i.e. saving. In a money economy saving and investment are generally separate, the more so as they are usually carried out by different kinds of economic unit. In order to finance investment, funds have to be accumulated by households, by enterprises and by government.

Investment can also be financed by the creation of money or by dishoarding (monetary financing) on behalf of firms producing capital goods. With the additional money these firms are then able, in conditions of full employment, to pay higher wages and thus attract workers from firms producing consumer goods. As the number of workers in such firms is reduced, the supply of consumer goods declines, and this sends prices up so that total consumption falls (provided a rise in income does not offset higher prices). Since expenditure consists only of consumption and investment (in a closed economy), the decline in consumption makes an increase in investment possible. In order to avoid inflation (Chapter 9.10), saving is to be preferred to this monetary restriction of consumption. As P. Hennipman has pointed out, this should not be confused with forced saving (Chapter 4.6e) – though the confusion is made by some writers.

So as not to be dependent on financing institutions or affected by government action on the supply of credit, many firms prefer self-financing, which is also a means of avoiding the disadvantage of being too deeply in debt. By holding sufficient liquid resources, firms hope to be able to face up to unforeseen circumstances and, more important, to keep their independence.

The firm's cash flow, sometimes erroneously called gross profit, is important in this respect: this is composed of net profit (after tax) plus depreciation allowances. Dividend payments (the minimum considered normal) are sometimes deducted from profit as well. So cash flow is an indication of what funds are available for investment (and for paying off any debts). Cash flow is important to any forecast of financing potential. It is also taken into account in the analysis of securities because it is not affected by subjective views about reserves and thus gives a more objective picture than operating results. But again, cash flow cannot be projected with any accuracy for a number of years ahead.

e. Other factors

Especially where the rate of interest is relatively low, other factors are of greater importance to the investment decision – changes in technology, the growth rate of demand, the probable trend of costs (fluctuations in the price of production factors), the attitude of government (tax policy, promotion of external economies – Section 3). Demand is a particularly significant factor; after all, it is closely connected with income, the influence of which we have already discussed.

If demand does not go up, for instance, there will be added difficulty in finding outlets and a price cut may be necessary in order to stimulate sales. Account must be taken of the reactions of other producers: if their market share is threatened, they too will make efforts to invest and the result of this may be excess capacity. A decision to invest is often made simply because it proves technically necessary. The urge to have greater power and psychological motives may also play a role (see Section 6a).

f. Conclusion

All this shows that the entrepreneur's investment decision cannot normally be based on a few simple criteria: too many subjective elements come into play. It is unwise to cover risk by increasing the target rate of interest or reducing the payoff period without good reason; it is much more advisable to build up general reserves. For the most part, deciding what investment should be made is still what A. I. Diepenhorst calls a refined form of fortune telling.

3 The location of industry and regional concentration

The selection of the place at which a plant should be built is really part of the investment decision. A plant will normally be set up where the maximum profit can be expected. Although their importance has diminished over the last twenty or thirty years, freight costs need to be taken into account. Because these are sometimes lower for parts than for finished products, motor manufacturers often set up assembly plants in other countries. Depending on the type of industry, plants may be located in the vicinity of centres of consumption, near raw material deposits or places to which raw materials are brought. In other cases, the appropriate region may be where there is sufficient skilled labour or cheap fuel. The circumstances underlying a decision may change in the course of time. General rules are difficult to lay down.

In the nineteenth century the discovery of coke made possible the extraordinary growth of the metallurgical industries. These and other industries found it advantageous to set up in the neighbourhood of coal mines, the output of which had been stepped up thanks to the steam engine. As it became easier to transport coal and to bring in rich iron ore from abroad, firms became independent of the coal-mining areas as places to set up coke and steel plants. The main attractions for industry nowadays are big seaports and centres of consumption.

Initially, the concentration of different industries in one region has its benefits: supplies of semimanufactures and raw materials are better assured, and more public utilities (transport, electricity, gas and water) are available. These are known as external economies – direct if a price can be put on them, indirect if not. When concentration round the major centres increases, we also find external diseconomies such as an increase in the price of production factors and services. Where these cannot be expressed in terms of money (delays caused by traffic jams, air pollution etc.), they are known as indirect external diseconomies.

These externalities (both economies and diseconomies) reflect the influence of economic acts on those who are not involved in them. For instance, the noise coming out of a factory may be a nuisance to the households in its immediate vicinity.

The increasing and injudicious use of land for non-agricultural purposes (weekend houses, roads or parking lots) is leading to the gradual disappearance of open country, and this has been attacked by E. J. Mishan and others.

The government can combat excessive concentration by opposing the establishment of new plants and by promoting the industrial development of other regions (as we see in the attitude of the British and French governments towards concentration in the London and Paris areas). Results cannot be guaranteed, because the entrepreneur is also swayed by considerations other than profitability when deciding where to set up a business (educational and recreational facilities, for instance). The government should also take action against external diseconomies (by increasing taxation on traffic and on industries which pollute air and water or make excessive noise), but unfortunately this is done in a few countries only – and even there the authorities do not go far enough.

The government can affect the location of industry by granting tax incentives, setting preferential rates on the railways and opening industrial estates. A policy of this kind in favour of areas with high

185

unemployment can only be justified if economic considerations such as competitiveness are not completely disregarded.

4 The consequences of increasing scale

In discussing returns in Chapter 5, we assumed that only one factor was variable. We can also examine the impact on production and costs of increasing the scale of a firm over the long run (when all factors will be variable).

Here we speak of economies and diseconomies of scale, returns to scale or the economies of large-scale production. These returns should not be confused with the returns discussed above: they are obtained in quite different circumstances (the ratio between factors is assumed to be constant, but the quantity of each factor increases). If, for instance, the quantity of each factor is increased by 10 per cent and production goes up the same, we have constant returns to scale. If the increase in production is more or less than 10 per cent, we have increasing and decreasing returns to scale respectively.

In the case of complementarity the ratio between factors is necessarily kept constant, at least if we want to avoid waste. In the case of substitutability new combinations of factors are generally used in the course of expansion, so the consequences of expansion with the same factor ratio are difficult to establish.

Generalizations about the consequences of corporate expansion are dangerous because the figures we have are very sparse and heterogeneous. According to the Cobb-Douglas function, constant returns to scale are obtained (always provided the increase in labour and the increase in capital are the same). Increasing and decreasing returns to scale will be obtained if the sum of the two exponents is greater and smaller than unity respectively. For the whole of industry in the United States, α has been estimated at 0·75 and therefore $1 - \alpha$ at 0·25. If the utilization of both factors is increased 1 per cent, production will go up 1 per cent (0·75 per cent because of the increase in the labour input, 0·25 per cent because of the increase in the quantity of capital employed; if only one of the factors is increased, then production will go up only by the corresponding percentage). The returns to scale, then, are independent of the volume of production: in either a small or a big plant, doubling the quantity of factors will double output. This seems rather unlikely at first sight. The Cobb-Douglas assumptions can only be accepted over a limited range of output,

186

especially from the macroeconomic standpoint (the whole of manufacturing industry or a single industry).

Firms generally obtain increasing returns to scale at the beginning, constant returns for a time and eventually decreasing returns. Once a certain level of production is attained, constant or even decreasing returns may be obtained from the outset. Experience alone can show which will be the case.

a. Increasing returns to scale

A ton of cement costs $16·4 (£6·8) to produce in a 900,000-ton plant, $19·8 (£8·2) in a 450,000-ton plant and $27 (£11·2) in a 50,000-ton plant. The cost of rolling flat products in a steel mill is $199·99 (£83·3) a ton if the plant has an annual capacity of 100,000 tons of finished products, $139·17 (£57·9) a ton with a capacity of 400,000 tons and $103·44 (£43·1) a ton if the capacity is 1·5 million tons.

What is the explanation of increasing returns to scale and decreasing costs? In the first place, the indivisibility of factors. The bigger the plant, the easier it is to adjust the capacity of machinery to production, the less production capacity is left idle and the cheaper it is to produce. This is particularly true when a number of different machines are being operated. For example, where there are three machines with a capacity of 10,000, 40,000 and 100,000 units a year respectively, there will be no unused capacity if production is set at the lowest common multiple of these figures, i.e. 200,000 units. This means that production will be at the optimum with twenty, five and two machines of each type. For a small plant a policy of this kind will be more difficult to pursue; although leasing of machinery is possible and it can employ part-time labour, the facilities are limited.

Even when there is some degree of divisibility (e.g. in the case of machines with a small capacity), it is usually cheaper to have one big machine rather than ten small ones because it takes up less room and costs less in overheads such as maintenance, heating and lighting.

The higher the cost of installation, the greater the advantages of mass production. Moreover, the cost of setting up a large factory is relatively lower than that of setting up a small one in most cases. This is true of shipbuilding, for instance. While a giant tanker of 200,000 tons costs about $14 million (£5·8 million) the combined cost of two 100,000 ton tankers will be over $15 million (£6·2 million).

In a big plant the division of labour can be organized more efficiently: workers can increase their skill by concentrating on a single

187

task, and the same quantity can be produced in less time (learning by doing may occur but should not be equated with increasing returns to scale: even if the level of production goes down, the benefits of learning by doing will be retained). Division of labour is only profitable where each activity keeps a worker occupied for a whole day, so there is a close link with the possibility of finding outlets for the goods produced. It should not be confused with specialization (Chapter 1.1*a*), though the two concepts are closely related.

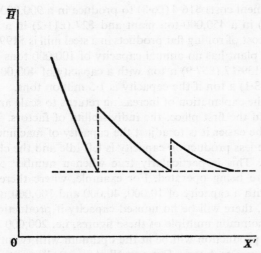

Figure 32: Average total cost in an expanding firm (through the addition of optimal production units)

Technology itself should not normally cause costs to go up when production increases: once costs have been minimized, a similar plant can be set up as often as is necessary (Figure 32). The optimal scale will differ from industry to industry, depending on technological circumstances. Since technology does not induce diseconomies of scale but the organization of the business does, a distinction is sometimes made between economies of large-scale production and economies of large organizations. The latter may sometimes turn into diseconomies of large organizations if the appropriate action is not taken.

Large organizations can pay their senior staff more and consequently attract the best people, especially as there will be better chances of promotion as well. By diversifying its output, the large firm can spread its risk. It has more money to spend on basic research and advertising. Buying and selling also become relatively cheaper when large quantities are involved. Of course, a small firm can specialize and reduce costs in that way, but it will be at a disadvantage in comparison with a large firm which is able to offer a large range of goods.

Finally, only big firms can spend as much as is needed on research and development – for which at least a team of scientists is required – and accept the risks involved. As invention has become a professional activity (since 1900), these risks have become smaller and smaller: 'To an increasing degree, especially in the new science-oriented industries such as the chemical and the electrical, it was becoming possible to invent almost any device or system needed by industry, and to produce new synthetic materials to meet any given specifications' (M. Kranzberg and C. W. Pursell, Jr). The firm's research and development division is especially important at the outset before the production process has been finally settled. Later, when the commercial departments are responsible for selling the products, the R & D people have to develop new products in order to widen the firm's range of production; this is particularly necessary at a time when demand for the older products has fallen off or disappeared.

b. Decreasing returns to scale
It will be clear from the foregoing that decreasing returns to scale are chiefly attributable to inefficient management. The entrepreneur himself cannot always guarantee coordination of his immediate staff's activities (see also Section 5 below). The firm may come up against serious difficulties in increasing sales. Transport costs go up (new customers are generally farther away). More effort has to be put into advertising and servicing. There are also limits to the availability of raw materials, labour and capital; the price of factors rises. The drawbacks can, however, be avoided. These are points which have caused many American businesses to set up plants in different parts of the United States. The most efficient plant size differs, of course, from industry to industry. According to investigations carried out by J. S. Bain in twenty American industries, the optimal scale of plant in six industries (fountain pens, tractors, copper, gypsum products, typewriters and automobiles) is 10 to 20 per cent of the market supply, in five industries (cigarettes, soap, rayon fibre, farm machinery and

189

steel) 5 to 6 per cent and in the others less than 5 per cent. (The figure is below 2 per cent in the flour milling, liquor distilling and meat packing industries.) Depending on the industry, inefficient plants are supplying 10 to 30 per cent of the market.

5 Business organization

A business has to be organized in such a way that functions and tasks and the powers and responsibilities associated with them can be accurately described.

The Frenchman Henri Fayol (1841–1925) was one of the first to study the management of a firm scientifically. Fayol was chief executive of a large combine that was on the verge of bankruptcy, and he managed to get the firm on its feet again by reorganizing the administration. He made the distinction between six types of activity that he considered essential to management and called functions – the technical, commercial, financial, security, accounting and managerial functions. The managerial function predominates over the other five, and to exercise it the entrepreneur must be able to plan ahead, to organize, to command, to co-ordinate and to control.

1. He first needs to work out a well-considered plan.

2. He must then check what is necessary for the smooth operation of the firm (e.g. raw materials and personnel). Fayol's main concern was the organization of management. He described the different relationships, organized the employees along rational lines and ensured that every man was doing the job for which he was most fitted. His requirements of the entrepreneur were health, initiative, strength of will, general education and the appropriate administrative and professional skill.

3. Once organization is taken care of, the enterprise has to be put into operation. This is done by means of properly thought-out and clearly formulated instructions. Giving orders requires a thorough-going knowledge of people. The entrepreneur is not concerned with details. In order to avoid the disadvantages of the line of command – Fayol was an advocate of the system known as line organization – departments may contact each other direct in urgent cases.

4. Coordination can be ensured by regular conferences between heads of division, with the chief executive in the chair.

5. The controlling function of the entrepreneur consists in ensuring that everything is done according to the original programme.

190

We shall first discuss line organization, then committee organization and finally functional organization.

a. Line organization

The essential feature of line organization (Figure 33), where the line of command goes from the chief executive or general manager through heads of division to foremen and supervisors, is unity of authority (one man, one boss).

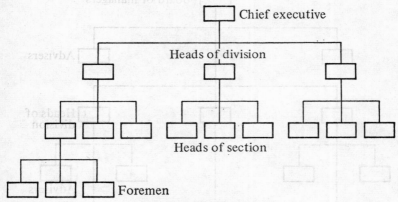

Figure 33: Line organization

This system will not operate efficiently if a superior at any level has too many subordinates reporting direct to him (too broad a span of control), so that he is overworked and cannot do his job properly. This should be avoided by establishing the optimum span of control. It is difficult to lay down general rules: everything depends on individual cases. It is generally assumed that the span of control should be three to four at top level, five to six at intermediate level, and more in the lower echelons.

The task of the line executives can be lightened, at least in large firms, by giving them staff executives with specific advisory responsibilities (Figure 34). This should not, however, be allowed to undermine the authority of the line executives or (where line executives are weak) to lead to direct intervention by staff in management. Staff executives must be aware that their purpose is only to give advice and should not feel frustrated if their advice is rejected.

In the line organization it is essential that top management delegate

191

enough responsibility and authority so as to have ample time to reflect on fundamental problems and to give effective leadership. As H. J. van der Schroeff has said, the art of leadership consists in knowing what to delegate and what not to delegate, and this is at the same time the therapy for overwork. In the same context he also cites the French sally: '*ne rien faire, tout faire faire, jamais laisser faire.*'

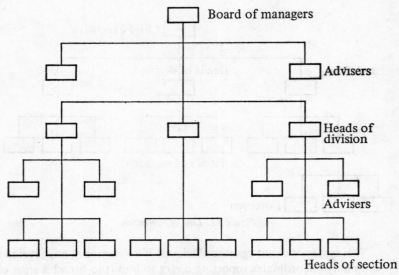

Figure 34: Line and staff organization

Useless links must be avoided at all costs, and most of all 'Parkinson's law' must not be allowed to operate. One of the axiomatic statements underlying 'Parkinson's law' is that any official will try to have two assistants assigned to him (two because the rivalry between them will ensure that he has greater authority). In order to enhance their status, the two assistants will also find that they need the assistance of subordinates, and the multiplication of officials can go on *ad infinitum.*

b. Committee organization
In this type of organization all the members of top management take part in decisions and the consultations preceding them. Each member

is generally at the head of a department, but it is responsible to the collective management (Figure 35). Decisions may perhaps be taken by majority vote. Although decisions under this system will sometimes be better grounded than with other forms of organization, there is the risk that they will be taken too slowly (or not at all) or that they will result from a compromise between the various managers that may not be arrived at rationally, since strong personalities are obviously more likely to make their views prevail. Another feature of this type of organization is a reduced willingness to take decisions – a frequent consequence of too many conferences. Line organization yields better results and is in fact the system generally used.

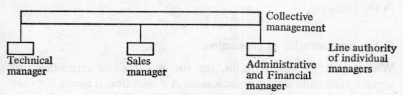

Figure 35: Committee organization

c. Functional organization

On the basis of experiments with skilled workers at the Bethlehem Steel Company and other firms, F. W. Taylor (1856–1915) established the minimum time in which each task was to be accomplished. He also worked out what was the best time for rest periods. In order to elicit maximum interest in the work to be done he also instituted a differential piece-rate system, lower rates being paid if performance did not measure up to the standard set. Taylor believed that 'functional foremanship' is necessary so that foremen are not subjected to excessive demands. The task to be performed is prepared by an order of work and route clerk, an instruction card clerk and a time and cost clerk. The work itself is supervised by a gang boss, a speed boss, a quality boss, a repair boss and a disciplinarian, which means that the worker has eight bosses and there is little chance of unity of command and co-ordination in the performance of tasks. Taylor's functional organization is no longer used. His piece-rate system was improved by H. L. Gantt (1861–1919) and H. Emerson (1853–1931): in order to ensure co-operation from the shop floor (something that Taylor did not manage to achieve), both of these guaranteed a

193

minimum hourly wage. Further systems for calculating wages by results were worked out after World War II. One of the most well known is the system instituted by C. Bedaux who, unlike Taylor, laid down not the minimum time for a specified job but the normal time that a job should take. A more modern idea is to allow wages to fluctuate as a function of productivity gains. This is behind the celebrated method developed by J. Scanlon and M. Rucker, where the workers receive a percentage of the value of production or the value added by manufacture respectively.

In general, workers are against the piece-rate system and favour wage stability. The bosses too give up payment according to the work produced whenever this leads to jealousy and harms the atmosphere in the business.

6 The concentration of production

Where there is concentration, the size and relative importance of certain economic data are increased. A distinction is made between plant and firm concentration, concentration of income and assets, regional concentration and concentration of financial power. Here, we are concerned only with the concentration of production (in plants and firms). Again, there is a great deal of terminological confusion in this field. Some writers equate concentration with cooperation pure and simple.

A number of different criteria are used to measure concentration, including numbers employed, assets and sales. A good deal of attention is paid to the number of employees, particularly in studying the social consequences of concentration. In a country where the level of technology is extremely varied and there are both capital-intensive and labour-intensive industries, the employment criterion is less useful. The same holds good for raw materials and energy consumed. Difficulties also arise in comparing assets: how, for instance, are we to estimate the valuation of each plant's assets accumulated over a considerable length of time in which there have been fluctuations in the value of money? Since mechanization has gone further in big firms, concentration is thus generally overstated (the converse is the case if the number of employees is used as the measure of concentration). In measuring sales, vertical links between plants (see Section 7) need to be taken into account. Of two plants with the same sales figure one may manufacture everything itself while the other does assembly work alone. None the less, sales are the most reliable measure of concentration.

As a number of firms are controlled by financial groups, financial concentration is often higher than concentration of production (see Section 7).

Corporate expansion does not *ipso facto* result in concentration of ownership. In fact, the share system may mean that ownership is distributed even more widely after a merger: in such cases there is concentration of the assets available to the acquiring firm but no

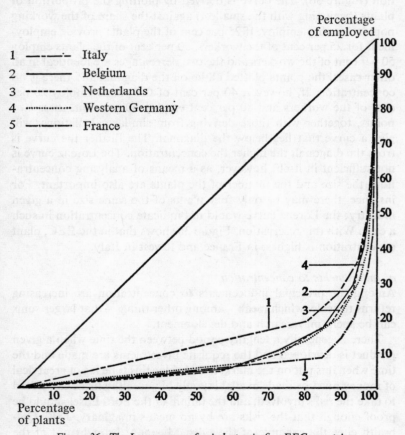

1	———·—	Italy
2	————	Belgium
3	- - - - - -	Netherlands
4	···········	Western Germany
5	—·—·—·—	France

Figure 36: The Lorenz curve for industry in five EEC countries

Source: Based on data from Statistical Office of the European Communities, *Industrial Statistics*, 1965, No 3, pp. 40–6.

195

concentration of ownership. However, this does not rule out concentration of authority, since small shareholders do not attend general meetings and the large shareholders with minority holdings are thus given the opportunity of gaining control of the firm.

The importance of concentration varies with the degree of competition with foreign companies in that industry. The larger the competing imports, the less significance should be attached to concentration.

The Lorenz curve is a device frequently used to measure concentration (Figure 36). The curve is derived by plotting the proportion of plants (beginning with the smallest) against the share of the working population they employ. If 25 per cent of the plants provide employment for 25 per cent of the workers, 50 per cent of the plants employ 50 per cent of the workers and the two percentages are identical in all other cases, the points plotted all lie on the diagonal and there is no concentration. If, however, 40 per cent of the plants employ 20 per cent of the workers and 80 per cent employ 50 per cent, these two points, together with those deriving from similar calculations, will give a curve that lies below the diagonal. The further the curve is from the diagonal, the higher the concentration. The Lorenz curve is not sufficient in itself, however, as a means of analysing concentration: the size and the number of the plants are also important. For instance, there may be only four plants of the same size in a given industry; the Lorenz curve would not indicate concentration in such a case. With this reservation, Figure 36 shows that in the EEC, plant concentration is highest in France and lowest in Italy.

a. Inducements to concentration

Among the principal inducements to concentration are increasing returns to scale, which mean – among other things – that larger sums can be spent on research and development.

There is generally a lengthy period between the time when a given product is developed and the requisite investments are made and the time when it is put on the market. To bridge this time lag, a great deal of money must be made available; only big, wealthy firms can afford to take the risks involved, and the failure of the Ford Edsel should be proof enough that the risks are by no means imaginary. J. K. Galbraith cites the example of the Ford Mustang: brought out at the beginning of 1964, it took three and a half years and $59 million to develop.

196

Investigations in the United States and elsewhere have shown, however, that it is not concentration as such but rather specialization that brings costs down. Concentration does not imply that each of the firms involved manufactures one single product. Of the thousand biggest firms in the United States, there are only 78 that manufacture a single category of product and 134 that consist of a single plant. The importance of these firms is due not so much to their dominance of the market in a single commodity as to a diversified range of products.

A firm's desire to be competitive on world markets increases as international economic integration proceeds. In recent years more and more firms in the various EEC countries have merged in order to stand up to competition from big foreign concerns. In the United Kingdom the Industrial Reorganization Corporation was set up in 1966 to promote amalgamation with the aid of government loans.

Another cause of concentration is that firms attempt to drive out their smaller competitors and obtain a monopoly position, which enables them to force up their prices. Now while the first of these inducements – the desire to lower production costs – is in the public interest (provided lower prices ensue), this does not necessarily hold good for the second. However, it should be pointed out that there is no general correlation between the level of profit and the size of plants or firms (as has been established in Britain, for instance).

Finally, psychological factors sometimes play an important part. Concentration may result not so much from the profit motive as from the entrepreneur's thirst for power and esteem (see Section 2e above), including his desire to keep his share of the market. It has also been shown that mergers may be dictated simply by a desire to increase sales and at the same time the manager's salary (which depends partly on sales: in the United States, for instance, doubling sales has been shown generally to entail a 20 per cent increase in management's salary).

b. Concentration in industry

Investigating the trend of concentration, like comparing concentration in different countries, is made more difficult by the lack of comparable statistics. It is generally agreed that concentration steadily increased until 1930. Opinions differ about the years thereafter. Concentration did in fact slacken off, but in some countries this was

HOUSEHOLDS AND FIRMS

mainly because of wartime conditions and antitrust legislation. Western European integration has brought with it an increase in concentration.

In the United States the share of the hundred biggest industrial corporations in total assets rose only from 28 per cent in 1935 to 29·8 per cent in 1958. In the growth industries the size of plants is increasing rapidly; this does not mean that concentration in these industries is increasing, because the number of plants is increasing more rapidly still.

Concentration is highest in manufacturing industry. If we rank plants by size (numbers employed), we find that in Belgium (1963) 3·4 per cent of the industrial plants (starting with the biggest) employed 60 per cent of the workers; in the Netherlands (1962) the equivalent percentages were 1·6 and 51, in Italy (1961) 1·0 and 39, in France (1962) 1·4 and 55 and in West Germany (1961) 2·4 and 59. And concentration has gone up further since that time. In West Germany, for instance, the fifty biggest firms accounted for 33·4 per cent of total sales in manufacturing industry in 1961 and 38·9 per cent in 1966.

There are appreciable differences from one industry to another. Concentration is higher in the oils and fats industry and in the sugar industry, for example, than elsewhere.

In the United States only 0·1 per cent of individual corporations account for 56·5 per cent of total assets (1962). There is a high degree of concentration in a large number of industries, including primary aluminium (three firms accounting for 100 per cent of output in 1963), cigarettes (six firms also accounting for 100 per cent of output; 1963), telephone and telegraph equipment (four firms and 96 per cent; 1963), automobiles (four firms and 94 per cent; 1964), electric bulbs (four firms and 94 per cent; 1963), gypsum products (four firms and 84 per cent; 1963). Although size alone is not an adequate measure of concentration, Table 22 is nevertheless of considerable interest. Of the biggest three hundred firms, 62·3 per cent are established in the United States; the United Kingdom comes second with 8·3 per cent, followed by Japan with 7·3 per cent, Germany with 6·3 per cent, France with 5·3 per cent and Canada with 2 per cent.

According to the Gibrat distribution, the proportional change in the size of the firm should be independent of its absolute size, but this is not the case: the percentage increase is generally bigger for small firms than for large ones.

198

TABLE 22: Sales and net income of the largest industrial corporations of the world (excl. USSR); £m., (1969)[a]

Company	Sales	Net Income
1. General Motors (US)	10,123	713
2. Standard Oil (NJ) (US)	6,222	437
3. Ford Motor (US)	6,148	228
4. Royal Dutch/Shell (Netherlands/UK)	4,058	420
5. General Electric (US)	3,520	116
6. International Business Machines (US)	2,999	389
7. Chrysler (US)	2,938	37
8. Mobil Oil (US)	2,759	181
9. Unilever (UK/Netherlands)	2,513	82
10. Texaco (US)	2,445	321
11. International Tel. & Tel. (US)	2,281	98
12. Gulf Oil (US)	2,064	255
13. Western Electric (US)	1,870	95
14. US Steel (US)	1,981	90
15. Standard Oil of California (US)	1,594	189
16. Ling-Temco-Vought (US)	1,563	16
17. Du Pont (E.I.) de Nemours (US)	1,523	148
18. Philips Gloeilampenfabrieken (Netherlands)	1,499	60
19. Shell Oil (US)	1,474	121
20. Volkswagenwerke (West Germany)	1,474	53
23. British Petroleum (UK)	1,427	97
25. ICI (Imperial Chemical Industries) (UK)	1,355	96
32. British Steel (UK)	1,195	23
33. Hitachi (Japan)	1,190	63
42. Montecatini Edison (Italy)	1,035	28
44. Siemens (West Germany)	1,009	26
48. Daimler-Benz (West Germany)	961	26
49. Fiat (Italy)	950	9
52. Toyota Motor (Japan)	947	45
57. Renault (France)	906	13
60. Nestlé (Switzerland)	893	48
62. Tokyo Shibaura Electric (Japan)	889	28
69. Rhône-Poulenc (France)	820	39
83. AKU (Algemene Kunstzijde Unie) (Netherlands)	733	35
90. Cie Française des Pétroles (France)	677	49
91. Ente Nazionale Indrocarburi (Italy)	674	7
135. Alcan Aluminium (Canada)	510	34
146. ARBED (Luxembourg)	486	14
167. Petrofina (Belgium)	439	18

[a] After the twenty largest companies in the world, the biggest in certain countries are listed (all in the 250 largest).

Company	Sales	Net Income
170. Brown, Boveri (Switzerland)	436	4
181. Pemex (Pétroleos Mexicanos) (Mexico)	414	10
183. Hoffmann – La Roche (Switzerland)	408	10
187. Massey-Ferguson (Canada)	402	13
209. Volvo (Sweden)	355	13
214. SKF (Svenska Kullagerfabriken) (Sweden)	340	17
216. Canada Packers (Canada)	339	4
233. Solvay (Belgium)	315	23

Source: Fortune, May 1970, pp. 184–99 and August 1970, pp. 143–6

Small industrial businesses are holding their own everywhere. This is because their managements – provided they are capable – identify themselves with the business more easily than management in big firms, keep costs down and discourage waste. Labour relations are often better in small firms (where the boss knows everybody). The boss also values the greater independence he enjoys. The drawbacks of such family businesses are regularly made clear, however. There may be too much nepotism, for instance, and the sons of the family will not necessarily have as much intelligence or strength of will as the father. It has been said of this kind of business that 'nine out of ten bankruptcies are because of drink, gambling or women' (H. Townsend).

c. Concentration in agriculture
Small and medium-sized businesses are also relatively important in agriculture. The reasons for this are:

1. the risks inherent in single-crop farms, which are sensitive to business fluctuations and generally call for mechanization;
2. the variety of work that has to be done from one season to the next, which makes division of labour difficult;
3. the opportunity of making large profits on a relatively small area (as in horticulture);
4. the fact that cooperation enables small farms to enjoy the same benefits as big ones (machinery that would normally be profitable only over extensive areas can be used by small farms through the intermediary of the co-operative);
5. preference for a relatively independent way of life even if earnings are low; and

200

6. most of all the protection afforded agricultural markets.

The biggest farms in the EEC countries are in France, where the average size is 44 acres (as against 25 acres in West Germany, the Netherlands and Belgium and 17 acres in Italy). Farms are generally bigger in the United Kingdom (100 acres on average) and even more so in the United States (300 acres). Farms of under 25 acres account for 45 per cent of the total in France, 85 per cent in Italy and 66 per cent in Belgium. Fragmentation is greatest in West Germany and Belgium, with 10·98 and 6·24 plots of land per farm respectively.

In the United States most farms whose annual sales total less than $5,000 are not considered profitable. But this is a category that includes nearly 1 million farms – 40 per cent of all commercial farms (i.e. excluding part-time holdings etc.).

d. Concentration in retailing

Concentration in the retail trade was begun by the big stores that started up in Paris in the mid-nineteenth century. Department stores of this kind need a large market and are generally found in the big urban centres, but they sometimes combine the advantages of large and small firms by setting up branches.

Departmental organization was introduced into retailing in the United States in 1826, with the 'one price system' (all prices marked, no haggling) used in A. T. Stewart's store. These techniques spread after the Civil War, a further development being the vertically integrated chain store and F. W. Woolworth's variant the 'five-and-ten-cent store', selling low-price goods only. By the turn of the century these low-price chain stores were established in Britain too (Penny Bazaars, Marks and Spencer), and by 1925 the 'magasins à prix unique' had come to continental Europe. A later development was self-service in supermarkets (selling foodstuffs and sometimes other standard consumer goods) and superettes, which imitated the methods of the department stores and their branches.

Despite the success of large stores with their ease of access, broad range of goods and displayed prices, small businesses still have an appreciable share of retail trade. With rising standards of living, many people would rather pay a little more in the neighbourhood shop than take the trouble to seek farther afield. This – together with the fact that the commercial centres of large towns are not normally residential areas – explains the tendency to set up department stores in the densely populated suburbs, where it is also easier for customers to park their cars. The personal touch and familiarity with the market also militate in favour of the small business. Another reason for the excessive number of intermediaries is that the consumer cannot be bothered to look after his own interests.

Mainly because of the excessive number of intermediaries, output per employee in retailing has increased much less than in manufacturing industry over the last ten or twenty years. The cost of distribution accounts for 35 to 50 per cent of the price of consumer goods in European countries. This is a consequence of the low turnover of individual traders (the number of inhabitants per retail outlet is 152 in the United States, 86 in Britain, 84 in West Germany, 82 in Sweden, 70 in Switzerland, 65 in the Netherlands, 59 in Italy, 57 in France and 34 in Belgium), and to some extent of the demands made by purchasers, which require the retailer to stock a wider range of goods. In USSR the organization of trade is poor; trade margins are about 10 per cent.

Self-employed workers or small businessmen might have a better defence against concentration if they were less individualistic and had thorough vocational training. They should seek safety in grouping together (voluntary chains) and in undergoing appropriate training (in accounting, for instance).

e. Concentration in banking

As we saw in Chapter 3.10, concentration has made great strides in banking as well. Savers have greater confidence in the big banks, partly because they offer better opportunities for spreading risks. Another development is that more and more international financial institutions are being set up by banks in different countries. In 1960, for example, the Eurosyndicat Investment Research Bureau was set up by banks in the EEC countries and Britain, in 1964 Midland and International Banks (MAIBL) by the Midland Bank, the Commercial Bank of Australia, the Standard Bank and the Toronto-Dominion Bank, and in 1967 the Société Financière Européenne by the Bank of America, Barclays Bank, the Banque Nationale de Paris, the Banca Nazionale del Lavoro, the Dresdner Bank and the Algemene Bank Nederland. In 1968 the European American Banking Corporation and the European American Bank and Trust Company were set up in New York by agreement between the Amsterdam-Rotterdam Bank,

oblige outside firms to comply with the terms of the agreement. The first time that this happened was in Japan in 1931 and in Italy in 1932.

And since 1935, any group undisputedly representing the majority of a given industry in Belgium and the Netherlands has been entitled to make application for commitments they have entered into voluntarily to be imposed on non-participating firms.

Action against trusts and agreements in restraint of trade was taken at an early stage in the United States (with the Sherman Act of 1890, supplemented by the Clayton Act of 1914), and antitrust enforcement has become steadily more stringent. Even firms whose pricing policies are the same or whose market conduct is parallel in some other respect, although no formal agreement exists, may be infringing the antitrust laws, and since 1957 action has been taken against vertical integration too. Restrictive business agreements are unlawful *per se* in West Germany, Australia and Japan as well (this is also the case with certain price-fixing agreements in the United Kingdom).

In most countries, including Belgium and the Netherlands, it is only abuse of economic power that is unlawful. Large firms, even if they have monopolistic features, may have their advantages, as we have seen, and this needs to be taken into account in judging them. For example, high profits (and prices) may or may not be used to finance new investment. The EEC is attempting to implement a common policy on business agreements and monopolies.

d. Corporate groups and conglomerates
By pursuing a policy of buying up shares, a holding company (whose assets comprise shares in other companies) may gain control of a number of other companies. The holding company and the firms it has set up or gained control of constitute a corporate group such as the Unilever and Royal Dutch/Shell groups. It is sometimes difficult to distinguish these groups from trusts. They can comprise both horizontal and vertical links. It is cheaper to form a group of this kind than to effect a merger, and the risks involved are smaller too since the parent company is not liable for the debts of the subsidiaries.

In a conglomerate there is no thought of establishing a closely knit industrial group. The purpose is to maximize profits and/or to send up the stock prices of the firms involved. So a conglomerate can be a disparate amalgam without horizontal or vertical links; plants are bought and sold for purely financial reasons. Conglomerates have become popular since the 1950s in particular in the United States (Litton Industries) and Britain (Tube Investments).

8 Bibliography

a. Technological advance

For a survey starting far back in time: *Technology in Western Civilization*, 2 volumes (ed. M. Kranzberg and C. W. Pursell Jr, New York 1967); see also Chapter 5 of W. Woodruff, *Impact of Western Man: A Study of Europe's Role in the World Economy 1750–1960* (New York 1966).

W. E. G. Salter, *Productivity and Technical Change* (2nd ed., brought up to date, after the author's death, under the direction of W. B. Reddaway, Cambridge 1966), investigates the rapidity with which inventions are applied and compares the advantages and disadvantages connected with new and existing capital goods; J. Schmookler, *Invention and Economic Growth* (Cambridge, Mass. 1966) points to the fact that '. . . invention results from specific need and demand'. See also B. R. Williams, *Technology, Investment and Growth* (London 1967); *Gaps in Technology* (OECD, Paris 1968); E. Mansfield, *The Economics of Technological Change* (London 1968); J. Jewkes, D. Sawers and R. Stillerman, *The Sources of Invention* (2nd ed., London 1969).

The Organization for Economic Co-operation and Development (OECD) has organized two conferences on automation (Washington, December 1964; Zürich, February 1966). *The Requirements of Automated Jobs* (Paris 1965) contains the proceedings of the first conference, *Manpower Aspects of Automation and Technical Change* (Paris 1966) those of the second. For numerous examples: B. B. Seligman, *Most Notorious Victory: Man in an Age of Automation* (New York 1966).

b. The investment decision

F. and V. Lutz, *The Theory of Investment of the Firm* (Princeton 1951), integrate the theory of capital accumulation in the individual firm with the theory of production. The authors deal with the different standards used with regard to profit maximization: they favour the maximization of the difference between the present value of future returns and the present value of costs (Chapter 2), the difficulties involved in compiling an investment-demand scheme (Chapter 13) and the Ricardo effect (Chapter 11).

Based on the above but more practical: P. Massé, *Le choix des investissements: Critères et méthodes* (2nd ed., Paris 1964). Not so exhaustive: E. Schneider, *Wirtschaftlichkeitsrechnung: Theorie der Investition* (4th ed. ,Tübingen 1962) and a related article – E. Schneider, 'Kritisches und Positives zur Theorie der Investition', *WA* 1967, Vol. 98, No. 2. Especially on the financing aspects: E. Gutenberg, *Grundlagen der Betriebswirtschaftslehre*, Vol. 3: *Die Finanzen* (2nd ed., Berlin 1969). For the practical aspect: *Manual of Industrial Project Analysis in Developing Countries* (OECD, Paris 1968).

A. Lamfalussy, *Investment and Growth in Mature Economies: The Case of Belgium* (London 1961) makes a distinction between 'defensive' and 'enterprise' investments. The former take place in 'declining industries' (where there is not necessarily disinvestment); a distinctive feature of defensive investments is their 'exclusive reliance upon minor innovations, upon the improvement of existing capital growth and upon rationalization'.

W. H. White, 'Interest Inelasticity of Investment Demand: The Case from Business Attitude Surveys Re-examined', *AER*, September 1956, discusses seven inquiries, conducted in several countries, into the relationship between investment and interest; he believes, on account of imperfections in the inquiries, that no final conclusions can be drawn. In *Oxford Studies in the Price Mechanism* (ed. T. Wilson and P. W. S. Andrews, Oxford 1951), Chapter 1, the limited significance of interest for investment is pointed out.

J. R. Meyer and E. Kuh, *The Investment Decision: An Empirical Study* (Cambridge, Mass. 1957) conclude – on the basis of investment decisions of some 600 industrial corporations during the period 1946–50 – that the necessity of extending productive capacity is the decisive factor in the expanding phase of the cycle, liquidity considerations in stable circumstances or a downturn. See also E. Kuh, *Capital Stock Growth: A Micro-economic Approach* (Amsterdam 1963); J. R. Meyer and R. R. Glauber, *Investment Decisions, Economic Forecasting and Public Policy* (Boston 1964).

G. J. Stigler, *Capital and Rates of Return in Manufacturing Industries* (Princeton 1963), establishes that the annual rate of return (after tax) amounted to 7·2 per cent on the average from 1938 to 1956 in the United States. The concentration ratio proved to have no influence on the profit level.

On the importance of business prospects: J. S. Duesenberry, *Business Cycles and Economic Growth* (New York 1958), Chapters 4 and 5; M. Kalecki, *Theory of Economic Dynamics: An Essay on Cyclical and Long Run Changes in Capitalist Economy* (London 1954), Chapters 6 to 10. See also G. Terborgh, *Dynamic Equipment Policy* (New York 1949).

Concerning the USSR: J. M. Colette, *Politique des investissements et calcul économique: L'expérience soviétique* (Paris 1965); T. Khachaturov, 'Effectiveness of Capital Investment', *PE*, March 1968 (translated from *Voprosy ekonomiki* 1967, No. 7).

The quotation from A. I. Diepenhorst's *Structuur en politiek* (Purmerend 1956) was found in H. J. Kruisinga, *Het selecteren van investeringsprojecten: Een bedrijfseconomische beschouwing van enige aspecten van het investeringsbeleid* (Leiden 1957).

c. *Location. External economies and diseconomies*
Theory: M. Beckmann, *Location Theory* (New York 1968).

On town and country planning: L. H. Klaassen, *Methods of Selecting Industries for Depressed Areas* (OECD, Paris 1967); H. Möller *Der Boden in der politischen Ökonomie* (Wiesbaden 1967).

On external economies, the brief but good study of P. Bohm, *External Economies in Production* (Stockholm 1964). In addition, K. Heinemann, *Externe Effekte der Produktion und ihre Bedeutung für die Wirtschaftspolitik* (Berlin 1966); J. S. Chipman, 'A Survey of the Theory of International Trade: Part 2, The Neo-classical Theory', *Em*, October 1965 (see Section 2.8). On external diseconomies: J. Mishan, *The Costs of Economic Growth* (London, 1967).

d. *Increasing scale*
A short introductory work: H. Townsend, *Scale, Innovation, Merger and Monopoly: An Introduction to Industrial Economics* (London 1968).

The difficulties encountered in determining cost in the long run are put forward by J. Johnston, *Statistical Cost Analysis* (New York 1960); this contains, apart from the author's own research, a brief survey with critical comments of similar investigations since 1940. See also P. J. D. Wiles, *Price, Cost and Output* (Oxford 1956), Chapter 12.

The benefits of increasing scale for the division of labour are stressed by E. H. Chamberlin, 'Proportionality, Divisibility and

Economies of Scale', *QJE*, February 1949, reprinted as Appendix B to his *The Theory of Monopolistic Competition: A Reorientation of the Theory of Value* (7th ed., Cambridge, Mass. 1958). See also F. T. Moore, 'Economies of Scale: Some Statistical Evidence', *QJE*, May 1959.

C. A. Smith, 'Survey of the Empirical Evidence on Economies of Scale' (in *Business Concentration and Price Policy*, see below) shows that generalizations in this field are dangerous on account of the scarce and heterogeneous data. See J. Jewkes, 'Are the Economies of Scale Unlimited?' in *The Economic Consequences of the Size of Nations* (ed. E. A. G. Robinson, London 1960).

The advantages of big over small firms are summarized or illustrated in the following works: J. Steindl, *Small and Big Business: Economic Problems of the Size of Firms* (Oxford 1945); more elaborate: P. Sargent Florence, *The Logic of British and American Industry: A Realistic Analysis of Economic Structure and Government* (London 1953) and A. Beacham, *Economics of Industrial Organisation* (4th ed., London 1962), Chapter 3. See also E. T. Penrose, *The Theory of the Growth of the Firm* (Oxford 1959), who distinguishes 'economies of size' from 'economies of growth'. W. Adams and J. B. Dirlam, 'Big Steel, Invention and Innovation', *QJE*, May 1966, point out that inventions are not necessarily developed in big firms only.

On the different stages in the evolution of the sales of the firm: E. Heuss, *Allgemeine Markttheorie* (Tübingen 1965).

On the 'Horndal effect': K. J. Arrow, 'The Economic Implications of Learning by Doing', *RESt*, June 1962, and the work of E. Lundberg mentioned therein; see also E. Lundberg, 'The Profitability of Investment', *EJ*, December 1959.

e. Business organization
See E. Dale, *Planning and Developing the Company Organization Structure* (American Management Association, New York 1965); H. L. Sesk, *Principles of Management* (Cincinnati 1969); M. S. Wortmann and F. Luthans, *Emerging Concepts in Management* (London 1969). For Parkinson's 'law', see: C. Northcote Parkinson, *Parkinson's Law or the Pursuit of Progress* (London 1958). For a series of case studies: K. White, *Understanding the Company Organization Chart* (American Management Association, New York 1963). The quotation from H. J. van der Schroeff is drawn from *Leiding en organisatie van het bedryf* (4th ed., Amsterdam 1968).

f. Production concentration
Die Konzentration in der Wirtschaft (ed. H. Arndt, Berlin 1960), is a
volume of papers in three parts. Part 1 (*Stand der Konzentration*) provides an introduction to the concept of concentration, the different
forms and statistical problems; it is especially concerned with Germany
but also contains contributions on the United Kingdom and the United
States. Part 2 (*Ursachen der Konzentration*) outlines the influence
exerted by technology, law, economic and, more specifically, social
and tax policy. Part 3 (*Wirkungen und Probleme der Konzentration*)
deals with the influence of concentration on economic development,
the market and market prices, and on government and society, and
with regional concentration. The work contains an elaborate bibliography (not annotated). Especially concerning West Germany, see
also: H. O. Lenel, *Ursachen der Konzentration unter besonderer
Berücksichtigung der deutschen Verhältnisse* (2nd ed., Tübingen
1968).

Business Concentration and Price Policy (Princeton 1953) also contains a number of papers which deal with the different forms and the
consequences of concentration.

On the influence of taxation: A. S. Mackintosh, *The Development
of Firms: An Empirical Study with Special Reference to the Economic
Effects of Taxation* (Cambridge 1963).

On distribution: J. B. Jefferies and D. Knee, *Retailing in Europe:
Present Structure and Future Trends* (London 1962). H. Barger,
Distribution's Place in the American Economy since 1869 (Princeton
1955), demonstrates the gradual increase of the share of people
employed in distributive trade and the rise in productivity (1·0 per
cent per annum from 1869 to 1949; but 1·9 per cent in agriculture,
2·3 per cent in the manufacturing industry and 2·6 per cent in mining).
Concerning the United Kingdom: C. Fulop, *Competition for Consumers: A Study of the Changing Channels of Distribution* (London
1964); K. D. George, *Productivity in Distribution* (Cambridge 1966).

On concentration in the United States: *Industrial Concentration
and Product Diversification in the Thousand Largest Manufacturing
Companies* (Federal Trade Commission, Washington 1957); J. S.
Bain, *Industrial Organization* (2nd ed., New York 1968), especially
Chapters 4, 5 and 6; G. J. Stigler, *The Organization of Industry*
(Homewood, Ill. 1968); N. R. Collins and L. E. Preston, 'The Size
Structure of the Largest Industrial Firms, 1909–1958', *AER*, Decem-
ber 1961; M. A. Adelman, 'Monopoly and Concentration: Com-

210

parison in Time and Space', *RISEC*, August 1965; on mergers since 1895: S. R. Reid, *Mergers, Managers, and the Economy* (New York 1968).

J. K. Galbraith, *The New Industrial State* (Boston 1967), shows how the market system is being replaced by the decisions of big corporations; he believes that everything related to the *US* industrial system (social security, town and country planning) has been neglected far too much.

On the United Kingdom: R. Evely and I. M. D. Little, *Concentration in British Industry: An Empirical Study of the Structure of Industrial Production 1935–1951* (Cambridge 1960), consider that no irrefutable conclusion can be drawn in relation to concentration tendencies during the period covered. Industries with strong elements of monopoly in their structure employ 10 per cent of the labour force; those with monopolistic characteristics only, 65 per cent and finally, those where competition prevails, 25 per cent.

On the USSR: L. Berri and I. Shillin, 'Economic Efficiency of the Concentration of Production in Industry', *PE*, February 1966, investigate the relationship between, on the one hand, the increase in scale and, on the other, production, fixed assets and electricity-consumption per worker and the production/assets ratio; S. Mikhailov and N. Solov'ev, 'Small and Medium-size Cities and the Location of Industry in the USSR', *PE*, May 1966; G. W. Nutter, 'The Relative Size of Soviet Industry: A Comment', *JPE*, October 1966.

J. S. Bain, *International Differences in Industrial Structure: Eight Nations in the 1950s* (New Haven 1966).

On Gibrat's 'law': R. Gibrat, *Les inégalités économiques* (Paris 1931); P. E. Hart, 'The Size and Growth of Firms', *Ec*, February 1962; E. Mansfield, 'Entry, Gibrat's "law"', Innovation and the Growth of Firms', *AER*, December 1962.

g. The different types of concentration
R. Lewinsohn, *Trusts et cartels dans l'économie mondiale* (Paris 1950): mainly about the origins of the leading international trusts and cartels in different industries. However, the survey goes back no further than 1940.

The inducements and impediments to international industrial combination, together with its consequences and the outlook in this field are (somewhat incoherently) dealt with in A. Plummer, *International Combines in Modern Industry* (3rd ed., London 1951). *Les cartels internationaux* (La Documentation Française, Paris 1957) gives examples of abuse of power in international restrictive agreements (including price, quality and market-sharing agreements), describes more extensively the origins and operation of the most important cartels, and summarizes policy towards restrictive agreements.

Internationales Handbuch der Kartellpolitik (ed. G. Jahn and K. Junckerstorff, Berlin 1958) is a series of papers on government policy towards restrictive agreements in Canada, the United States, Argentina, Uruguay, Australia, Japan and most European countries. See also C. Kaysen and D. F. Turner, *Antitrust Policy: An Economic and Legal Analysis* (Cambridge, Mass. 1959). A. Neale, *The Anti-trust Laws of the United States of America: A Study of Competition Enforced by Law* (2nd ed., New York 1967), gives a lucid exposition of American law and a discussion of its effectiveness. Concerning the United Kingdom, see also the complementary works of A. Hunter, *Competition and the Law* (London 1966), and C. K. Rowley, *The British Monopolies Commission* (London 1966); in addition: A. Sutherland, *The Monopolies Commission in Action* (Cambridge 1969).

Prices and Incomes

PART 3.

Prices and Incomes

7 Prices

*It occurs that economic science has not yet solved
its first problem – what determines the price of a
commodity?*

Joan Robinson

The study of prices is introduced by a number of definitions concerning the market, after which the accepted theory of prices under pure competition, monopoly, monopolistic competition and oligopoly is set out. Attention then turns to price determination in practice and to related matters including price discrimination, resale price maintenance and commodity agreements. After this, the connection between market structure and conduct on the one hand, and market performance on the other, is examined. In addition, the role of the consumer is considered (in respect of the role of government the same is done in Chapter 13). Finally there are some considerations on price indices.

1 The market

Buyers and sellers of the same commodity meet in a market. To begin with, this may be thought of as a marketplace, where the goods, and their potential buyers and sellers, are actually present. The area of the market is greater for expensive goods, since these can bear transport costs more easily. The extension of trade has enlarged this concept, bringing in numerous intermediaries. Rapid means of communication, e.g. telegraph and telephone, have substantially expanded the geographical concept of the market. The term has now evolved to mean the general system of exchange by which buyers and sellers of a given commodity come into contact.

On markets in a single commodity or group of commodities, the goods may be replaced by samples, and exchanges arise where even samples are superfluous on account of known standards of quality. An exchange is a regulated market for fungible goods – those which are accepted as uniform and interchangeable and can thus be traded

215

sight unseen. In addition to the commodity exchanges (metals, wheat, cotton, etc., graded on an internationally accepted scale), there are stock exchanges, where shares and bonds are entirely fungible, trade fairs (international exchanges held at intervals for various industrial products) and vertical fairs, which are generally open to producers only.

a. Market organization and market structure

The circumstances in which a product changes hands can be considered under two aspects – market organization and market structure. Market organization relates to the technical means by which buyers and sellers can come into contact (e.g. exchanges, shops, travelling salesmen), the route followed by goods and services between producer and consumer (intermediate trade) and the government regulations affecting transactions.

Market structure relates to the features of the market that determine the nature of the relations between buyers and sellers, particularly power relationships.

These two types of market conditions have an influence on each other: just as a given organization will facilitate or put obstacles in the way of a specific structure, so will a given structure entail a specific organization.

b. Market conduct

Market conduct or policy comprises the means employed by economic transactors (particularly sellers) to achieve their aims. This can be subdivided into market strategy and market tactics – action of a general and of a more limited scope respectively. Many authors equate market conduct and market 'strategy'; we do not see why a departure from common usage should be made.

Restrictive agreements are best studied from the angle of market conduct (not market structure). Although agreements of this kind affect the powers of the various transactors, the actual number of transactors is not changed (as it is in the case of a trust or a joint sales agency).

Again, there is a close link between market organization and structure, and market policy: the former have an impact on policy options, and market policy is often used in an attempt to determine both the organization and the structure of the market.

216

c. Market performance

Market performance refers to the way in which the market fulfils its function and, for instance, contributes to the efficient operation and growth of the economy, full employment and an equitable distribution of income (Chapter 13.1). More particularly, market performance is judged by prices because the objectives just named can hardly be attained if prices are not stable. Account must also be taken, however, of other factors such as the quality of the goods sold. Investigation of market performance thus entails an examination of healthy or effective competition where selling prices do not deviate too greatly from a level which is considered normal (see Section g).

The connection between market structure and conduct on the one hand, and market performance on the other, is discussed later (see Section 11).

d. The perfect market

A perfect market is a market where there is only one price for any given commodity at any given time. For this to be possible, any two examples of the same commodity must be utterly identical (so that they can be exchanged at will) and buyers and sellers must have perfect knowledge of market conditions (market 'transparency'). There must be no scope for the expression of personal preference. (Though L. Baudin neatly remarks, 'it takes no more than a sales girl's smile to disrupt competition'.)

Producers of a given commodity or type of good differentiate their products from those of their competitors by details of, for instance, taste, smell, colour, durability, packaging and brand name. Advertising (see Section 7b) is an important factor here. Differentiation is found not only in virtually all consumer goods but also in many capital goods; however, the output of agriculture is still mostly homogeneous.

A commodity can be defined narrowly or broadly. Increasing product differentiation has ensured that the broader concept is the more widely accepted. For instance, a commodity does not comprise one particular brand of (say) cigarettes alone but all the other brands denoting substitute products as well. In other words, varieties with the same basic features but showing incidental differences constitute a market as long as they satisfy identical wants; the firms producing them constitute a single industry.

In a 'transparent' market buyers know the prices at which

217

suppliers are willing to sell, and sellers know the prices buyers are prepared to pay. This need not mean that participants know and can foresee everything but that they are sufficiently informed to take advantage of any difference in price – and are ready to do so. Split-second reactions are not needed and, moreover, rather unlikely since consumer habits do not change overnight. In addition, changes in production take time, especially when new production factors are to be introduced. Distance will hamper the mobility of labour. Terms of delivery can delay the availability of raw and accessory materials. However, these factors do not necessarily impair the uniformity of prices at a given moment and consequently do not affect the perfection of the market.

Contact between buyers and sellers is not obstructed. Where transparency of the market is lacking, price disparities can be maintained. Transparency is connected with the homogeneity of commodities; where there are many differentiated products, it is difficult to assess market conditions. Perfect knowledge of the market is in any case unlikely if we take spatial considerations into account: distance can be an impediment.

e. Kinds of market structure
Various criteria can be employed to indicate the nature of the relationship between buyers and sellers, particularly the degree of perfection of the market and freedom of entry to the market, together with the number and relative importance of buyers and sellers.

1. Perfect and pure competition
There is perfect competition when the following conditions prevail:

a. perfection of the market (market perfection does not necessarily imply perfect competition; even in the case of a monopoly or oligopoly there may be only one price on a given market);

b. free entry to the market (no barriers to the establishment of new firms);

c. a large number of buyers and sellers, so that no one can influence total supply or total demand substantially by changing his own demand or supply; in other words, each buyer or seller regards the market price as independent of his personal decisions;

d. complete mobility of the factors of production.

Where only the first three of these conditions prevail (but without

218

market 'transparency'), there is pure competition. Even this type of competition existed only to a limited extent in the mid-nineteenth century.

2. *Imperfect and impure competition*
The conditions for perfect and pure competition are in fact never fulfilled; in practice, it is invariably a case of imperfect competition.

a. As we have noted, there are no perfect markets. Product differentiation gives every producer a monopoly in his own products, though this situation is seriously challenged by the many possibilities of substitution. Here we speak of monopolistic or heterogeneous or differentiated competition (oligopoly or duopoly where there are a small number of sellers or only two: see below). In addition, inter-commodity or inter-industry competition (by means of close substitutes) is also strong in some cases – e.g. between metal and plastic products.

b. Established firms or the financing institutions linked with them do their utmost to exclude new firms. Increasingly large sums are needed to set up a firm. And then there is no certainty that a new firm will immediately be able to produce under optimum circumstances since this requires a minimum output. Moreover, additional factors of production (e.g. skilled workers) are not always available. And account must be taken of buyers' preference for existing brands.

c. Many producers go out of business as a result of competition itself, and this knowledge gives rise to such things as trusts and restrictive agreements between competitors. Depending on the number of sellers, we have monopoly (one seller), duopoly (two), oligopoly (few) and polypoly (many); on the buyers' side we have mono-, duo-, oligo- and polypsony. A monopoly is thus a logical outcome of active competition (see below). There are various possible combinations. Table 23 shows a simple example, first from the supply side, then from the demand side.

The indistinct boundary between 'many' and 'few' is determined by considering what influence a single seller (or buyer) has on other sellers (or buyers). If his influence is perceptible, we have 'few' sellers (or buyers), otherwise 'many'.

The relative importance of buyers and sellers (or their market share) is also a significant factor. Where there is a single big seller and few or many small sellers, we have a partial monopoly; where there are two (or few) big and many small sellers, we have a partial

219

TABLE 23: Market structure

		One seller	Few sellers	Many sellers
SUPPLY	One buyer	limited (bilateral) monopoly	limited oligopoly	limited polypoly
	Few buyers	limited monopoly	limited (bilateral) oligopoly	limited polypoly
	Many buyers	monopoly	oligopoly	(bilateral) polypoly
DEMAND	One buyer	limited (bilateral) monopsony	limited monopsony	monopsony
	Few buyers	limited oligopsony	limited (bilateral) oligopsony	oligopsony
	Many buyers	limited polypsony	limited polypsony	bilateral polypsony

duopoly (or partial oligopoly); where the oligopolists are of gradually declining size (with every firm having to take account of smaller competitors), we have proposed the term 'pyramid' oligopoly.

Oligopoly is the most frequently occurring market structure in the manufacturing industry. It is difficult to give precise details on the point because the concept of oligopoly is not clear-cut. An arbitrary boundary always has to be drawn.

About a third of American industries are oligopolies in which the largest eight firms make at least 50 per cent of shipments and the largest twenty firms at least 75 per cent. Another third are weaker oligopolies (with the eight leading firms making at least 33 per cent of shipments and the top twenty less than 75 per cent). In the other industries, with a lower degree of concentration, the biggest eight firms make less than 33 per cent of shipments.

f. Types of market conduct

Where there is pure competition, the firm really cannot take any independent action. Price is determined by the market, and there is little point in advertising (since there is no product differentiation). In the case of impure competition, particularly oligopoly, there is a greater range of options (see below). The instruments of market conduct (e.g. price and advertising) which are lacking in pure competition can now be used.

Competition as a type of market structure, or pure competition, should therefore be carefully distinguished from competition as a type of market conduct, or active competition. The latter can only exist where pure competition is absent.

Active competition, which implies rivalry and conflict, can take two forms:

1. effective, healthy or performance competition, and
2. non-performance competition.

The latter can be of various types, including unfair competition (e.g. copying a trade mark), disorderly competition (when prices are too low owing to inadequate costing) and margin competition (competition in dealers' margins).

g. Assessment of market performance

In order to assess whether prices are 'normal' (or whether competition is effective), various criteria may be used, including the level of profits and selling costs, the flexibility of prices, and plant size.

1. Profits

High profits are not objectionable in themselves: they may be needed to finance new investment or more research. But if they become permanent and are mainly used to pay out dividends, prices could be reduced instead.

2. Selling costs

This term refers to the outlay made to promote sales. Selling costs and distribution costs coincide in distributive trade, but there are no distribution costs in collecting trade.

High promotional costs often make it difficult to cut prices. The bigger the sums involved, the more unlikely it is that prices will be cut. Market entry is also hindered in industries where selling costs are high. Nevertheless increasing returns may be possible as a result of advertising.

3. Plant size

A study needs to be made of whether plants produce in optimum circumstances. Many plants are too small, but big ones do not *ipso*

221

facto produce more cheaply than small ones (Chapter 6.4*b*). Plants should be run almost at full capacity, though a small volume of unused capacity is justifiable in anticipation of periods of more intensive demand. Generalization on this point is difficult.

4. *Price flexibility*

Price flexibility may be calculated in various ways. In the relative approach, relative changes in price are compared with the relative changes in other factors which have given rise to the price change – usually the relative change in quantity (flexibility in this definition being the reciprocal of price elasticity of demand). The concept is also used to refer to the extent of price variability. These variations are sometimes compared with cost movements. Permanent cost reductions should normally be reflected in selling prices. Such costs are difficult to determine, however, and this approach takes no account of fluctuations in demand even though these together with cost fluctuations, determine the price. It is for this reason that the absolute price variations are mostly followed. Prices showing great changes are characterized as flexible, and those showing little change as rigid. Rigid prices appear to preponderate, and this flows logically from the fact that most prices are 'administered' (see Section 9). The boundary between flexible and inflexible prices is nevertheless an arbitrary one.

2 Sales and revenue

Demand has already been examined from the buyer's point of view, and it is now time to consider it from the seller's side. We may take the matter in two parts: pure competition and impure competition.

In a market where pure competition obtains, the individual producer (a cotton or potato grower, for instance) has no influence on the market price. Demand for his own produce is very elastic, appearing on a graph as a horizontal straight line (the individual sales curve or the firm's demand curve). For the producers as a whole, of course, the aggregate demand curve represents the aggregate sales curve.

In the case of monopoly, on the other hand, the sales curve matches the demand curve for the sole supplier's production. In monopolistic competition the supplier can alter his prices within certain limits (his 'monopolistic range') without experiencing exceptional changes in the quantities sold. Beyond these limits demand is more elastic.

The sales curve is at the same time the average revenue curve. In pure competition marginal revenue and average revenue are the same. In monopolies, and impure competition in general, increased quantities sold bring a fall in prices and consequently a drop in average revenue too. Marginal revenue must always be less than average revenue, otherwise the latter could not fall (Table 24, in which infinitesimal changes in revenue are not considered, consequently relates to differential revenue; Figure 37).

TABLE 24: Average, total and differential revenue under pure competition and monopoly

Quantity sold	Pure competition			Monopoly		
	Price (average revenue $= \overline{R}$)	Total revenue R	Differential revenue R_d	Price (average revenue $= R$)	Total revenue R	Differential revenue R_d
1	10	10	10	15	15	15
2	10	20	10	14	28	13
3	10	30	10	13	39	11
4	10	40	10	12	48	9
5	10	50	10	11	55	7
6	10	60	10	10	60	5
7	10	70	10	9	63	3
8	10	80	10	8	64	1
9	10	90	10	7	63	−1
10	10	100	10	6	60	−3

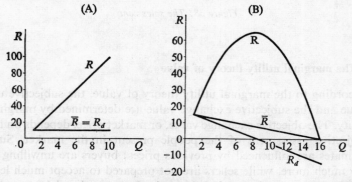

Figure 37: The revenue curves under pure competition (A) and monopoly (B)

Appraisal
Bearing in mind the remarks on demand, it is seen that the concept of the sales curve does not lead very far in practice. The supplier should be guided by an estimated curve, and he has in fact no concrete data to draw on in making this estimate. In view of his uncertainty, he should start rather from a demand or sales zone (Figure 38). Generally, however, the supplier does not know all these concepts. In the end, the quantities sold do not depend on price alone, and in many cases the price is not a decisive factor (see Section 7b).

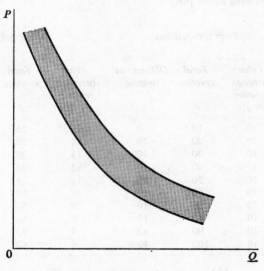

Figure 38: The sales zone

3 The marginal utility theory of value

According to the marginal utility theory of value, the subjective use value and the subjective exchange value are determined by marginal utility. The objective exchange value, or market price, depends on the subjective assessment of the people present in the market. Such estimates are influenced by previous prices: buyers are unwilling to pay much more, while sellers are not prepared to accept much less. The more transactions take place, the better and quicker market circumstances are known and the narrower the limits within which market prices fluctuate.

In the marginal utility theory of value, utility (demand) and the scarcity of the factors of production (supply) combine to account for the value. The costs of production are a reflection of the scarcity of the factors, at least with arbitrarily multipliable goods. For those which are not, demand is always the predominant factor.

Value is consequently determined by marginal utility on the

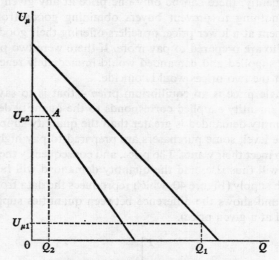

Figure 39: The marginal utility of gold and water

demand side, and largely by the costs of production on the supply side.

The marginal utility theory of value serves to explain the paradox that water, in spite of its great utility, has a low value; since a large number of units is available, the marginal utility is relatively small, or even practically negligible ($OU\mu_1$). Gold, whose utility is less ($OQ_2AU\mu_2$), has a high value ($OU\mu_2$); the marginal utility is substantial (for those wishing to possess gold) because of the relatively small stock (Figure 39).

Appraisal

Considerations regarding the basis of value should not be given undue importance. Psychological and philosophical arguments of this kind

225

are of no use in practice, and one should rather restrict the field to the study of prices.

4 Prices *under* pure competition

According to the generally accepted theory of pure competition prices are determined by the intersection of the supply and demand curves.

Consequently, there can be only one price at any given moment. There is nothing to prevent buyers obtaining goods from sellers offering them at a lower price, or sellers offering their goods to purchasers who are prepared to pay more. If there were two prices, the quantities supplied and demanded would immediately react in such a way that the two prices would coincide.

This single price is an equilibrium price – that is to say, a price where the quantity supplied corresponds to the quantity demanded. When quantity demanded is greater than the quantity supplied, at a given price level, some purchasers are prepared to pay higher prices in order to meet their wants. The price, and consequently the quantity supplied, will thus rise, and the quantity demanded will fall until it tallies with supply (Figure 40, which reproduces the data from Tables 8 and 14 and shows the difference between quantities supplied and demanded at a given price).

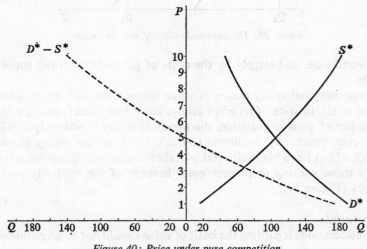

Figure 40: Price under pure competition

a. Price in the market period

Here suppliers can only let their stocks fluctuate (provided, of course that they are dealing in non-perishable goods). Prices are higher when only part of the stock is put on the market.

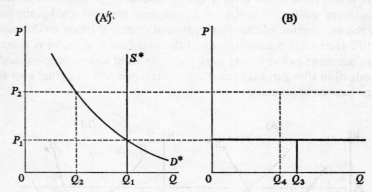

Figure 41: Price under pure competition in the market period: industry (A) and firm (B)

In Figure 41, D* represents the demand curve (in the very short term) and OQ_1 the aggregate stock. The (inelastic) supply curve is Q_1S^* and the price OP_1. Where OQ_2 only is put on the market, the price is OP_2. The main factors governing the decision whether to market the complete stock or not are the expected short-run prices of all the suppliers (who need not necessarily agree) and, as already mentioned, the possibility of storing the goods. The available stock OQ_3 of an individual firm is illustrated in the right-hand figure (the x axes for industry and individual supply are, of course, to different scales). When only part of the aggregate stock is put on the market, a firm can offer OQ_4, for instance (where everyone does not do the same, it can also offer the same quantity OQ_3).

b. Price in the short and the long term

Here, production costs play a part in the firms' supply. Figure 42 shows, on the left, supply and demand in industry, and on the right the cost curves of a single firm; both graphs refer to the short run. The scale for the vertical axes is the same in both graphs, while the horizontal axes are to different scales: a unit on the left-hand graph consequently represents a far greater quantity than a similar unit on the right-hand graph. The industry's aggregate supply schedule S^* represents the sum of the supply schedules of the individual firms.

When a price OP_1 obtains through the action of S^* and D^*, the individual firm, as already stressed, can bring no influence to bear on this price. How much does it then produce? The output at which maximum profits are realized or a minimum loss sustained is shown by the intersection of marginal costs and marginal revenue (Chapter 5.10). Here only the rising part of the marginal cost curve is taken into account; in the falling part, the only valid course is to expand production (the gap between marginal revenue and marginal cost is then becoming greater).

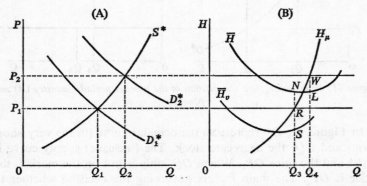

Figure 42: Price under pure competition in the short term: industry (A) and firm (B)

Application of this principle does not, however, determine whether the firm is making (excess) profits (Chapter 8.8b) from the production of every unit. Marginal costs do not take account of fixed costs. For this reason it must be ascertained whether the average total costs are covered.

For price OP_1, this does not appear to be the case, as $OP_1 < Q_3N$. Quantity OQ_3 is determined by the intersection of marginal costs and marginal revenue – in this case the horizontal straight line P_1R. While $OP_1 > Q_3S$, output can be temporarily carried on, provided financial reserves permit; fixed costs must still be borne, and this method is cheaper than bringing production to a halt.

The supply curve for an individual firm should consequently be determined by marginal costs, provided the latter are higher than the average variable costs.

228

With a demand curve D_2^*, the output of the industry is increased to OQ_2, and that of the individual firm to OQ_4. An (excess) profit of LW per unit is realized.

Such profits cannot be maintained in the long run because they lead to expanded production and new entrants are attracted. At the very least the price must be equivalent to average total costs (otherwise firms will close down, causing a trend towards increased prices).

c. Shifts in supply and demand curves

We must now consider what effect a change in supply or demand has on prices. The repercussions of prices on quantities were examined in the study of supply and demand, and we should turn now to the influence of supply and demand on prices.

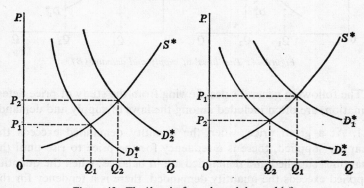

Figure 43: The 'laws' of supply and demand (A)

As prices stand at the point where the quantity supplied balances the quantity demanded, the following laws may be formulated:

1. As a rule, increased demand will lead, where the supply is constant, to a rise in prices and reduced demand to a fall in prices. The quantity sold will generally change in accordance with demand (Figure 43).

2. Increased supply will usually lead, where the demand is constant, to a fall in prices and reduced supply to a rise in prices. The quantity sold will generally change in accordance with supply. Upward movements in both supply and demand curves are indicated by a shift to the right.

229

3. A variation in demand, however, will virtually always elicit a change in supply and a variation in supply a change in demand. Rising demand may thus be conducive to an increase in supply, where the additional output makes a reduction in the cost price possible. In this event there is no price increase, and there may even be a reduction (Figure 44).

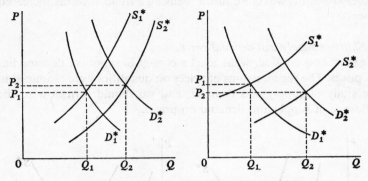

Figure 44: The 'laws' of supply and demand (B)

The following general rules, flowing from the study of price determination, are often included among the laws of supply and demand:

1. At a given price, when the quantity demanded exceeds the quantity supplied, there is a tendency for the price to rise until the quantities supplied and demanded are in balance; when the quantity supplied exceeds the quantity demanded, there is a tendency for the price to fall until the quantities supplied and demanded are in balance.

2. A rise in prices will usually cause an increase in the quantities supplied, and a reduction in the quantities demanded; a fall in prices will usually cause a reduction in the quantities supplied, and an increase in the quantities demanded.

The Davenant-King 'law'

We have just seen that, where demand (supply) is constant, reduced supply (demand) will lead to a rise (fall) in prices. We can now examine the relation between the percentage reduction in supply (demand) and the relative change in the price.

Charles Davenant studied this relation at the end of the seventeenth century. Drawing on the similar investigations of Gregory King, he found that with corn shortages of 10, 20, 30, 40 and 50 per cent the prices rose by 30, 80, 160, 280 and 450 per cent respectively. Prices rose more steeply than the ratio of the shortage to the normal crop.

These calculations were later attributed to Gregory King alone and the phenomenon, observed for other goods too, was called King's phenomenon or 'law'. It is only equitable, however, that Davenant's name should be included.

Similar observations were made when output exceeded consumption. A small surplus can lead to a fall in price proportionately greater than the rise in output. This frequently means that the overall value of the harvest falls as the quantity rises, and increases as the quantity falls, accounting for the conflicting interests, in many cases, of consumers and producers (and leading to destruction of the harvest surplus).

Although the prices of certain industrial raw materials (tin, zinc) also show reactions of this kind, the law applies chiefly to agricultural produce for which there is an inelastic demand and whose output cannot be expanded or contracted at will. Moreover, the goods in question must be traded on a market which is free but, except from a universal point of view, isolated.

The law is merely an application of the general principle that the degree by which a price changes, following a shift in the supply or demand curve, depends on the elasticity of supply and demand.

d. Dynamic supply and demand relations

So far the time factor has played only a subsidiary role. Although varying periods were mentioned, the length of time was neither specified nor implicit in the theory. In the analysis of the consequences of variations in supply and demand in the previous sections, it was assumed that the mutual adjustment of supply and demand occurs instantaneously.

The new level – for instance, the equilibrium needed following an increase in demand – does not in reality establish itself straight away, since supply can only partly adapt to the new demand there and then. Adaptation to changes in supply and demand requires a certain lapse of time, varying from product to product and longest for goods with an inelastic supply. This is the case for much agricultural produce (cocoa, coffee), but also for some capital goods.

Although the period concerned is rather short, livestock production (especially the pig cycle) was the first to be studied in this connection. When prices are high, pig farmers are encouraged to breed more

231

pigs. Eighteen months or more must pass before the pigs can be put on the market. The actual 'production' period – approximately sixteen months, including four months' gestation – is usually followed by a few months in which the pig farmers appraise the market situation. As every breeder reacts in the same way when prices rise, the quantity supplied at the end of this time is substantially greater. This leads to a price fall which, after a corresponding period, causes supply to contract.

The appearance of graphs showing the successive reactions of quantities supplied and demanded has led to this being called the cobweb theorem.

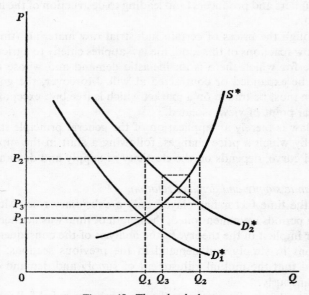

Figure 45: The cobweb theorem

In Figure 45, S^* is the long-run supply curve, and D_1^* and D_2^* represent the previous and current demand curves. The new equilibrium is not established immediately because the producers are unable to increase output OQ_1 overnight. OQ_1 is taken up by the buyers at a higher price OP_2. Believing that this price will be maintained, the producers expand their output and at the end of the period required for this there is a quantity OQ_2 on the market. The consumers are only prepared to take up this increased output at price

OP_3, and output subsequently contracts to OQ_3. The damped oscillations continue until the new balance is struck. Disturbance of this balance will in turn cause similar phenomena with a delayed adaptation of the quantity supplied to the quantity demanded or *vice versa*.

According to the shape of the supply and demand curves, however, uniform or even explosive (antidamped) oscillations may arise (Figure 46). In the case of uniform oscillations, the new equilibrium is never achieved; in the case of explosive oscillations a situation arises which must inevitably be ended (by removal of the circumstances that produced it).

The cobweb theorem is a typical example of dynamic analysis (cf. Chapter 1.10).

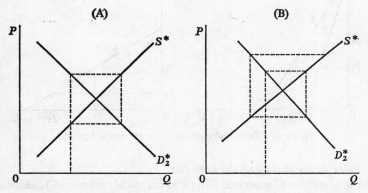

Figure 46: The cobweb theorem: uniform (A) and explosive (B) oscillations

5 Prices under monopoly, monopolistic competition and oligopoly

a. Monopoly

Besides the public monopoly, where the government controls production of certain goods or services and excludes private individuals from such activities, a distinction may be drawn between technical monopoly (where one company owns a specific patent) and natural monopoly. The latter is based on the fact that minerals are found only in certain areas and that specific properties are linked to certain places (wine, spas). We speak similarly of the shopkeeper's local monopoly.

1. Price in the market period

With a given (estimated) demand, the entrepreneur who is free to set his prices will aim at the highest possible total revenue ($OQ \times OP$).

233

Where the demand is elastic, low prices are in his interest. High prices are to his advantage, however, where demand is inelastic (Figure 47), since prices can rise further in these conditions than with elastic demand without causing revenue to fall through a reduced volume of sales. In fact, maximum revenue is determined by the intersection of marginal revenue and x-axis. Starting from OQ_1 additional output is not profitable any longer. It can thus be to the advantage of monopolists, in some circumstances, to withhold part (Q_1Q_2) of their stocks, or destroy part in the case of perishables.

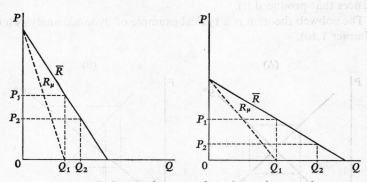

Figure 47: Price under monopoly in the market period

2. *Price in the short and the long run*

The intersection of marginal costs and marginal revenue (K) indicates the optimum output OQ_1 and the corresponding price $(OP_1$ or $Q_1L)$ (Figure 48). Since each unit of OQ_1 carries with it costs to an amount of Q_1M or ON, the monopoly profits are equal to $OQ_1 (OP_1 - ON)$ and are represented by the rectangle NP_1LM. L is known as Cournot's point (Appendix 8). In the long run the same principle applies as in the short run: optimum output is determined by marginal costs and marginal revenue. Where these are identical, the most profitable capacity of the firm has been selected. (Marginal revenue is then also identical with the short-run marginal costs.)

b. Monopolistic competition

The situation in the retail trade may be taken as an example of monopolistic competition (or equally of heterogeneous oligopoly). Each tradesman (cf. also the dairy trade) holds a relatively powerful (local) monopoly that depends among other things on personal relations.

234

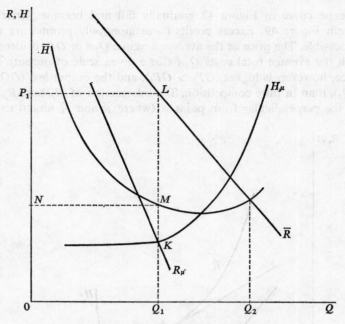

Figure 48: Price under monopoly in the short run

This allows him to set prices slightly higher, and less efficient businesses are thus kept in existence.

1. *Price in the very short and the short run*
Here each supplier enjoys monopoly profits, the level of which depends on the preferential demand for the goods in question. Figure 48 thus applies for the short run; profits are lower than in a monopoly because monopoly power is less intense.

2. *Price in the long run*
When the price gap between the desired brand and its competitors is too great, purchasers will choose the latter even when they are less well known: the producers cannot abuse their monopoly position. In addition, new firms are encouraged by the high profits to enter the industry.

These two factors mean that abnormal profits eventually disappear and a position arises in each firm in which the demand curve forms a tangent with the average total cost curve (Figure 49). By making the

235

revenue curve in Figure 48 gradually fall and become flatter we obtain Figure 49. Excess profits (here monopoly profits) are now impossible. The price or the average revenue Q_1A or OP_1 is identical with the average total costs Q_1A (for a given scale of output). The price, however, is higher ($OP_1 > OP_2$), and the output less ($OQ_1 > OQ_2$), than in pure competition. The intersection of H_μ and R_μ lies on the perpendicular from point A (where $\bar{R}$ and $\bar{H}$ touch) to the

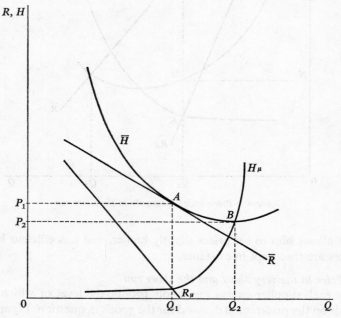

Figure 49: Price under monopolistic competition in the long run

x-axis. If this were not so – and A shifted to left or right – then the average costs would be greater than the price. The optimum position, which is given by the intersection of H_μ and R_μ, corresponds solely to point A.

However, high prices and easy market entry may also cause excess capacity and production on too small a scale.

c. Oligopoly

In an oligopoly the entrepreneurs do not know how their competitors will react to a given decision, such as to alter prices (but see 'co-

236

ordinated oligopoly' below). There is no such uncertainty in the case of monopoly or pure competition.

Following accepted hypotheses concerning both the aims of the firm concerned and its competitors' reactions, numerous divergent theories can be developed. The term oligopoly in fact covers highly divergent market situations; some oligopolies, for instance, involve three competitors, others twenty. The size of the firms may vary (cf. the pyramid oligopoly). Oligopolies may be homogeneous (aluminium, cement) or heterogeneous (cigarettes, cars), uncoordinated (there is no tacit or explicit agreement among the suppliers) or coordinated. Consequently, it is not easy to formulate a general statement, and the lack of a satisfactory theory is not surprising. Oligopoly is 'the real blind spot in price theory' (D. C. Hague). Here follow, however, a few considerations on uncoordinated and coordinated oligopoly (a distinction that is possible for both homogeneous and heterogeneous oligopoly). In each case market entry is difficult.

The situation as regards price setting and profits may be compared to that in a heterogeneous polypoly. Profits are eliminated in the case of the weakest oligopolists but are high for those in a strong position. As in monopolistic competition prices will normally be higher, and output lower, than in pure competition.

1. *Uncoordinated oligopoly*

Since an oligopolist does not know how his competitors will react he has to make conjectures; an oligopoly has been likened to a game where various combinations are open to the players.

An oligopolist may assume that his competitors will follow him if he carries through either a price cut or an increase (often accepted in homogeneous oligopoly); on the other hand, he may assume that a cut will be followed but a rise not.

The latter hypothesis introduces the theory of the kinked demand curve. With a price cut the quantity sold undergoes little change; an increase, however, will affect sales. In Figure 50 the demand curve D^* is kinked (where the price is higher than Q_1A or OP_1 elastic demand is to be expected, and inelastic demand with a lower price). D^*AD^* is matched by the marginal revenue curve $R_\mu BCR_\mu.R_\mu B$ corresponds to D^*A and CR_μ to AD^*.

The shape of the marginal revenue curve causes price inflexibility within a certain range. This can be explained by the vertical part CB

of the marginal revenue curve. Let us assume that H_μ^1 represents the marginal costs and cuts the marginal revenue curve at B. This results in the price OP_1. When the marginal costs are lower and, for instance, are represented by H_μ^2 which cuts the marginal revenue curve at C, the price OP_1 is again obtained. Marginal costs may cut CB at any point without a change in price.

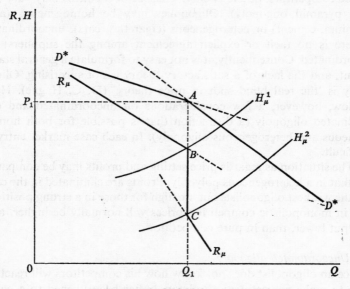

Figure 50: The kinked demand curve

The assumption underlying the thesis of the upward kinked demand curve is only valid, however, in a buyers' market. In a sellers' market opposite reactions, resulting in a downward kinked curve, are to be expected (Figure 51).

2. *Coordinated oligopoly*

Uncoordinated oligopolies are in fact rare. A certain degree of cooperation is the general rule, more especially in concentrated oligopolies. The kinked demand curve does not then apply.

Businessmen in a given sector generally meet to discuss their common interests (cf. the well-known Gary dinners in the American steel industry between 1907 and 1911). Such meetings lessen competition, and business associations themselves often frame 'codes of conduct' which may provide guidelines for the calculation of prices.

Cooperation among oligopolists is not always ideal. Lower prices are often set in secret. As a rule, coordination affects the level of prices only; oligopolists wish to remain free to increase their market share, for example through advertising.

It is often hard to distinguish between uncoordinated and coordinated oligopoly.

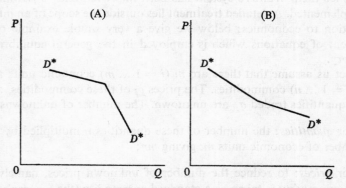

Figure 51: The kinked demand curve in a buyers' (A) and a sellers' market (B)

In many cases the price is fixed by the dominant firm (price leadership). The remaining firms simply apply these prices. They accept the leadership because 'rebellion' may mean disaster for them, especially when the dominant firm has substantial financial reserves allowing it to wage a long price war. Even when the likely outcome is not clear, firms avoid the dangers involved in a price war. Price leadership is often 'barometric': the price set by one firm is regarded as a reliable reflection of market circumstances. The price leader fulfils his task with the consent of the other oligopolists; he cannot compel them to follow.

In a pyramid oligopoly the small and medium-sized competitors follow price variations only when they deem it advantageous. They show a tendency towards undercutting to compensate for their lower repute and limited product range (see Section 7b). They are often encouraged to do so by a need for liquid assets. On account of their small share of the market they expect no reaction from the major firms.

239

6 Price interdependence and general equilibrium

It has been assumed hitherto that prices, whose determination was not studied, remained unaltered. This is not the actual case. Demand for a commodity does not depend solely on the price of that commodity but on the prices of every other item. The first thorough analysis of this problem was conducted by Léon Walras (Appendix 8).

Since then, Walras's system has been improved and substantially supplemented. A detailed treatment lies outside the scope of an introduction to economics; below we give a very simple example of a system of equations which is employed in the general equilibrium theory.

Let us assume that there are m $(i = 1 \ldots m)$ economic units and n $(j = 1 \ldots n)$ commodities. The prices p_j of these commodities, and the quantities traded q_j, are unknown. The number of unknowns is:

for *quantities*: the number of these quantities n multiplied by the number of economic units m, giving mn;

for *prices*: to reduce the number of unknown prices, namely n, one commodity is taken as a standard commodity (the *numéraire* of Walras); this way the prices of the other commodities are reduced to relative prices. If we take the first commodity as *numéraire* its price becomes $p_1/p_1 = 1$, while the prices of the other commodities are p_j/p_1 hereafter simply represented by p_j. The number of unknown prices p_j $(j = 2 \ldots n)$ is thus $n - 1$.

In all there are thus $mn + n - 1$ unknowns.

To find these unknowns, a set of equations with as many equations as unknowns is needed. First there are utility equations (consumers' priorities are assumed) wherein the marginal utilities are in proportion to prices:

$$U\mu_1 = \frac{U\mu_j}{p_j} \text{ for } j = 2 \ldots n.$$

For each economic unit there are $n - 1$ utility equations; from these $n - 1$ supply or demand equations (selling or buying) may be deduced. Since there are m economic units, we have $m(n - 1)$ supply or demand equations.

Further, for each economic unit a budget balance equation can be formulated which, since the sum of the values received and disbursed equals zero, takes the following form:

$$\Sigma_j p_j q_{ji} = 0 \text{ for } i = 1 \ldots m \text{ and } p_1 = 1.$$

Finally, it is possible to formulate a market equation for each commodity (on each market the sum of all quantities received is identical to the sum of all quantities disbursed):

$$\Sigma_i q_{ji} = 0 \text{ for } j = 1 \ldots n.$$

In all there are $m(n-1) + m + n$ or $mn + n$ equations. There is thus one equation more than there are unknowns. However, by totalling the budget balance equations for all individuals, we obtain:

$$\Sigma_i \Sigma_j p_j q_{ji} = 0$$
$$\Sigma_j p_j (\Sigma_i q_{ji}) = 0.$$

For commodity 1 we have $\Sigma_i q_{1i} = 0$. One of the market equations is already produced as a budget balance equation; this equation is redundant and finally $mn + n - 1$ equations are left.

This system can be extended to include production factors. Here the (unknown) prices of the production factors and the (known) quantities of the latter available must be taken into account. The technological coefficients are then assumed to be constant. It is again shown that the number of unknowns corresponds to the number of independent equations. This last development leads to input-output analysis (Chapter 13.2a).

Appraisal
It is no longer accepted that a system of simultaneous equations with the same number of equations as unknowns will yield an equilibrium solution (no forces at work to upset the equilibrium). Equality is neither a sufficient nor a necessary condition for the existence of a solution (even for the existence of one single solution). Attempts have accordingly been made in recent years to determine the conditions for a general equilibrium. So far these have all been based on perfect or pure competition (and other unrealistic hypotheses). The statement of U. Ricci (1924) on the theory of general equilibrium is still valid: 'a marvellous castle . . . but of no help in solving the housing problem'.

7 An appraisal of marginal analysis

According to marginal price theory, the entrepreneur attempts to equate marginal cost and marginal revenue in order to maximize profits. As will be shown below, firms actually employ other methods in pricing. In general, entrepreneurs apparently do not even know these marginal concepts.

The marginal method does not determine whether fixed costs, and hence average total costs, are covered. So this requires further examination. Sales promotion costs, moreover, are given little weight. While the technique proceeds as though producers and consumers were in direct contact, this is rarely the case. Frequently it is even the wholesaler who actually sets prices. Marginal costs (especially in the long term – accounting for the brief treatment of prices in this period in the present chapter) and above all marginal revenue cannot as a rule be calculated, and the countless attempts to determine the demand curve empirically have been unsuccessful (Chapter 4.3).

One of the other objections to marginalism is that it attaches no importance to stability considerations. It assumes that changes in marginal cost and revenue are immediately reflected in changes in price. The continuous price fluctuations that result, however, encourage speculation. Both dealers and consumers prefer price stability, which also makes it easier for firms to plan ahead. In other words, it is often better to let a short-term advantage go in order to safeguard long-term interests (*inter alia* with an eye to potential competition, which may come from either new or existing firms). Hence, the monopolist (or oligopolist) sets a 'limit price' which is not exceeded in order to check new market entries.

What are known as administered prices meet these requirements. They are not determined by the interplay of supply and demand but fixed by corporate (single firm or group) or government decision.

The marginal method can also be objected to on the grounds that it establishes the most profitable level of output (not price). In reality the businessman first sets his price; only then does he consider what quantity he will be able to sell. In determining this quantity, marginal theory does not even make allowance for the need to use as much as possible of the capacity available. It is in no way concerned with unused capacity.

A detailed critique of the marginal price theory cannot be given here. In addition, it may, however, be mentioned that when higher prices are ascribed to monopolistic competition and oligopoly than to pure competition, this applies only provided the cost curves remain unchanged. Greater output on the other hand, generally brings costs down. When the primary aim, as with government agencies, is to satisfy wants, the equality of average costs and average revenue should be preferred. In such cases no (excess) profits will be made.

The real drawbacks to the marginal theory of price, however, are the two major assumptions on which it rests; although it is mentioned incidentally that businessmen can have objectives other than profit maximization, it is assumed that profit maximization is the only important aim; it is also assumed that price is the businessman's chief policy instrument, even when it is admitted that he may sometimes have others to rely upon. We shall deal with these two assumptions in turn.

The marginal principle is not applied in the Soviet Union, where the enterprises proceed from average costs. The most important prices are imposed or approved by the central government while the remainder are fixed by the production units involved, which since 1965 have enjoyed greater liberty in this area. Prices are so fixed as to recover manufacturing and distribution costs while giving (normal) profit in a normally functioning plant. Provided too detailed and centralized intervention is avoided. 'There is much to be said in favour of the system of prices which are not distorted by selfish monopolists and myopic consumers, but in which long-run macrosocial cost-benefit considerations can be reflected.' (J. Wilczynski).

a. Corporate objectives

An examination of corporate behaviour is the only means of studying how a firm reaches its decisions. Empirical studies have shown that as a general rule a variety of aims are pursued.

Among the most prominent objectives of major corporations in the United States are a target return on investment, stable prices and profit margins, gaining or holding a given market share, and meeting or forestalling competition. In Denmark the small firms appear to pursue maximization of profits in the short run while the large firms, though their aims are the same give more attention to long-term considerations. The behaviour of the small firms is due, in some cases, to a shortage of liquid assets.

W. J. Baumol regards maximizing sales as the foremost objective,

243

at least provided total profits do not fall below a specified minimum. More particularly, the aim should be maximization of the rate of growth of sales. Maximizing sales is a matter of prestige, and a firm will endeavour to preserve or increase its share of the market. At the same time, managers seek to demonstrate their ability, and this – especially in the most common case where they hold little or none of the firm's capital – may lead to higher salaries in that company or elsewhere.

Occasionally, the main aim of the entrepreneur is, especially in independent firms, simply a quiet life. He prefers leisure to higher profits, security to more risks, good relations with his colleagues to rivalry. This is by no means fanciful: the slow rate of economic growth in some countries may partly be attributed to it.

In many cases the need for a minimum of liquid assets is in conflict with the target of maximizing profits: a firm usually tries to avoid substantial indebtedness and preserve its independence, hence the preference for self-financing. Moreover, as we have already seen, the avoidance of potential competition is incompatible with a policy directed at maximizing profits. This in fact also applies to firms wishing to maintain good relations with consumers, suppliers, investors, trade unions and above all the government.

Anyway, profit maximization cannot be regarded as the major objective of the firm; other objectives, relating to sales, production and stocks, are by no means subsidiary. The importance of these aims varies from case to case, and no general rules can be formulated here. Within the firm, the various objectives themselves often give rise to conflicts between the heads of different divisions. The determination, persuasiveness, or other qualities of one executive will sometimes turn the scales.

b. Instruments of corporate policy

Although it is not the only instrument of marketing policy, almost exclusive attention is given to price in economic theory. Often, however, price is of subordinate interest, and the other policy instruments such as quality (very often closely related to R & D expenditure), sales promotion, distribution channels and product-line policy, are more important. The extent to which the different instruments are used, i.e. what the marketing mix is, has not yet been examined very closely. We shall concentrate on these instruments further. The choice of instruments depends first of all on the nature of the goods offered for sale. The financial situation may also be of great significance. Time and again it is seen that a firm obtains better results by attaching importance to such items as advertising and packaging rather than by lowering the selling price.

1. *Price*

Price sensitivity varies from product to product, from consumer to consumer. There are many goods (or types of good) for which the consumer pays little attention to price; on the other hand, there are others for which price is of great significance. Most consumers do little in the way of comparing prices. They seem to remember only a limited number of prices.

Price increases should not necessarily be objected to. They can be explained as being due to improved quality or greater demand. In certain cases (even for homogeneous goods), however, firms systematically price their products above their competitors' (this is made possible by product differentiation) to create the impression that they are offering better quality. On account of the (largely irrational) behaviour of consumers, insignificant changes are often made to a product in order to sell it at a higher price (product variation: see below).

Price reductions are sometimes thought to signify a decline in quality, an unsuccessful line, difficulties in maintaining liquidity, or the imminent introduction of a new model. A price cut may in fact appreciably reduce sales of a product through the snob effect, when a certain class of consumer is attracted precisely on account of its price. Even the price of a new product can be regarded as too low. When electric alarm clocks were first marketed in the United States they were not successful. Consumers thought they were priced too low in comparison with the conventional clock; they felt that a quality product could not be sold at such a price. The clocks were withdrawn and later put on sale at a higher price – and this time with better results.

2. *Quality*

This is a concept that can cover industrial design, packaging, servicing, delivery times and product variation. For many goods and services – dry cleaning, for instance – price is not as important as quality and speedy delivery. The quality of durable goods is often kept low deliberately in order to make them wear out sooner and thus promote replacement purchases. In proceedings brought against General

K

Electric in 1939 it was found that the life of light-bulbs had repeatedly and deliberately been reduced. When the consumer is accustomed to a price that is a good round figure, the quality (or the weight) of a product (bar of chocolate) is often reduced as an alternative to increasing the price (a practice known as price line pricing). Packaging and servicing are becoming steadily more important. This also applies to product variation. By this we mean not the distinction of a firm's products from those of its competitors (product differentiation) but the way a firm makes temporary, minor changes in its own products in order to give the consumer the impression that new products are being brought out. This is a practice that causes considerable waste. In the United States at least 5,000 million dollars a year are spent on automobile model changes.

It is no simple matter to determine optimum quality and the corresponding selling price.

3. *Sales promotion*

Sales promotion is the practice whereby firms employ representatives and advertising to inform dealers and consumers of the qualities of their products and to encourage them to buy. The word is used in its narrower sense here, since price and quality are also means of stimulating sales.

Marketing costs are only indirectly linked with the level of production; the figure differs from industry to industry. Huge amounts are spent on advertising in many industries. Annual expenditure on advertising in the United States totals about 22,000 million dollars – the proportion on soap and other toiletries amounts to 15–20 per cent of the cost price and on cigarettes and alcohol about 10 per cent. Advertising, in addition to its useful function of providing information, can force prices up. In many cases advertising does not increase a firm's market share because of the compensatory effect of advertising by competing firms. Firms are often put out of business by competitors whose products are inferior but who put a bigger effort into sales promotion. In particular, advertising for homogeneous or virtually homogeneous products (aspirin and petrol, for instance) is tantamount to waste from the national point of view.

4. *Distribution*

A firm can see to the distribution of its own products or can give the job to outsiders. Everything here depends on the consumers to be reached, the need to provide information (e.g. with consumer durables), and the type and status of the product. Prestige, for example, will probably rule out distribution through chain stores, although it must be borne in mind that these are becoming increasingly important.

The main drawback to distribution through independent retail firms in fact lies in the margin competition resulting from resale price maintenance (see below) – competition shifts from the consumer to the distributor. As the retailer stimulates sales of the most profitable products, the producer tends to set prices at a level which permits distribution margins at least equal to or, preferably, higher than those granted by his competitors. This tendency explains the possibility of 'rebate wars' (especially during a depression).

5. *Product range*
Firms are often constrained to increase the number of types of goods which they produce – in other words, to widen their product range. This strengthens their bargaining position *vis-à-vis* competitors with only a few products and *vis-à-vis* the distributors handling their products.

Other considerations are also of importance. A few years ago an American firm found itself unable to increase its market share for low-priced fountain pens. To induce the public to associate its brand name with better quality, the corporation brought out an expensive pen (for which, in the first instance, profit considerations were disregarded). The result was satisfactory: sales of the low-priced pen showed a substantial rise. This brings to mind G. Tarde's dictum *'Ce n'est pas la loi de l'offre et de la demande qui fixe le prix; c'est l'opinion'*.

c. *Price setting in practice*
Prices are not an instrument in pure competition, where a firm has control only of the quantity it sells, and not of prices. As there is no product differentiation, advertising serves no useful purpose except for collective advertisements. However, pure competition is rare, apart from the stock exchange and a number of world markets. Even there producers and governments endeavour to counter what they consider excessive price fluctuations – by commodity agreements, for instance.

Although monopolists are free, in principle, to set their prices as high as they wish, caution is still required. First and foremost they have to bear possible government reactions in mind. The consumers

247

may turn to substitute products. And potential competition from new producers cannot be ruled out. Cases of pure monopoly – railways, water, gas and electricity supply – are rare, too.

In oligopoly, the most common market structure, prices are fixed as in a monopoly and are consequently administered prices. Once prices are set they generally are only changed following more or less permanent changes in cost price or demand. Short-term fluctuations in demand (which often cancel out in the long term) generally have little or no impact on prices. The existence of (excess) profits makes this possible. Administered prices are thus characterized by a certain inflexibility.

As a rule the producer works from the standard cost price, at least when he makes only one product. Where more than one product is involved direct costing is appropriate, but the standard cost price may still be of use since direct costing is not a method of calculating cost prices.

Since the standards used (quantities, prices) may be undervalued, the standard cost price is supplemented in many cases to allow for business risks. The variable standard cost price may also be increased by such supplementary charges, which are constant in cost-plus pricing and variable in flexible-markup pricing.

The full standard cost price merely indicates the minimum selling price in the long run; in the short term this function is performed by the variable standard cost price. It does not indicate the level at which the selling price should be set, for demand must be considered and here, as has been seen, the producer has no firm data to go on. This explains why experts agree that setting prices is more of an art than a science. In certain cases – price discrimination (see below) or a slump – products may be sold at a loss; many factories produce different commodities to which varying margins are applied; profits are greater on one article than on another, according to the (fluctuating) potential of the market. New products especially can sometimes be priced far above cost, as was the case with the first ballpoint pens. Psychological considerations also play a part: consumers are, for instance, more sensitive to a price increase from £0·95 to £1·05 than to a rise from £0·75 to £0·85.

A. R. Oxenfeldt has rightly stated, 'the detailed analysis of prices . . . suggests that every price is unique in some important respect. No fairly simple explanation of price, like the law of supply and demand, has been uncovered'. The 'law' of supply and demand, which in fact applies only in pure competition, merely indicates trends. In present-day society the working of the economy is regulated not by some automatic mechanism but by the planning of major corporations and possibly of the government; '. . . our economy is not organized by the market mechanism. The market is organized by the economy' (C. E. Ayres). In a certain sense the major firms first manufacture goods (production planning requires several years), then set the prices, and finally ensure a demand for the goods by marketing techniques.

8 Price differentials and price discrimination

Price differentials occur when identical products are sold at the same time at different prices, on account of divergent selling costs. For instance, discounts are generally allowed for large orders, cash payment, or orders placed well before delivery is required (thus countering seasonal fluctuations in production). The differences that occur in price discrimination are due not to cost-price differences but to differences in the consumers' purchasing power. A surgeon, for example, may charge a rich patient higher fees, a cinema may admit children at half price, a railway company may offer lower rates for cheap goods, and an electricity board has different rates for peak and off-peak use. When price differentials do not apply to everyone who is in the same circumstances, this is discrimination too.

A certain degree of monopoly power is consequently required where price discrimination is practised, and the market must be divisible into several segments or submarkets between which communication is impossible or at least thought to be so. A surgical operation, for instance, cannot be resold. As regards goods, discrimination is often effected by selling various brands at different prices. Stocking manufacturers, for instance, market the same nylons at a high price (e.g. producer brand), a middle-range price (distributor brands) and a low price (unbranded). T. Scitovsky quotes the example of the same watches and perfume sold under two different names (Longines and Wittnauer; Lanvin and Le Galion). Where there is the merest impression of quality differences even brands may become unnecessary. G. H. Bousquet wrote in 1936 that Mozabite traders in Algiers were selling oil at different prices, running it off from taps which connected with the same barrel concealed behind a curtain only a few inches away.

Discrimination will normally lead to greater sales – since other categories of consumer can be reached – higher profits, and some-times lower prices.

We also speak of price discrimination when the sale of one and the same product gives rise to divergent costs which are not expressed in the selling price. A well-known example is the basing-point system which was applied, for instance, in the American steel industry between 1916 and 1948. A single basic price for delivery to Pitts-burgh (and later other cities as well) was determined for all steel pro-ducers; the cost of transport on to the final destination then had to be added in. Even a Chicago steelmaker charged a customer in the same city the Pittsburgh price plus the Pittsburgh-Chicago rail freight. He could thus supply a customer in Pittsburgh at a lower price than a customer in his home town. The system prevented a choice of opti-mum location and thus shielded the less favourably situated firms.

9 Resale price maintenance

One type of administered pricing is resale price maintenance (as opposed to horizontal price fixing among competitors dealing in one article – for instance, a restrictive price agreement). Here the selling price – uniform for all consumers – is fixed by the producer or importer and not by the seller. In other words, the manufacturer himself controls the price at which his products are sold to the con-sumer by means of a predetermined minimum or maximum or a single set level. This in turn presupposes a certain monopoly power resulting from product differentiation or, with homogeneous goods, restrictive agreements.

Resale price maintenance generally occurs with branded products, and a distinction is drawn between 'strong' and 'weak' brands. The public asks for the strong brand by name, but not for the weak one; sales also depend sometimes on the persuasiveness of the dealer.

There are various opinions on this subject. Fixed prices are a particular subject of discussion. They are chiefly found with con-sumer goods, 25 to 80 per cent of which (depending on the industry) are fixed.

Those retailers who find it difficult to introduce a self-service system are usually advocates of resale price maintenance (provided that distribution margins are considered satisfactory), since price competition is eliminated.

Large department stores and supermarkets, which aim at high

turnover through low prices, are averse to price fixing. They consequently establish their own brands (distributor brands) for products supplied by manufacturers. Department stores can thus sell virtually the same products at lower prices. Such non-brand deliveries are to the advantage of the producers, since output is increased and the cost price reduced.

The producers themselves often favour resale price maintenance since distributors do not always pass on price reductions, using them to raise their margins. Moreover, they are afraid that their products may be retailed at a loss to attract customers. In such cases the traders sell the loss leader together with other products from which more profit can be obtained, more than compensating for the loss. Even when the product is not sold at a loss but simply at an abnormally low price, this practice cuts back sales of the same item in other shops. Moreover, after the sales drive the low price will not stimulate further sales for the distributors, and the producers suffer. The importance of this argument should not be overstressed. It is difficult to determine whether sales are being made at a loss or at an abnormally low profit. The price cuts are usually temporary and local. Not all products will serve as loss leaders; only convenience goods (those bought regularly and almost automatically) are suitable. Finally, countermeasures can be taken by the manufacturers.

Via the fixed retail prices, the producers themselves determine the distributors' margins. Excessive margins are thus avoided. However, larger margins are increasingly granted because this encourages the seller to stimulate sales of the products in question. This applies particularly when the influence of intermediaries is more important and the demand is less sensitive to price. However, high margins also mean that substantial discounts are sometimes granted.

Competition among producers contributes to the continual raising of margins. Only in oligopolistic industries where collusion is practised is there any restriction on this. Fixed prices are conducive to (overt or tacit) restrictive agreements. It is particularly easy to check whether an agreement is being observed where prices are uniform.

It is sometimes argued that resale price maintenance (through adequate margins) allows distributors to offer better service. This does not bear examination. Not all consumers desire such service. It would be more logical for the price of this service to be expressed separately (bread and milk delivered to the doorstep should be more expensive than in the shop).

251

Since it generally leads to higher prices – or prevents price cuts – resale price maintenance is as a rule prohibited in Canada, Denmark, France, the United Kingdom, Norway and Sweden. Other countries make a distinction between individual systems of resale price maintenance and collective ones, where a number of producers agree to pursue or enforce maintenance in order to restrict price competition; collective systems, for instance, are not permitted in the Netherlands or the United States.

The Netherlands prohibits individual price fixing for goods such as radio and television sets, refrigerators, vacuum cleaners, private cars, cameras, and records. To preclude the use of these articles as loss leaders, the ban does not apply when the relevant selling price is lower than the purchase price.

10 Commodity agreements

The pronounced fluctuations in the prices of most primary products, related to business cycles and, with agricultural produce, especially contingent on climatic conditions, have given rise to agreements to regulate prices. Such agreements were in existence before 1939, and after World War II the United Nations Economic and Social Council recommended that consumer interests should also be represented on the appropriate agencies. Where this is done, we speak rather of commodity agreements, although the term is also used less restrictively (in the sense of international producers' agreements). Governments generally conclude such agreements for primary products where output exceeds demand and where each country has numerous producers who would not otherwise conclude an agreement.

Up to the present, endeavours to achieve stabilization of commodity prices have assumed three forms – the multilateral contract (International Wheat Agreement), the international quota (International Sugar Agreement, International Coffee Agreement) and the buffer stock (International Tin Agreement).

a. The first International Wheat Agreement was ratified in 1949, and has been revised and renewed on numerous occasions since then. The latest in the series, running for three years from 1 August 1968 and now restyled the International Grains Arrangements, set limits of $1·73 and $2·13 per bushel. As soon as prices approach or touch the floor, the Wheat Council adopts counter-measures. The Council also proposes adjustments where an exporting country has a poor harvest or an importing country urgently requires wheat.

As long as the market prices fluctuate within the price limits, the importing countries are obliged to effect a specific proportion of their annual purchases in the exporting countries. Importing countries may buy from non-participants when the ceiling is exceeded; no account is taken of such purchases in calculating the stated percentages. The obligation to purchase from the exporting countries is not applicable when prices fall beneath the minimum level.

When the ceiling is exceeded the exporting countries, which include the United States, Canada, Australia and Argentina, are still under an obligation to offer the agreed quantities (or the remaining balance) at a price not higher than the specified maximum.

b. The first International Sugar Agreement became operative on 1 January 1954, and the second, again of five years' duration, on 1 January 1959. Export quotas were established, which were subject to adjustment when given limits were exceeded. Although the second agreement was provisionally extended, the most important provisions were not implemented between 1962 and 1968, on account of the dispute between the United States and Cuba. A new agreement came into force on 1 January 1969, but neither the United States nor the EEC participated.

c. Following a series of annual agreements starting on 1 October 1959, a five-year International Coffee Agreement became operative on 27 December 1963; this is also based on export quotas. A new agreement took effect on 1 October 1968, and a Diversification Fund was set up to counter overproduction.

d. The first International Tin Agreement came into effect on 1 July 1956. The fourth, also running for five years, commenced on 1 July 1971. The stabilization provisions included a buffer stock of 20,000 tons in tin metal.

When the market price falls below the floor of £1,260 per ton, the stockpile is replenished; to support the floor price, and provided that there are 10,000 long tons in the buffer stock, export quotas are established. When the ceiling of £1,605 is exceeded, or this threatens to be the case, tin from the stock is sold to the market (as long as the market price does not fall below the ceiling). In the event of a shortage, the stocks may be equitably apportioned, but producers must increase their output by as much as possible.

Operation

It is difficult to assess the effectiveness of such agreements. The United States' support policy has contributed to the stability of the wheat price, whose level is, however, undoubtedly excessive. Political factors sometimes predominate, as in the sugar agreements. One drawback of export quotas is that stable prices are obtained at the expense of stable output, benefiting the least efficient producers. A buffer stock rises beyond measure or falls sharply as soon as large price movements occur. It is not easy to determine a reasonable price range.

For commodity agreements to succeed, all the major producers must participate and the governments must be able to control their operation. Such supervision is particularly hard with agricultural produce.

Finally, when concluding agreements it must be realized that complete stabilization of prices is not possible, or in fact desirable: the quantities supplied and demanded must balance in the long run, and the necessary adjustments to the economies concerned should not be impeded.

11 The effects of market structure and conduct on performance

a. Market structure

While monopolies and oligopolies may present many drawbacks, such as excessively high prices, profits and outlay on advertising, their inhibiting effect on technological progress, and their opposition to new market entries, they frequently offer corresponding advantages in lower prices or higher expenditure on research – and this is conducive to industrial innovation (cf. the advantages and drawbacks of trusts).

It is difficult to make general pronouncements; divergent types of market structure yield satisfactory performance.

There has been little research in this field. J. S. Bain concluded from surveys of twenty American industries that high concentration brings higher profits, and more so when market entry is difficult. Product differentiation also goes together with high profits, less efficient plants, and higher selling costs.

Finally, the structure of demand will affect market performance. In a bilateral monopoly there is normally bargaining between the two parties, and bargaining power is of predominant significance. Compared with a monopoly, a bilateral monopoly may give a lower price level. This is also possible when a coordinated oligopsony (as in the pooling of raw-material purchases) confronts a monopoly.

A 'pyramid' oligopsony, however, gives rise to individual purchases, which the monopolist will turn to advantage in price discrimination. Department stores thus buy their products at lower prices than non-integrated retailer firms. In a sellers' market the advantages of a dominant position are not always expressed in the form of lower purchase prices, but as guaranteed supplies.

When a 'pyramid' oligopoly is confronted by an oligopsony, the major suppliers cannot impose their terms to the same extent as a monopolist can, since the buyers have some choice of sources of supply. Moreover, substitute products are generally available. In a market where supply is atomistic and demand concentrated, even greater pressure can be brought on prices. To quote G. H. Bousquet again, in an example taken from a report which the French explorer F. Foureau published in 1902 (the quotation refers to Agadès; *Mission Foureau-Lamy: D'Alger au Congo*): 'For a few days, Lamy had indeed tried to allow the market to operate freely and let the soldiers buy according to their wishes; but prices of all kinds of items had immediately started rising in such a way that he reverted to the more rational system of buying through one person for the whole community'.

b. Market conduct

Here again there is great difficulty in showing any connection with market performance. Conduct that appears to be directed at maximum joint profits in fact takes other considerations into account, such as fear of potential competition, mistrust of competitors, the possibility that less efficient firms may be better equipped on account of the high profits.

Administered prices are becoming more and more common. Product differentiation is the pre-eminent method of competition. Actual price competition is practised to some degree among department stores, but not as fully as their organizaton would allow.

More evidence concerning structure and performance is obtained when there is aggressive market conduct. In a price war – a rare occurrence – small competitors are sometimes squeezed out of the market and potential entrants discouraged. Identical results are obtainable by securing control of distribution channels. In such cases the market structure (greater concentration or more difficult market entry) and the market performance (prices) are directly affected by market conduct.

12 The role of the consumer

Partly on account of greater product differentiation, consumers are less able to determine the properties of goods themselves. They often believe that the most expensive is necessarily the best. They need objective information setting out the results of thorough comparative surveys of the various brands.

The first effective consumer organization was set up in the United States in 1928; this was Consumers' Research, publishing the *Consumers' Research Bulletin*; 1936 saw the foundation of a second organization, the Consumers Union, which has since become the larger; it publishes *Consumer Reports*. Research is conducted without any assistance from the manufacturers, and the results of the surveys may not be used for advertising purposes.

The majority of such organizations in Western Europe were set up in the 1950s. In France there is the Union Fédérale de la Consommation (1951; *Que Choisir?*) and the Organisation Générale de la Consommation-Orgeco (1959; *Orgeco*); in the Netherlands, the Nederlandse Consumentenbond (1953; *Consumentengids*); in West Germany a number of local associations joined forces in the Arbeitsgemeinschaft der Verbraucherverbände (1953; *Verbraucher Rundschau*); in the United Kingdom, the Consumers' Association (1957; *Which?*); in Belgium, the Association des Consommateurs (1957; *Test-achats*) and the Union Féminine pour l'Information et la Défense du Consommateur-Ufidec (1959; *Ufidec*); and in Italy the Unione Nazionale Consumatori (1955; *Le scelte del consumatore*).

In some countries the consumer organizations issue quality labels, while other countries have separate organizations for this, such as the Varudeklarationsnämnden-*VDN* (1951) in Sweden.

To give some idea of the results of the tests we may give a few examples. On the Belgian market, out of ten brands of vacuum cleaner examined, not one satisfied the national or international requirements for powered domestic appliances (*Ufidec*; 1965). The cheaper brands of petrol are not of inferior quality (*Ufidec*; 1966). In spite of the regulations, some coloured pencils had a dangerous lead content (*Ufidec*; 1969). On the British market, the more expensive the binoculars, the better they did in the tests, while on the other hand the most important difference found between twenty-eight brands of baked beans was their price (*Which?* 1969).

13 Price indices

Price indicators for primary products traded on the international market include the Moody Index, based on the price movements (weighted average of the spot quotations) of eight agricultural and seven industrial items on the New York exchange (31 December 1931 = 100), and the Reuter Index for 21 raw materials on the London market (18 September 1931 = 100). Prices of primary products, being pure goods prices, are very sensitive. Since they are expressed in the major currencies (dollars, sterling), they follow the fluctuations in the latter's value.

Most countries produce wholesale (cf. Table 1), retail and consumer price indices, and also a cost-of-living index.

Retail price indices did not come into use until about 1910. The chief aim was to follow cost-of-living movements more closely and study the relationship of wholesale and retail prices. Since they relate to finished products, retail prices are less sensitive than primary-product and wholesale prices. They include more fixed factors, such as wages and the retailer's profit margin. Furthermore, domestic goods are protected to some degree from foreign competition. The influence of currency fluctuations is likewise less. For these reasons retail prices do not usually go up so quickly in the rising phase of the business cycle and they fall more slowly at the downturn; they may still continue to rise when wholesale prices have begun to decline.

The inadequacy of retail prices as a yardstick for the cost of living led to the introduction of further indices, taking account not only of all the items which affect the cost of living (rent, entertainment) but also of the relative importance of the various products (weighted indices). Budget surveys were first of all required (Chapter 4.7). However, the indices for retail prices and the cost of living generally follow a parallel course, partly because the retail price indices are in many cases indirectly weighted (various qualities).

Based on budget surveys, indices for consumer prices or the cost of living are published in Belgium (base year 1966), West Germany (1963), France (1962), the United Kingdom (1963), Italy (1966), the Netherlands (1960) and the United States (1957–63).

257

14 Bibliography

On price theory in general, see as a first initiation G. J. Stigler, *The Theory of Price* (rev. ed. New York 1952); in addition the more elaborate M. M. Bober, *Intermediate Price and Income Theory* (rev. ed. New York 1962); S. Weintraub, *Intermediate Price Theory* (Philadelphia 1964) and D. S. Watson, *Price Theory and its Uses* (2nd ed. Boston 1968) with annotated bibliography.

The quotation from L. Baudin is taken from his *La monnaie et la formation des prix* (3rd ed. Paris 1947).

a. Competition
The distinction between pure and perfect competition was made in 1932 (1st ed.) by E. H. Chamberlin, *The Theory of Monopolistic Competition* (Cambridge, Mass.), appendix to Chapter 2 – a work in which the concept of monopolistic competition was also introduced; cf. *id.*, *Towards a More General Theory of Value* (New York 1957). A quarter of a century later, on the same subject: *Monopolistic Competition Theory: Studies in Impact: Essays in Honor of Edward H. Chamberlin* (ed. R. E. Kuenne, New York 1967). See also: J. Robinson, *The Economics of Imperfect Competition* (London 1933; the second edition of 1969 differs only in its preface), and *id.*, 'Imperfect Competition Revisited', *EJ*, September 1953.

The concept of *workable competition* was introduced by J. M. Clark, 'Toward a Concept of Workable Competition', *AER*, June 1940; see the concise paper by J. S. Bain, 'Workable Competition in Oligopoly: Theoretical Considerations and Empirical Evidence', *AER*, May 1950; further elaborations in J. S. Bain, *Industrial Organization* (New York 1968). See finally S. H. Sosnick, 'A Critique of Concepts of Workable Competition', *QJE*, August 1958; the extensive J. M. Clark, *Competition as a Dynamic Process* (Washington 1961).

On The Davenant-King law, see G. J. Stigler, 'The Early History of Empirical Studies of Consumer Demand', *JPE*, April 1954; G. H. Evans Jr, 'The Law of Demand: The Roles of Gregory King and Charles Davenant', *QJE*, August 1967.

For a brief mathematical exposition of the cobweb theorem: R. G. D. Allen, *Mathematical Economics* (London 1962), Chapter 1. G. Åkerman, 'The Cobweb Theorem: A Reconsideration', *QJE*, February 1957, points out (in a short article) that the theorem only applies to a limited extent in the case of industrial products. M. Nerlove, 'Adaptive Expectations and Cobweb Phenomena', *QJE*, May 1958, thinks that producers will, indeed, pay due regard to practical experience.

The concept of the *sales zone* was introduced by W. J. Eiteman, *Price Determination: Business Practice versus Economic Theory* (Ann Arbor, Mich. 1949), though he uses the term 'output zone' rather than 'sales zone'.

b. *Monopoly*

To the question 'Monopoly: Impediment or Stimulus to Economic Progress?' (in *Monopoly and Competition and their Regulation*, ed. E. H. Chamberlin, London 1954), no answer in unambiguous terms can be given, according to P. Hennipman. Neither theory nor the facts permit any generalizations. See also L. J. Zimmerman, *The Propensity to Monopolize* (Amsterdam 1952).

Monopoly power is difficult to evaluate (one criterion is not sufficient): see E. H. Chamberlin, 'Measuring the Degree of Monopoly and Competition', in *Monopoly and Competition and their Regulation*.

See also J. K. Galbraith, *American Capitalism: The Concept of Countervailing Power* (Cambridge, Mass. 1952): the economic power of monopolies can be neutralized by the countervailing power of customers and workers grouped in powerful buyers' organizations and trade unions. It is the government's duty to help organize this countervailing power. For criticism of this point of view, see, *inter alia*, G. J. Stigler, 'The Economist Plays with Blocs', *AER*, May 1954.

c. *Oligopoly*

The kinked demand curve was first examined in R. L. Hall and C. J. Hitch, 'Price Theory and Business Behaviour', *OEP*, May 1939, reprinted in *Oxford Studies in the Price Mechanism* (ed. T. Wilson and P. W. S. Andrews, Oxford 1951); P. M. Sweezy, 'Demand under Conditions of Oligopoly', *JPE*, August 1939, reprinted in *Readings in Price Theory* (ed. G. J. Stigler and K. E. Boulding, Homewood, Ill. 1952); see also in this volume the paper by G. J. Stigler. For criticism of this last contribution: C. W. Efroymson, 'The Kinked Oligopoly Curve Reconsidered', *QJE*, February 1955.

W. Fellner, *Competition among the Few: Oligopoly and Similar*

Market Structures (New York 1949): fear of the reactions of the other oligopolists leads to price agreements (attempts to maximize aggregate profits); an essentially unmodified reprint was published in 1960.

A. D. M. Kaplan, *Big Enterprise in a Competitive System* (Washington 1954) expounds the advantages of big corporations and believes that these firms ultimately favour competition.

A. D. M. Kaplan, J. B. Dirlam and R. F. Lanzillotti, *Pricing in Big Business: A Case Approach* (Washington 1958): the big firms are conscious of the dangers attaching to a price war, so that competition is more concerned with quality, servicing and design. W. J. Baumol, *Business Behavior, Value and Growth* (New York 1959), studies the conduct of oligopolist firms (mentioning the deliberate limitation of profits and the efforts to maximize sales, and developing a growth theory on this basis).

The quotation from D. C. Hague can be found in 'The Task of the Contemporary Theory of Pricing', in *Price Formation in Various Countries: Proceedings of a Conference held by the International Economic Association* (ed. D. C. Hague, New York 1967).

d. The theory of games

The theory of games, based on the measurability of utility, was expounded in J. von Neumann and O. Morgenstern, *Theory of Games and Economic Behavior* (Princeton 1944). Simple introduction: J. D. Williams, *The Compleat Strategyst: Being a Primer on the Theory of Games of Strategy* (New York 1954); more in the mathematical field: J. McKinsey, *Introduction to the Theory of Games* (New York 1952).

M. Shubik, *Strategy and Market Structure: Competition, Oligopoly and the Theory of Games* (New York 1959), analyses oligopoly by means of the theory of games.

e. General equilibrium

This theory was first elaborated by L. Walras, *Eléments d'économie politique pure* (Lausanne 1874), and V. Pareto, *Manuel d'économie politique* (Paris 1909).

See also E. Schneider, *Pricing and Equilibrium* (London 1962), Part 2; J. R. Hicks, *Value and Capital* (2nd ed., Oxford 1946), Chapters 4 to 8; D. Patinkin, *Money, Interest and Prices: An Integration of Monetary and Value Theory* (2nd ed., Evanston Ill. 1965);

P. A. Samuelson, *Foundations of Economic Analysis* (Cambridge, Mass. 1947), Chapter 9.

R. E. Kuenne, *The Theory of General Economic Equilibrium* (Princeton 1963), gives a (difficult) survey of the relevant literature; *id., Micro-economic Theory of the Market Mechanism: A General Equilibrium Approach* (New York 1968). The quotation from U. Ricci can be found in: 'Pareto e l'economia pura', *Giornale degli Economisti*, February 1924.

f. Marginal price theory
The application of the full cost price is discussed in *Oxford Studies in the Price Mechanism* (especially in the paper by R. L. Hall and C. J. Hitch, 'Price Theory and Business Behaviour'); W. J. Eiteman, *Price Determination* (importance of changes in stocks for the entrepreneur's decisions); P. J. D. Wiles, *Price, Cost and Output* (Oxford 1956); B. Fog, *Industrial Pricing Policies: An Analysis of Pricing Policies of Danish Manufacturers* (Amsterdam 1960).

The 'normal' price (account is taken of potential competition) is considered in P. W. S. Andrews, *Manufacturing Business* (London 1949), and J. Dean, *Managerial Economics* (New York 1951).

For refutation of the foregoing criticism: F. Machlup, 'Marginal Analysis and Empirical Research', *AER*, September 1946.

In order to promote optimal factor allocation, the application of the marginal principle is also recommended for public services. If losses are suffered they can be compensated by a subsidy. This subsidization is defended by H. Hotelling, 'The General Welfare in Relation to Problems of Taxation and of Railway and Utility Rates', *Em*, July 1938. Like I. M. D. Little, *A Critique of Welfare Economics* (Oxford 1950), Chapter 11, C. J. Oort concludes in *Decreasing Costs as a Problem of Welfare Economics* (Amsterdam 1958) that in this event no uniform solution is possible, on account of the allocation problems mentioned (financing of the subsidies through taxation).

See in this connection: *Marginal Cost Pricing: Fundamental Economic Principles Employed to Determine Pricing, Operating and Investment Policies* (ed. J. R. Nelson, Englewood Cliffs, N.J. 1964) – a series of papers, translated from the French, on the application of the marginal principle in determining prices of the nationalized enterprise Electricité de France (prepared by officials or former officials of this concern, especially by M. Boiteux).

g. Prices and the instruments of corporate policy
For a brief survey: M. A. G. van Meerhaeghe, *Price Theory and Price Policy* (London 1969), Chapter 2.

Most of the numerous recent works on advertising are of a descriptive nature and aimed at the practical. See C. J. Dirksen and A. Kroeger, *Advertising Principles and Problems* (rev. ed., Homewood, Ill. 1964); J. S. Wright and D. S. Warner, *Advertising* (2nd ed., New York 1966); J. F. Engel, H. C. Wales and M. R. Warshaw, *Promotional Strategy* (Homewood, Ill. 1967); *International Handbook of Advertising* (ed. S. W. Dunn, New York 1964) – numerous contributions on the principles and the method to be adopted, including a discussion of certain geographical markets (e.g. the United States, Latin America, the United Kingdom, France, West Germany, the Benelux countries).

L. G. Telser, 'Advertising and Competition', *JPE*, December 1964, concludes that the two are incompatible. See also the celebrated work of V. Packard, *The Hidden Persuaders* (New York 1957).

On quality competition: L. Abott, *Quality and Competition: An Essay in Economic Theory* (New York 1956). The cases cited in text were drawn from: F. M. Fisher, Z. Griliches and C. Kaysen, 'The Cost of Automobile Model Changes since 1949', *AER*, May 1962; J. A. Menge, 'Style Change Costs as a Market Weapon', *QJE*, November 1962; J. Pen, *Harmony and Conflict in Modern Society* (London 1966). The quotation from G. Tarde is drawn from his *Psychologie économique* (Paris 1902); the quotation from J. Wilczynski from his *The Economics of Socialism* (London 1970).

h. Price setting in practice
For a general survey on the relationship between price theory and reality: *Models of Markets* (ed. A. R. Oxenfeldt, New York 1963). For the divergent methods followed by entrepreneurs in setting prices: A. R. Oxenfeldt, *Industrial Pricing and Market Practices* (New York 1951); *id.*, *Executive Action in Marketing* (New York 1966); *Creative Pricing* (ed. E. Marting, New York 1968).

Certain writers are opposed to the view that administered prices bring about inflation: H. W. Briefs, *Pricing Power and 'Administrative' Inflation: Concepts, Facts and Policy Implications* (Washington 1962); H. J. Depodwin and R. T. Selden, 'Business Pricing Policies and Inflation', *QJE*, April 1963.

The quotation from C. E. Ayres is drawn from his work *The*

Industrial Economy: Its Technological Basis and Institutional Destiny (Cambridge, Mass. 1952).

i. Price discrimination and price differentials
See the general works on price theory mentioned above, especially J. S. Bain, *Industrial Organization*. On price differentials and the basing-point system respectively, U. W. Ellinghaus, *Die Grundlagen der Theorie der Preisdifferenzierung* (Tübingen 1964) and F. Machlup, *The Basing-Point System* (Philadelphia 1949).

The example by T. Scitovsky is drawn from his *Welfare and Competition: The Economics of a Fully Employed Economy* (Homewood, Ill. 1951). The quotations from G. H. Bousquet are drawn from his work *Institutes de science économique*, Part 3: *La production et son marché* (Paris 1936).

j. Resale price maintenance
S. Gammelgaard, *Resale Price Maintenance* (OEEC, Paris 1958), sets out the relevant law in the OEEC countries, the United States and Canada, discusses the causes and consequences of r.p.m. and concludes that prices imposed by industry have adverse effects.

P. W. S. Andrews and F. A. Friday, *Fair Trade: Resale Price Maintenance Re-examined* (London 1960), defend resale price maintenance; *Resale Price Maintenance* (ed. B. S. Yamey, London 1966), gives an introduction to r.p.m. studies on Canada, the United States, Sweden, Denmark, the *EEC*, Ireland and the United Kingdom.

k. Commodity agreements
M. A. G. van Meerhaeghe, *International Economic Institutions* (2nd ed., London 1971), Chapter 4 and bibliography.

l. The effects of market structure and conduct on market performance
Especially for the United States: J. S. Bain, *Industrial Organization*; L. W. Weiss, *Case Studies in American Industry* (New York 1967); more concise, R. E. Caves, *American Industry: Structure, Conduct, Performance* (Englewood Cliffs, NJ 1964).

m. Prices in communist countries
USSR: M. Ellman, *Economic Reform in the Soviet Union* (London 1969), on recent reform.

Czechoslovakia: G. R. Feiwel, 'The Era of Economic Reforms of Socialist Planning', *EI*, February 1969.

Hungary: 'First Experiences Gained in the Implementation of the Economic Reform in Hungary', *Acta Oeconomica* (Hungarian Academy of Sciences), 1969, No. 1; B. Csikos-Nagy 'The Monetary Framework of a Socialist Economy', *New Hungarian Quarterly,* 1969, No. 33.

For all East European countries: the annual *Economic Survey of Europe 19–* (of which the most recent, with subtitle 'The European Economy in 1968', New York 1969).

8 Incomes

The present state of the theory of income distribution is generally considered unsatisfactory, and it is rightly so considered.
W. Fellner and B. F. Haley

This chapter deals with the distribution of national income. The general introduction is followed by an analysis of wages and interest. Economic rent and profit are also briefly dealt with. The conclusion consists in a brief discussion of the principles of the marginal theory of distribution.

1 Distribution of income

The revenue from the sale of goods produced is used by the entrepreneur to pay for the factors which have contributed to production. This primary distribution of national income (which is related to the respective contributions to the national product) is concurrent with the production process. After collection of taxes and allowance for transfer payments or the deliberate redistribution of income by the authorities, a secondary distribution takes place. This distribution is studied from the personal and functional points of view.

a. Personal distribution

Personal distribution refers to the distribution of national income to different persons without reference to the source of the income; the same person may receive both a salary and a return on capital. The more even this distribution, the closer the Lorenz curve will be to the diagonal (see Figure 36).

In 1962, 5 per cent of the households in the United States (counting from those with the largest incomes, after tax) received 19·6 per cent of the total personal incomes (in 1929, 30 per cent), and 20 per cent received 44 per cent (54·4 per cent in 1929). The distribution of after-tax income in the United States, then, is less even than in Britain, where, in 1957, 5 per cent received 14 per cent (as against 24 per cent

265

in 1938) and 20 per cent received 38 per cent of the income (46 per cent in 1938). This may be explained in part by the large number of farmers and unskilled workers in the United States and by a better system of social security in Britain (in the distribution of wealth the situation is reversed: more Americans are owners of their houses). The tendency towards levelling has become apparent since World War I: it would appear even more strongly if the increase in free social services were to be taken into account (e.g. education).

Distribution in the USSR is the 'great enigma' (H. F. Lydall). No data have been published since 1934. On the basis of several postwar publications, H. F. Lydall concludes, '. . . we may guess that the dispersion of all employee incomes in the Soviet Union is . . . less – on a pre-tax basis – than in the United States or most of Western Europe; but the dispersion of manual workers' earnings may well be greater than in Western Europe.'

Statistics on personal distribution are generally scarce and not too reliable.

b. *Functional distribution*

Functional distribution is based on the compensation received by individuals according to the function they fulfil in the production process (wages for the workers, interest for the owner of capital). Functional and personal incomes coincide if an income is provided by only *one* function. Functional distribution may be reviewed both in its individual and its collective aspects.

The following sections of this chapter are devoted principally to the analysis of individual incomes (wages and interest).

The collective aspect of functional distribution, then, is the proportional division of national income over the various categories of functional income: aggregate wages, interest, rent and profits for a fixed period.

In the United States the share of wages in national income rose from an 1899–1908 average of 54 per cent to 69 per cent in 1954–60, and in Britain from 47 per cent in 1860–9 to 70 per cent in 1954–60. In 1967 the share of wages in national income in the EEC countries was fairly uniform: West Germany 67 per cent, Netherlands and Luxembourg 66 per cent, Belgium 64 per cent, France 62 per cent and Italy 59 per cent.

Fluctuations in aggregate wages may be explained partly by changes in the importance of the different sectors (aggregate wages are higher in administration than in industry, and higher in industry than in agriculture) and partly also by the organization of society (especially the influence of trade unions and government). J. Pen finds the explanation more particularly in the relation between money wages and prices (in other words, real wages) and labour productivity:

$$\frac{\text{aggregate wages}}{\text{national income}} = \frac{\text{wage} \times \text{employment}}{\text{price} \times \text{production}} = \frac{\text{wage}}{\text{price}} \times \frac{1}{\text{production}/\text{employment}}$$

$$= \frac{\text{real wage}}{\text{labour productivity}}.$$

It can similarly be claimed that the share of capital in the national income should be determined by the relation of real interest to capital productivity.

In order to maintain the share of labour in the national income, real wages would have to keep pace with labour productivity. The movement of this share is not quite a measure of the welfare of the population group concerned since the number of earners may vary and the hours worked may change. It is further supposed that the 'price' derived from national income agrees with the 'price' in which the consumer is interested. This is in fact not the case, since the national income 'price' refers also to the prices of goods for export, capital goods and public services. Finally, it is accepted that no influence is exerted by export and import prices (or their mutual relationship – the terms of trade; see Chapter 11.2). Whenever, for example, a cut in import prices is not fully reflected in the price to the consumer, profits rise and the distribution of national income is affected. J. Pen then concludes: 'In open economies the effect of changes in the terms of trade on the prices and incomes structure is, next to the relation between real wages and labour productivity, the most important factor controlling distribution'. In this connection we should recall the reservation formulated in the use of the concept of productivity (a rise in labour productivity is not necessarily explained in terms of the labour factor; the increase is in many cases due only to new machinery).

In a number of countries after World War II it was asserted that the share of wages in the national income was remaining fairly stable. It was frequently claimed in explanation that with every drop in this share the trade unions would increase their activity.

Some authors, such as N. Kaldor and M. Kalecki, rely in part on the degree of monopoly power to explain the relation between aggregate wages and profits. Apart from the fact that there are many factors influencing this relation, the degree of monopoly (e.g. the power of the unions) cannot be measured.

2 Wages

A wage is the price of labour services.

Only real wage is important, although the wage earner may be influenced by the 'money illusion' (the assumption of constant purchasing power of the money unit) of his money wage. As a measure of standard of living real wages must give way to real income, which will include, for example, family allowances. It is also necessary to make a distinction between net and gross income and wages, according to whether or not taxation is taken into account. Finally, the average wage of a country, industry or firm is worked out by dividing the aggregate wages by the number of workers.

The workers may be divided into numerous non-competing groups. Skilled and unskilled workers, for example, do not compete with each other. For the first group, a division by industry is necessary (only certain trades such as joiners and electricians can find employment in all industries without retraining).

Wages in the past were very low and fluctuated around the bare subsistence level. While the employers were easily able to reach agreement, the employees were individually isolated: in France the Le Chapelier Enactment of 1791 had prohibited the formation of unions and was only repealed after more than seventy years (France 1864, Belgium 1866, and the Netherlands in 1872). The North German Confederation legalized unions in 1869. In the United Kingdom the ban on unions lasted for twenty-five years up to 1825 under the Combination Acts of 1799 and 1800. Strikes were long considered an offence.

The development of trade unions introduced a basic change in the situation. The point was stressed that a worker's wage is not a *price* but an income on which his livelihood depends. It is clear that labour, even from a theoretical viewpoint, cannot be regarded as a commodity: for one thing, it cannot be stored (if work stops, the lost working time can never be made up 'from stock'), and production costs for labour (food, clothing etc.) are not taken into account.

a. Demand

Demand has a characteristic derivative nature here in that it arises not directly from the consumer but from the entrepreneur. Demand for a factor reflects not only the circumstances of production and the supply of the other factors but also the demand for the commodity in the production of which that factor is required. In the short run the elasticity of the demand for labour is determined by the possibility of change in the factor combination and is consequently slight.

Although for the worker his wage is primarily an income, for the employer it continues to retain the character of a price. Furthermore, the wage level almost always differs according to employee and employer, since for the latter social charges form part of wages (78 per cent in Italy, 51 per cent in France, 48 per cent in Belgium, 40 per cent in the Netherlands, 32 per cent in West Germany, approximately 20 per cent in the USA, and 9 per cent in the United Kingdom).

b. Supply

The quantity of labour individually supplied increases normally as the wage rises, up to a given point at which leisure time is valued more than a higher income. One is then presented with a backward-sloping supply curve.

The aggregate supply is governed by the individual supply schedules (the number of workers and hours worked, the quality of the work carried out). Here again an increase in wages can produce a greater quantity supplied until a certain income is reached, at which point a decrease in supply may also occur (though not necessarily, since new workers may appear, particularly women). The same uncertainty applies with respect to a cut in wages (however unlikely): if a decrease in the quantity supplied appears normal, an income effect usually comes into play (in so far as a greater quantity of labour can be supplied).

With reference not to the aggregate labour supply of a country, but to the supply per industry or per firm, one would expect at first glance that the wage fluctuations could have greater repercussions. If in a certain industry there is no unemployment, a firm can tempt workers away from competing firms by means of higher wages so long as counter-measures are excluded. In judging the elasticity of supply in an industry or in a firm, the degree of (un)employment is therefore of importance. The possibility of drawing labour away from a different industry is usually slight owing to lack of the required skills. The

269

nature of the work may also have repercussions on the elasticity of supply (e.g. in mining).

In developed countries the concept of supply loses its meaning – quite apart from our criticism of supply and demand in general – since the quantity supplied is determined by institutional circumstances. Maximum hours of work are fixed by government, partly as a result of trade union activity, and overtime is permitted only under certain conditions. On the other hand, absenteeism is quite possible. The aggregate supply in a country is thus relatively inelastic. Wage increases that endanger the competitive position of a country that is to a large extent dependent on foreign connections can, however, disadvantageously affect employment (see below).

Fluctuations in the wage level usually have little repercussion on the distribution of the labour supply over the different industries, since a change in the wages structure generally does prompt reactions. Non-financial motives are more important.

c. *The labour market*

Today's labour market usually evidences a bilateral monopolistic character in which one or more trade unions negotiate with one or more employers' associations to fix uniform wages in each industry. To determine in advance what wages will result is not possible, since this depends on strength of character, the competence of the negotiators, public opinion and the entrepreneur's fear of a substitute product gaining ground in the event of a strike.

Social, political and psychological factors are becoming as important as purely economic considerations. The growth of production per employee, the cost of living and profits are, however, taken into account; the wages in key industries and the competitiveness of the economy (degree of dependence on foreign trade) also exert an influence. When negotiations between employees and employers prove fruitless, the government is often compelled to play the role of arbitrator.

Partly owing to the activity of the unions, the wage level has generally experienced a sharp rise. Without government intervention, however, wages remain low when a continual supply of new workers is available (for example through immigration) and when non-union workers are prepared to work for a lower wage.

In the USSR wages are set by the central government, but market relationships (scarcity of some sorts of worker) result in government directives often being bypassed in the industries themselves. With a view to increasing production, industry was empowered, from the beginning of 1966, to devote a proportion of profits (cf. Chapter 5.1c) to increasing wages. In the factories 'socialist rivalry' is organized (Stakhanovism) and the 'winners' are rewarded.

Only since 1956 has it been possible to change jobs (on condition that the new work is started less than a month after leaving the old), and since then there has been a greater tendency towards labour mobility. The place of work of university graduates may be fixed by the government for a period of three or four years and members of the communist party may equally be obliged, on pain of expulsion, to work wherever the government may choose.

Wages and unemployment

Several authors are of the opinion that a relation exists between wages and unemployment, J. Rueff believes that when wages rise more than wholesale prices, this will lead to an increase in unemployment because the competitive position worsens and exports fall off (which is possible for a country greatly dependent on foreign connections). On the other hand, A. W. Phillips traces the influence of unemployment on wages; according to him, there exists (as in the United Kingdom from 1861 to 1957) a relation between the level and the percentage change of unemployment and the percentage change in wages (except in or shortly after the years in which important prices experience a sharp rise). Thus, for example, an unemployment level of 5·5 per cent would be necessary to prohibit an increase in wages (and consequently higher prices), and a 2 per cent unemployment would cause wages to rise by 2 per cent per year (which would not increase prices if productivity were also to increase at a rate of 2 per cent). A. W. Phillips' research methods and conclusions are, however, open to criticism. Unemployment is not a determining factor of the wage level in the industrialized countries, though it does influence negotiations between employers and employees. The negotiating power of the unions is indeed stronger in times of full employment.

In a tight labour market wage drift arises, the difference between agreed rates and actual earnings. Wage drift is in part the result of bypassing decisions reached by collective bargaining (and ratified by government) by such means as additional bonuses and changes in the various qualification requirements which amount to concealed wage rises. This primary wage drift is to be distinguished from the secondary

271

drift which attempts to restore the wage differences existing before the primary drift (at a higher level).

3 Trade unions

The trade unions have as their primary purpose the defence of their members' interests. They strive in particular for the highest possible wage and are firmly opposed to any drop in income. Through associated political parties they also aim at the improvement of social legislation (e.g. maximum working hours and paid holidays). It is sometimes claimed that they should also check 'exploitation'. According to some, this arises when the wage is less than the marginal revenue of labour; according to others when the wage is smaller than that required to enjoy a certain minimum standard of living. In both cases it is very difficult to determine the degree of 'exploitation'.

In order to keep or to consolidate their position, the unions have sometimes declared against technological advance (in the USA, unions opposed painting by spray-gun) and even (in the USA and Britain) against the abolition of obsolete functions (firemen on diesel locomotives). They often succeed in preventing the import of cheaper goods.

Negotiations with employers are now carried on according to a regular procedure. The threat of strike action does arise in discussions but is seldom put into effect. With this end in view, however, the union must dispose of considerable cash reserves. Strikes in key industries can cause grave damage to the economy, so governments endeavour to prevent them. In the United States a strike can be postponed for 80 days whenever 'national health or safety' is in danger. In order to avoid corruption there has been an obligation on unions since 1959 to make public their financial position, and union representatives may receive no payment in kind from employers.

For reasons of negotiating strength the unions try to achieve a monopoly position and to represent the great majority of the workers. From this follows the emphasis on 'closed shops' in which no one may take up work if he is not already a member of the union and intends to remain one. In the 'union shop' prior membership of the union is not required, but workers must undertake to join within one or two months of starting work in the firm. These two systems occur in about 75 per cent of American factories; in Western Europe they are exceptions.

Generally speaking, at most half of the wage and salary earners of developed countries are members of a union (in Sweden 95 per cent, Belgium 65 per cent, a third in West Germany and the Netherlands, a quarter in the United States, and a fifth in France and Italy).

In the USA the oldest union federation (1881) is the American Federation of Labour (AFL). Because of legal impediments unions have only been able to develop since 1935, when the Congress of Industrial Organizations (CIO) was also founded. In 1955 the AFL and the CIO merged (together they include some 12 million members). In the United Kingdom there are about 8 million members affiliated to the Trades Union Congress (TUC). The most important union federations of the other West European countries are listed below.

Belgium:	Confédération des Syndicats Chrétiens – CSC (0·9 million members);
	Fédération Générale du Travail de Belgique – FGTB (0·8 million members);
France:	Confédération Générale du Travail – CGT (1·7 million members);
	Confédération Générale du Travail – Force Ouvrière – CGT-FO (1 million members);
	Confédération Française Démocratique du Travail – CFDT (0·7 million members);
Germany (West):	Deutscher Gewerkschaftsbund – DGB (6·5 million members);
Italy:	Confederazione Italiana Sindacati Lavoratori – CISL (2·1 million members);
	Unione Italiana del Lavoro – UIL (0·8 million members);
Netherlands:	Nederlands Verbond van Vakverenigingen – NVV (0·6 million members);
	Nederlands Katholiek Vakverbond – NKV (0·4 million members).

In the USSR the unions have only an advisory function, and striking is forbidden. They do, however, administer social funds: the advantages are greater for members than for non-members.

In 1902 an International Confederation of Trade Unions (ICTU) was established. In 1950 it split into the communist World Federation of Trade Unions (WFTU) and the International Confederation of Free Trade Unions (ICFTU). In 1968 the International Federation of

273

Christian Trade Unions (IFCTU) changed its name to World Confederation of Labour (WCL).

On the employers' side it is most of the time only the groups of industrialists that are strongly organized, such as the American National Association of Manufacturers and in Western Europe the Fédération des Industries Belges (Belgium), the Bundesverband der deutschen Industrie (West Germany: dealing with economic problems), the Bundesvereinigung der deutschen Arbeitgeberverbände (West Germany: dealing with social matters), the Conseil National du Patronat Français, the Confederation of British Industry, the Confederazione dell' Industria Italiana, the Nederlands Verbond van Ondernemingen (Netherlands).

4 Joint councils of workers' and employers' organizations

Alongside the above-mentioned aims, unions may pursue other, albeit closely associated, objectives. For instance, they attach much importance to the establishment of economic and social democracy – the possibility of participating in the direction of the national economy on an equal footing with employers. Moreover, governments themselves have in certain instances a vested interest in taking the advice of workers' and employers' organizations, the more so in that these have access to a number of means of influencing public opinion.

As early as 1925 the Conseil National Economique was set up in France, which developed in 1958 into the Conseil Economique et Social, with wider powers. The council must be consulted on draft legislation and on economic and social planning (but not on budgetary receipts and expenditures) and a member of the council may voice its views in parliament.

The Dutch Sociaal-Economische Raad (1958) must also be consulted by ministers elaborating any social or economic measure. This council possesses regulatory authority (e.g. executive decisions with respect to works councils). A third of it is made up of 'Crown members' – experts who are appointed by the Crown but are not responsible to the government for their activities in the council.

In Belgium two councils have been set up: the Conseil Central de l'Economie (1948; for economic problems), and the Conseil National du Travail (1952; social questions). Logically the two should be merged. Consultation of the councils is not obligatory, with the exception that in certain instances the Conseil National du Travail must be consulted.

In Italy a Consiglio Nazionale dell' Economia e del Lavoro was established at the beginning of 1957 and may be consulted by the government and parliament except on budgetary matters. The council may itself bring legislation before parliament via the prime minister.

In most countries the fixing of wages is left to the parties concerned, but approval by the government is generally required before collective agreements can be declared binding.

5 Wage differentials

Differences in wages may be partly explained by one or more of the following factors:

a. A difference in inherited aptitude or environment.

b. The nature of the work (it is only by higher wages that labour is attracted to dangerous or difficult work; for regular and secure employment a smaller remuneration is sufficient); even in the USSR a prominent wage difference has had to be introduced; this difference was even higher than in most western countries in the mid-1950s. Presently the wage and salary structure is very similar in communist and western countries, although 'successful managers and professional people in large firms, and persons with special skills in temporarily short supply earn relatively more in capitalist ... countries' (J. Wilczynski).

c. The length of training (without the prospect of higher wages a worker will not attend training courses).

d. Age (professional skill may increase or decrease with age).

A preparedness to perform equal work for less pay is sometimes encountered if the future prospects are good, and one trade has more prestige value than another (white-collar as against blue-collar jobs).

Even so, it is difficult always to find an explanation of wage differences. In the same groups and in the same places differences are found (between men's and women's wages). Account must be taken of the varying power of different unions, which is itself associated with the varying profit position of different industries or firms. Thus in the same industries the wages often vary depending on the district. Usually, the higher the concentration of production, the better the wages are in the industries concerned. In other words, wage differentiation (different wages for the same work) often occurs. Demographic pressure also influences this common phenomenon.

Since the unions usually have easy success in rapidly growing industries (e.g. petroleum), the main need for them is in the backward industries, although in many countries it is precisely here that they have less influence.

Job classification is an attempt to fix a firm's wage structure on the basis of certain criteria. The various functions in a firm are investigated from a number of different viewpoints (the required degree of knowledge, skill, independence etc.), and each assessment is given a figure adjusted by a (not easily determined) weight. Difficulties arise, however, when the final figures have to be converted into wages.

Usually there exist a number of functions in the same industry that are paid the same (the key rates); in relation to these wages a whole series of others are determined (job clusters or groups of job classifications).

In spite of the attempts that have been made to determine the optimal wage differences scientifically, the wages structure is still governed not only by the scarcity of labour but also by habit and tradition. What A. Ross says of the United States – 'The "national wage structure" seems to consist of little islands of rationality in a sea of anarchy' – is equally valid for other countries.

6 Interest

Interest is the price paid for the use of assets made available by other economic units for periods of varying length (cf. lucrative capital).

Whenever a given sum is put at the disposal of firms (to procure social capital), households (consumer credit) or government (national debt), a return is expected: this is the interest expressed as a percentage of the funds loaned. If no interest were forthcoming, the owner would prefer to buy capital goods himself or to devote the sum to consumption or to hold it over against unforeseen circumstances. Interest is therefore also to be regarded as the price of giving up liquidity preference – at least where money and not goods is made available. It is frequently overlooked that all assets, including capital goods, can yield interest. If 100 lb of grain currently available is equivalent to

108 lb in a year's time, then the interest, expressed in grain, is (108 — 100) ÷ 100 = 8 per cent (this is called 'own interest' since it is given in terms of the asset itself). In order to avoid waste, capital and land are no longer considered free resources in the USSR since the 1960s (cf. Chapter 5, 1c).

The following discussion is mainly concerned with money interest. It may be kept relatively brief since important and indispensable points in the analysis of interest, such as the investment decision, the motives for holding cash balances and the credit market, have already been dealt with (see also Chapter 13.4a).

a. The demand for loanable funds

Borrowers will be prepared to pay interest when it can be offset by advantages accruing to the use or disposal of the borrowed assets. These assets can of course consist of either goods or money, but the demand is almost entirely for loanable funds. The demand for money can operate:

1. In order to satisfy a liquidity preference (Chapter 3.1; see also Chapter 9.13): this is important when a rise in interest is expected (the speculative motive);

2. In order to invest in securities; the presumed returns are important. This involves many possibilities, and the question which assets are to be preferred (asset preference) is not easily answered, partly because future returns are difficult to estimate. Considerations in connection with the spreading of risk and the fixity of value (avoidance of the consequences of inflation) are also relevant. Because of the difficulty of finding precise criteria, F. H. Hahn's statement is not surprising: 'It might well be argued that in situations in which rational behaviour is so difficult individuals will adopt rules of thumb';

3. In order to invest in capital goods and stocks (Chapter 6.2); demand is dependent on the internal rate of return and even more on the desired stock of capital goods. As has already been pointed out, the influence of interest on investment is slight. Thus the demand for investment purposes may rise in spite of a rise in interest if the profit expectations rise even faster. Similarly, demand may decrease notwithstanding a cut in interest;

4. In order to consume more than current income permits, consequently revealing a time preference.

L

b. The supply of loanable funds

Suppliers require an interest in order to overcome their time and/or liquidity preferences. Here again both money capital and, less frequently, goods are made available.

The supply of loanable funds finds its origin in newly formed or dishoarded savings from households or firms, and in the creation of money (e.g. extension of credit). The liquidation of assets is a form of demand for money.

As regards the influence of interest on savings, a distinction must be made between the substitution and the income effects. If interest rises, savings can increase by the encouragement of the replacement of present by future wants (substitution effect), but there is also the possibility of a decrease in savings because higher returns on invested capital in the future admit a better satisfaction of needs (income effect). The same effects appear in a lowering of interest, and it is not possible to say in advance which of them is the greater.

The consequences of fluctuations in interest are very small in respect of low and high income. In the first case the returns are in any event of little importance and in the second case savings take on a residual character, regardless of the interest rate. With respect to the middle incomes there is normally a fixed proportion saved from income, and this habit is also little influenced by changes in interest. Other considerations are sometimes weightier, such as stability in the value of the assets formed.

c. The market for loanable funds

The classical authors explained the interest level in terms of saving and investment. It was later pointed out that hoarding (influenced by liquidity preference) and the additional supply of money (understood as independent of interest, which is not necessarily the case) must also be taken into account. The interest would then be determined by $I + H^*$ (investment and hoarding) on the side of demand, and by $S + M^*$ (saving and the additional money supply) on the supply side (Figure 52). This explanation is valid only in the long run and in the absence of monopolistic tendencies and government intervention. Since in the market for loanable funds there is no question of pure competition, it is not possible to determine the interest level by means of the supply and demand curves (which imply pure competition).

Just as in the labour market, various submarkets appear; in fact there is no such thing as *the* interest rate. For simplicity's sake only the general condition of the money market and the capital market are considered here, although it would be possible to distinguish a number of submarkets for each.

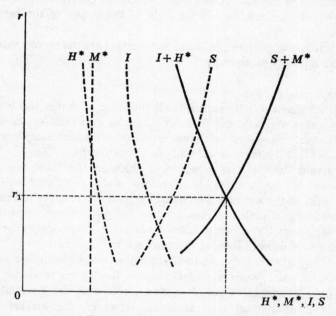

Figure 52: Determination of interest

1. *The money market*

Although more funds are traded on the capital market, from the economic viewpoint the money market is more important; '... it constitutes the first stage in the process of capital formation. The manner in which the funds will be appropriated remains uncertain for some time, and it is on how they are used that the economic situation will be largely dependent...' and again '... according to the volume of the funds which can be invested at a given moment, the money market is undoubtedly more important. The funds administered by the capital market are more considerable, but locked up to a large extent and thus assigned a passive role' (F. Baudhuin).

Interest is normally lower than in the capital market because the relevant period is shorter and the corresponding risk less. The banks are the major suppliers.

279

The central banks play a dominant role on the money market; they exert influence through discount policy and even more by their other directives (Chapter 13.4). They deal in fact with a limited number of participants in the market (the banks and some government bodies), who determine their rates in the light of the policy of the central banks.

Of primary importance in the money market are the money supply and the liquidity preference.

2. *The capital market*

The government usually superintends the issue of shares and bonds (the primary market), and in most countries also exercises control over fluctuations in stock-exchange quotations (the secondary market or the market for securities already in circulation).

In recent decades the government share in the total quantity demanded has become steadily larger; this is also associated with the relative fall of the amounts demanded by firms as a result of increased self-financing. If cash holdings are low the government demand is often inelastic with respect to interest variations (the reserves needed in order to wait until interest rates fall are non-existent).

With regard to supply, the institutional investors (insurance companies and government agencies' pension funds) are becoming increasingly important. They often deal direct with the government without using market intermediaries. However, the market still influences these transactions.

Just as the quantity of money and liquidity preference are the most decisive elements in the money market, so are saving and investment in the capital market. Though interest appears to have little influence either on saving or on investment, a greater repercussion on the level of interest may be attributed to saving and investment. As has been mentioned previously, the classical school in fact explained the level of interest only in terms of saving and investment. J. M. Keynes was later to indicate the importance of liquidity preference. This, however, is primarily of importance in the money market.

Both in the money and in the capital market the influence of international conditions has increasingly been felt. The liberalization of international capital movements (cf. also the Eurodollar market: Chapter 12.1c) has given rise to vast capital flows, partly induced by differences in interest rates.

3. *The structure of interest*

Although the whole range of interest rates usually move in the same direction, this is not necessarily the case; neither do they rise or fall in the same proportion: 'The rates vary in absolute spread, in relative spread, in direction of movement, and in the degree of movement' (E. Marcus). The business cycle has an effect: in a recession, for example, (see Chapter 9) the spread is greater than during a boom and the interest on the money market can even exceed that on the capital market.

The interest structure itself is not very clear: even the specialist first has to make all sorts of calculations in order to find the actual interest rates. Divergent conditions (e.g. in the case of issue or redemption of bonds), or deliberate misrepresentation (e.g. with reference to consumer credit or personal loans) mean that only the specialist is able to assess opportunities for investing in securities with real knowledge of the facts. A report by the Organization for Economic Cooperation and Development rightly concludes: 'In the present state of affairs, the "market process" in many countries is basically distorted by the fact that the majority concerned are unable to ascertain the real rate.'

International comparison of interest rates is equally difficult since the degree of liquidity and, particularly, taxation vary from one country to another. The higher interest on bonds in continental Europe may, for example, be explained by the fact that the banks there sell directly to the individual through a chain of branches; in the United States and Britain, on the other hand, the issues are placed chiefly in the hands of the institutional investors; there are in fact no direct sales to households. If this is taken into account, it is questionable whether there is a great difference in the level of interest.

4. *Conclusion*

It will be apparent from the foregoing sections (see also Chapter 13.4*a* for a summary of the consequences of interest-rate changes) that general statements on interest are very difficult. These sections explain also why it has, with a certain exaggeration, been said that '... the rate of interest can be forgotten, at least in aggregative analysis' (R. Turvey). G. L. S. Shackle concluded a survey of the theories of interest in like vein: 'It seems likely that the interest rate, or the system of rates, will continue to receive from theoreticians the homage due to a ceremonial monarch, without in fact counting for more than such a monarch in the real affairs of western nations.'

At the moment, international capital movements cause the market for loanable funds to be less inflexible than the labour market. These movements often make it impossible for the governments of western countries to make use of certain instruments of monetary policy: the freedom of capital movements hampers the efficacy of these measures. That general pronouncements in connection with interest are extremely difficult is a point that also holds good for these international capital movements. Capital exports to Switzerland, for example, are explained not by a higher rate of interest but by greater confidence in the Swiss currency.

The theory of interest remains one of the most difficult and debatable areas of economic science: 'the theory of interest has for a long time been a weak spot in the science of economics, and the explanation and determination of the interest rate still gives rise to more disagreement among economists than any other branch of general economic theory' (G. Haberler).

7 The relation between saving and investment

Saving and investment have been mentioned repeatedly in the above sections. Because of the terminological confusion which has arisen around these concepts, it is desirable to discuss further their relation to each other.

There is frequent mention of a difference between saving and investment, but they are in fact always (*ex post*) identical with each other.

The effect of an increase in investment in a state of equilibrium may be taken as a starting point. The national income is then increased by the same amount. If this amount is not spent, it represents saving (also if it is deposited in banks or savings institutions). If the additional income is in fact spent, three cases may be distinguished:

a. the consumer goods purchased are provided from stocks: dissaving is compensated by an equal amount of disinvestment;

b. the prices of consumer goods rise and thus also profits: dissaving is matched by an equal rise in entrepreneurs' saving;

c. the additional demand leads to an increase in production: dissaving is coupled with equal saving since the national income increases through the rise in production.

In the case of increased saving, it can be shown by the same reasoning that investment and saving must always be equal:

a. the stocks of consumer goods increase: saving is compensated by an equal amount of investment;

b. the prices of consumer goods decrease: this leads to dissaving by entrepreneurs;

c. production decreases, which causes a drop in the national income. If the consumption level is maintained, dissaving equal to the original saving occurs.

In the first hypothesis, the increase in investment appears to go together with either an unforeseen fall in stocks or an unexpected rise in saving. In the second supposition, the increase in saving is followed by an unexpected rise in stocks or an unforeseen fall in saving.

The disturbance of equilibrium is thus coupled with an unexpected change in saving or investment (passive instead of active saving and investment). An inequality is valid only for the projected (*ex ante*) saving and investment.

8 Economic rent and profit

a. Economic rent

By rent is understood the difference between the actual price of a factor and the price with which the seller would be satisfied (the minimum supply price).

When supply is constant and cannot therefore be increased, a rise in demand leads, under pure competition, only to a rise in price and an enrichment of the current owners by the creation of economic rent (Figure 53). In the case of a monopoly, the entrepreneur sets prices in consideration of the (estimated) elasticity of demand (Chapter 7.5).

The term quasi-rent is used when the supply, although not absolutely fixed, can still be increased only after a relatively long period (e.g. specialized workers, coffee). A quasi-rent also arises from industrial advance (since the other entrepreneurs are unable immediately to put a more advantageous production method into operation). There is no essential difference between this and economic rent proper. The period during which economic rent can be received is dependent on the elasticity of supply. The market circumstances (competition, monopoly) are again of importance here.

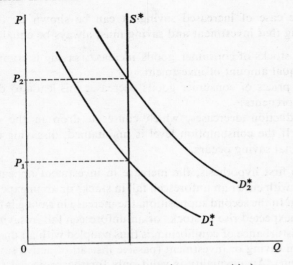

Figure 53: Economic rent (pure competition)

b. Profit

By the entrepreneur's profit is understood the (positive) difference between revenue and costs for a given period. If costs are greater than revenue, the result is a loss. Costs (cf. Chapter 5.7) consist of:

1. The entrepreneur's remuneration, or the normal payment to the entrepreneur as a manager;
2. The normal return on capital belonging to the entrepreneur;
3. Premiums covering risks that can be insured against;
4. Depreciation;
5. All other expenditure devoted to production (interest, wages, raw materials).

Contrary to what is customary in economic theory, in accounting practice the two first cost items are not taken into account in calculating the firm's profit. In economic theory profit is therefore sometimes referred to as surplus or excess profit.

Profits are derived from:

1. A monopoly position (monopoly profits);
2. Speculation (speculative profits);
3. Cyclical conditions (cyclical profits);

4. Personal achievement on the part of the entrepreneur. A new combination of factors can reduce costs and lead to an advance over other firms. The entrepreneur's profit proper, the result of his initiative and success in keeping costs as low as possible, is transitory, since others will adopt the new form of organization (provided there are no such barriers as business secrets or patents; monopoly profits).

The profits that appear in the official or published annual accounts of limited companies often do not tally with their actual profits. In the official accounts, for example, secret (or hidden) reserves are often included (stocks and buildings valued too cheaply).

In the USSR profits are naturally not attributable to all the above elements (e.g. speculative and cyclical profits would not occur).

9 Distribution according to marginal theory

Since the customary theory of distribution is still to a large extent influenced by marginal theory, it is appropriate to deal with it here. According to this theory, the first principle underlying demand for factors of production is that the marginal products created by the factors should be in proportion to the sums paid for them. In the demand for a given factor, therefore, the price of the other factors must be taken into account if an optimal combination of factors is to be realized. If, for example, the price of capital rises, the demand for labour can increase to the extent of the possible substitution of capital by labour (substitution effect). Since capital goods cannot be completely excluded, costs and prices will rise, so that a cut in production and in the demand for labour is not impossible (production effect).

Further, marginal costs are always compared with marginal revenue. As long as the marginal revenue yielded by the marginal production is greater than the marginal cost, it is advantageous, say, to introduce an infinitesimal quantity of capital. The marginal revenue depends on the output potential of the additional products (derived demand) or, in other words, on market structure. The marginal costs also vary according to the degree of competition. In the labour market, for example, under pure competition the marginal cost is the factor price. Under impure competition the demand of the firm exercises an influence on the factor price and the marginal costs are usually greater: if a higher wage is necessary to attract more workers, this must also be paid to the workers already employed.

Borrowed capital may be used for various purposes. Care is taken in any case that marginal cost should not exceed marginal revenue, while the various marginal revenues are compared with each other.

The unreal nature of the marginal theory has already been indicated, (Chapter 7.7). Marginal costs and revenue are here likewise very difficult to calculate. This is also the case whenever the productivity of labour and capital goods must be compared. Labour productivity is moreover linked to the nature of the capital goods at its disposal. Thus, the productivity of a worker may be low because he is employed in a labour-intensive industry. The elaboration of the marginal theory of distribution is very weak as regards supply (labour is supplied until the increasing reluctance to work becomes greater than the decreasing marginal utility of the wage; the possibility of a steady satisfaction in work itself is lost sight of).

The classical theory of distribution rested on the contributions to production of the three factors. The entrepreneur was later regarded as a separate factor apart from the factor 'capital', and eventually four factors of production were distinguished – land (rent), labour (wages), capital (interest), and entrepreneurship (profits). This division remained the basis for later models. A. Marshall, however, emphasized that the characteristics of the production factor 'land' did not necessitate separate analysis of its remuneration since not only the supply of land but also the supply of other factors can remain constant. Rent is a general phenomenon attributable to scarcity and appearing whenever supply is not, or is only slightly, elastic. But an analogous remark is valid for interest: whenever anyone devotes money to his own training, a part of his income later on can be regarded as interest.

From the definitions of rent and entrepreneurial profits, it appears that no essential difference exists between the two: they often coincide. Rent has, in fact, usually a more permanent character, and profits are not necessarily associated with a contribution to production; they can, for example, as already mentioned, be the result of speculation.

10 Bibliography

a. Distribution of income
Apart from the works on price theory in general: G. J. Stigler, *Production and Distribution Theories: The Formative Period* (New York

1941): a historical analysis; *Readings in the Theory of Income Distribution* (ed. W. Fellner and B. F. Haley, Philadelphia 1946) with a classified bibliography by F. E. Norton, Jr; *The Theory of Interest Rates: Proceedings of a Conference held by the International Economic Association* (ed. F. H. Hahn and F. P. R. Brechling, London 1965).

N. Kaldor, 'Economic Growth and the Problem of Inflation', *Ec*, August and November 1959 (in some ways a summary of a series of papers by the same author published since 1955), completes Keynesian theory on distribution.

K. E. Boulding expounds a controversial theory in Chapter 14 of *A Reconstruction of Economics* (New York 1950; with new preface in the 1962 reprint): distribution depends on a set of distinct but mutually connected decisions concerning, *inter alia*, investment, consumption and liquidity. Thus, the analysis is not primarily determined by wage bargaining (except when it influences the decisions mentioned).

Kaldor's theory is considered by K. W. Rothschild, 'Themes and Variations: Remarks on the Kaldorian Distribution Formula', *Ky*, 1965, No. 4.

On the determination of aggregate wages see also J. Pen, *Harmony and Conflict in Modern Society* (London 1966); M. Kalecki, *Theory of Economic Dynamics* (London 1954), Chapter 2; S. Weintraub, *An Approach to the Theory of Income Distribution* (Philadelphia 1958); M. Reder, 'Alternative Theories of Labor's Share', in *The Allocation of Economic Resources: Essays in Honor of B. Haley* (ed. M. A. Abramovitz, Stanford 1959).

Actual data can be found in S. Kuznets, *Modern Economic Growth: Rate, Structure and Spread* (New Haven 1966), Chapter 4; *The Behavior of Income Shares: Selected Theoretical and Empirical Issues* (Princeton 1964) – a series of papers of a conference held in 1961; H. F. Lydall, *The Structure of Incomes* (London 1968).

On the United States: Volumes 13 and 15 of the *Studies in Income and Wealth* (New York 1951 and 1952); R. M. Solow, 'A Skeptical Note on the Constancy of Relative Shares', *AER*, September 1958; H. F. Lydall and J. B. Lansing, 'A Comparison of the Distribution of Personal Income and Wealth in the United States and Great Britain', *AER*, March 1959; S. F. Goldsmith, 'Size Distribution of Income and Wealth in the United States', in *Die Konzentration in der Wirtschaft* (ed. H. Arndt, Berlin 1960), Part 1.

b. Wages

R. Mossé, *Les salaires* (Paris 1952) – a brief and comprehensive introduction, in which the importance of political factors in wage determination is stressed (with annotated bibliographical list of 192 works); K. W. Rothschild, *The Theory of Wages* (Oxford 1954) – clear, but only few examples and little attention paid to non-economic factors.

J. Pen, *The Wage Rate under Collective Bargaining* (Cambridge, Mass. 1959), develops, on the basis of psychological factors, a theory according to which wages *are* determined in the case of bilateral monopoly (by which he means that the determining factors are indeed apparent, but not measurable).

See also: *The Theory of Wage Determination: Proceedings of a Conference held by the International Economic Association* (ed. J. T. Dunlop, London 1957).

The difficulties arising in comparing real incomes are dealt with from a theoretical point of view in *International Comparisons of Real Wages: A Methodological Study* (International Labour Office, Geneva 1956).

J. T. Dunlop, *Wage Determination under Trade Unions* (2nd ed., Oxford 1950), opposes the view according to which wage determination is solely a political and social matter (the aim of trade unions: maximize aggregate wages); A. Ross, *Trade Union Wages Policy* (Berkeley 1948), on the other hand, supports this opinion: he views a trade union in the first place as 'a political agency operating in an economic environment'.

L. G. Reynolds, *Labor Economics and Labor Relations* (4th ed., New York 1965) – based on American conditions. Unenthusiastic judgment of trade-union action.

H. J. Laski, *Trade Unions in the New Society* (London 1950) – four lectures, given in the United States. Considers the changed attitude of society and judicial authorities towards trade-unionism, points to the necessity of their action in political life.

A. Rees, *The Economics of Trade Unions* (Chicago 1962), and J. E. Maher, *Labor and the Economy* (Boston 1965), relate to the United States. See also *The Structure of Collective Bargaining* (ed. A. R. Weber, New York 1961). On bargaining procedures: J. Barbash, 'American Unionism: From Protest to Going Concern', *Journal of Economic Issues*, March 1968.

I. Deutscher, *Soviet Trade Unions: Their Place in Soviet Labour*

Policy (London 1950), especially for historical developments, which show that the role of the USSR trade unions cannot be compared with that prevailing in the western world; they are of secondary importance.

c. Wages and unemployment

On Rueff's law: J. Rueff, 'Les variations du chômage en Angleterre', *Revue Politique et Parlementaire*, December 1925; *id.*, 'L'assurance-chômage, cause de chômage permanent', *REP*, March–April 1931; *id.*, 'Nouvelle discussion sur le chômage, les salaires et les prix', *REP*, September–October 1951. For criticism: M. Parisiades, *Essai sur les relations entre le chômage, les salaires les prix et le profit: Etude critique de la loi de M. Rueff* (Paris 1949); P. Lambert, 'Chômage et niveau des salaires', in *Recueil de travaux du Centre Interfacultaire du Travail de l'Université de Liège* (Liège 1950).

On the Phillips curve: A. W. Phillips, 'The Relation between Unemployment and the Rate of Change of Money Wage Rates in the United Kingdom, 1861–1957', *Ec*, November 1958. Criticism can be found in B. Corry and D. Laidler, 'The Phillips Relation: A Theoretical Explanation', *Ec*, May 1967; J. K. Gifford, 'Critical Remarks on the Phillips Curve and the Phillips Hypothesis', *WA*, 1969, Vol. 102, Part 1.

Wages and Labour Mobility: A Study of the Relation between Changes in Wage Differentials and the Pattern of Employment (OECD, Paris 1965): only prudent and general conclusions are possible.

On wage drift: E. H. Phelps Brown, 'Wage Drift', *Ec*, November 1962.

d. Wage differences

Besides the works mentioned: L. R. Salkever, *Toward a Wage Structure Theory* (New York 1964); *Wage Structure in Theory and Practice* (ed. E. M. Hugh-Jones, Amsterdam 1966).

Internal Wage Structure (ed. J. L. Mey, Amsterdam 1963) – six papers on wage differences within the firm (including material on Soviet conditions and trade-union influence).

e. Interest

Apart from general works on price theory: F. A. Lutz, *The Theory of Interest* (Chicago 1968) – a translation from the second German language edition – and J. W. Conard, *Introduction to the Theory of*

Interest (Berkeley 1959), are (especially the former) principally comments on previous theories. See also R. Turvey, *Interest Rates and Asset Prices* (London 1960), and S. Homer, *A History of Interest Rates* (New Brunswick, N.J. 1963).

More difficult and very theoretical: D. Patinkin, *Money, Interest, Prices* (2nd ed., Evanston, Ill. 1965), also criticizes classical and Keynesian views; mathematical expositions are comprised in the annex (about one half of the book).

Source of the quotation: E. Marcus, 'The Interest-Rate Structure', *RES*, August 1948.

G. L. S. Shackle, 'Recent Theories Concerning the Nature and Role of Interest', *EJ*, June 1961 – a survey stressing the slight influence exerted by interest.

On the Wicksell effect (a higher rate of capitalization causes an increase in interest rates – which is in no way certain): I. M. D. Little, 'Classical Growth', *OEP*, June 1957, Appendix; J. Robinson, 'The Real Wicksell Effect', *EJ*, September 1958.

A general fall in prices causes a rise in the real value of assets (cf. the Pigou effect), as a result of which it becomes possible – there is no question of certainty – that more liquid funds are supplied, interest rates decline and thus investment increases. In such a case, we speak of the Keynes effect. See D. Patinkin, *Money, Interest, Prices*.

On government influence on the determination of interest rates: *Capital Markets Study: Structure of Interest Rates in Some OECD Countries* (OECD, Paris 1967) and *Capital Markets Study: General Report* (OECD, Paris 1967).

e. *Profit and rent*

The different meanings and theories of profit are considered by J. Weston, 'A Generalized Uncertainty Theory of Profit', *AER*, March 1950, and 'The Profit Concept and Theory: A Restatement', *JPE*, April 1954.

Standard books are F. H. Knight, *Risk, Uncertainty and Profit* (Boston 1921; reprints published in 1933, 1948 and 1957 with a new preface by the author), in which profits are explained by uncertainty, and J. A. Schumpeter, *The Theory of Economic Development: An Inquiry into Profits, Capital, Credit, Interest and the Business Cycle* (Cambridge, Mass. 1934) – translation of German ed. – in which they are explained by entrepreneurial innovation.

J. Marchal, 'The Construction of a New Theory of Profit', *AER*,

September 1951, thinks that the entrepreneur does not make any distinction between his remuneration as manager and the revenue resulting from the capital he owns: he is supposed to identify himself with the firm.

In addition to general works on income distribution, see on rent: K. E. Boulding, 'The Concept of Economic Surplus', *AER*, December 1945; Chapter 18 of A. P. Lerner, *The Economics of Control: Principles of Welfare Economics* (New York 1944).

9 Fluctuations in the level of national income and of prices

> *... all the other forces affecting the distribution of income – the rise of the labor movement, the development of agricultural policy, the tariff, even the progressive income tax itself, all taken together have not achieved half the revolution in distribution of both income and wealth that decades of successive inflation, deflation and inflation have achieved.*
>
> Kenneth E. Boulding

This chapter deals with the most important elements determining the level of national income and its fluctuations and affecting the general level of prices. As a first step, the concept of monetary equilibrium is explained as primarily dependent on the macroeconomic data – saving and investment. In this respect it is useful to examine the multiplier and the accelerator and the interaction of the one upon the other. Say's law of monetary equilibrium is considered at the beginning of the chapter. Four sections on the business cycle follow later.

After the connection between monetary equilibrium and the general price level has been shown, the classical (and more static) theory on the matter is discussed; the equation of exchange, the quantity theory and its most recent version are dealt with in that order.

1 Monetary equilibrium

The production of goods and services provides the production factors, as we have seen, with an income by means of which it is possible to buy those goods and services. The entrepreneurs dispense this income and receive expenditure, i.e. the total expenditures for consumption and investment.

There is monetary equilibrium when expenditure is equal to current income. If expenditure is greater than current income, the explanation is to be found in creation of money, dishoarding or sale of property

292

(e.g. securities). In the alternative situation (expenditure less than current income) the explanation lies in destruction of money, hoarding or the purchase of property (mainly securities). It may thus be seen that money itself has an important function in monetary equilibrium.

Since current income is equal to consumption plus saving $(C + S)$, and expenditure is equal to consumption plus investment $(C + I)$, there is monetary equilibrium whenever saving is equal to investment. If investment is greater than saving (aggregate demand greater than aggregate supply), a stimulating influence is exerted on the economy, while the opposite case has a braking effect. In the first situation, the entrepreneurs find it in their interest to expand production where possible (their income is greater than their expenditure) and in the second case to contain their activities. Naturally, what is meant here is planned saving and investment (Chapter 8.7). If the plans of firms and households are not in accordance, unforeseen disparities arise. Only in the case of self-financing can the same persons determine both saving and investment.

So far nothing has been said of the influence of the rest of the world and of government. Government spending is also expenditure, government receipts also income.

In a situation where exports are greater than imports, the difference is equated with investment; where imports are greater, the deficit is regarded as equivalent to a saving (Chapter 2.3c). The various items of importance for monetary equilibrium are expressed in the national product and expenditure account in Example 6. The condition for equilibrium is therefore:

$$C + I_\beta + E - M = Y + D + T_i - W$$
or
$$C + I_\beta + E - M = C + S_\alpha + D + T_i - W$$
or
$$I_\beta + E + W = S_\beta + M + T_i$$
or more generally
$$I + E + G_o = S + M + G_t.$$

a. Monetary equilibrium and equilibrium of expenditure

The income level given by saving and investment (assuming equilibrium in the balance of payments – Chapter 11.6 – and in the government budget) does not necessarily guarantee full employment. In the case of unemployment, total expenditure has to be raised in order to increase the demand for labour. The government must therefore stimulate either private consumption or investment – by adjusting monetary and tax policy, for instance, or increasing its own spending. The equilibrium between S and I or $C + S$ and $C + I$ then occurs at a higher level. We can then speak of an equilibrium of expenditure: there is enough spending to provide full employment. The prior situation is one of underexpenditure.

When, in the case of full employment, planned expenditure exceeds the national income (overexpenditure), this leads only to price increases.

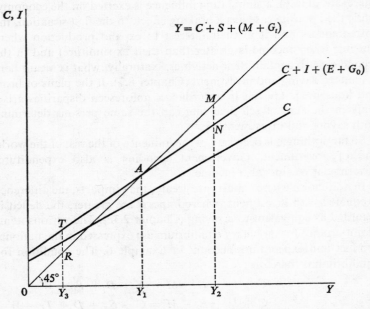

Figure 54: Determination of national income (A)

b. Graphical representation

It is customary to recapitulate the above explanation in a graph showing the consumption, investment and saving curves. The monetary equilibrium is then determined by the intersection of the $(C + I)$ curve with the 45° line (if government and foreign influences are disregarded). At point A (Figure 54) the national income (OY_1 or Y_1A) is equal to the sum of consumption and investment.

In the case of a higher national income (OY_2) firms' expected

294

receipts (expenditure) are less than their expected spending (income; $Y_2N < Y_2M$) and economic activity is restrained. In the case of a lower national income (OY_3), conversely, production is expanded ($Y_3T > Y_3R$). If consumption is subtracted from both data, the comparison is reduced to the investment and savings curves. This is also apparent in the following numerical example (Table 25), where the differential propensity to consume is taken as constant and where investment increases in each period by the same amount. In Figure 55, which reproduces mainly the data from Table 25, the point of equilibrium is indicated both at A and B. In the case of a national income of more or less than £75,000 million, $C + I$ is respectively smaller or greater than $C + S$. Thus, for example, FD (consumption, or the difference between the national income LD and saving LF) plus LG (investment) is less than the national income LD. The saving curve usually lies above the investment curve for higher incomes.

TABLE 25: Determination of national income (£'000m.)

National income	Planned consumption	Planned investment	Planned expenditure received back by firms	Planned expenditure of firms	Planned saving
Y	C	I	$C + I$	$C + S$	S
0	10	5	15	0	−10
60	46	17	63	60	14
65	49	18	67	65	16
70	52	19	71	70	18
75	55	20	75	75	20
80	58	21	79	80	22
85	61	22	83	85	24

If full employment accords only with the national income OL, expenditure is not high enough; what is known as a deflationary gap (the difference between actual expenditure and the expenditure required in order to create full employment) then appears (ED here). In order to reach OL, C or I or government spending G_o or exports E have to be increased. The new curve of total expenditure $C + I + G_o + E$ then intersects the 45° line at D.

When the planned expenditure $C_1 + I_1 + G_{o_1} + E_1$ exceeds the national income under full employment, there is an inflationary gap

DK – the difference between the production demanded and the actual production with full employment (money income is always expressed along the x axis of the graphs; in a stable price situation this corresponds to real income, in other situations a separate function is needed for the relation of real to money data).

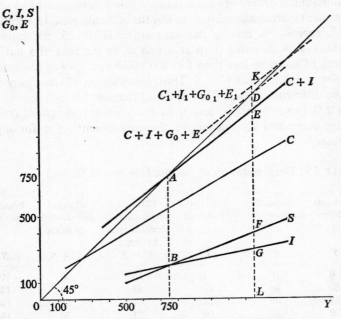

Figure 55: Determination of national income (B)

Appraisal

The difficulties involved in determining the consumption, savings and investment curves have already been indicated (Chapter 4.6*f*; Chapter 6.2*c*). The process implies *ex ante* data that are related to expectations and intentions and which are not statistically determinable. To attempt to explain monetary equilibrium (and the level of national income) on the basis of these curves solves little, since the shape of these curves itself requires an explanation. In fact, the level of national income depends on numerous elements, such as the quantity and quality of production factors, technological

296

progress and institutional circumstances (see further Chapter 10.7). These elements *are* reflected in saving and investment, but not in a systematic way.

2 Say's 'law'

According to Say's 'law' *loi des débouchés* – which could more justifiably be called James Mill's 'law' – a general sales crisis is impossible since production gives the production factors a purchasing power corresponding to the value of, and in fact being paid out for, the goods produced in the same period. So there is always monetary equilibrium. If the demand for a given commodity declines, the demand for another commodity increases. The necessary adjustments occur through variations in the prices of goods and factors. The price, for example, of the commodity required less begins to decrease and producing it becomes less well paid. The supply of and demand for labour are then brought into equilibrium by the level of wages; everyone satisfied with the market-determined wages can find work, and involuntary unemployment is impossible.

J. B. Say and the writers (L. Walras and A. Pigou, among others) who elaborated this point of view did in fact recognize that saving detracts from purchasing power, but this saving, they claimed, is normally invested (in capital goods), so that income is completely spent and initiates a corresponding production.

If the saving is not invested in capital goods, but is offered on the market, there follows a cut in interest on the credit market (where saving is supplied): consumers are then encouraged to save less and producers to invest more. In other words, changes in interest rates take care of the equilibrium between saving and investment. As was the case with wages, the rate of interest is assumed to be highly flexible.

Appraisal

As will be clear from what we said in Section 1 of this chapter, Say's 'law' does not hold good. Saving, for example, is not necessarily invested (in capital goods). Prices – and particularly wages – are inflexible and do not contribute to a restoration of equilibrium. On the basis of the classical theory the Great Depression of the 1930s was explained in terms of an unsatisfactory adjustment of wages to the lowered prices. A similar interpretation was reflected in the economic policy pursued at the time (wage cuts). The explanation has to be sought in insufficient spending (Section 1), aggravated precisely by the loss in purchasing power due to the cuts in wages.

J. B. Say equally wrongly assumed that the quantity demanded and the quantity supplied of money are always equal to each other (irrespective of the level of prices or the quantity of money); his 'law' is therefore incompatible with the quantity theory (see Section 12). L. Walras, on the other hand, is of the opinion that the aggregate demand for all goods, including money, is equal to total supply of all goods, also including money (Walras's 'law').

3 The investment multiplier

Since investment forms part of total expenditure, changes in it influence the level of national income. This influence is generally greater than the original change in investment.

a. A single investment

Let us assume that investment at the beginning of a given period increases by £10,000 million. It might be concluded at first glance that the national income increases by the same amount; however, as a rule it increases more. With a differential propensity to consume of $\frac{2}{3}$, £6,667 million of the additional income (£10,000 million) is consumed in the following period. The factors that have contributed to the production of the consumer goods demanded thus receive a supplementary income of £6,667 million. Of this a further $\frac{2}{3}$ is appropriated for consumer purposes (as long as the differential propensity to consume remains constant). Total increase in national income thus reaches:

$$\Delta Y = £10,000 \text{ m.} + (\tfrac{2}{3}) £10,000 \text{ m.} + (\tfrac{2}{3})^2 £10,000 \text{ m.} +$$
$$(\tfrac{2}{3})^3 £10,000 \text{ m.} + ...$$
$$= £10,000 \text{ m.} [1 + \tfrac{2}{3} + (\tfrac{2}{3})^2 + ...]$$
$$= £10,000 \text{ m.} \ \frac{1}{1 - \tfrac{2}{3}} = £30,000 \text{ m.} \tag{1}$$

An income of £100,000 million rises first to £110,000 million (a £10,000 million increase), but falls during the following periods to £106,667 million (a £6,667 million increase), £104,448 million (£4,448 million increase) and so on. The sum of all the increases is £30,000 million. The original increase in investment of £10,000 million (over a very long period) gives, then, rise to growth in the national income (divided over very many periods) of £30,000 million. In such a case the investment multiplier w, or the figure by which the change in investment must be multiplied in order to arrive at the (total) change in the national income (over a very large number of periods), is said to be 3 ($w = \Delta Y/\Delta I$).

The investment multiplier is the reciprocal of the marginal propensity to save. The greater the latter, the smaller the multiplier; equation (1) may therefore be expressed generally as follows:

$$\Delta Y = \frac{\Delta I}{1 - c_\mu} = \frac{\Delta I}{s_\mu} \tag{2}$$

$$\frac{\Delta Y}{\Delta I} = w = \frac{1}{s_\mu}.$$

When imports are also taken into account (rising owing to an increase in income; *induced* imports, determined by the marginal propensity to import, m_μ), it is possible to express the relationship between the various influencing factors (assuming that exports and autonomous consumption and imports remain constant) by means of a supplement to equation (2):

$$\Delta Y = c_\mu \Delta Y + \Delta I - m_\mu \Delta Y$$

$$\Delta Y(1 - c_\mu + m_\mu) = \Delta I$$

$$\frac{\Delta Y}{\Delta I} = \frac{1}{1 - c_\mu + m_\mu} = \frac{1}{s_\mu + m_\mu}.$$

Other multipliers

An analogous line of reasoning can be followed for exports (assuming constant investment, autonomous consumption and imports). It leads to increases in income and consumption (the latter depending on the marginal propensity to consume), but also to a rise in imports:

$$\Delta Y = c_\mu \Delta Y + \Delta E - m_\mu \Delta Y$$

$$\Delta Y(1 - c_\mu + m_\mu) = \Delta E$$

$$\frac{\Delta Y}{\Delta E} = w_E = \frac{1}{1 - c_\mu + m_\mu} = \frac{1}{s_\mu + m_\mu}.$$

In this last case the term 'export multiplier' is used. In a similar way, the consumption multiplier, the government-spending multiplier and the general expenditure multiplier can all be determined. By this last term we mean the figure by which all variations in expenditure must be multiplied in order to arrive at the variation in national income. The multiplier concept can also be applied to employment and, for example, thereby determine what influence on employment is exercised by the incorporation of extra labour in the production process.

Through the stimulating influence exerted by the original investment, many entrepreneurs approach the future with a greater degree of trust and may in turn decide on additional investment. This induced investment reinforces the principle: the multiplier which also takes into account the effect of this investment is called a supermultiplier.

If i_μ represents the marginal propensity to invest, then $i_\mu \Delta Y$ represents induced investment (assuming constant exports), and the following equation is valid:

$$\Delta Y = c_\mu \Delta Y + \Delta I + i_\mu \Delta Y$$
$$\Delta Y (1 - c_\mu - i_\mu) = \Delta I$$
$$\frac{\Delta Y}{\Delta I} = \frac{1}{s_\mu - i_\mu}.$$

The export supermultiplier then becomes

$$\frac{1}{s_\mu + m_\mu - i_\mu}.$$

If all possible influences – including those of the rest of the world – are taken into account, the above equations naturally take on a more complicated appearance.

b. Successive investments

Following a single investment the national income, after the lapse of a certain length of time, returns in fact to its previous level. This is not the case if the same sum is invested in each time period: if, for example, £10,000 million is expended each time for investment purposes, the national income eventually reaches a permanent level of £30,000 million more than before (Table 26, Figures 56 and 57). The operation of the multiplier is shown in Table 26. This may also be expressed graphically, for example, by drawing a parallel to the investment curve in Figure 55.

TABLE 26: The pattern of change in national income resulting from one single investment and from equal successive investments (£'000m.)

Period	One single investment	Successive investments					
1	10·00	10·00					= 10·00
2	6·67	6·67 +	10·00				= 16·67
3	4·45	4·45 +	6·67 +	10·00			= 21·12
4	2·96	2·96 +	4·45 +	6·67 +	10·00		= 24·08
5	1·98	1·98 +	2·96 +	4·45 +	6·67 +	10·00	26·06
6	1·32	1·32 +	1·98 +	2·96 +	4·45 +	6·67 + ...	= 27·38
7	0·88	0·88 +	1·32 +	1·98 +	2·96 +	4·45 + ...	= 28·26
8	0·59	0·59 +	0·88 +	1·32 +	1·98 +	2·96 + ...	= 28·85
9	0·39	0·39 +	0·59 +	0·88 +	1·32 +	1·98 + ...	= 29·24
10	0·26	0·26 +	0·39 +	0·59 +	0·88 +	1·32 + ...	= 29·50
11	0·17	0·17 +	0·26 +	0·39 +	0·59 +	0·88 + ...	= 29·67
12	0·11	0·11 +	0·17 +	0·26 +	0·39 +	0·59 + ...	= 29·78
13	0·08	0·08 +	0·11 +	0·17 +	0·26 +	0·39 + ...	= 29·86
00	0·00	0·00 +	0·00 +	0·00 +	0·00 +	0·00 + ...	= 30·00

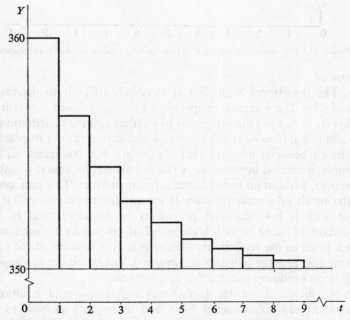

Figure 56: The change in national income after one single investment

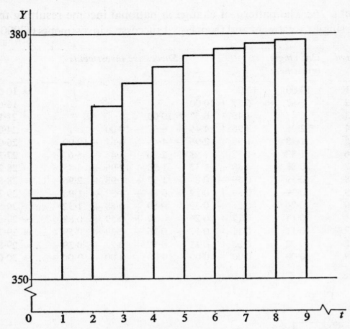

Figure 57: The change in national income after equal successive investments

Appraisal

1. The investment multiplier is extremely difficult to determine statistically. The marginal propensity to consume is not constant; it differs from one population group to another and the distribution of the additional income is not known. A distinction cannot in practice be drawn between incomes that are or are not the result of, for example, increased investment. A rise in national income is possible, moreover, without an initial increase in expenditure. This may occur as the result of a redistribution of income (to the disadvantage of those with a low marginal propensity to consume, and to the advantage of those with a high marginal propensity to consume), which gives us the redistribution multiplier (the relation of the total income effects to the redistributed income). The multiplier can appear only in an economy without full employment.

2. As shown above, the (sometimes slight) results of additional investment are counteracted by a rise in imports as well as by the claims made by the government on part of the additional

income. Fluctuations in stocks frequently cancel out the multiplier effect.

3. Particularly where the investment multiplier is applied to macro-economic questions, it is overlooked that alongside the quantitative changes there also appear qualitative differences and that in many cases the first of these are merely the result of the second. H. Hegeland correctly draws attention to the fact 'that the multiplier theory loses much of its relevance when applied to social aggregates and that it can be fruitfully applied chiefly to problems of microeconomics, i.e., when applied to the effects of changes in a single flow of expenditure within a limited sector of the economy'.

4 The accelerator

The accelerator theory analyses the influence of income and more particularly the influence of income variations on investment. The theory was originally formulated in microeconomics (first by J. M. Clark).

Let us assume, for example, that the yearly production of shoes reaches a value of £100 million and that the value of the machinery required is £300 million; this machinery is replaced every ten years, so that a depreciation allowance of £30 million must be made each year (on the assumption that the stock of machinery has been gradually built up).

What happens if demand rises and production has to be increased to £110 million? The stock of capital goods must be raised by 10 per cent, i.e. by £30 million (£300 million $\div$ 10). The value of the gross production of the machines will total 60 million pounds instead of 30 million, representing an increase of 100 per cent as against a rise of 10 per cent for the consumer goods (Table 27).

If in the following year production has to be raised not by 10 per cent but only by 5, the production of the machines shows a fall of 17·5 per cent (£330 million $\div$ 10 = £33 million; £330 million $\times$ 5 $\div$ 100 = £16·5 million; £33 million + £16·5 million = £49·5 million; (49·5 $\div$ 60) $\times$ 100 = 82·5; 100 − 82·5 = 17·5).

The production of capital goods appears more liable to substantial fluctuation than the production of consumer goods. The fluctuations are greater in proportion to the length of the depreciation period. The figure by which the additional production or the additional income in a given period must be multiplied in order to arrive at the consequent

TABLE 27: Fluctuations in the production of consumer and capital goods (acceleration principle) (£m.)

Period	Production of consumer goods	Capital goods required	Depreciation	Increase in production capacity	Production of capital goods
1	100	300	30	0	30
2	110	330	30	30	60
3	115·5	346·5	33	16·5	49·5

(induced) investment I_t^l in the following period is called the accelerator, or the acceleration coefficient. In the above example it has a value of 3 ($10 \times 3 = 30$; 5·5 (or 5 per cent of 110) $\times 3 = 16·5$).

$$v = \frac{I_t^l}{Y_t - Y_{t-1}}.$$

In order to ascertain the total of all induced investment, all previous income fluctuations have to be taken into account:

$$I_t^l = v_1 (Y_t - Y_{t-1}) + v_2 (Y_{t-1} - Y_{t-2}) + \dots v_n (Y_{t-n+1} - Y_{t-n}).$$

The following formula is also often taken a basis:

$$v = \frac{I_t^l}{Y_{t-1} - Y_{t-2}}.$$

Whenever the necessary investment does not follow immediately on an increase in income but is spread over a number of years, there is reference to the flexible or partial accelerator (as opposed to the actual or fixed accelerator).

The accelerator is not a synonym for the differential capital-output ratio (sometimes called incremental capital-output ratio: $ICOR$). The capital-output ratio (also called capital coefficient) expresses the relation of the value of the capital goods to that of production ($k = K/X$). The differential capital-output ratio k_d – also often referred to as the marginal capital-output ratio – is then represented by $\Delta K/\Delta X$ or $I/\Delta X$; analogous definitions are given for the labour-output ratio $l = L/X$ and the differential labour-output ratio $l_d = \Delta L/\Delta X$. The differential capital-output ratio itself must not be confused with the percentage profit accruing from the new investment (the relation of profits to the additional capital involved). If an investment of

£100 million leads to a production of £25 million (including a profit of £6 million), the differential capital-output ratio amounts to 4 and the profit on the new capital is 6 per cent.

If there is no autonomous investment, the accelerator (not the flexible accelerator) and the differential capital-output ratio coincide, although their nature is entirely different: the accelerator indicates a (very simple) business policy, and the capital-output ratio a technical relationship. Moreover, the capital-output ratio refers to one single period, and the accelerator to successive periods. When autonomous investment is also taken into account, the differential capital-output ratio is then greater than the accelerator.

Appraisal

1. The acceleration theory is valid only so long as all machines are in use (no excess capacity), overtime is excluded, the relation between production factors cannot be altered (unchanged technology), sufficient raw materials and labour are present and the entrepreneurs command the necessary financial means. Since such is not the case (the machines, for example, are usually replaced by better ones), the accelerator is of little significance. The attempts to measure the accelerator have yielded little result. This is in part attributable to the difficulty of distinguishing between autonomous and induced investment (particularly on the macroeconomic level).

2. In order to explain entrepreneurs' investment behaviour, numerous other factors must be taken into account (Chapter 6.2). Future expectations play a particularly important part (a shortage of capacity is not made up immediately; stocks are drawn on instead). Investment is made which has nothing to do with changes in income (e.g. under pressure of increased real wages), while autonomous investment is becoming more important (new inventions, public works).

3. The theory is based upon 'balanced' growth: income and the stock of capital goods increase in the same proportion. This is not the case. Economic growth, furthermore, is not only dependent on capital (cf. Chapter 10).

4. As in the case of the multiplier, the pitfalls of macroeconomic data must be pointed out. A rise in investment can follow on increased consumption in a given industry while the general level of consumption has nevertheless remained the same. This investment could then incorrectly be classed as autonomous. The accelerator is therefore

not competent to explain changes in aggregate investment. Only under special circumstances and in the short term is there a proportional relationship between output and the stock of capital goods.

5. The acceleration principle is less general than the multiplier. Whereas the latter operates in both directions, the acceleration principle is effective only in the upward direction and then only when the firm concerned is operating at full capacity (in the downward direction only to the extent that replacement investment is not provided for).

5 The interaction of multiplier and accelerator

Various attempts have been made using a multiplier and accelerator to explain the unstable character of economic activity.

As has already been emphasized, the influence of certain economic phenomena is not felt during the same period. The repercussions have a delayed operation.

Consumption is influenced by the income of the previous period:

$$C_t = C_z + c_\mu Y_{t-1}.$$

The consumption of period t is equal to a constant part C_z (below which consumption does not fall) and a fraction that fluctuates according to the income level of the preceding period. The consumption lag covers approximately one year in the case of farmers (who receive the greater part of their income yearly, after the harvest) and only a few days in the case of workers paid weekly.

For investment the time lag in the use of income is longer still. It is accepted that autonomous investment remains constant over the short term and that induced investment is dependent on the increase in income during the preceding period:

$$I_t = I_z + v\,(Y_{t-1} - Y_{t-2}),$$

where v represents the accelerator. The greater expenditure lag stems from the fact that firms try to cope with a rise in demand without new investment. Only if the expansion persists do they initiate new investment. Individuals also hold over the money intended for investment longer than that intended for consumption. Since the production of capital goods usually requires more time than that of consumer goods (with the exception of agricultural products), the output lag is also generally longer.

306

A rise in income usually works on investment with a delay of three to six months. The longer this time lag, the more the cumulative growth of income is hindered. Everything here depends on the size of the accelerator and multiplier. This is apparent from the accompanying table (Table 28), which sets out the influence of an increase in autonomous investment according to the formula

$$Y_t = C_z + c_\mu Y_{t-1} + I_z + v (Y_{t-1} - Y_{t-2}),$$

C_z being disregarded.

Beginning with period 1, autonomous investment is increased at a rate of £10,000 million in an economy in a situation where monetary

TABLE 28: The interaction between multiplier and accelerator (£'000 m.)

Period	Autonomous investment	Additional consumption ($c = 0.6$ or $w = 2.5$)[a]	Induced investment ($v = 0.8$)[b]	Changes in income
(1)	(2)	(3)	(4)	(5)
1	10·00	0·00	0·00	10·00
2	10·00	6·00	8·00	24·00
3	10·00	14·40	11·20	35·60
4	10·00	21·36	9·28	40·64
5	10·00	24·36	4·48	38·84
6	10·00	23·28	−1·44	31·84
7	10·00	19·08	−5·60	23·48
8	10·00	14·10	−6·64	17·46
9	10·00	10·50	−4·80	15·70
10	10·00	9·42	−1·44	17·98
11	10·00	10·80	1·84	22·64
12	10·00	13·56	3·68	27·24
13	10·00	16·32	3·68	30·00
14	10·00	18·00	2·24	30·24
15	10·00	18·12	0·16	28·28
16	10·00	16·98	−1·52	25·46
17	10·00	15·30	−2·24	23·06
18	10·00	13·86	−1·92	21·94
19	10·00	13·14	−0·96	22·18
20	10·00	13·32	0·24	23·56
21	10·00	14·16	1·12	25·28
22	10·00	15·18	1·36	26·54

[a] Figures for the previous period from column (5) multiplied by 0·6.
[b] Difference between the figures for the two previous periods from column (5) multiplied by 0·8.

307

equilibrium prevails. It is assumed that the (constant) differential propensity to consume is 0·6 (the multiplier therefore 2·5) and the accelerator 0·8. In period 2 induced investment equals £8,000 million and the additional consumption £6,000 million. The change in income then amounts to £24,000 million. Of this, 60 per cent (£14,400 million) is expended during the following period.

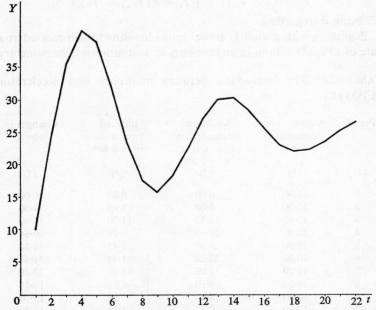

Figure 58: Income variations through the interaction of multiplier and accelerator

The variations in income arising from the interaction of multiplier and accelerator (Figure 58) are expressed by damped fluctuations. According to the assumed magnitudes of accelerator and propensity to consume, anti-damped movements and fluctuations of about the same amplitude may be obtained.

Appraisal
Attention has already been drawn to the limited validity of the multiplier and particularly of the accelerator. Furthermore, a statistical determination of them is out of the question: neither the accelerator nor the multiplier (marginal propensity to consume) remains constant. In a recovery period, for example, the accelerator

308

would have to be very low, since there is excess capacity available; it would have to rise rapidly as soon as the economy is working at full capacity. The opposite would have to take place with respect to the multiplier.

Whenever it is sensible to include the multiplier in the analysis (recovery), it is less convenient for the accelerator. In the case of full capacity operation, on the other hand, the inclusion of the accelerator in the reasoning is justified, while that of the multiplier is not.

The above explanation of income fluctuations is purely mechanical and does not take sufficient account of qualitative and psychological factors (such as the entrepreneurs' future prospects and the changing power of pressure groups over the business cycle).

6 The business cycle

The succession of a period of higher and lower national income is called a business cycle. Figure 58 is a schematic representation of this. In reality the cycles show a much greater degree of variation (Figure 59).

A 'boom' is a situation of high national income coupled with full employment. A 'depression' or 'slump', on the other hand, is characterized by a lower national income and an appreciable unemployment figure. In some cases a low income does not, however,

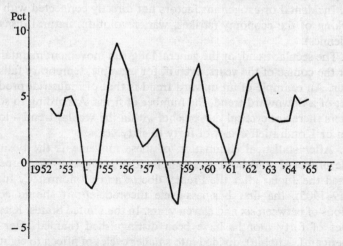

Source: *World Economic Survey, 1964* (UN, New York 1965), p. 167

Figure 59: Percentage quarterly variation in the gross national product of the USA (1952–64)

M

309

cause an increase in visible unemployment (only in disguised unemployment).

The transition from boom to depression is termed 'crisis' whenever it occurs rapidly and strikingly (stock-exchange crash, many bankruptcies, sudden fall in prices and incomes). The term 'recession' is used to cover a temporary slowing down in a rising cycle or a gradual transition from boom to depression.

The four phases (depression, recovery or revival, boom, and crisis or recession) together form the business cycle. This terminology is misleading to the extent that the phases mentioned do not necessarily occur in cyclical progression.

A recession can remain limited and afterwards turn into a period of recovery; the latter does not always develop into a boom. The lengths of the phases sometimes vary considerably. Although fairly substantial fluctuations still arise, government action generally prevents serious depressions (cf. Chapter 13).

Economic fluctuations are the result of various influences. The following distinctions are made:

a. Seasonal fluctuations caused by the time of year, the weather, customary methods of payment or holidays. The economy, as a rule, easily accommodates these foreseeable fluctuations.

b. Incidental or exogenous factors not directly connected with the working of the economy (strikes, war, revolution, natural disaster, epidemics).

c. The secular trend, or the general long-run movement maintained over the course of the years, even if, for example, temporary falls do occur. An example of an upward trend is that of industrial production; of a downward trend, the number of firms. According to some writers there are cyclical movements within the secular trend – longterm or Kondratieff cycles of forty to sixty years.

d. After statistical elimination of these movements the business cycle proper should become apparent; this business cycle proper is named the Juglar after the French doctor and economist C. Juglar (1819–1905), the first business-cycle theoretician; it should cover periods of between six and eleven years. In the United States, Kitchin cycles of forty months have been distinguished (named after the American J. Kitchin), divided into smaller cycles of fifteen to eighteen months.

In fact the above distinctions are difficult to make in practice and often pointless. The statistical data to prove the existence of Kondratieff, Juglar and Kitchin cycles are in any case insufficient.

7 The overinvestment and underconsumption theories

Although it is generally agreed that in an upward phase of the business cycle planned investment is greater than planned saving, and that in a downward phase, on the contrary, investment is smaller, there is a lack of agreement on the explanation of the transition from over to underinvestment. Some authors believe that the unusual rise in the demand for capital goods (the acceleration principle) is the prime cause of the crisis (overinvestment theory); according to others, consumption is not sufficiently geared to the increasing production capacity and sales difficulties therefore arise, provoking a crisis (underconsumption theory).

a. The overinvestment theory

According to this theory, the large demand for capital goods during a boom causes imbalance on the financial and material levels. The increased demand for credit brings about a money shortage, as a result of which interest rates rise; this prompts the abandonment of investment projects. Meanwhile, the output of the capital-goods industries continues to increase. Since entrepreneurs always have to take a possible further rise in demand into account and carry out their plans for expansion independently of each other, excess capacity necessarily results. When orders fall off, partly under the influence of the rise in the rate of interest, the industries producing capital goods find themselves in difficulties and a crisis becomes unavoidable.

b. The underconsumption theory

This theory maintains that consumption rises insufficiently to absorb the increased production resulting from investment. Whenever it becomes clear that the additional output of consumer goods sold is less than had been expected, entrepreneurs cut down on investment, giving rise to a general fall in demand and ushering in the crisis.

A rise in consumption is impossible, since the national income is unevenly distributed; those with larger incomes save too much, profits rise more than wages, so that the marginal propensity to save increases.

c. The consequences for economic policy

While the origin of the crisis according to the underconsumption theory is insufficient consumption and too much saving, the over-investment theory claims that there is not enough saving to finance planned investment. Depending on the theory accepted, one of two irreconcilable policies is necessary.

On the basis of the overinvestment theory, an attempt must be made to prevent exaggerated investment. The crisis could be avoided by a selective credit policy ensuring in time that overcapacity does not arise in any single industry. In order to increase the volume of funds supplied, saving also has to be encouraged in boom periods.

According to the underconsumption theory, attempts must be made during a boom to increase consumption, if necessary by extension of consumer credit. Consumption must also be increased to combat depression: by this means an increase in investment will be achieved, albeit with some delay.

Appraisal

In an assessment of the two theories their basic assumptions are important, and more particularly whether they presuppose full employment.

Under full employment (maximum production) a rise in invest-ment is possible only by means of a fall in consumption: saving is indispensable to increasing investment (saving and consumption being in competition). Also, an increase in consumption is disadvan-tageous to capital accumulation (by enticing of workers away from the capital-goods industries). If the volume of investment can be maintained, every attempt to increase consumption will lead to a rise in prices.

So long as full employment is not achieved, saving is not necessary for investment. Too much saving is even harmful (the so-called saving paradox: a microeconomic virtue is not necessarily a macro-economic one) when it gives rise to a cut in consumption and indirectly in investment. Here the multiplier operates in a downward direction. The national income then falls to a level at which almost no saving or investment is possible and where extensive unemployment is the rule. The level at which the equilibrium of saving and invest-ment is realized is thus not without importance.

8 The course of a 'cycle'

We have already said that a genuinely cyclical movement does not occur. Each fluctuation in economic activity has its own characteristics. Each country reacts differently to given phenomena depending on its structural circumstances: 'every cycle is a historical individual *to some extent* and . . . unique combinations of circumstances must enter largely into every analysis of a particular case' (J. A. Schumpeter). What follows below is only an outline and must not be considered universally applicable.

a. Depression and recovery

A depression – characterized by low prices and income (though the fall in income is less than that in prices in comparison with the preceding period of boom), scant production, insignificant or even negative returns on investment, and pronounced unemployment – usually comes to an end because:

1. the decreased stocks eventually make increased production necessary (in spite of reduced consumption);

2. depreciation, without matching efforts to invest, results in a considerable accumulation of liquid assets, which causes firms to decide to invest (in capital goods);

3. productive equipment must be adapted to technological progress in order to keep costs down, and a minimum of replacement investment is indispensable.

These endogenous forces may still be too weak to bring about a recovery. Particularly in a severe depression, it is possible that consumption falls so low that stocks hardly decrease at all, in spite of decreased production. At the same time, the entrepreneurs shrink from increasing production capacity by means of technological improvements. A sharp fall in prices often hinders normal depreciation allowances so that liquid assets do not necessarily increase. Exogenous factors (public works, armament production) then often give the impetus towards recovery.

As soon as the national income rises, consumption rapidly increases to satisfy the numerous wants that could not be satisfied during the depression (backlog demand). The increase in demand provokes in turn a series of price increases by means of which the entrepreneurs' trust in the future is encouraged and investment is extended. Since

313

further price increases are expected, manufacturers and dealers build up speculative stocks whereby demand is increased still more.

The expansion of investment (including stockbuilding) quickly absorbs the liquid assets of firms, so that the demand for credit rises; this leads to a rise in interest rates.

Production follows the increase in demand with some delay (cf. output lag) and eventually a state of full employment is reached.

b. Boom and crisis

Wages, which have lagged behind prices, rise rapidly. Demand pull is reinforced by cost push (see Section 10a). The latter is favoured by a decrease in output per worker due to the recruitment of less skilled workers. If the increase in prices is not slowed down in time by credit restriction, a boom arises characterized by a 'flight from money' (because of the inflationary tendency).

The increasing demand for shares prompts stock-exchange speculation, and that for real estate an extension of activity in the building industry. The considerable rise in the demand of credit, both for consumption and for investment, leads to a further increase in interest rates. In order to maintain their liquidity, the banks finally have to adopt credit restriction.

Because of this, some investment projects have to be interrupted before they have yielded any result. Firms that have borrowed too much go bankrupt, and the sale of their fixed assets and stocks exercises a disadvantageous influence on the market. If a large proportion of security purchases have also been financed by bank credit, a stock-exchange crash also becomes possible: quotations running too high owing to speculation may suddenly drop, and the consequent losses force many individuals and firms to convert their stocks and claims into cash in order to meet their commitments.

A further restriction of credit possibilities thus results, along with an excessive supply of goods, so that prices may fall while interest rates continue to rise.

The fall in prices is accompanied by a rise in real wages and a sharp decrease in profits. The prospects for the establishment or extension of firms become poor, causing the demand for capital goods to sink to a minimum, a large number of firms manufacturing them to close down, and unemployment to increase. This in turn gives

314

rise to a fall in consumption and a further drop in demand and output.

If the banks counter the excessive granting of credit in time, the boom and its consequent crisis can usually be avoided. If they are short of funds, firms must restrict their investment during the upward phase so that the demand for goods is held in check and prices, after a possible rise, return to a more normal level. The boom is then transformed into a mild recession, after which an immediate recovery is possible.

c. Normal correlations

In the course of the business cycle the following correlations are usually found to hold:

1. except in agriculture, prices and production move in parallel;
2. major changes in total production, employment or price level are most of the time accompanied by prominent changes (in the same direction) in the quantity and the velocity of money circulation;
3. expenditure on durable goods fluctuates more than that on non-durables; also, spending on capital goods shows greater fluctuation than that on consumer goods;
4. current expenditure devoted to stockbuilding fluctuates more than aggregate sales;
5. fluctuations in profits are more pronounced than those in other types of income.

9 Business cycle indicators

It is of importance to the government, households and firms to be able to foresee the course of the business cycle. The government can prevent serious economic fluctuations by taking action early enough (e.g. by initiating public works or changing credit policy); firms can safeguard themselves in time against loss. For these reasons attempts are made to predict the turning points in economic activity.

The three-market, or Harvard, indicator was originally the best-known: from the analysis of various economic data for the period 1903–14 in the USA it was ascertained (Figure 60) that some curves move in a similar pattern (trends, seasonal fluctuations and incidental influences being first removed), but with a time lag. These curves represented:

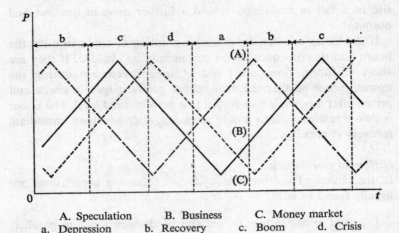

A. Speculation   B. Business   C. Money market
a. Depression   b. Recovery   c. Boom   d. Crisis

Figure 60: Stylized representation of the Harvard index chart

a. speculation (stock prices);
b. business (wholesale prices);
c. money market (short-term interest rates).

On the average, the speculation curve led the business curve by eight months, while the business curve led the money-market curve by four months. Since the business curve represents the cycles, it was sufficient to follow the course of the stock-market curve in order to predict cyclical fluctuations. Until 1929, this method yielded satisfying results; the crisis and Great Depression of 1929–34 were not predicted, however, and afterwards the recovery was regularly heralded without appearing until much later.

Other, more complicated, indicators (sometimes called barometers) have been constructed, each of them geared to the economy of the country concerned. Statistical data referring to orders, stocks and prices of basic industrial products (e.g. cast iron, steel) have often been used, and demand for these commodities is in fact closely connected with the volume of investment, which is of great importance for the behaviour of the business cycle.

In recent years more importance has been attached to the results of surveys of planned investment, expansion of production and accumulation of stocks by the major firms. Managements are not always prepared to divulge their plans: they fear that pessimistic prospects would prompt their buyers to withhold purchases. From

316

this it follows that these data are not always reliable. Surveys of this kind had already been started in the United States before the First World War. Most European countries followed this lead after 1950 (West Germany first: the Ifo-Institut für Wirtschaftsforschung in Munich). In the United Kingdom cyclical research is done by the National Institute of Economic and Social Research; in Belgium by the Banque Nationale; in France, Italy and the Netherlands by the national statistical offices. Nowadays the 'Klein-Goldberger model' (see Section 14) is used in the United States in November each year to make reasonably accurate predictions for the gross national product of the following year.

That it has not yet proved possible to construct infallible business cycle indicators should come as no surprise: unforeseeable psychological factors have an important hand in this. D. B. J. Schouten rightly believes that, '. . . any forecast concerning the pattern of the business cycle has only a limited value. Even the best-equipped cyclical-research bureau is unable at the present time to construct a reliable business-cycle prognosis for any longer period than a year.'

10 Monetary equilibrium and the general level of prices

It was pointed out above (see Section 1.*a*) that when planned expenditure exceeds income in a closed economy this leads to a general rise in prices if there is full employment. This general, if persistent, rise is called inflation. As is the case with many other economic concepts, inflation is used with numerous meanings. For most authors, inflation is equivalent to a continuous rise in the prices of consumer goods (whatever the cause).

a. The causes of inflation

1. A rise in the general price level is usually caused by overspending (demand-pull inflation). Overspending that does not cause price increases leads to what is sometimes termed 'reflation'. 'Bottleneck inflation' is the result of disequilibrium arising between quantities supplied and demanded in one or more basic industries and spreading from these into other industries.

2. Autonomous increases in wages and profits also lead to increases in costs and prices, out of which a cost-push inflation develops. Prominent in this respect are exaggerated claims on the part of the trade unions. In most cases these are only a reaction against inflation

317

due to overspending, which is itself a product of, *inter alia*, a budget deficit, an exceptional credit expansion or a rise in exports. The cost push, however, reinforces the demand pull. The two are difficult to distinguish in a period of expansion. Since competitiveness has to be taken into account, the dangers of cost push vary from country to country. When profits provide the basis of a cost push, 'markup inflation' is the term used. Particularly those firms with administered prices make use of a rise in wages to readjust their profit margin.

3. Both demand-pull and cost-push inflation can be imported from abroad (Chapter 12.4).

Whatever the cause of inflation, it is usually coupled in practice with an increase in the quantity of money.

b. The degree and consequences of inflation
There are, of course, different degrees of inflation (Table 29); it may seem almost harmless (1 to 1·5 per cent a year) and can sometimes be offset by an improvement in the quality of production. If the annual increase in the general price level is less than 4 per cent, the term 'creeping inflation' is applied; higher percentage increases are known as trotting, galloping or runaway inflation. Whenever spending is

TABLE 29: The percentage annual increase in the cost-of-living index for various countries (1960–8)

1.	Venezuela	1·2	18.	Netherlands	3·7
2.	Iran	1·5	19.	Portugal	3·7
3.	Greece	1·9	20.	Sweden	3·8
4.	United States	2·0	21.	Norway	3·9
5.	Australia	2·2	22.	Italy	4·8
6.	Luxembourg	2·3	23.	Finland	5·5
7.	Mexico	2·3	24.	Japan	5·6
8.	Canada	2·4	25.	Denmark	5·7
9.	South Africa	2·4	26.	Turkey	6·0
10.	Germany (West)	2·7	27.	India	7·1
11.	Belgium	2·8	28.	Philippines	7·4
12.	France	3·0	29.	Spain (1961–8)	7·4
13.	Ecuador	3·1	30.	Iceland	10·6
14.	New Zealand	3·3	31.	Colombia	11·9
15.	Pakistan	3·4	32.	Argentina	24·2
16.	United Kingdom	3·6	33.	Chile	25·3
17.	Austria	3·6	34.	Brazil	50·6

Source: calculated from *BSUN*, December 1968 and November 1969

restricted by the government (e.g. by means of price control and rationing), the term 'repressed (or suppressed) inflation' is used (the price increase cannot be completely expressed).

Even if a mild inflation, such as usually accompanies a boom, is less dangerous, any form of inflation is still disadvantageous for those with a fixed money income (though wages too are adjusted only after a time lag) and for creditors. The 'forgotten groups' (small rentiers, pensioners) in particular generally find themselves the victims. Debtors, on the other hand – including the government (national debt) – benefit from inflation. Because there is a close relationship between the internal and external value of the currency (Chapter 12.5), inflation is accompanied by a decrease in the value of the currency, known as depreciation (on depreciation and devaluation: Chapter 12.6). Likewise a general price decrease leads to an increase in its value, or appreciation.

When inflation begins to assume large proportions, distrust of the value of the currency sets in, and prices and the quantity of money both rise still further. The German currency in 1923 was worth 10^{22} times less than in 1914, that of Hungary after the Second World War 3×10^{22} less than in 1940.

c. Deflation

Deflation is usually described as a decrease in money supply: there is, in other words, no mention of the consequent price movements as was the case in the definition of inflation (although some authors define inflation merely as an increase in money supply; every increase in supply thus becomes an inflation, even if compensated for by a parallel rise in goods and services). If income is greater than planned expenditure, a contraction of economic activity, employment and the national income indeed follows, but usually not a lowering in prices: the rigidity of wages and prices, along with monopoly situations, prevent this from happening. Only where there is extensive unemployment can the wage level drop. As long as the deflation does not cause major unemployment, it may sometimes be termed 'disinflation' (though this term is also used to indicate the end of an inflationary development).

11 The transactions equation of exchange

When the values of all money transactions during a given period are added together, their sum is equal to $\sum_{i=1}^{n} = p_i q_i$ (the value of each sale is equal to the price per unit multiplied by the number of units). The actual quantity of money M^* may be used several times throughout the same period to make payments. The figure by which M^* must be multiplied in order to arrive at the total value of transactions, is represented by V^* and is termed the velocity of circulation, so that $M^*V^* = \sum_{i=1}^{n} p_i q_i$. While M^* represents the quantity of money at a given moment (or the average quantity available over a given period), M^*V^* represents the money supply, or the total expenditure on goods and services within a given period.

If all prices are represented by an average P^* (general level of prices) and the volume of sales (total goods sold, not produced) by T^*, the exchange or Fisher equation is obtained:

$$M^*V^* = P^*T^*$$

or, separating notes and coin (M_1^*) from deposit (M_2^*) money:

$$M_1^*V_1^* + M_2^*V_2^* = P^*T^*.$$

Starting from the equation of exchange, it can be stated that the variations in general price level are directly proportional to the quantity of money and its velocity of circulation and inversely proportional to the volume of goods and services purchased with the money. On the basis of the equation, inflation can also be defined as a situation in which the money supply increases more than the corresponding goods and services, the consequence of which is a general rise in prices; deflation arises if the money supply increases more slowly than the quantity of goods and services sold, and a general decrease in prices is caused.

Appraisal

a. The equation needs no proof. The goods are exchanged for each other: the money available is equal to the amounts needed to pay for the transactions.

b. The formula enables us to express any one of the factors as a function of the others $(M^* = P^*T^*/V^*;\ V^* = P^*T^*/M^*;\ P^* = M^*V^*/T^*;\ T^* = M^*V^*/P^*)$, though this does not tell us anything about the factors themselves. M^*, for instance, is partly determined by the structure of the banking system, V^* by the way the economic units normally make payments, P^* by monopolistic conditions, and T^* by the quality and quantity of the factors of production.

c. The time element is disregarded. Present funds are sometimes used to pay for past transactions, often at prices differing from the current ones. Moreover, M^* is a stock at a point in time (although an average can be calculated for a given period), while T^* is a flow over a period of time.

d. A reminder must be given of the dangers of using aggregated data. As has already been pointed out, various price indices have been compiled on account of the heterogeneity of the various commodities. The 'general' level of prices gives no explanation of the price levels of the different commodity groups. The influence of an increase in the quantity of money is not the same in all price categories. The equation should be written as follows:

$$M^*V^* = p_1q_1 + p_2q_2 + p_3q_3 + \dots + p_nq_n$$

where n commodity groups can be distinguished.

12 The quantity theory

The oldest and best-known explanation of the value of money and the changes in that value is the quantity theory.

Starting from the exchange equation, the supporters of the modern version of the quantity theory – the most widespread form of which was postulated by I. Fisher (1867–1947) – claim that every change in M^* has a repercussion on the general price level. At first these consequences were described as automatic and proportional, but a less rigid relationship was later accepted whereby the influence on P^* only gradually appears and nothing guarantees a proportional change or an even spread of the price variation over all commodities.

I. Fisher assumes that V^* is constant and dependent on institutional circumstances. V^* does not normally reflect changes in M^* or T^*.

Money is regarded purely as a medium of exchange. The (aggregate) quantity of money serves to procure the total quantity of goods. The greater the quantity of money, the more currency units can be offered for each commodity (assuming the total quantity of goods to be constant) and the higher the prices. When the quantity of money decreases, prices fall. This theory is termed 'quantity' theory because of the causal role attributed to the quantity of money.

Appraisal

a. The theory suffers from the weakness of the exchange equation. The two may not be confused, however: the exchange equation itself is neutral and says nothing of the causal relationship between the four components.

b. Since moderate price fluctuations appear possible without a rise in M^*, the theory can be valid only in the long run.

c. Not only the level of absolute prices can be influenced, but also the relation between the various prices (the relative prices), without altering the general level of prices. Stability, therefore, is not necessarily a guarantee of the neutrality of money (relative prices remain unchanged).

d. The relationship between M^* and P^* can naturally best be studied when V^* and T^* are constant. Particularly since 1930, however, it has been more common for an increase in M^* not to lead to a price rise, because V^* has decreased (hoarding). A fall in M^* usually does not lead to a price cut because of the rigidity of prices. In other words, the quantity theory seems to be applicable only in the case of full employment.

e. The direction of causality (M^* is the independent variable) is usually correct, but psychological factors and autonomous changes in profits and wages can cause a rise in P^* to bring about an increase in M^*. During periods of sharp price rises (e.g. in Germany after the two world wars) confidence in the currency is lost and a preference shown for goods over money. By this process prices are raised again, and this causes a further increase in M^*. Finally, there is also the possibility of indirect action (M^* influences interest rates and thereby production costs and P^*).

f. The quantity theory has in fact contributed to the statistical determination of the factors concerned. In practice it is advisable to interpret the equation of exchange by means of four index numbers with the same reference period. The velocity of circulation of money is particularly hard to follow. The velocity of circulation of deposit money is usually determined by, for example, dividing the demand-deposits turnover by the average daily demand deposits in private bank accounts.

13 The cash-balance theory

The supporters of the quantity theory regard money as only a medium of exchange. Money is also demanded for its own sake: it is a means of saving, a precautionary store of wealth against the uncertainties of the future.

D. H. Robertson points out that the value of money may be explained according to the general theory of value, i.e. as the result of supply and demand. The value then must be such that supply and demand correspond. The demand for money is determined by the quantities of money that people require in order to dispose of a certain purchasing power.

The quantity of money M^* is at any given moment equal to the aggregate of cash balances held by the economic units (for a given *period*, the *average* quantity of money equals the aggregate of *average* cash balances). These cash balances also represent a given share b of the total value of goods traded so that:

$$M^* = bP^*T^*$$

This is known as the cash-balance equation of exchange.

Attention is now placed on the amount of money it is felt desirable to hold. Price expectations are of great importance in this respect. The (aggregate) quantity of money is regarded as given.

From the comparison of the two formulas $M^*V^* = P^*T^*$ and $M^* = bP^*T^*$ it follows that $b = 1/V^*$. The average velocity of circulation and the average resting-time of money are reciprocals.

Appraisal

a. As was the case with the transactions equation of exchange, the cash-balance (Cambridge) equation expresses an evident truth: the value of the supply of money is equal to the value of the goods for which purchasing power is retained in the form of money.

b. While in the transactions equation of exchange attention is paid exclusively to that part of the quantity of money destined for current transactions, in the cash-balance equation it is paid principally to that part retained for unforeseen expenditure. And V^* or b is different for each part – rather stable for the first but not for the second.

c. The objections to the quantity theory remain valid. The cash-balance theory is likewise a monetary approach to the explanation of the variations in economic life. For this purpose, both theories are based on the fluctuations, respectively, of M^*V^* and M^*/b – particularly on the various motives for holding cash balances. In modern expenditure analysis, on the other hand, changes in the economic activity are explained by means of investment and consumption decisions, by the fluctuations of $C + I$ (but $C + I$ and $M*V*$ are not equivalent: $C + I$ only includes expenditure for end products; $M*V*$ covers all expenditure, also for production factors and semi-finished products, and is therefore larger than $C + I$). Depending on the approach adopted, the government uses different instruments of economic policy: on the one hand monetary policy, and on the other, control of the circular flow.

The quantity theory and the cash-balance theory are too limited as general analytical tools, though they may provide useful indications. It must be remembered that the equations concerned 'are nothing more or less than short-hand expressions designed to indicate the nature of the variables whose operations can be shown to influence prices' (A. W. Marget), and that these variables have still to be thoroughly investigated. Psychological factors are of great importance here: 'It appears difficult to arrive at a full understanding of fluctuations in the value of money . . . without taking qualitative considerations and psychological analyses into account' (A. Aftalion).

14 Bibliography

On the macroeconomic aspect of the subjects dealt with in this and the following chapter: G. Ackley, *Macroeconomic Theory* (New York 1961); T. F. Dernburg and D. M. McDougall, *Macroeconomics: The Measurement, Analysis, and Control of Aggregate Economic Activity* (3rd ed., New York 1968) and T. F. Dernburg and J. D. Dernburg, *Macroeconomic Analysis: An Introduction to Comparative Statics and Dynamics* (Reading, Mass. 1969).

a. Monetary equilibrium

The foundations of modern income analysis were laid by J. M. Keynes, *The General Theory of Employment, Interest and Money* (London 1936). There are good commentaries on this not very clear work, including D. Dillard, *The Economics of John Maynard Keynes: The Theory of a Monetary Economy* (New York 1948); L. R. Klein, *The Keynesian Revolution* (2nd ed., London 1968); A. H. Hansen, *A Guide to Keynes* (New York 1953). The last two have no bibliography. *Post-Keynesian Economics* (ed. K. K. Kurihara, London 1955) examines to what extent the most important features of Keynes' theory have been supplemented or modified. The first exposition on monetary equilibrium was given by J. G. Koopmans, 'Zum Problem des neutralen Geldes', in *Beiträge zur Geldtheorie* (ed. F. A. von Hayek, Vienna 1933). See also D. J. Botha, *A Study in the Theory of Monetary Equilibrium: A Comparative Analysis* (Leiden 1959).

b. Say's 'law'

See J. B. Say, *Traité d'économie politique ou simple exposition de la manière dont se forment, se distribuent et se consomment les richesses* (Paris 1803); A. H. Hansen, *A Guide to Keynes*, Chapter 10; D. Dillard, *The Economics of John Maynard Keynes*, p. 18. From an historical point of view: P. Lambert, 'The Law of Markets Prior to J. B. Say and the Say-Malthus Debate', *International Economic Papers*, No. 6 (London 1956); see also further: A. S. Skinner, 'Say's Law: Origins and Content', *Ec*, May 1967.

c. The multiplier

H. Hegeland, *The Multiplier Theory* (Lund 1954), after lucid criticism of the relevant theories, including those of R. F. Kahn and J. M. Keynes, and a consideration of different kinds of multiplier, stresses the limited practical significance of this concept; on the supermultiplier: J. R. Hicks, *A Contribution to the Theory of the Trade Cycle* (Oxford 1950).

d. The acceleration principle·

P. Winding, *Some Aspects of the Acceleration Principle* (Copenhagen 1957) is a purely theoretical work ('some of the results . . . tend to reinforce the idea of the acceleration principle. But others work in the opposite direction, and the importance of the latter may well prove to be stronger'). See also Chapter 12 of H. Hegeland, *The Multiplier Theory* (see p. 210 for the difference between accelerator and multiplier); the bibliography in D. Smyth, 'Empirical Evidence on the Acceleration Principle', *RESt*, June 1964. Finally, A. E. Ott, 'The Relation between the Accelerator and the Capital-Output Ratio', *RESt*, June 1958.

A comprehensive explanation of the concept of the capital-output ratio is given by J. Tinbergen, *The Design of Development* (Baltimore 1958), p. 13 and appendix 1; see also *Problems of Capital Formation: Concepts, Measurement and Controlling Factors* (*Studies in Income and Wealth*, Vol. 19, Princeton 1957), Part 2.

See the publications on the business cycle (for the multiplier also). The most exhaustive analysis of the interaction of multiplier and accelerator is given by J. R. Hicks, *A Contribution to the Theory of the Trade Cycle*; H. Neisser, 'Critical Notes on the Acceleration Principle', *QJE*, May 1954. For the mathematical aspects, see W. J. Baumol, *Economic Dynamics: An Introduction* (2nd ed., New York 1959).

e. The business cycle

The theories of Kondratieff, Juglar and Kitchin were expounded respectively in N. D. Kondratieff, 'Die langen Wellen der Konjunktur', *Archiv für Sozialwissenschaft und Sozialpolitik*, 1926, No 3 (an English translation was published in *Readings in Business Cycle Theory*, ed. G. Haberler, Philadelphia 1944); C. Juglar, *Des crises commerciales et de leur retour périodique en France, en Angleterre et aux Etats-Unis* (2nd ed., Paris 1889); J. Kitchin, 'Cycles and Trends', *The Review of Economic Statistics*, January 1923.

G. Haberler, *Prosperity and Depression: A Theoretical Analysis of Cyclical Movements* (3rd ed., Geneva 1949), a standard work, comprises a general survey of business-cycle theories and of the causes and consequences of business cycles.

Good introductions: J. Tinbergen and J. J. Polak, *The Dynamics of Business Cycles* (London 1950), is a revised translation by J. J. Polak of a Dutch publication by J. Tinbergen dating from 1946; A. H. Hansen, *Business Cycles and National Income* (New York 1951); J. A. Estey, *Business Cycles: Their Nature, Causes and Control* (3rd ed., New York 1956); M. W. Lee, *Economic Fluctuations: Growth and Stability* (rev. ed., Homewood, Ill. 1959), and especially R. C. O. Matthews, *The Trade Cycle* (Cambridge 1959).

On the empirical investigation of the business cycle: A. F. Burns and W. C. Mitchell, *Measuring Business Cycles* (New York 1946). A purely econometric investigation: L. R. Klein, *Economic Fluctuations in the United States 1921–1941* (New York 1950). Further elaborated in L. R. Klein and A. S. Goldberger, *An Econometric Model of the United States 1929–1952* (Amsterdam 1955). A. S. Goldberger, *Import Multipliers and Dynamic Properties of the Klein-Goldberger Model* (Amsterdam 1959), investigates the practical value of this model. More extensive and based on quarterly figures: *The Brookings Quarterly Econometric Model of the United States* (Chicago 1965).

An inquiry especially concerned with the 1947–61 period: T.

Hultgren, *Cost, Prices, and Profits: Their Cyclical Relations* (New York 1965).

A general analysis of the fluctuations in the relevant economic data (national product, consumption, etc.) can be found in C. Clark, *The Conditions of Economic Progress* (3rd. ed. London 1957).

On the part played by stocks: M. A. Abramovitz, *Inventories and Business Cycles, with Special Reference to Manufacturers' Inventories* (New York 1950), and T. M. Stanback, Jr., *Postwar Cycles in Manufacturers' Inventories* (New York 1962), are concerned respectively with the interwar and 1947–56 period.

The quotation from J. Schumpeter is drawn from his *Business Cycles* (New York 1939).

f. Business cycle indicators
Business Cycle Indicators (ed. G. H. Moore, Princeton 1961), Part 1: *Contributions to the Analysis of Current Business Conditions*; Part 2: *Basic Data on Cyclical Indicators*. The first volume is a collection of twenty papers of which fourteen were published from 1950 to 1959 and one in 1938. Eight articles are by G. H. Moore, based on North American data. *The Quality and Economic Significance of Anticipations Data* (Princeton 1960) is another series of papers on various relevant methods.

F. Newsbury, *Business Forecasting: Principles and Practice* (New York 1952), gives a more systematic outline. See also *Techniques of Economic Forecasting: An Account of the Methods of Short-Term Economic Forecasting used by the Governments of Canada, France, the Netherlands, Sweden, the United Kingdom and the United States*, with an introduction by C. W. McMahon (OECD, Paris 1965).

The comment of D. B. J. Schouten is from *Conjunctuurtheorie*, Part 1 of his *Dynamische macro-economie* (Leiden 1967).

g. Inflation
G. Haberler, *Inflation: Its Causes and Cures: revised and enlarged edition with a new look at inflation in 1966* (Washington 1966) – a booklet in which this prominent economist gives a general outline of the problem, with particular reference to American conditions. Another simple but more extensive exposition: W. L. Thorp and R. E. Quandt, *The New Inflation* (New York 1959). See also: M. Bronfenbrenner and F. D. Holzman, 'Survey of Inflation Theory', *AER*, September 1963; A. J. Hagger, *The Theory of Inflation: A*

Review (Melbourne 1964) – a good analysis of recent studies including B. Hansen's work mentioned below); H. G. Johnson, *Essays in Monetary Economics* (London 1967), Chapter 3.

Especially on repressed inflation: B. Hansen, *A Study in the Theory of Inflation* (London 1951), theoretical, brings disequilibrium on the labour market within the scope of analysis (Hansen adheres to the demand-pull theory), and H. K. Charlesworth, *The Economics of Repressed Inflation* (London 1956), a theoretical work of about a hundred pages, based on insufficient literature.

F. Machlup, 'Another View of Cost-Push and Demand-Pull Inflation', *RES*, May 1960, also distinguishes different categories for each type of inflation.

On cost-push theory: W. G. Bowen, *The Wage-Price Issue: A Theoretical Analysis* (Princeton 1960).

See also the last two chapters of R. J. Ball, *Inflation and the Theory of Money* (London 1964), on the causes and combating of inflation.

G. Maynard, *Economic Development and the Price Level* (London 1962): holds that secular price inflation is difficult to avoid.

The Course and Control of Inflation: A Review of Monetary Experience in Europe after World War I (League of Nations, Geneva 1946). Part 1, prepared by R. Nurkse (some 80 pages), investigates the causes of inflation, and Part 2 (some 40 pages) considers the stabilization of European currencies.

See also Chapter 13.8*d*.

h. The quantity theory

The transactions equation of exchange was set forth in I. Fisher, *The Purchasing Power of Money* (2nd ed., New York 1913), especially in Chapter 2; the cash-balance equation of exchange in D. H. Robertson, *Money* (London 1928, rev. ed., 1948).

A. W. Marget, *The Theory of Prices: A Re-examination of the Central Problems of Monetary Theory*, Vol. 1 (New York 1938), is a standard work, though attaching too much importance to the views of Keynes.

H. Hegeland, *The Quantity Theory of Money: A Critical Study of its Historical Development and Interpretation and a Restatement* (Göteborg 1951), is mainly historical in Part 1; Part 2 (more concise, of about 40 pages) explains the difference between the Fisher and Cambridge theories by means of the various functions of money.

Studies in the Quantity Theory of Money (ed. M. Friedman,

Chicago 1956): after a brief introduction by M. Friedman, in which the Chicago version of the quantity theory is explained (related to the cash-balance theory but also taking the influence of interest into account), four articles on its application, especially in the United States and West Germany. See also M. Friedman, *The Optimum Quantity of Money and Other Essays* (London 1969).

D. Patinkin, *Money, Interest and Prices* (Evanston, Ill. 1965) argues that the validity of the quantity theory is more general than is asserted most of the time.

In connection with the influence of psychological factors: A. Aftalion, *Monnaie, prix et change* (3rd ed., Paris 1950; the first edition was published in 1927). Aftalion also pointed to the importance of income as a determining factor; a change in *MV* which has no influence on income has no influence on prices.

See also *The Controversy over the Quantity Theory of Money*, ed. E. Dean (Boston 1965); R. T. Selden, 'La théorie quantitative de la monnaie contre l'optique des dépenses et du revenu', *Bulletin d'Information et de Documentation de la Banque Nationale de Belgique*, October 1965.

10 Economic growth

> *No attempt is made ... to present a Theory of Economic Growth ... which is to be defended as the theory, superior in every respect, or even in every important respect, to any other. I do not think that there is such a theory; I much doubt if there can be.*
>
> Sir John Hicks

Partly because governments have succeeded in mitigating the fluctuations in the business cycle, more attention has been given to economic growth since the Second World War. The business cycle is now seen in the context of economic growth. After defining economic growth, we shall review the various theories advanced to explain it. We shall examine, in particular, the problems pertaining to the less-developed countries, since much of the enhanced interest in growth theory can be related to these countries' struggle to attain a higher standard of living.

1 The factors of economic growth

a. Definitions
Economic growth is a long-term concept. In our analysis of the business cycle, we mostly ignored the possibility of an increase in production capacity because the short-term effects of this increase would be negligible. In other words, the study of the business cycle is concerned with the changes in the extent to which a given production capacity is utilized. In the long run, the expansion of capacity must also be taken into consideration. Economic growth could therefore be defined as a constant raising of production capacity. In general, however, economic growth is not measured against production capacity, which is very difficult to estimate, but against national production. It must be remembered that an increase in national production is due not only to the expansion of production capacity but also to the changes in the extent to which this capacity is utilized.

The influence of price fluctuations must be eliminated. We can study the changes either in total production or in production *per capita* of the population, *per capita* of the labour force or per hour worked. In the following pages, we take economic growth to mean a sustained increase in the net real national product (or income) per inhabitant.

Some authors draw a distinction between economic growth (production and population increase at the same rate) and economic development (production increases faster than population). Others define economic growth also as a continuous increase in real *per capita* national income or product but consider that economic development has a wider meaning, including structural change and technological progress. It is difficult to achieve economic growth without economic development if this distinction is adopted. The two terms will be regarded as synonyms in this text.

Economic growth is underestimated if the national product per head of the population is used as criterion (the caution with which this concept should be employed having been stressed in Chapter 2). In the last hundred years, the proportion of the active population to the total population has increased by about 2 per cent every decade. On the other hand, the number of hours worked per head of the active population has decreased, from 1·1 per cent to 4·5 per cent per decade according to the country (estimates of Simon Kuznets).

Growth theory is designed to explain the long-term changes in the factors determining the national product and the influence of these factors on the national product and the national product *per capita* (where capacity changes also occur).

The compilation of data with a view to studying economic growth is a recent phenomenon. S. Kuznets in particular has done pioneering work in this field. It can be seen from Table 30 (cf. Figure 61) that, in countries where statistics are available, total production rises at between 2 and 4 per cent a year, the real national product *per capita* at between 1·4 and 2·8 per cent. It is only in the USSR between 1928 and 1958 that higher rates were achieved.

Obviously, growth rates were not constant during the periods in question. It is generally accepted that economic growth has occurred mainly since 1750. Whether there was a significant increase in living standards at that time may be doubted: economic growth has usually been a gradual process.

During the period following the Second World War (1950–67), the growth rate in less-developed countries was 2·4 per cent in comparison to 3·1 per cent in developed countries (see Section 6).

b. The factors

As the level of the national product can be explained by the quantity and quality of the factors of production, the way in which they are used, and the institutional framework, so the growth of the national product can be explained by the changes in these factors. Numerous growth theories, however, some of which will be examined later, are based essentially on only *one* determining factor.

TABLE 30: Growth per decade of national product and *per capita* product of some countries (in constant prices)

Country	Period	Total product	per capita product
1. Russia (European)-USSR	1860 to 1913	30·2	14·4
	1913 to 1958	35·7	27·4
	1928 to 1958	53·8	43·9
2. Sweden	1861–5 to 1960–2	36·9	28·3
3. Japan	1879–81 to 1959–61	42·0	26·4
4. Denmark	1870–4 to 1960–2	31·8	19·4
5. Norway	1865–74 to 1960–2	29·0	19·0
6. Italy	1861–5 to 1898–1902	9·7	2·7
	1898–1902 to 1960–2	26·8	18·7
7. Canada	1870–4 to 1960–2	40·7	18·1
8. France	1841–50 to 1960–2	20·8	17·9
9. Germany (West)	1851–5 to 1871–5	17·6	9·2
	1871–5 to 1960–2	31·1	17·9
10. United States	1839 to 1960–2	42·5	17·2
11. Switzerland	1890–9 to 1957–9	25·7	16·1

Country	Period	Total product	per capita product
12. United Kingdom	1780 to 1881	28·2	13·4
	1855–9 to 1957–9	21·1	14·1
13. Netherlands	1900–4 to 1960–2	29·7	13·5
14. Australia	1861–5 to 1959–60 1961–2	34·1	8·0

Source: S. Kuznets, *Modern Economic Growth: Rate, Structure, and Spread* (New Haven 1966), pp. 64–5

1. *Population*

Table 30 shows that there is no connection between the growth rate of the national product and that of the population. In all these countries, population went up less than total production – otherwise, there could have been no increase in *per capita* product – but in varying degrees from one country to the next. The population increase was low in France but high in Australia, the United States and Canada (owing to immigration).

Since the number of hours worked per day (and year) has fallen by about 25 per cent on average since 1870 (see also the figures for hours worked per head of population), the real product per hour worked has increased even more than real *per capita* product, so the increase in the latter cannot be explained by an increase in the number of hours worked *per capita*.

2. *Natural conditions*

It is difficult to generalize on the connection between soil conditions or mineral resources and economic growth. The possession of rich ore deposits is not a sufficient condition of economic development, nor is the lack of them any hindrance (e.g. New Zealand): the extension of transport in particular has made for cheapness in the shipment of raw materials. Whereas in some countries with abundant natural resources the average national income has not in fact shown an increase (e.g. Indonesia), countries not so well off in this respect have shown steady progress.

3. *Capital*

It is generally accepted that the stock of capital goods in western

333

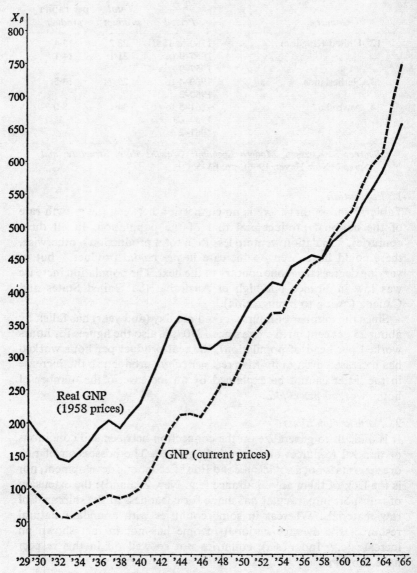

Figure 61: The gross national product of the United States ($000m.; 1929–65)

countries has increased more than the active population (capital deepening). This is reflected in industrialization and the increasing importance of the tertiary sector. In the United States agriculture represented 20 per cent, industry 33 per cent and services 47 per cent of the national product in 1869–79: in 1966 the corresponding percentages were 13, 39 and 58. There was a similar trend in the United Kingdom, where agriculture's share was 45 per cent in 1770, 22 per cent in 1841 and 3 per cent in 1966, while that of industry increased from 21 per cent in 1770 to 47 per cent in 1966. Agriculture accounts for a bigger proportion of national product in most less-developed countries: Congo (Kinshasa) 28 per cent (1959), UAR 29 per cent (1965), Brazil 28 per cent (1965), Turkey 37 per cent (1966), Pakistan and India 49 per cent (1966), Indonesia 56 per cent (1964).

The ratio of reproducible capital to output rose from 4·1 to 5 in the United Kingdom between 1865 and 1933, from 1·9 to 2·1 in the United States between 1850 and 1950, from 2·8 to 3 in Japan between 1905 and 1935. S. Kuznets arrives at the following conclusion on the basis of these and other scarce data: 'the trends in the ratios of reproducible capital to product have been upward, though tempered by recent declines, often to particularly low levels in the post-world war II years'. However, when he takes 'total capital', including raw materials (e.g. minerals), into consideration he finds that the (total) capital-output ratio has been falling, owing to the reduced importance of the non-reproducible part of the stock of capital goods. For further discussion, he feels it is possible to assume that the (total) capital-output ratio remains constant (but see Section 2).

4. *Other factors*

Among other factors that should be mentioned are technological progress (see Section 3*b*) and the institutional, political and social circumstances (see Section 7) in which production takes place.

2 The Harrod-Domar theory

Sir Roy Harrod, an Englishman, and E. Domar, an American, were among the first to construct growth models. Although there are slight differences between the two, they are generally referred to as the Harrod-Domar theory. We shall only give the essential points here, concentrating on growth theory proper (business cycles are also included in the theory, but this is its weakest part).

Investment (the increase in the stock of capital goods) is the primary cause of growth: the relation between the stock of capital goods and output (production, national income) can be expressed as follows:

$$K = kY$$

in which k, the capital-output ratio, is assumed to remain constant. Saving too (the supply of money available for investment in capital goods) makes up a constant proportion of the national income:

$$S = sY$$

Since k is constant, the effect of a change in K on Y can always be determined:

$$\Delta K = k\Delta Y \tag{1}$$

By definition, ΔK is the amount of investment in a given period, it being assumed that all saving is invested:

$$\Delta K = I = S = sY. \tag{2}$$

Substitution of (2) in (1) gives:

$$sY = k\Delta Y$$

or:
$$\frac{\Delta Y}{Y} = \frac{s}{k}.$$

The relative change in the national income, or $\Delta Y/Y$, which henceforth is shown by g, is thus:

$$g = \frac{s}{k}.$$

When $k = 5$ and $s = 0.20$, the relative increase in Y is equal to $0.20 \div 5 = 0.04$. How growth proceeds is shown in Table 31. An original stock of capital goods of 500 yields an income of 100, of which 80 per cent is consumed and 20 per cent saved. The savings are invested, so that in the succeeding period the stock of capital goods rises to 520. This rise in capital leads to an increase in production, which is divided in the same way between S and C. As $g = 0.04$, it is clear that K must also increase by 4 per cent. If the increase in population (or the labour input) which is exogenously determined, is 2 per cent (as in the example), capital deepening results.

Changes in the labour input must be taken into consideration in

336

order to establish the trend of national income *per capita g**. This makes the increase not 4 per cent but approximately 2 per cent (last column in Table 31), or also by the simplified formula:

$$g^* = \frac{s}{k} - l^* \text{ or } g^* = g - l^*.$$

TABLE 31: Schematic outline of the Harrod-Domar growth model ($k = 5; s = 0.20$)

Period	K	Y	S	C	L'	Y/L'
1	500·00	100·00	20·00	80·00	100·00	1·0000
2	520·00	104·00	20·80	83·20	102·00	1·0196
3	540·80	108·16	21·63	86·53	104·04	1·0396
4	562·43	112·48	22·49	89·99	106·12	1·0599
5	584·92	116·98	23·39	93·59	108·24	1·0807
6	608·31	121·66	24·33	97·33	110·40	1·1020
7	632·64	126·53	25·30	101·23	112·61	1·1236

In conditions of full employment, and taking technological progress into account, R. Harrod calls the percentage increase in labour input the natural rate of growth. For *g* to go up by the same figure (and the workers concerned to be integrated in the production process), the propensity to save must be $0.02 \times 5 = 0.10$ (in which case the *per capita* national income remains constant in view of the fact that both *Y* and *L'* increase by 2 per cent); this means that there is capital widening. The propensity to save must be $(0.02 + 0.02) 5 = 0.20$ if the *per capita* national income is to rise by 2 per cent. The actual or historical rate of growth can be lower than the natural rate of growth. When this is the case, the government must take the necessary measures to ensure a rise in saving. Saving and the concomitant investment provide the momentum for economic growth.

Appraisal

1. Like the equation of exchange, the formula gives the factors which are relevant for an analysis, but it tells us nothing about the factors themselves.

2. The theory is based on unrealistic assumptions. The capital-output ratio does not remain constant. Authors, such as S. Kuznets, who find it an acceptable working hypothesis to regard the capital-output ratio as constant, are relying on excessively limited material.

In so far as reliable data are available (the calculation of macro-economic capital is quite a feat), the ratio – and changes in the ratio – differs from country to country. Special circumstances have repeatedly played a role. Technological progress is frequently embodied in the formation of capital, so that production is compared not only with capital but also with the technological progress embodied in capital goods. If this technological progress is not maintained, then the capital-output ratio will be too low in the next period.

Normally, a difference in growth between labour and capital provokes substitution phenomena. This substitution is considered impossible in the Harrod-Domar theory, where the growth rate of the national product is identical with that of the stock of capital goods. This is more a hypothesis for the short than for the long run.

It is surprising that the Harrod-Domar theory does not try to show a link between an increase in the exogenously determined total or active population and the increase in the derived demand for labour which results from the increase in the stock of capital goods (labour and capital are assumed to be in a fixed ratio to each other).

3. A similar observation may be made about the propensity to save. Some authors, including N. Kaldor and J. Robinson, have pointed out that the propensity to save differs in the case of income from employment and income from entrepreneurship, and they have supplemented the Harrod-Domar theory accordingly.

3 The neoclassical theory of growth

a. The Solow-Swan theory

Neoclassical growth theory is also based on a constant propensity to save but does not assume a fixed capital-output ratio. R. Solow and T. W. Swan, who were the first to formulate the theory, consider that economic development depends not on one but on two production factors (labour and capital). These factors are wholly substitutable. The rate of growth of labour or population l^* is determined exogenously, that of capital by the ratio s/k:

$$\frac{\Delta K}{K} = \frac{I/Y}{K/Y} = \frac{S/Y}{K/Y} = \frac{s}{k}.$$

When the increase in s/k is greater than that in l^*, each worker has more capital goods at his disposal (capital deepening). The increase in the quantity of capital coincides, however, with a decrease in marginal product (the additional production resulting from additional capital declines: decreasing returns occur). The capital-output ratio or k thus increases; in other words, the growth rate of capital s/k diminishes. This reduction in s/k will continue till the growth rate of capital coincides with that of labour: steady-state growth is achieved, where the growth rate of national product equals those of labour and capital.

Prices – and particularly the remuneration of production factors – are assumed to be extremely flexible. They ensure that the available factors of production are fully utilized and that the growth rates of labour and capital coincide: a capital-intensive production, for example, will bring interest rates down and increase wages.

Appraisal

Once more it must be stressed that the propensity to save is not constant. We found in our study of prices that most prices and wages are rigid; to assume flexible prices is therefore unrealistic (unemployment is not absorbed when wages fall). The ratio between capital and labour has not been fixed once and for all, and perfect substitutability is not possible either.

b. Technological advance in the theory of growth

On the basis of the Cobb-Douglas function with $\alpha = 0.75$ (three quarters of income going to labour, one quarter to capital), which assumes perfect substitutability, the conclusion would be that the growth of production depends 75 per cent on growth of labour and 25 per cent on growth of capital. A quarter of the growth of *per capita* production, then, is accounted for by 25 per cent of the growth of capital per head. This is why economic growth is ascribed chiefly to technological advance.

According to R. Solow, technological advance accounted for 85 per cent of the growth in the American economy (national income per employee) between 1909 and 1945. E. F. Denison quotes 62 per cent for the United States in the period 1950–62 and 80 per cent for northwestern Europe (where the highest figure for any one country was 86 per cent for West Germany).

Technological advance here is a broader concept than the technological advance in the strict sense to which we have referred hitherto. The latter is a consequence of microeconomic innovation, while the former is a macroeconomic residual factor. That part of the growth

339

rate of the national product which cannot be explained by the increase in labour and capital is attributed to technological advance – not only technological advance in the strict sense but also improvement in the quality of production factors (e.g. a higher standard of education) and the way in which factors are combined to make for efficient production (e.g. more efficient management, economies of scale, external economies). The sum of these changes entails increased production per unit of input. Thus, the national income rises because there are changes in factor inputs and because output per unit of input increases (i.e. technological advance in the broader sense). It would be preferable to speak of productivity or simply of production per unit of input to avoid confusion with technological advance proper.

It should be mentioned at this point that there are numerous other definitions of technological advance and that technical and technological advance are usually synonymous (though 'technological' is perhaps preferable since it is more suggestive of the application of *scientific* knowledge or research to the economic process). There are also various definitions of neutral technological advance – which is attained, according to R. Harrod, for example, when the capital-output ratio remains constant (and the profit rate is constant) or, according to R. Solow, when the labour-output ratio remains constant (and the wage rate is constant).

Although the relevant literature is of recent date, a number of theories have been put forward concerning the role of technological advance in economic growth. R. Solow, for instance, holds that technological advance can be seen in or is incorporated in the investment of the current year ('the latest vintage of capital'). Others remark that technological advance need not necessarily be embodied in labour or capital but should rather be considered a third production factor. K. Arrow sees technological advance as a consequence rather than a cause of economic growth (see Chapter 6.4a: learning by doing and the Horndal effect). Others again are investigating whether technological advance should be considered an exogenous or endogenous factor (e.g. as a result of expenditure on education and research). In the last case, technological progress is considered to be part of the production process, on account of the institutionalization of the search for new production processes (see Chapter 6.4a). Technological progress is then no longer considered to be among the 'data'; or, in other words, not to be an element of the economic structure (see Chapter 1.8).

Appraisal

The fact that theories on technological advance have so far proved unsatisfactory is partly because there is little information on which to test the assumptions made. This can also be seen in the heroic efforts to measure the residual factor, which is already so 'difficult to analyse' (J. Johnston), and especially to allocate it to various components such as education and increasing returns to scale (as in E. F. Denison's work). The very rough estimates concerned could as well be replaced by other, quite different, estimates. The hypotheses (e.g. pure competition) on which the method is based are indeed very unrealistic. Technological advance has, without question, been important in economic growth, but it is impossible to ascertain exactly to what extent the one explains the other.

c. Conclusion

Economic growth is a difficult and complicated matter. J. H. Adler quite rightly points out that 'the experience of the postwar period shows the complexity and manysidedness of the process of economic development, on the one hand, and how little we know and how much we still have to learn about it, on the other'. It should not surprise us that 'we seem as far from a *general* theory as ever' (B. Higgins). Theory implies generalization. But to try to explain economic growth by one criterion will not do. The significance of each growth factor differs from country to country – the institutional circumstances in particular.

This last point is especially true of the less-developed countries. It is a fact that there are relatively few features common to the economies of these countries: small stock of capital goods and little technological knowhow, few good entrepreneurs or managers. And there are great differences in natural resources, institutional circumstances and population. It stands to reason that economic policy in a densely populated country (with substantial disguised unemployment) will differ from that in a thinly populated country.

A theory that will serve for one particular country or group of countries is not necessarily applicable to another. India, for instance, is often regarded, wrongly, as *the* example of a less-developed country. In view of this misconception, more attention is now paid to a classification of the different countries – with a theory for each type. There is no need to look for a special development theory for the less-developed countries: economic growth is a universal phenomenon.

Attempts made along these lines have had little result. With the exception of W. W. Rostow's theory (see Section 4) we have been offered only partial explanations (some of which we shall come back to later in discussing the stimulation of growth in the less-developed countries). The economic dualism assumed by some authors, for instance (coexistence of a relatively small, modern, capital-intensive sector and a traditional, mainly agricultural sector), can be found in developed countries too, though to a lesser extent.

4 The stages of economic growth

As long ago as the second half of the nineteenth century, a number of writers took the view that economic growth inevitably follows a fixed pattern and that it is not possible to skip any of the stages (Appendix 5). According to one of the newer theories on the subject, that of W. W. Rostow, there are five distinct stages. In Rostow's theory, unlike many modern theories of growth, more attention is given to psychological and political factors.

a. The preconditions for take-off
In a traditional society (the first stage) a number of expanding industries (e.g. commerce, mining, plantations) grow up, generally under foreign influence, and an active minority is formed which sets itself the aim of developing the country's economy. It is frequently xenophobia, more than any quest for gain, that motivates this élite. Investment accounts for 5 to 10 per cent of the national income.

b. Take-off
A start can be made with the development process when the forces referred to above have acquired predominance in both the political and the economic sphere. The rise in the national income, which was irregular during the preceding stage, becomes a permanent feature. Whether by private enterprise or by official action – sometimes a combination of the two – care is taken to ensure that at least 10 per cent of the national income is invested.

Considerable attention is paid to the improvement of the economic infrastructure (in order to make possible external economies). Industry turns this to account and employs more manpower; so does agriculture, which no longer works solely to meet its own requirements, but for the market. Industry, which in most cases is protected

against foreign competition, undergoes a rapid expansion and the
bulk of the profit is ploughed back.

The 'take-off' dates were 1783–1802 in the United Kingdom, 1830–
60 in France, 1833–60 in Belgium, 1843–60 in the United States,
1850–73 in Germany, 1890–1914 in Russia and 1896–1914 in Canada.
The start of this process has been established as 1935 for Argentina,
1937 for Turkey and 1952 for India and China. (In the case of the two
last-named countries, Rostow suspends judgment on the success of
the take-off.)

c. The drive to maturity

The ruling class which arose during the take-off (entrepreneurs and
financiers in the capitalist countries, officials in the communist
countries) causes an increasing proportion of the national income
(10 to 20 per cent) to be saved and invested. Through the growth of
the population, wages are kept low and the necessary workers are
found for the many new occupations.

Some sixty years, on average, after the take-off (forty years after
the beginning of the drive to maturity) a state of economic maturity
is reached, the salient features of which are a high *per capita* income
and the application of modern technology in most sectors of the
economy.

d. Mass consumption

During the last few years of the drive to maturity, it is usual for trade
unions and political movements to be set up in order to increase the
workers' share in the national product. As the national product rises,
so can this pressure be the more readily yielded to without jeopardiz-
ing investment. Thus by degrees the way is cleared for a high level of
consumption, which leads to increasing production of durable
consumer goods (domestic equipment). At the same time, the birth
rate is seen to follow a gradual downward trend. Most industrialized
countries may probably be said to be still in this phase. In the United
States, the postwar 'baby boom' would appear to indicate a sixth
stage, in which the standard of living virtually stabilizes as a consequence of the fresh expansion of the population.

Appraisal

Rostow's thesis does not concur with the statistical material available.
The process of growth and the trend of investment are gradual: they

343

do not advance by fits and starts. The industrial 'revolution' in England 'was the cumulation of a four-century period of advance in techniques' (E. E. Hagen). It is not clear what criteria can be used in order to distinguish one stage from another. In recent years, for instance, the American baby boom has seemed to be coming to an end. Nor is it possible to establish in advance what industries should provide the thrust to set off economic growth.

Rostow's scheme fails to take sufficient account of the fact that the less-developed countries can now avail themselves of western experts and up-to-date equipment and thus avoid not a little trial and error and misdirected investment. They experience difficulties in exporting, however, because in the matter of quality and price higher demands are made than, for instance, at the beginning of the nineteenth century, when Britain was the only exporter on an international scale. Lack of financial means is another factor that frequently restrains accelerated development, despite the aid which is provided by national and international institutions in this field (see Section 7e).

5 Foreign trade and economic growth

There is an interrelationship between external trade and economic growth: just as economic growth may have an effect on foreign trade, so may foreign trade exert an influence on growth.

Initially, economic growth usually brings about an increase in external trade, since requirements of capital and consumer goods rise. Once some of these goods begin to be produced at home as a policy of industrialization takes effect, a decline is liable to set in.

Foreign trade itself frequently stimulates economic growth. The economic progress achieved by England at the end of the nineteenth century was due to an expansion of exports. The less-developed countries which succeed in raising their exports generally achieve a high growth rate. Opportunities vary from case to case, however, so that divergent types of policy are pursued – depending on the economic system.

a. Isolation

In order to make more resources available for investment, consumption has to be kept as low as possible. In many of the less-developed countries this is difficult to manage without import restrictions. The ruling classes especially are eager to follow western consumer habits for prestige reasons (demonstration effect), so they save little, even in the event of a substantial rise in income. Again under the influence of the West, the workers insist on certain measures (education for all, social security) which in Western Europe were only implemented at the end of the nineteenth or in the course of the twentieth century, when there was already a higher level of prosperity. The governments concerned find themselves obliged to spend an appreciable proportion of their available resources on projects of this kind.

Nor does the training of university graduates in the developed countries yield much in the way of results. Once they are accustomed to a higher standard of living, the graduates have little inclination to return to their own country; they are only interested in diplomatic posts or positions in international organizations. Over 90 per cent of the Asians who go to the United States to study stay there after graduating. In New York alone there are more Iranian doctors than in Iran itself, and nearly half the National Health Service doctors in the United Kingdom are Indians and Pakistanis.

Isolation is a means of ensuring that foreign goods, newspapers and tourists do not encourage the indigenous population to imitate other countries' living standards. It is then possible to increase the propensity to save and build up basic industries without having to pay very much heed to consumers' wishes.

This is how the USSR achieved its economic progress in a relatively short time, despite its heavy losses in the Second World War.

b. Limited isolation

However, most of the less-developed countries, China being an exception, are too small to aim at economic independence or to pursue a completely autarkic policy. They have to settle for limited isolation: cultural and tourist relations are still permitted and exports are encouraged, but protectionist measures are taken against foreign industrial products.

Such a development technique was successfully applied by the United States and Germany in the nineteenth century. The propensity to save in these countries was swelled by high entrepreneurs' profits, which were themselves derived from the monopolistic or oligopolistic position of the protected industries. If, however, savings are not put to good use – perhaps because of a lack of competent entrepreneurs – there is no stimulus to economic progress.

c. Specialization in goods for export

Instead of being geared to the home market, industrial development can be organized from the outset for selling abroad. The export industry then becomes the driving force in the national economy. As exports increase, purchasing power on the home market rises, thus clearing the way for the establishment of other industries (foodstuffs, building).

This method is eminently suitable for countries which are able to offset the drawbacks of the initial stage because wages are low, this in turn being the result of high population density. Compared with the policy described under (*b*), it has the advantage that there is no danger of the growth of less-competitive industries.

Countries with a relatively sparse population and high wages can only apply this policy if natural advantages make specialization in exports a profitable activity (Australia, Canada, Venezuela).

As with the protectionist method, success is only assured where capable entrepreneurs are available. If this is not the case, the country has to rely on foreign capital and technicians, so that a good deal of the profit is exported and internal purchasing power increases at a slower pace. Moreover, the success of this policy hinges on the industrial countries' trade policies: for instance, no discrimination may be exercised against the low-wage countries. One final point: the proceeds from the leading exports must not fluctuate unduly, for without sufficient stability in purchasing power, it is not possible to set up consumer-goods industries.

Initially, the result of growth in less-developed countries will be a tendency towards the gradual contraction of the world market because the demand for some manufactures is being satisfied by home production. Sales of industrial goods by the western countries may go down, while the price of raw materials may rise because some of them will be processed in their country of origin.

The changes entailed by economic progress, however, stimulate demand for other imported goods, so that it is generally assumed that industrialization promotes international trade. This is true only if there are no quantitative restrictions on trade. Since 1913, then, industrialization in the less-developed countries has been shown to work to the disadvantage of other industrial countries, especially the United Kingdom.

The best way in which industrialized countries which are highly dependent on exports can defend themselves is to adapt their economic

346

structure to changed circumstances by producing more sophisticated, science-based goods, especially capital goods, and leaving the production of less elaborate goods to the less-developed countries.

6 International differences in welfare

We noted in Chapter 2 that real national product and *per capita* income are only approximate indicators of welfare. The *level* of *per capita* national income alone should be considered, but all countries – and the less-developed countries in particular – attach as much importance to the *growth rate* of *per capita* national income too because the level is influenced by it.

The level of *per capita* national income is notably higher in developed countries (Table 32). With 19 per cent of the world's population, the non-communist developed countries produce about 64 per cent of its gross domestic product. The corresponding figures are 35 per cent and 22 per cent for the communist countries, 46 per cent and 14 per cent for the non-communist less-developed countries (Kuznets's figures for 1958). The richest countries and areas are the United States and Canada, New Zealand and Australia, Scandinavia and Western Europe (Table 33).

Growth data for the less-developed countries are available only for the postwar period. The increase in gross domestic product there is higher than in the developed countries. Owing to the faster increase in population, however, the increase in product *per capita* is lower (Table 32). The situation is more favourable in Southern Europe and the Middle East. Growth in North America (2·1 per cent) is lower than in the less-developed countries as a whole (2·4 per cent). Countries with a high rate of growth (more than 4 per cent per year) include Libya, Liberia, Jordan, Saudi Arabia, Taiwan and Angola. A yearly increase of 3 per cent to 3·9 per cent in average domestic product is attained by Mozambique, Tunisia, Syria, Thailand and Iran. These last three countries have to face an annual increase in population of at least 2·5 per cent. Although poverty is not on the increase in the less-developed countries, the difference in welfare is being felt more strongly than before – partly as a result of more intensive political and economic relations between the different parts of the world. Hence the efforts being made to raise their level of living as quickly as possible. Some of the means of realizing this aim are dwelt upon in the following pages.

TABLE 32: Level of gross domestic product (1967) and annual rate of growth of gross domestic product and population (1950–67) by regions (excluding communist countries)

Group	Gross domestic product *per capita* in $	Gross domestic product *per capita* in £	Real gross domestic product	Population	Real gross domestic product *per capita*
			Average rate of growth in per cent		
Less-developed countries	170	71	4·8	2·3	2·4
of which Southern Europe[a]	692	288	6·0	1·4	4·5
Middle East	390	163	6·5	3·0	3·4
Developed countries	2,020	842	4·3	1·2	3·1
of which North America	3,570	1,488	3·8	1·7	2·1
Western Europe	1,420	592	4·5	0·8	3·7
Other developed countries[b]	1,121	467	7·6	1·4	6·1

[a] Greece, Spain, Portugal, Cyprus

[b] Australia, Japan, New Zealand, South Africa, Puerto Rico

Source: IBRD, Annual Report 1969 (Washington 1969), p. 46 and derived from UNCTAD, Handbook of International Trade and Development Statistics 1969 (New York 1969), p. 168

TABLE 33: Population (in million, mid-1970) and gross national product per capita (1966, in $ and £)

Country	Population	GNP per cap.		Country	Population	GNP per cap.	
		in £	in $			in £	in $
United States	205	1,467	3,520	Romania	20	271	650
				Spain	33	267	640
Sweden	8	946	2,270	South Africa	20	229	550
Switzerland	6	938	2,250	Chile	10	213	510
Canada	21	933	2,240	Jugoslavia	21	213	510
New Zealand	3	804	1,930	Mexico	51	196	470
Australia	13	767	1,840	Portugal	10	158	380
Denmark	5	763	1,830	Peru	14	133	320
France	51	721	1,730	Turkey	36	117	280
Norway	4	713	1,710	Colombia	21	117	280
Germany (West)	59	708	1,700	Iran	28	104	250
				Brazil	93	100	240
Belgium	10	679	1,630	Morocco	16	71	170
United Kingdom	56	675	1,620	United Arab Republic	34	67	160
Finland	5	667	1,600	Philippines	38	67	160
Netherlands	13	592	1,420	South Korea	32	63	150
Germany (East)	16	508	1,220	Thailand	36	54	130
Israel	3	483	1,160	South Vietnam	18	50	120
Austria	7	479	1,150	Sudan	16	42	100
Italy	54	429	1,030	Indonesia	121	42	100
Czecho-slovakia	15	421	1,010	India	555	38	90
USSR	243	371	890	Pakistan	137	38	90
Japan	104	358	860	China	760	35	84
Venezuela	11	355	850	Nigeria	55	33	80
Hungary	10	333	800	Afghanistan	17	29	70
Argentina	24	325	780	Ethiopia	25	25	60
Poland	33	304	730	Congo (Kinshasa)	17	25	60
Greece	9	275	660	Burma	28	25	60

Source: World Bank Atlas. Population, per capita product and growth rate (IBRD, 4th ed., Washington 1969); concerning China (1958): Simon Kuznets, Modern Economic Growth, p. 360; Trends in development countries (IBRD, August 1970).

7 The promotion of economic growth in the less-developed countries

a. Population

In many less-developed countries, as we have seen, it would be sufficient to bring down the rate of population growth in order to see the standard of living go up. The use of western methods in public health and medicine have resulted in a population explosion in many of these countries. For example, in India the death rate (see Chapter 1.8*b*) was reduced from about 43 at the beginning of the century to 17 in 1970, and in Chile from about 40 in the middle of the last century to 10 in 1967 (see also Table 2). At the same time, the birth rate has not decreased. In the less-developed countries, the population increases on average by 2·3 per cent a year as compared to 1·2 per cent in developed countries (Table 32). Thus, the annual increase of population in less-developed countries is 37 million, in communist countries 13 million and in developed non-communist countries 6 million. The world population, which was 250 million at the beginning of the Christian era, 550 million in 1650, 725 million in 1750, 900 million in 1800, 1,600 million in 1900 and 3,592 million in 1970, might therefore reach a figure of 6,000 to 7,000 million by the year 2000.

Although demographic expansion can contribute to economic growth by inducing new investment, it acts rather as a brake when the growth of population does not give rise to an increase of demand. This is the case in most less-developed countries.

There are many less-developed countries which have come to the conclusion that a policy of birth control must be adopted although a surplus of manpower can help industrialization. In other words, they are unwilling to wait for a spontaneous reduction in the birth rate, such as came about in the western countries fifty or sixty years after the reduction in the death rate. Japan made abortion legal in 1948; the number of abortions is now reported to exceed the number of births. In India and China too, the governments officially favour policies to keep the population in check. The difficulties do not stem so much from religious conviction. The ignorance of the population hampers the spread of contraceptives, which need to be both cheap and easy to use.

b. Investment
Industrialization makes it possible to absorb some of the disguised unemployment in agriculture, and these 'unlimited supplies of labor' (W. A. Lewis) themselves facilitate industrialization. But the thinly populated less-developed countries also seek industrialization in order to become less dependent on business cycles through having a wider range of production. Without a lively home market, the harmful

effects of a drop in the prices of a few export goods are felt much more seriously.

Capital formation in both industry and agriculture must be preceded by investment in two major sectors – transport and hydroelectric power. An effective investment policy is inconceivable without an advanced transport system and the necessary motive power, especially in industry. It is because essential public works (which benefit production only indirectly) must be carried out that the (macroeconomic) capital-output ratio is generally high in less-developed countries. It can be kept down by using labour-intensive production methods as far as possible.

Theoretically, preference should be given to investment in as many industries as possible. There are many risks involved in capital investment in only one industry; income must also be raised elsewhere to absorb that industry's increased production. A big push is needed, then, to achieve balanced growth. In fact, balanced growth cannot be realized because there are insufficient financial means and a scarcity of entrepreneurs; and in some cases it would thwart the international division of labour. Some authors, including A. O. Hirschman, even advocate deliberately unbalanced growth.

Whereas some progress has been achieved in industry (see Table 34) – though not without difficulty – on the whole little result has been produced in agriculture, despite the fact that it is still the main source of income. As a matter of fact, industry will not necessarily absorb all the disguised unemployment in agriculture. It is only in recent years that some of the less-developed countries (e.g. Pakistan, Turkey) have realized that there is much that can be done in agriculture too.

Where we invest is not without importance: expanding exports is a useful exercise if foreign loans have to be serviced, and agriculture is often the appropriate sector for doing so.

c. Financing investment
A rise in investment normally means a curtailment of consumption. As individuals will not voluntarily increase their saving, government action is needed (where possible). Industrialization was pushed through in the USSR by cutting down on consumption for a whole generation. Similar methods are needed in the less-developed countries (at least if faster growth is the objective). Thus, 'contrary to popular belief, the rigorous pursuit of economic development policies designed to raise the level of material income in the future

may frequently intensify, rather than reduce, the existing level of discontent in developing countries' (H. Myint).

In spite of the lower savings potential in these countries (see Table 34), every effort should be made to find the necessary funds in the countries themselves, since otherwise the balance-of-payments burden (see Chapter 11.6) becomes too heavy. To assert that less-developed countries are incapable of doing this will not bear examination: Egypt's pyramids and Europe's cathedrals were not built in wealthy countries either. Tax evasion, moreover, is very common (and the relative differences in income are more pronounced than in western countries), partly because of inefficient administration. The average net outflow of Latin American funds is estimated at more than $600 million a year.

Financing investment by means of inflation is tempting at first sight: revenue from taxation goes up, higher prices provide an incentive for further investment. On the other hand, consumption by the underprivileged is reduced while producers make high profits, saving declines, speculative investment is encouraged, there is a flight of capital and exports are handicapped.

Foreign capital could have a part to play. The industrialization of the United States was initially made possible by the investment of British capital, that of Canada by capital from the United States and the United Kingdom. The less-developed countries reproach foreign investors, however, with not being concerned to ensure a balanced economic structure: their only aim is to export, and the wages they pay are no higher than in other parts of the economy (which means that purchasing power remains low and cannot have a stimulating effect). This criticism relates to the colonial period. While not wishing to deny its drawbacks, we must point out that in many cases the colonial system laid the foundation for economic growth.

Consequently, the less-developed countries often prefer to borrow from countries other than the former colonial power or from international agencies, so that they can decide independently how new investment should be directed.

Given the tremendous needs of the less-developed countries and the limited resources of international organizations, however, a substantial contribution must still come from private investors. But the willingness of risk capital to go abroad has diminished in recent years for fear of political complications and restrictions on income transfers. This is the reason why some countries (in particular West

Germany, but also Switzerland, the United States, France, Belgium, Denmark and Japan) have concluded bilateral agreements to protect private investment.

TABLE 34: Gross investment, saving in per cent of average gross national product (1960–7), by regions

Region	Gross investment	Savings
Less-developed countries	17·8	15·0
Africa	16·7	13·1
East Asia	15·6	11·0
South Asia	13·9	11·3
Southern Europe	24·9	21·5
Latin America	17·7	16·3
Middle East	19·8	14·8
Developed countries	21·2	21·7
North America	18·0	18·8
Western Europe	23·1	23·7
Other developed countries	33·0	32·0

Source: IBRD, Annual Report 1969, Washington 1969 p. 47

d. Other factors

An increase in investment is only possible where there is efficient management and skilled labour – factors which are not normally available. Hence the importance of education (and technical assistance: see below). Here, however, a minimum of planning is required – as in the developed countries. For example, there are too many lawyers and too few engineers in the less-developed countries, and primary and secondary education are often neglected in favour of higher education, so that the number of university graduates is in excess of the openings for them.

In agriculture, where methods are in use which have been out of date for centuries, the population is illiterate and often opposed to all change. Nevertheless, output can be increased by means of relatively simple tools and devices (seed selection, drainage and fertilizers). A change in mentality is what is needed. There is no point in erecting a dam for irrigation if the people concerned refuse to give up their nomadic way of life.

General obstacles to economic growth ensue from the political structure, as a result of which large areas often remain uncultivated (where big landowners control the legislature), and from mal-administration (bribery is a common practice).

The fragmentation of certain regions (as in Africa) as a consequence of colonial frontier-demarcation also hinders economic expansion. Economic integration (Chapter 11.5) is indicated in such areas.

e. Foreign aid

Foreign aid can be understood in a strict or a broad sense. In the wider sense it covers grants, private investment, export credits and loans but excludes repayment of loans, interest and capital exports from the recipient countries. In the narrower sense it only covers outright grants and loans on favourable terms ('soft loans'). In the publications of international organizations such as the United Nations and the Organization for Economic Cooperation and Development, which give comparative figures each year for aid to less-developed countries, the broader definition is used.

The developed countries have contributed an ever-increasing amount of aid: public and private net capital assistance rose from about $4,500 million (£1,875 million) in the fifties to about $13,300 million (£5,416 million) in 1969 (excluding technical assistance). Multilateral assistance constituted $1,100 million (£500 million) of this last sum – most of it supplied by the International Bank for Reconstruction and Development (IBRD) and its two affiliates the International Finance Corporation (IFC) and the International Development Association (IDA). Bilateral grants (about $3,400 million – £1,458 million) and bilateral loans (about $3,100 million – £1,000 million) are provided mainly by the United States, France and the United Kingdom.

There is not much international coordination, and there is no point in looking for any general 'policy'. The USA is motivated by both moral and political aims, but her political efforts so far have not been attended by much success. Other countries, including France, are mainly concerned to keep their cultural influence in their former colonies; small countries concentrate on technical assistance. Economic considerations are relatively unimportant and must not constitute an incentive for the developed countries to provide assistance; humanitarian considerations are a weightier factor.

The technical assistance provided by industrial countries makes it possible to send technicians to the backward territories or – and this

is generally less recommendable – to train groups from these territories in the industrial countries. If this kind of assistance now seems
normal to us, we should just remember that it was not until 1824 that
Britain, for instance, lifted restrictions on the export of machinery
and the emigration of skilled workers.

The United States endeavours to stimulate the private sector more
particularly, the USSR (which provides much less aid – about one
tenth that of the United States) the public sector and heavy industry.
Since distributing aid to all the less-developed countries would have
little result and allocation to the least favoured become a permanent
burden and would not be much of an incentive, the donor nations
generally concentrate on a small number of countries (the United
States, for instance, assisting India, Vietnam, Brazil).

Initially, assistance was of the 'project approach' type (the World
Bank method): a contribution was made to carrying out a given
project. It was soon realized that the beneficial results of investment
of this kind could be thwarted by general economic policy in the
recipient countries. Moreover, foreign aid was sought only for
'marginal' projects. Projects which perhaps were much less interesting
but were considered indispensable by the governments concerned had
been financed beforehand from their own resources. It was for this
reason that more attention was subsequently paid to programme aid,
which was provided on the basis of a comprehensive development
programme (Chapter 13.2). Unlike project aid, however, programme
aid inevitably implies constant involvement with the general economic
policy of the recipient country, which is often reluctant to follow the
directives laid down (a *sine qua non* for assistance). Most of the less-
developed countries are in fact incapable of drawing up serious
development programmes because they lack reliable basic statistics.
They cannot carry out much more than project planning.

Where development programmes are nevertheless worked out, they
are generally conceived on much too ambitious a scale, and it is
immediately obvious that they can never be implemented. Governments then calculate the amount of foreign aid they need on the basis
of the resulting balance-of-payments gap. Previously, we heard more
about the savings gap, but the emphasis has thus been shifted: a
savings gap implies a failing on the part of the less-developed
countries, a balance-of-payments gap a deficiency on the part of the
developed countries. It is often forgotten that both approaches
amount to the same thing in the end (both indicating the difference

between the resources employed and those generated at home and received from abroad). As we have already said, whether the planned investment can be carried out (whether the managerial potential and skilled workers are available) is a point to which too little attention is normally paid. The calculations of the gap are generally on the imaginative side.

Experience so far with development aid has shown 'the limits to the power of foreign aid and the overwhelming importance of political and economic efforts in the less-developed countries themselves' (G. Ohlin). Nevertheless, the developed countries could provide real assistance in the efforts being made to introduce birth control in the less-developed countries: 'The modest contributions that rich countries might make to facilitate this crucial part of the modernization process could well count for more than all they are prepared to do in the realm of conventional aid, (G. Ohlin).

Lastly, some writers observe that foreign aid is not essential to economic growth (Japan is a case in point) and that it may even have a harmful influence: '. . . the flow of unearned grants generally obstructs the development of the qualities, attitudes and efforts which make for material advance and diverts attention from these prime determinants of development' (P. T. Bauer). It should be noted here that American food aid to India is hindering the reform of Indian agriculture. If certain countries spend much more on their armies than on education (Pakistan, India), if religion forbids the killing of animals (India), if nothing is done to cut back an excessive increase in population – these are the internal affairs of the countries involved. But then they must be aware of the consequences for economic growth. It may be doubted, however, whether the people of some of the less-developed countries 'are willing to change their ways of life, values and attitudes towards matters such as work, saving or size of family to enjoy a higher material level of income' (H. Myint). It is precisely because it is impossible to theorize about how such attitudes will change that a general theory of economic growth will be a long time coming.

8 Bibliography

A voluminous, but good textbook on economic growth: B. Higgins, *Economic Development: Principles, Problems and Policies* (rev. ed., New York 1968), considers successively the general theories, the

lessons from the past, the theories of underdevelopment, the different
forms of economic policy and some case studies. The following
introductions are mainly (even when also referring to rich countries,
as in the case of Higgins) or completely concerned with the less-
developed countries: W. A. Lewis, *The Theory of Economic Growth*
(London 1955): literary-historical introduction (no analysis of the
theories concerned); P. T. Bauer and B. S. Yamey, *The Economics of
Underdeveloped Countries* (Cambridge 1957); C. P. Kindleberger,
Economic Development (2nd ed., New York 1965); G. M. Meier and
R. E. Baldwin, *Economic Development: Theory, History, Policy* (New
York 1957); H. Myint, *The Economics of Developing Countries* (rev.
ed., London 1967), comprises two parts relating to less- and overpopulated areas respectively; E. E. Hagen, *The Economics of Development* (Homewood, Ill. 1968), in which 'empirical materials are
generously' used.

A survey of the theories since the Second World War (excluding
growth in respect of foreign trade and less-developed countries) is
given by F. H. Hahn and R. C. O. Matthews, 'The Theory of
Economic Growth: A Survey', *EJ*, December 1964.

Sound readings are to be found in G. M. Meier, *Leading Issues in
Development Economics. Studies in International Poverty* (2nd ed.,
New York 1970).

A synthesis of much statistical material, with comment: S. Kuznets,
Modern Economic Growth (New Haven 1966); similar data for the
postwar period: E. F. Denison, *The Sources of Economic Growth in
the United States and the Alternatives Before Us* (New York 1962);
*id., Why Growth Rates Differ: Postwar Experience in Nine Western
Countries* (Washington 1967).

a. Growth theories

The most recent version of Harrod's work, itself based on articles by
P. A. Samuelson and others, is contained in R. F. Harrod, *Towards a
Dynamic Economics: Some Recent Developments of Economic Theory
and their Application to Policy* (London 1948), especially Chapter 3
(based on an article published in *EJ*, March 1939); the concept of
dynamics is investigated in Chapter 1; *id., Economic Essays* (London
1952), essay 14; *id.*, 'Second Essay in Dynamic Theory', *EJ*, June
1960; *id.*, 'Are Monetary and Fiscal Policies Enough?', *EJ*, December
1964.

Domar's most important contributions (articles published since

1947) are collected in E. D. Domar, *Essays in the Theory of Economic Growth* (New York 1957), and stress the importance of depreciation and replacement investment.

For a comment on the Harrod-Domar theory: D. Hamberg, *Economic Growth and Instability: A Study in the Problem of Capital Accumulation, Employment, and the Business Cycle* (New York 1956); more simple – K. K. Kurihara, *National Income and Economic Growth* (London 1961), Part 3.

H. G. Johnson, *International Trade and Economic Growth* (London 1958) applies the Harrod-Domar theory to international trade. M. Dobb, *An Essay on Economic Growth and Planning* (London 1960) examines the relation between the growth models of Harrod and Domar and economic planning. It is an introduction to a subject that has been little studied.

A small but clear work (in which the Harrod-Domar formulae are illustrated): L. J. Zimmerman, *Poor Lands, Rich Lands: The Widening Gap* (New York 1965).

For an attempt to determine normal relationship between investment and national income: J. S. Duesenberry, *Business Cycles and Economic Growth* (New York 1958). B. R. Williams, *International Report on Factors in Investment Behaviour* (OECD, Paris 1962) denies any relationship between investment and economic growth (report based on national surveys relating to Belgium, the United Kingdom, France, West Germany, the Netherlands and Sweden).

Neoclassical viewpoints are found in R. M. Solow, 'A Contribution to the Theory of Growth', *QJE*, February 1956; T. W. Swan, 'Economic Growth and Capital Accumulation', *Economic Record*, November 1956.

Criticism in relation to the distribution of national income: N. Kaldor, 'Capital Accumulation and Economic Growth', in *The Theory of Capital: Proceedings of a Conference held by the International Economic Association* (ed. F. A. Lutz and D. C. Hague, New York 1961).

The importance of technological progress (also the so-called residual factor) is stressed by M. A. Abramovitz, 'Resource and Output Trends in the United States since 1870', *AER*, May 1956; R. M. Solow, *Capital Theory and the Rate of Return* (Amsterdam 1963); M. Brown, *On the Theory and Measurement of Technological Change* (London 1966).

See, finally, the well-known work of J. R. Hicks, *Capital and Growth* (Oxford 1965).

Among the purely mathematical growth theories (for which the basis was laid down by L. Walras: see Chapter 7.6), the following warrant special mention: J. von Neumann, 'A Model of General Economic Equilibrium', *RESt*, February 1946; M. Morishima, *Theory of Economic Growth* (Oxford 1969).

In addition to J. A. Schumpeter, *The Theory of Economic Development: An Inquiry into Profits, Capital, Credit, Interest and the Business Cycle* (Cambridge Mass. 1934), A. Cole also puts forward the view in *Business Enterprise in its Social Setting* (Cambridge, Mass. 1959) that the entrepreneur is the central figure in economic growth.

The quotation from R. E. Johnston is taken from his 'Technical Progress and Innovation', *OEP*, March 1966.

b. Stages of economic growth

W. W. Rostow set forth his theory in *The Stages of Economic Growth: A Non-Communist Manifesto* (Cambridge 1960). A considerable part of this work, not dealt with in this Chapter, is devoted to naturally subjective forecasts about the future economic growth of the United States and the USSR. *The Economics of Take-off into Sustained Growth* (ed. W. W. Rostow, London 1963) – papers of a congress held in 1960; see also G. M. Meier, *Leading Issues in Development Economics*, Part 1.

On development methods applied in the past by the industrial states: N. S. Buchanan and H. S. Ellis, *Approaches to Economic Development* (New York 1955). An interpretation of development problems influenced by Marxist doctrine is given by P. A. Baran, *The Political Economy of Growth* (New York 1957).

c. Economic policy in the less-developed countries

This subject is considered in many of the above-mentioned works. See also: G. Ohlin, *Population Control and Economic Development* (OECD, Paris 1967); F. Harbison and C. A. Myers, *Education, Manpower and Economic Growth: Strategies in Human Resource Development* (New York 1964) – separate analyses of the less-developed, the partly developed, the half-developed and the developed countries.

The financing of investment is dealt with in R. Nurkse, *Problems of Capital Formation in Underdeveloped Countries* (Oxford 1953), and

W. Brand, *The Struggle for a Higher Standard of Living: The Problem of the Underdeveloped Countries* (The Hague 1958) – the revised translation of a Dutch work dating from 1954.

The examples in Section 5a were drawn from *The Brain Drain* (ed. W. Adams and H. Rieben, London 1968).

On balanced growth: R. Nurkse, *Problems of Capital Formation in Underdeveloped Countries.* On unbalanced growth: A. O. Hirschman, *The Strategy of Economic Development* (New Haven 1958), who also points to the importance of psychological factors. Comment on the literature on these two aspects: G. M. Meier, *Leading Issues in Development Economics*, Part 5.

On growth by means of disguised unemployment in agriculture: W. A. Lewis, 'Economic Development with Unlimited Supplies of Labour', *Manchester School of Economics and Social Studies*, May 1954; J. C. H. Fei and G. Ranis, *Development of the Labor Surplus Economy: Theory and Policy* (Homewood, Ill. 1964).

The comment by J. H. Adler is from his paper in *Finance and Development* (1968, No 4): 'Poverty Amidst Wealth: Trends in the World's Economy'.

On aid to the less-developed countries: G. Ohlin, *Foreign Aid Policies Reconsidered* (OECD, Paris 1966); P. T. Bauer, 'Foreign Aid: An Instrument for Progress?' in B. Wootton and P. T. Bauer, *Two Views on Aid to Developing Countries* (London 1966); D. Avramovic *et al.*, *Economic Growth and External Debt* (Baltimore 1966); A. Krassowski, *The Aid Relationship* (London 1968); A. O. Hirschman and R. M. Bird, *Foreign Aid: A Critique and a Proposal* (Princeton 1968).

On planning methods: see the bibliography of Chapter 13.

PART 4

External Relations and Government

11 External relations

*National frontiers as such are basically irrelevant
to economic analysis; it is only government policies
that make them relevant. And yet a political boundary line may be useful to the economist because
it forms, as it were, a zone of light through which
economic processes pass and at which at least
some of them can best be observed.*

Ragnar Nurkse

Chapter 2 brought out the significance for a country of its relations
with the rest of the world. Yet there is no essential difference between
internal and external trade. In both cases, the aim is to bring goods to
the place where they are wanted.

Even so, the theory of international exchange is studied apart
because trade between the various countries:

a. must take account of the existence of different foreign currencies
(problem of exchange rates); and

b. is influenced far more by trade policy; customs tariffs can even
be prohibitive.

The present chapter begins with an exposition of the theory
accounting for foreign trade and the associated policy problems,
going on to give an explanation of what is meant by 'balance of
payments' and 'exchange rate'.

1 Comparative cost and the Heckscher-Ohlin theory

a. The theory of comparative cost

The founder of the theory of comparative cost is R. Torrens. It was,
however, through the work of D. Ricardo that it became known.
According to this theory, it is not the absolute but the comparative
cost which constitutes the decisive factor in determining which goods
are traded with other countries. Even if a country were able to
manufacture everything more cheaply than any other country, it

would be in its interest to concentrate upon the output of commodities which, comparatively speaking, it produced in the most favourable conditions and to leave to other countries those lines which it found comparatively less profitable to engage in.

This can be illustrated (Table 35) by a simple example (only two countries and two commodities), which involves in particular the following assumptions: complete factor mobility within the national frontiers, complete international immobility; labour costs only; fixed costs; unchanged technological knowledge; full employment; no trade barriers; same wants.

TABLE 35: Quantity of two commodities produced in one working hour

Country	Commodity x	Commodity y
δ	2	10
ε	1	2

In country δ the exchange ratio for the two commodities is $2x/10y = x/5y$; in country ε it is $x/2y$. As soon as country δ receives a unit x for just under 5 units y at most, it is to its advantage to specialize entirely in the production of y; as soon as country ε has acquired just over 2 units of y at least for one unit x, it too can benefit from complete specialization in the production of x. The international exchange ratio must then be somewhere between $\dfrac{x}{2y}$ and $\dfrac{x}{5y}$; the closer the ratio comes to $\dfrac{x}{2y}$, the more favourable it is for country δ; the more it approaches $\dfrac{x}{5y}$, the more advantageous it is for country ε.

International trade is advantageous if

$$\frac{f_L^{\delta_x}}{f_L^{\delta_y}} \neq \frac{f_L^{\epsilon_x}}{f_L^{\epsilon_y}}. \tag{1}$$

In the event of inequality between the foregoing terms

$$\frac{f_L^{\delta_x}}{f_L^{\delta_y}} < \frac{f_L^{\epsilon_x}}{f_L^{\epsilon_y}}. \tag{2}$$

country δ will concentrate on the production of y and country ε on production of x.

364

Appraisal

a. The assumptions on which the theory proceeds have no basis in fact. For example, costs are not due to labour alone. Moreover, labour is not homogeneous (otherwise there could be no international differences in costs). Again, calculations are not made with costs in kind, but with currency units. The concept of 'opportunity cost', or 'substitution cost', introduced by G. Haberler therefore offers no solution. (The opportunity cost of producing an additional unit of x is the value of the units of y which must be given up for it; this is because factors of production involved in the production of y are transferred to the production of x.)

b. While the theory tells us within what limits the exchange ratio must lie, it gives no indication as to the actual ratio, nor as to the quantities traded. This is because it disregards the importance of demand. At a later date, attempts were made (notably by J. S. Mill) to take account of demand, but here too the initial assumptions made were unrealistic.

c. Since it was from the theory of comparative cost that the need for international division of labour and free trade was derived, it was not surprising that protectionism was justified because certain hypotheses in the theory were inconsistent with the hard facts (see Section 4).

d. Comparative costs, moreover, do not account *per se* for the development of trade: they themselves have to be explained.

b. The Heckscher-Ohlin theory

The explanation was first advanced by the Swedish economist E. F. Heckscher (1879–1952) and elaborated by his fellow countryman B. Ohlin. Hence what has come to be known as the Heckscher-Ohlin theory (Appendix 9).

The basis now used is not one but several factors of production. The production functions are assumed to be the same in every country: a commodity that is produced capital-intensively in one country is produced in the same way in other countries. In addition, reasoning is not in real terms but in terms of money costs. The other hypotheses in the classical theory, however, have been adopted (such as constant returns and pure competition).

Both domestic and export prices are conditioned by a variety of factors. Buyers' income and preference for specific commodities helps to determine the types of production which are undertaken.

365

Also of particular importance are the money costs, which depend on the prices and the productivity of the factors of production. Factor prices are determined by the quantity and quality of the manpower, capital goods and raw materials available in the various regions, and also by climatogical conditions and the state of the soil. If labour is the relatively abundant and consequently cheap factor, it is the one used to the greatest extent and the resultant commodities are exported.

Specialization by any country, and consequently international and inter-regional trade, is thus due in large measure to unequal distribution of the factors of production and its corollary in the form of unequal remuneration.

B. Ohlin endeavours to incorporate the theory of international trade in the theory of general equilibrium, pointing to the interaction of factor endowments, demand for goods, production conditions and – as regards more particularly international equilibrium – the rate of exchange and the necessity of a balance between merchandise imports and exports.

Appraisal

a. Analysis on the basis of two or more factors is certainly more realistic, but the difficulties persist because these factors are not homogeneous.

b. Production techniques are not the same everywhere. Many goods can be produced, either capital-intensively or labour-intensively, at the same cost. A change in the ratio of factor prices may cause entrepreneurs to organize production differently. In such a case there is said to be a reversal of factor intensity.

c. More than half international trade is between countries with roughly the same factor ratios. For this the Heckscher-Ohlin theory can provide no explanation. Nor, since the factor endowments is assumed to be unchanged, can it account for substantial short-term changes in the pattern of trade. In the longer term, however, trade has an effect on factors: instead of factor distribution accounting for the pattern of international trade, it is the latter which may give an idea of the former.

d. Factor prices do not necessarily reflect the relative scarcity differences accounted for by government action (e.g. the fixing of minimum wages and social legislation). For that matter, such scarcity differences are not always accorded the attention they deserve. For prestige reasons, preference is sometimes given to capital-intensive production where labour-intensive production is called for.

c. A general theory?

From the foregoing it emerges that neither the theory of comparative cost nor the Heckscher-Ohlin theory can really be called satisfactory. The fact is that an explanation has to be found for differences in prices, as the decisions made by importers and exporters are based on them. The theory of comparative cost would hold water if prices in international exchange were a reflection of such costs. This implies in particular that the price system operates in a highly flexible manner (pure competition), that exchange rates are selected appropriately and that there are no barriers to trade (which, as already pointed out, are unrealistic hypotheses). In many cases, international division of labour can only be accounted for by historical or political circumstances. International restrictive agreements frequently influence international trade. The Heckscher-Ohlin theory applies in a certain degree to natural resources, but the influence of this factor is steadily declining as a result of the downward trend of transport costs.

In recent years, all sorts of attempts have been made to adjust the theory of international trade to the realities. S. B. Linder maintains that the basis of exports is the satisfaction of domestic wants: goods are produced first for the home market and only after that for the foreign market. Without a large market which makes possible large-scale production, exporting is frequently inconceivable. Since domestic demand is determined by income, exports normally go to countries with a comparable standard of living (whereas according to the Ohlin theory, they go to countries with different factor ratios).

Other economists consider that the explanation for the pattern of foreign trade lies mainly in changes in technology. A country which exploits an innovation and initially has a monopoly tends gradually towards mass production, but at the same time the production technique usually becomes known throughout the world as a result of the sale of licenses and the establishment of subsidiary firms. When the technological lead is lost, exports have to be kept up to scratch by further innovations (as was done around the middle of the nineteenth century by the United Kingdom, later on by Germany and the

United States, and after the Second World War mainly by the latter). It must not be forgotten, however, that innovations may have an adverse instead of a stimulating effect on international trade (a case in point being the substitution of nylon for silk).

The multiplicity of factors which may affect import and export prices 'cannot be reduced to a *meaningful* simple formula' (H. Bockelmann), and F. Devons is right in claiming 'that we are still far from having, either in theory or in industrial analysis, techniques which enable us to explain satisfactorily the main features of international trade'.

2 The terms of trade

Although the extent to which external trade relations influence the level of prosperity in the various states cannot be accurately determined, it is possible to calculate how much a country's position (in the example of comparative cost between $x/5y$ and $x/2y$) has changed in comparison with a given period.

This involves examining the ratio between average import and export prices. In theory, prices should relate to both goods and services. In practice, it is difficult to obtain data for prices of services, so that it is almost invariably the movement of merchandise prices that is studied. The ratio, expressed as an index value, of the index of the average export price (P_E) to the index of the average import price (P_M) is called the terms of trade:

$$N = \frac{100 \, P_E}{P_M}.$$

The terms of trade may also be reflected by the reverse ratio (of import price indices to export price indices), but we agree with J. Viner's view that a rise gives a better indication of a fundamentally improving situation. F. W. Taussig nevertheless opted for the import/export price ratio.

Changes in the terms of trade have to be ascertained together with changes in the quantities imported and exported. A deterioration of the terms of trade is in itself a setback, but this disadvantage is sometimes more than offset by a quantitative change. The average export price may be reduced by greater rationalization, in which case the result is often an increase in the quantity exported. An improvement in the terms of trade may be brought about by heavier foreign demand. It also frequently derives from increased costs; this, how-ever, usually causes a quantitative decrease in exports.

Thus France's terms of trade (1958 = 100) improved to 108 in 1969 but the export/import volume dropped to 88. In the case of Italy, on the other hand, the corresponding figures were 97 and 120.

3 Free trade and protectionism

At the end of the eighteenth century, free-trade ideas gained more and more ground, and in the mid-nineteenth century they predominated. Even protectionist France concluded a trade agreement with the United Kingdom in 1860 which involved a relaxation of its customs system. From 1880 onwards, the liberal tendency shown by most European countries in trade policy wilted before a resurgence of the protectionist mentality. This was mainly due to the depression of 1873–9 and the decline in the prices of agricultural commodities.

The depression in the early 1930s served to strengthen economic nationalism. There was a substantial increase in the United States tariff in 1930. From 1930 to 1935, most countries introduced severe protectionist measures. After the Second World War, attention was once again focused on the drawbacks inherent in restrictions on international trading (competition is frustrated and the creation of monopolies stimulated; a country's own exports suffer because its trading partners are not allowed to earn means of payment), and trade was liberalized to a very large extent.

a. The instruments of protectionism

The chief methods by which a country can protect its own goods are customs duties (levies on imports, and sometimes also on exports) subsidies to domestic producers (and their concomitant, dumping: see below), quantitative restrictions and state trading.

The first method, customs duties, has not only protectionist aims; it may also be designed to swell the treasury, restrict domestic consumption, cover a balance-of-payments deficit, etc. There are specific duties (a given amount per unit imported) and *ad valorem* duties (a certain percentage on the value of the relevant product). In industrial countries, it is nowadays mainly agriculture which is protected.

Whereas import subsidies are comparatively rare, export subsidies, and particularly dumping, are more widespread. Like export duties, quantitative restrictions on exports are for the most part applied to raw materials or semi-finished products which a country wishes to keep for its own industry. Similarly, import restrictions are aimed at giving priority to these categories of goods by restricting all other imports. There are tariff quotas (low customs duty for a specific quantity, high duty for additional imports), bilateral quotas (only operative with respect to a given country) and multilateral quotas (all countries collectively). In the communist countries, external trade is entirely conducted by the state; imports and exports serve the ends of economic planning. In many of the less-developed countries too, the government accounts for a considerable proportion of imports (e.g. about 45 per cent in India, Pakistan and Burma) and/or exports (e.g. about 45 per cent in Indonesia).

Protection can take less overt but none the less effective forms, e.g. arbitrary interpretation of customs laws by the authorities (e.g. in the United States) and complicated technical and health regulations governing imports.

b. Dumping

Dumping is the practice of selling commodities abroad at a lower price than that at which the same goods are supplied on the domestic market.

If the goods are not sold in the producing state, the basis for defining whether goods are being dumped is either the selling price in other countries or the cost price in the country of origin.

Discrimination occurs without the authorities intervening. By means of an export subsidy, a tax reduction or credit facilities, governments too can ease the task of domestic enterprises in capturing foreign markets. This is called subsidy-dumping. Like export subsidies, dumping calls for customs protection in the country practising it, as the exported goods could be reimported, unless transport costs rule this out.

It is frequently found that lower prices are charged abroad. An entrepreneur who obtains the equivalent of his fixed costs (for total production) on his domestic market may be satisfied with having his variable costs covered on the export market. He must, indeed, pay due heed to changing conditions on world markets (meeting competition). Provided it is done consistently, permanent dumping of this kind is accepted by many economists; in such cases, other countries can acclimatize themselves to the situation and derive benefit from the lower prices. This is what happens when the goods in question are not produced in the country in which they are dumped or where they are semi-finished products or raw materials. Production costs of finished goods are thus made more favourable compared with those in the dumping country.

Temporary dumping, on the other hand, sometimes causes marked disturbances – for instance, if the goods are sold at a loss abroad in order to eliminate competition. This is called 'dumping from strength', as distinct from 'dumping from weakness' (selling surplus production which cannot be disposed of on the domestic market).

To determine whether or not the dumping is of an acceptable temporary or permanent character is not easy. It presupposes knowledge of the exporter's costing methods and aims. The term 'social dumping' is frequently employed in the case of low priced imports from low-wage countries. Actually, this is in most cases not dumping at all.

On account of the difficulties mentioned in proving the occurrence of dumping practices, the so-called basic-price system is sometimes used (as in Sweden): in country A, export prices of country B are not compared with those ruling in the home market of country B but with the lowest domestic price of all foreign suppliers (of country A) where normal competitive conditions prevail.

While dumping implies favourable discrimination for foreign consumers, 'reverse dumping' (dual or multiple pricing) constitutes discrimination against foreign markets. The opportunity for such action arises in the event of internal price controls (and free price determination abroad) or increased external demand (sometimes through a domestic devaluation). Another occasion for such action may be the desire to bring down the profits of importers in countries where imports are restricted. Here again proof is difficult because in the price comparison due account must be taken of, for instance, transport costs and credit terms.

Protection against discriminatory government support (export subsidies) and against dumping can be effected by countervailing and anti-dumping duties respectively. Needless to say, more effective quantitative restrictions can also be applied.

A country must find itself seriously disadvantaged before taking reprisals. Practical experience shows that the domestic industries cry dumping whenever they experience intense but normal competition:

not the external but the domestic price is employed as a yardstick for comparison.

The government is frequently swayed by such complaints and introduces protectionist measures (this has happened in the United States). Hence it is that most writers are unenthusiastic about anti-dumping legislation.

c. General Agreement on Tariffs and Trade (GATT)

After the Bretton Woods decision to establish the IBRD and the IMF, efforts were directed towards setting up an International Trade Organization (ITO) for the purpose of eliminating international trade barriers and discriminatory provisions. It was resolved not to wait until the organization's Charter had been ratified (as the United States stopped short of this step, the organization was not in fact established) and in the meantime to start negotiations on the reduction of import and other duties. It was in this way that on 30 October 1947 the General Agreement on Tariffs and Trade came into being. Its main prohibitory provisions are summarized below.

1. Discrimination of any kind among the member countries is prohibited. Bilateral commitments concerning reductions and consolidations (no further increases to be introduced) of import duties are immediately and unconditionally extended to all member countries, under the terms of the most-favoured-nation clause; any country may claim most-favoured-nation treatment.

Preferential provisions are allowed in some cases, notably when a customs union or a free-trade area is set up, on condition that the new customs duties *vis-à-vis* non-member countries are on average no higher than before.

2. In principle, quantitative restrictions of any kind are ruled out. This prohibition does not in practice apply to the less-developed countries. For other states too there are numerous exceptions (in the event of scarcity; in connection with export control; in certain cases to assist agricultural production; in order to maintain balance-of-payments equilibrium; if a country is about to suffer a serious disadvantage through an unusually marked increase in imports). Any unnecessary prejudice to other countries' interests must be avoided, and possible remedial measures have to be discussed with the other contracting parties. Temporary deviations (five years) may be granted by a majority of the votes cast.

The non-discrimination principle also holds good for the application of quantitative restrictions, though here too exceptions are provided for (in particular with respect to scarce currencies).

3. Customs duties bound at their existing levels may only be modified after consultation with the states concerned. Withdrawal of a bound duty must as a general rule be compensated, as otherwise the countries affected have the right to take countermeasures with the same scope.

4. Any subsidy having repercussions on foreign trade must be notified. If it seriously damages the interests of a contracting party, the country granting the subsidy must examine, jointly with the other country concerned, the possibility of reducing it. Member countries may protect themselves by anti-dumping duties against dumping and by countervailing duties against direct and indirect production or export subsidies which have or threaten to have an adverse effect.

Operation
Numerous reductions and bindings of customs duties were brought about at the tariff conferences held at Geneva (1947), Annecy (1949), Torquay (1950–1) and Geneva (1956, 1960–2 and 1964–7). Particularly appreciable progress was made during the last conference (the 'Kennedy Round'). For the first time multilateral uniform tariff reductions were carried out.

If GATT can boast of no more spectacular achievements (e.g. in the field of quantitative restrictions), this is due to the many escape clauses and the difficulty of conducting a policy which is accepted by a large number of states with differing economic structures.

4 Arguments in favour of protection

The case for free trade is based on a number of assumptions (Section 1) which do not always ring true. If these hypotheses do not accord with the facts, protection of the domestic market is in the view of many economists admissible.

a. Full employment
In the event of unemployment the available manpower may be provided with work as a result of protective measures (an alteration in the exchange rate – see below – does not necessarily yield results) and the national prosperity increased. The same may be done with

o

hitherto unused, idle factors of production (an argument used by less-developed countries). Since it is the other country that suffers, reprisals (with effects on employment) cannot be ruled out. On the domestic market, consumers are faced with higher prices.

Especially in periods of recession, industries afflicted with appreciable unemployment tend to ask for government aid. Thus it happens that a decline in world prices – coinciding with a depression – is generally accompanied by greater protectionism and an upward trend of world prices by liberalization of trade.

A particular industry may also need to be protected when it has to cope with other transient difficulties – for example, if there are bumper crops throughout the world. It must be a genuine emergency to warrant measures for the relief of large-scale unemployment.

Because of the probable reaction in other countries, it is sometimes desirable to help industries in difficulties by means of production subsidies. These also have the effect of restraining imports but exercise a diametrically opposite influence on consumption; as no price increases are forthcoming, demand shows no contraction. Since such measures involve the Treasury in expenditure, supervision is usually stricter. Production subsidies can be better attuned to individual cases than, for instance, customs duties. If, however, they require vast administrative machinery and give rise to arbitrary allocation, it may be that the disadvantages outweigh the advantages. If their financing calls for a raising of taxes, this may still have its effect on demand.

b. Fixed costs

It is possible for costs to increase or decrease. In the first case, specialization becomes less profitable at a given moment; hence the fact that the same commodities are both produced domestically and imported. In the second case, specialization can only be turned to account by temporary protection of the domestic market. Thus it becomes possible to establish enterprises which in the normal course can rely upon propitious operating conditions but have to face keen competition from abroad. During the starting-up period, production costs are higher; personnel have to be trained, new processes have to be developed, market research is necessary. After the teething troubles have been overcome, 'infant-industry' protection is normally discontinued.

In point of fact, it is not easy to determine which industries have favourable prospects. 'Provisional' import duties in many cases assume a permanent aspect, as the example of the United States shows. After the transitional period, the firms concerned do everything they can to maintain their protected status; in this way, monopolistic conditions are frequently created. If the outlook is favourable it might be wondered why in that case no private capital is prepared to take risks (without temporary protection). These objections do not alter the fact that protectionist policy has undeniably contributed to speeding up the economic development of not a few countries.

Many of the less-developed countries, indeed, reject the comparative cost theory and the specialization it breeds, which they say prevents the diversification of their economies and causes greater instability on export markets.

c. Income distribution
Moreover, the theory of comparative cost does not take into account the effects of changed income distribution on prosperity.

The classical authors (Appendix 4) have already pointed out that international distribution of income may be influenced by restraint of trade. If a country has a monopoly of a certain type of production, exports in that sector can be made subject to export levies, which in turn can be passed on to another country (terms-of-trade argument). Where a monopsonistic position is held, an import duty is frequently paid by the foreign trading partner. Here, elasticity of internal and external supply and demand and the size of the profit margin are important factors.

Repercussions on national distribution of income also have to be taken into consideration. Thus an export levy benefits domestic consumers of the commodity concerned. An import duty involves discrimination in favour of the protected industry: selling prices and profits rise. Consumers experience beneficial or adverse effects, depending on the movement of consumer-goods prices.

Here again, allowance must be made for countermeasures. Reasonably accurate estimates of supply and demand coefficients of elasticity, however, are out of the question.

d. Other arguments
Reference has been made above to countervailing and anti-dumping duties which help to combat unfair competition. Cost differences as

375

such – e.g. in wages – may not be adduced as justification for a protectionist policy, since differences in cost are precisely the reason why there is international trade.

Other arguments in defence of a protectionist policy are of a non-economic character – the exigencies of national defence, for instance, and tactical considerations (designed to force other countries to withdraw or relax their restrictive trade measures). In a modern war, however, all goods are of importance to national defence, so that such a policy would lead to autarky, which for a small country is unthinkable. The smaller countries, moreover, are not alone and can obtain the commodities they require from their allies. In certain cases stockpiling is a better policy. In the conclusion of trade agreements, countries which do not apply quotas are at a disadvantage compared with others, which by contrast have a powerful negotiating instrument. It is for this reason that some countries have of necessity fixed import quotas.

5 International economic cooperation and integration

After the Second World War, there was a general realization of the need to eradicate the prewar uncertainty as to the pattern of other countries' trade policy and lay down rules for international exchanges. By reason of closer cooperation, efforts towards economic recovery were more orderly than after 1918. The IMF, the IBRD, GATT, the various commodity agreements and the Organization for European Economic Cooperation (OEEC) did a great deal to assist this process.

Although these forms of cooperation brought undeniable benefits, freely accepted rules were in many cases not observed. A multiplicity of escape clauses diminished the significance of the various agreements. On the one hand, the organizations concerned were not of a supranational type; on the other hand, their member countries had different economic and social structures. The larger the number of member states, the vaguer were the obligations involved and the greater the opportunities for evading them.

The less-developed areas are anxious not to have their economic expansion hampered by international obligations. Whenever they need to do so in order to stimulate their industrialization, they want to be able to avail themselves of protection and discrimination. The difference in the treatment accorded to the two groups of countries is particularly well illustrated in GATT. Even so, it was found necessary to organize a United Nations Conference on Trade and Development (UNCTAD), which in point of fact deals with the same problems as GATT.

The use made by the industrial states too of quantitative restrictions, e.g. in cases of balance-of-payments difficulties, frequently makes for an unsound monetary policy and proves indirectly detrimental to the interests of countries which show more self-discipline in this respect.

It is therefore no wonder that union has been sought between countries with similar economic structures, nor that more attention has been focused on the *need* for coordinated economic policy. This is what has happened in Western Europe in particular.

International economic integration (not to be confused with the integration of plants and firms referred to in Chapter 6.7) goes further than mere international cooperation. Efforts are made to remove all trade barriers and reap the benefits both of a wider market and of a coordinated economic policy. The main accent is laid on the greater opportunity for specialization and its concomitants, i.e. capital savings, optimum-scale plants, a better factor supply, more effective competition, and increased productivity and levels of living. This, of course, applies to associations between economically developed countries, a large market not being in itself sufficient to ensure the achievement of high prosperity (India). The difference between this and the type of cooperation referred to above lies in the fact that the removal of barriers is complete and there can normally be no backsliding, the same customs policy being pursued in relations with other countries. Sometimes, however, it is difficult to draw the dividing line.

a. Forms of integration

In the economic integration of two or more countries, the economies concerned are merged together, the free movement of persons, goods and capital is guaranteed (no customs duties or quantitative restrictions, same external tariff), a single currency circulates and a common budget is drawn up. Such economic unification without political unification is inconceivable. In most cases, moreover, the political incentives to integration are stronger than the economic.

Integration also connotes the tendency towards such unification. In order to implement this process gradually, horizontal and sectoral methods are applied; the free-trade area, the tariff union, the

377

customs union and the economic union are forms of the first-named method.

1. *Free-trade area*
In a free-trade area, internal trade barriers such as customs duties are abolished, but the member countries maintain their own tariff *vis-à-vis* the outside world. This calls for efficient control as regards the origin of goods.

2. *Tariff union*
In a tariff union, the same external tariff and customs legislation are accepted and import duties are abolished in trade between the participating states.

3. *Customs union*
A customs union involves, in addition to what applies in a tariff union, the standardization of excise duties and other consumer taxes and (if possible) of taxes on the transfer of movable property.

4. *Economic union*
In an economic union movements of persons, goods and capital are unrestricted; the necessary coordination is achieved in the determination and implementation of economic, financial and social policy; dealings with non-member countries are conducted as an economic, financial and social entity, save in purely domestic matters which have no effect on other member countries.

5. *Integration sector by sector*
In the sectoral approach to integration, the establishment of a common market only affects one industry or a small number of industries – as in the European Coal and Steel Community.

b. *The consequences of integration*
As regards the consequences of integration, it is difficult to make generalizations. The situation will vary from case to case. The free-trade argument upon which integration is so largely based is not wholly conclusive, as has been seen. Closer economic integration does not necessarily bring benefit to every one of the participating countries. Other countries too may be adversely affected owing to what is known as trade diversion. This occurs when, for instance, a member state of a customs union finds it advantageous, on account of the new tariff, to obtain its requirements from one of its partners, at

378

the expense of a former supplier who is not in the union. Trade creation, on the other hand, comes about through the abolition of duties among the partner countries: products are imported which have not been hitherto because the price was higher than that of the protected home-produced product.

c. Distortion

Difficulties arise in connection with the elimination of distortion – that is, differences in conditions of competition resulting from government measures.

Distortions of a specific nature influence prices of goods to an unequal extent. Generally speaking, they are caused by divergences in indirect taxes (e.g. excise duties). In order to avoid distortion of competition, these taxes need to be aligned or countervailing duties and rebates must be applied on imports and exports respectively.

In the case of general distortions, by which all commodities are advantaged or disadvantaged to the same degree, fewer problems are encountered. Possibly they can be removed by altering the exchange rate.

It is not easy to identify a distortion. All kinds of compensation are possible, and they are usually adduced in connection with differences in wages and social benefits. They need not be levelled out prior to integration: harmonization is expected to result from the development of the common market. Measures are only necessary if the international division of labour is obviously disrupted and productive activities are embarked upon in countries which are really not suitable for them. If this happens, consideration may be given to laying down international standards or standards acceptable in the union.

In the absence of integration, countries with higher wage levels or more progressive social policies already have to reckon with international competition. This is also the case in a customs union.

d. Achievements

The bulk of international economic integration has been carried out in Western Europe. The example was set by Belgium, Luxembourg and the Netherlands, which on 1 January 1948 entered into a customs union (the 'Benelux Union'). On 1 November 1966 the Treaty of Economic Union came into operation, but this does not in fact relate to an economic union, there being no, or not enough, coordination of economic policy. In the case of agricultural products, the frontier has

379

only been opened on certain conditions (minimum prices). Excise duties have not been equalized.

On 25 July 1952 the Treaty establishing the European Coal and Steel Community (ECSC) came into force. It was signed by the Benelux countries, West Germany, France and Italy. In this Community certain of the member states' rights were surrendered to a supranational body (High Authority) (e.g. it was given the right to raise its own revenue and power to eliminate discrimination, combat unfair practices and act against arrangements and combinations in restraint of competition).

The drawbacks of the ECSC arise from the fact that integration is only partial; measures in fields where the High Authority has no jurisdiction (e.g. foreign trade, wages policy) sometimes prevent a necessary alignment. That the other energy sources, which are continuously gaining in importance, do not come within the High Authority's ambit is in the final analysis a major handicap as regards the integration process, since the competitive position of coal is weakening all the time.

France subsequently proved unwilling to extend integration to other branches of the economy.

The Benelux Union was to a large extent eclipsed by the establishment of the EEC on 1 January 1958. Here too a customs union (without any real supranational organization) was gradually achieved – the last intra-Community customs duties were abolished on 1 July 1968 – but no economic union has yet come into being. Once again, liberalization of trade in agricultural products has been linked to a complicated system of frontier prices. Nor, mainly because indirect taxes have not yet been lined up and customs laws have not completely been harmonized, has trade in industrial goods become completely free.

On 8 April 1965 it was decided to merge the executive agencies of the EEC, the European Atomic Energy Community (Euratom) – which was also launched on 1 January 1958 but has accomplished little – and the ECSC. This was done on 1 July 1967. The Treaties themselves have not yet been unified.

As a result of the breakdown of negotiations with the EEC, a decision was taken by the United Kingdom, the Scandinavian countries, Austria, Switzerland and Portugal to set up a European Free Trade Association (EFTA), which came into operation on 3 May 1960. Finland became an associated member on 26 June 1961 and Iceland a full member on 1 March 1970. Customs duties between the original EFTA countries were gradually reduced and were abolished on 31 December 1966, Finland following suit on 31 December 1967. The Convention does not cover agricultural commodities. Owing to the lack of coordination of economic policy, many obstacles to trade have persisted.

6 The balance of payments

The balance of payments provides a systematic survey of all economic transactions which take place during a given period between residents of a particular country and those of other countries. The word balance is not used in its accounting significance here. The latter relates to a given point in time, the balance of payments to a given period of time.

For purposes of this discussion, a country's diplomats and servicemen abroad are not included among the residents of the host country (having no permanent domicile there). Transactions relating to branches of foreign firms or to international organizations are not taken into consideration; those relating to subsidiaries are. It is not always easy to draw the dividing line.

a. The components of the balance of payments
The balance of payments may be broken down as follows:

1. Balance on current transactions (current account):
   a. balance on goods or balance of trade (visible items),
   b. balance on services (invisible items),
   c. balance on investment income;
2. Balance on capital movements (capital account):
   a. balance on long-term capital movements,
   b. balance on short-term capital movements;
3. Balance on gold and foreign exchange.

Because of the difficulty of distinguishing short-term capital movements from gold and foreign-exchange transactions, it is also proposed that the capital account should cover only long-term capital movements. The cash account would then relate to short-term capital movements and to gold and foreign exchange, showing what changes take place in the gold and foreign-currency reserves (also called monetary reserves) and in short-term claims as a result of

381

current and capital transactions. The basic balance comprises current transactions and long-term capital movements. By the over-all balance is meant the balance on current transactions, and either all capital movements, or all capital movements excluding short-term government capital transactions (see further the Bernstein definition).

If the value of goods exported is greater than that of goods imported, there is said to be an active trade balance; in the reverse case, there is said to be a passive trade balance. Owing to the increasing importance of services, the significance of the trade balance has declined, though statistical data become available more quickly for the trade balance.

The balance on services relates in particular to transactions in the field of transport, tourism, insurance and transfers of migrants (workers employed abroad). In some countries, income from these sources is considerable; thus income from tourism accounts for 34 per cent of the value of exports in Austria, 28 per cent in Ireland, 19 per cent in Switzerland and 17 per cent in Italy. In Norway the corresponding proportion for freight and other services is 97 per cent. Invisibles of all kinds make up 42 per cent of the value of exports in Ireland, 42 per cent in Italy and 57 per cent in Israel. In 1968 all receipts from tourism added up to $11,000 million for all OECD countries; the highest figures were obtained by the United States ($1,800 million), Italy ($1,500 million) and Spain ($1,200 million). In relative terms, these receipts were highest in Ireland and Portugal (about 6 per cent of the gross national product), Spain and Switzerland (about 4 per cent).

The balance on investment income concerns payments of interest and dividends derived from lending of capital to or borrowing of capital from other countries. If a particular country has a positive balance on such transactions, it is said to be a creditor country; if a negative balance, it is said to be a debtor country.

Current capital movements are entered on capital account; in other words, this shows *changes* in external claims and debts and must not be confused with the debt position at a given moment. It may be subdivided according to whether it relates to short- or long-term capital. A creditor country is not necessarily a country that exports capital. The creditor position merely denotes that it did so at some previous period. A similar observation applies to a debtor country.

Long-term capital exports occur when, for instance, securities are purchased abroad (or foreign securities are offered for sale on the home market), loans are granted to other countries or credits previously granted by other countries are repaid.

The balance on monetary gold (transactions in non-monetary gold are included in merchandise trade) and foreign exchange shows what changes have taken place in the reserves of gold and foreign currencies This is connected with the financing of deficits in other sections of the balance of payments. Such financing can only be done by means of credits, gifts or changes in the gold and foreign currency reserves. As mentioned before the cash account is often used in this connection.

b. Record of foreign-exchange transactions

The balance of payments does not correspond with the record of foreign-exchange transactions between residents and non-residents through the country's banking system, since:

1. the balance of payments comprises those transactions which do not involve any transfer of money (barter transactions, gifts in kind) and those which are settled without the agency of a bank (exports the proceeds of which are not repatriated, imports paid for from private foreign-currency holdings);

2. imports and exports are recorded in the balance of payments on the same basis (fob frontier country of exportation), and therefore transactions relating to insurance and freight of goods are set apart. In a record of foreign-exchange transactions, freight and insurance costs are mostly included in the value of the exports or imports (cif);

3. in the balance of payments, account is taken of external transactions at the time at which they take place. If payment is on a forward basis, the economic transaction and the relevant credit are immediately entered in the balance; only later, at the time of settlement, is the credit deleted. In a record of foreign-exchange transactions, the international transactions are only incorporated when they have been paid and the proceeds repatriated through the national banking system. That is to say, credits are not recorded.

The designation 'balance of payments' is in fact more appropriate for the record of foreign-exchange transactions. It has already been proposed that the term should be employed in this sense and be superseded in its present significance by 'balance of transactions' or 'balance of accounts'.

c. Method of accounting

Each transaction is entered on the credit (usually the left) or the debit side of the balance sheet. Credit items arise where the transaction concerned involves payments *by* a foreign country; debit items originate from payments *to* a foreign country. Among the principal items shown on the credit side are exports of goods and services, transport of foreign merchandise in the country's own shipping and interest and dividend payments from abroad; those on the debit side include imports of goods and investment income due to other countries (Table 36).

TABLE 36: Accounting method of the main balance-of-payments transactions

Credit (+)	Debit (−)
Balance of trade	
Exports	Imports
Balance on services	
Services to other countries	Services from other countries
Balance on investment income	
Investment income due from other countries	Investment income due to other countries
Capital account	
Capital imports	Capital exports
Balance on gold and foreign exchange	
Decrease in gold and foreign exchange	Increase in gold and foreign exchange

Exports of capital (and foreign exchange) also involve external payments and must therefore be entered on the debit side (capital and foreign-exchange imports go on the credit side). Exports of gold (decreases in the gold reserve) are treated as exports of goods and services (imports of gold or increases in the gold reserve being treated as imports of goods). Through the use of this method of accounting, a balancing picture is obtained from a bookkeeping standpoint.

This method of accounting can also be explained by proceeding from the fact that on the credit side all transactions are shown which afford normal residents purchasing power in other countries; on the debit side appear all transactions through which normal residents use this purchasing power. All items can also be entered one below the other (the debit items in that case having a minus sign).

The balance of payments is (*ex post*) always in equilibrium, because opposite to each credit item there is a debit item (e.g. export on the one side, increase in gold and foreign exchange reserves or capital export on the other). Particular components of the balance of payments, however, are not necessarily in equilibrium. Temporary, minor balance-of-trade disequilibria are continually occurring, partly as a consequence of seasonal differences between imports and exports and changes in the movement of prices. A country's foreign-currency reserve, therefore, has to be maintained at a certain minimum level.

d. *Autonomous and compensating transactions*

An important factor is the breakdown into autonomous (also called 'independently motivated') and compensating transactions. Autonomous income and expenditure result from normal payments, which include, in addition to the balance on goods and services, autonomous capital movements (e.g. long-term credit granted to less-developed countries). Compensating capital transactions (mostly short-term) are aimed at redressing a disequilibrium in the autonomous items of the balance of payments. Differentiation between the two types of transaction is sometimes difficult. Short-term capital movements are often speculative ('hot money'). Where in the text below reference is made to a disequilibrium in the balance of payments, this relates to autonomous items.

A fundamental equilibrium is said to exist when autonomous income and expenditure accord with each other over a given period without either necessitating import restrictions or causing excessive unemployment. The period in question may be several years, as cyclical fluctuations may bring about transitory deficits. In practice, it is difficult to determine whether these criteria are fulfilled. In the IMF's Articles of Agreement, in fact, no definition is given of a fundamental equilibrium.

Since the balance on autonomous credit and debit items is difficult to determine, the basic balance is sometimes used as a starting point. A deficit in the basic balance is not necessarily detrimental; it is frequently the result of investment abroad which may subsequently have a beneficial influence on the basic balance.

Other balances too are in use. For instance, particular importance

385

may be attached to the liquidity position. In the United States (US Department of Commerce: balance on regular transactions), this is assumed to be given by the basic balance with the addition of the changes in the country's short-term external (private and government) debts (e.g. an increase in foreign deposits in American banks). No account is taken of the corresponding claims on other countries (deposits by Americans abroad), because it is assumed that they are not necessarily at the immediate disposal of the authorities. (On the contrary, it is postulated that all external claims might be presented at the same time and the government is liable for them.) There is also a 'balance settled by official reserves transactions', in which a distinction is made between short-term private and government claims and debts. The starting data here are the basic balance and short-term movements of private capital (the Bernstein definition).

The foregoing shows how necessary it is in every case to determine accurately which balance-of-payments figure is meant. This is no needless precaution: at an international economic discussion, one of the participants noted that no less than twenty-nine different definitions of balance of payments were used.

e. Some balance-of-payments examples

After the Second World War, the United States' overall balance showed a surplus for many years (the 'dollar gap'). Since 1958 there has been a virtually unbroken series of deficits (averaging $2,500 million for the 1958–65 period). These are mainly attributable to aid, military expenditure and foreign investment. Some writers, therefore, such as C. P. Kindleberger, do not consider the deficit to be so alarming. In their view, there is too great an obsession with the liquidity position and the fact that the United States' assets abroad are increasing is overlooked. Kindleberger sets the net creditor position for 1966 in this respect at $51,600 million ($112,000 million minus $60,400 million).

In Table 37, the United States balance of payments is calculated on the basis of official transactions. The 1969 surplus ($2,7000 million) is mainly due to increased liquid liabilities to foreign commercial banks. The decline in reserves of convertible foreign currencies is offset by a rise in gold reserves. The table contains an item designated 'direct investment'; in such investment, control continues to be exercised by the country of origin – in this case the

TABLE 37: United States: Balance-of-payments summary 1968–9 ($m.)

	1968	1969
A. Goods, services and unrequited transfers (excluding aid)		
Exports fob	33,588	36,473
Imports fob	−32,964	−35,835
Trade balance	624	638
Net military expenditures	−3,140	−3,336
Investment income	4,754	4,376
Other services, remittances and pensions (excluding aid and military transfers)	−886	−919
Total	1,352	759
B. Aid and nonmonetary sectors' capital		
Advance repayments on US government loans	269	−87
Other government capital and grants	−4,225	−3,741
Direct investment abroad	−3,209	−3,070
Portfolio investment abroad	−1,115	−1,588
Foreign direct and portfolio investment in United States	5,495	4,744
Total	−2,786	−3,742
C. Total (A plus B)	−1,434	−2,983
D. Net errors and omissions	−514	−2,924
E. Short-term capital, n.i.e.		
Foreign nonliquid capital	866	400
Foreign liquid capital	423	−503
US private assets (increase:—)	−1,087	−716
Total	202	−819
F. Liquid liabilities to foreign commercial banks	3,387	9,434
G. Total (D through F)	3,075	5,691
H. Total (C plus G)	1,641	2,708
I. Official settlements		
Liabilities to foreign official agencies		
Nonliquid liabilities	2,340	−996
Liquid liabilities	−3,101	−525
Net IMF accounts	−870	−1,034
US convertible currency holdings (increase:—)	−1,183	814
Monetary gold (increase:—)	1,173	−967
Total	−1,641	−2,708

Source: IMF, Annual Report 1970 (Washington 1970), p. 168

United States. On a liquidity basis, the 1969 balance was in deficit by $7,000 million – in other words a difference of $9,700 million. In 1968 the difference was smaller. The explanation of these differences partly lies in the fact that a substantial proportion of foreign investment is financed with Eurodollars (dollar deposits outside the United States). The difficulty of arriving at balance-of-payments estimates is illustrated by the need to introduce an item 'errors and omissions', which appears as a balancing item.

The United Kingdom too has experienced chronic balance-of-payments deficits (Table 38). Again, a major reason is the granting of gifts to other countries. Furthermore, the economic situation has been less satisfactory since the war, which has resulted in continuous speculation against the pound. In the EEC, West Germany is seen to occupy the strongest position.

TABLE 38: Industrial countries: Balance-of-payments summary 1967–9 ($'000m.)

	Current balance			Capital balance			Overall balance		
	1967	1968	1969	1967	1968	1969	1967	1968	1969
United Kingdom	−0·2	−0·3	1·4	−1·1	−2·7	−0·5	−1·3	−3·0	0·9
United States	4·0	1·4	0·8	−7·4	—	2·0	−3·4	1·4	2·8
Total	3·8	1·1	2·2	−8·5	−2·7	1·5	−4·7	−1·6	3·7
Germany (West)	3·3	3·9	2·9	−3·2	−2·2	−5·9	0·1	1·7	−3·0
France	0·7	−0·8	−1·8	−0·4	−2·9	0·8	0·3	−3·7	−1·1
Italy	1·8	2·9	2·6	−1·2	−3·0	−3·3	0·6	−0·1	−0·6
Belgium-Luxembourg	0·3	0·1	0·2	−0·1	−0·5	—	0·2	−0·4	0·2
Netherlands	—	0·1	—	0·2	−0·2	0·1	0·2	−0·1	0·1
Total EEC countries	6·0	6·2	4·0	−4·7	−8·7	−8·4	1·3	−2·5	−4·4
Canada	−0·3	0·1	−0·5	0·3	0·3	0·6	—	0·3	0·1
Japan	—	1·2	2·3	−0·1	−0·3	−1·6	−0·1	0·9	0·7
Switzerland	0·3	0·6	0·5	−0·2	−0·2	−0·5	0·1	0·4	—
Austria	−0·1	−0·1	0·1	0·3	0·1	−0·1	0·2	—	—
Denmark	−0·3	−0·2	−0·4	0·2	0·1	0·4	−0·1	−0·1	—
Norway	−0·2	0·2	0·1	0·4	−0·2	−0·1	0·2	—	—
Sweden	—	—	−0·1	−0·2	—	—	−0·2	—	−0·1
All industrial countries	9·1	8·9	8·2	−12·4	−11·5	−8·1	−3·2	−2·6	—

Source: IMF, Annual Report 1970 (Washington 1970), p. 74

7 The rate of exchange

The rate of exchange is the price of a foreign currency. It shows how many units of the national currency are needed in order to obtain one unit of a foreign currency (e.g. in Belgium, $1 = B.fr. 50$; in the United States, B.fr. $1 = \$0.02$ or B.fr. $100 = \$2$). The exchange rate is generally quoted with a fixed external value, though in the United Kingdom it is quoted with a fixed internal value showing the number of foreign currency units which can be obtained with one pound sterling (e.g. £1 = $2.40).

At one time, payments to and from other countries were usually made with bills of exchange; hence the term exchange rate, which was maintained when the bill of exchange, as in the case of internal transactions, fell into disuse for dealings with other countries. The instruments employed today for international payments are cheques and transfers. Such exchange operations are carried out almost exclusively by banks.

The whole exchange-rate system is determined by the debits and credits of the record of foreign-exchange transactions, since the latter involves demand for and supply of the foreign currency. Usually, there is no great difference between the balance of payments and the record of foreign-exchange transactions. On the other hand, exchange rates exercise an influence on the (autonomous) balance of payments: they are normally fixed in such a way that they lead to an equilibrium.

In order to form a balanced exchange system, the numerous rates must be reconcilable with each other in terms of foreign currencies. If it is possible to make a profit by purchasing a foreign currency and by converting this currency into another and back again into the national currency (arbitrage), these exchange rates are not in line with one another. Such transactions, however, tend to restore the equilibrium.

If all exchange rates fall, this evidences an appreciation in the value of the national currency. This is not necessarily the case when only one exchange rate declines, since it may be a sign of a depreciation of the foreign currency in question.

At present, fixed exchange rates are in operation everywhere. The members of the IMF have given an undertaking to prevent deviations of more than one per cent from the parity declared to that institution. This is done by intervention on the foreign-exchange market (purchase and sale of dollars against the domestic currency). The parities correspond to a given quantity of gold or (since the dollar is equivalent to a fixed quantity of gold) to a specific amount in dollars. Parity changes are permitted in certain circumstances (see Chapter 12.6). The United States is not obliged to take action on the exchange market since it buys and sells gold (at the rate of $35 per ounce) from and to the monetary authorities (see Chapter 12.1a).

Convertibility

If it is possible at any time for a country's own currency to be exchanged for that of any other country (and *vice versa*) without control by the monetary authorities over the use of the currency thus acquired, there is said to be full convertibility. The currency concerned is called a 'hard' currency. Where there is limited convertibility, on the other hand, the corresponding designation is 'soft' currency.

Convertibility is of little significance without free trade: it must be not only formal but also effective.

If convertibility only applies to certain currencies, transactions (mostly current and not capital) or persons, this is called partial convertibility. Where it is permissible for residents only, convertibility is designated internal; where it is enjoyed solely by non-residents, it is known as external convertibility.

The term transferability refers simply to the possible uses of specific currencies (transferable sterling within the sterling area).

Convertibility of the dollar derives chiefly from the fact that gold is purchased and sold freely at the request of the (western) foreign central banks at a fixed price of $35 an ounce; convertibility of other currencies is the result of intervention by the central bank on the foreign-exchange market (usually by means of transactions in dollars) in order to maintain the fixed exchange rates.

8 Bibliography

A comprehensible introduction: J. Pen, *A Primer on International Trade* (New York 1967); more extensive, but equally straightforward: S. J. Wells, *International Economics: A general Textbook* (London 1969); also C. P. Kindleberger, *International Economics* (4th ed., Homewood, Ill. 1968); P. T. Ellsworth, *The International Economy* (4th ed., New York 1969). Exclusively theoretical and more difficult: J. Vanek, *International Trade: Theory and Economic Policy*

(Homewood, Ill. 1962); R. E. Caves, *Trade and Economic Structure: Models and Markets* (Cambridge, Mass. 1960), is rather an extensive survey.

G. Haberler gives an intelligible summary in *A Survey of International Trade Theory* (2nd ed., Princeton 1961). A critical comment on postwar literature can be found in: J. Bhagwati, 'The Pure Theory of International Trade', *EJ*, March 1964; W. M. Corden, *Recent Developments in the Theory of International Trade* (Princeton 1965); J. S. Chipman, 'A Survey of the Theory of International Trade', *Em*, July and October 1965 and January 1966 (devoted to classical, neoclassical and modern theory respectively).

a. Comparative cost. Heckscher-Ohlin theory

In addition to the above mentioned textbooks and B. Ohlin, *Interregional and International Trade* (rev. ed., Cambridge, Mass. 1967), standard works that may usefully be consulted are G. Haberler, *The Theory of International Trade with its Applications to Commercial Policy* (London 1936), and J. Viner, *Studies in the Theory of International Trade* (New York 1937). On the closely related location theory: W. Isard, *Location and Space Economy* (New York 1956).

For attempts to illustrate the comparative-cost theory statistically, D. MacDougall, 'British and American Exports: A Study Suggested by the Theory of Comparative Costs', *EJ*, December 1951 and September 1952; see also the literature commented on in J. S. Chipman, 'A Survey of the Theory of International Trade; Part 2, The Neoclassical Theory'.

In connection with the Heckscher-Ohlin theory, mention must be made of the 'Leontief paradox'. On the basis of his input-output research and on the strength of questionable reasoning, W. Leontief came to the staggering conclusion that the United States is a country lacking in capital. Leontief's standpoint, which derives from two production factors, has been supplemented by J. Vanek, who distinguishes a third factor – nature. The substitution of raw materials would require a relatively large amount of capital, and United States imports might be capital-intensive. W. Leontief, 'Domestic Production and Foreign Trade: The American Capital Position Reexamined', *Proceedings of the American Philosophical Society*, September 1953; also in *EI*, February 1954; *id.* 'Factor Proportions and the Structure of American Trade: Further Theoretical and Empirical Analysis, *RES*, November 1956. See for comments hereon

S. Valavanis, R. Robinson, G. Elliott and B. Vaccara, and Leontief's reply in *RES*, February 1958 (supplement).

The article of J. Vanek appeared in *RES*, May 1959 ('The Structural Content of Foreign Trade 1870–1955, and the Relative Abundance of Natural Resources in the United States'). See the same author's *The Natural Resource Content of United States Foreign Trade 1870–1955* (Cambridge, Mass. 1963).

C. P. Kindleberger, *Foreign Trade and the National Economy* (New Haven 1962), illustrates the repercussions of foreign trade on the economy of the developed and less-developed countries and examines, *inter alia*, which influences cause changes in international transactions.

S. B. Linder, *An Essay on Trade and Transformation* (Stockholm 1961), demonstrates that production for exports will follow rather than precede production for the home market. Trade in industrial products is therefore on a larger scale between the developed countries than between the latter and new states.

The Soviet viewpoints are considered in *International Trade and Central Planning: An Analysis of Economic Interactions* (ed. A. A. Brown and E. Neuberger, Berkeley, Cal. 1968) and P. J. D. Wiles, *Communist International Economics* (Oxford 1968).

See also H. Bockelmann, *Zur Kritik der klassischen Tradition in der Aussenhandelstheorie* (Frankfurt/Main 1958); and E. Devons, 'Understanding International Trade', *Ec*, November 1961.

b. The terms of trade
C. P. Kindleberger, *The Terms of Trade: A European Case-Study* (New York 1956), examines the validity of the theories formulated in respect of the terms of trade and shows how difficult it is to make generalizations. On the same lines: M. A. G. van Meerhaeghe, 'Observations sur la signification des termes d'échange des pays sous-développés', *Ky*, 1969, No. 3.

c. Free trade and protectionism
For a simple exposition of the international aspects of trade policy, see L. B. Yeager and D. G. Tuerck, *Trade Policy and the Price System* (Scranton, Pa. 1966).

In an immoderately protracted exposition, based on numerous assumptions, J. E. Meade comes to the same conclusion as the classical authors: as a rule, free trade is the optimum form of commerce (*The Theory of International Economic Policy*, Part 2: *Trade and Welfare* with a *Mathematical Supplement*, London 1955); for the opposing view, see E. E. Hagen, 'An Economic Justification of Protectionism', *QJE*, November 1958. For a succinct mathematical-theoretical analysis (for advanced students) of free trade and protectionism: L. H. Janssen, *Free Trade, Protection and Customs Union* (Leiden 1961).

A plea for customs protection as a means to protect a high level of living: L. Lloyd, *Tariffs: The Case for Protection* (New York 1955); see also J. Black, 'Arguments for Tariffs', *OEP*, June 1959.

On pre-war international trade currents and policy, see the following publications of the League of Nations: *Europe's Trade* (Geneva 1941); *The Network of World Trade* (Geneva 1942); *Commercial Policy in the Interwar Period* (Geneva 1942); *Trade Relations between Free-Market and Controlled Economies* (Geneva 1943). The second of these works describes how, from 1870 onwards, international trade relations assumed the form of a multilateral system between different groups of countries. In the same connection: E. Thorbecke, *The Tendency towards Regionalization in Trends in International Trade 1928–1956* (The Hague 1960). Further, numerous data are found in A. Maizels, *Industrial Growth and World Trade: An Empirical Study in Trends in Production, Consumption and Trade in Manufactures from 1899 to 1959 with a Discussion of Probable Future Trends* (Cambridge 1963).

The restrictive trade policy of the less-developed countries is defended by G. Myrdal, *An International Economy* (New York 1956), Chapter 13. Classical theory in this connection (with the fundamental argument in favour of free trade) is outlined in J. Viner, *International Trade and Economic Development* (2nd ed., Oxford 1957). See also H. Myint, 'The "Classical" Theory of International Trade and the Underdeveloped Countries', *EJ*, June 1958, and G. M. Meier, *The International Economics of Development* (rev. ed. New York 1967).

H. G. Johnson, *Economic Policies towards Less Developed Countries* (London 1967), investigates what the policy of the United States towards the less-developed countries should be, and favours liberal trade policy.

d. Dumping
Anti-Dumping and Countervailing Duties (GATT, Geneva, July 1958) contains a survey of the laws and their application in eight countries

(including Belgium and the United States). This is supplemented by *Anti-Dumping and Countervailing Duties: Report of Group of Experts* (GATT, Geneva, March 1961). See finally *Agreement on Implementation of Article VI: Anti-Dumping Code* (GATT, Geneva 1969), which lays down under what conditions anti-dumping and countervailing duties can be applied.

e. GATT
See M. A. G. van Meerhaeghe, *International Economic Institutions* (2nd. ed., London 1971), Chapter 3; K. Kock, *International Trade Policy and the GATT 1947–1967* (Stockholm 1969).

f. Economic integration
J. Tinbergen, *International Economic Integration* (2nd ed., Amsterdam 1965), gives a straightforward description of the essentials of international economic relations and of the conditions for economic integration. On the same subject, but for greater detail: B. Balassa, *The Theory of Economic Integration* (Homewood, Ill. 1961). In *Social Aspects of European Economic Co-operation* (International Labour Office, Geneva 1956) – compiled by a group of experts under the chairmanship of B. Ohlin – it is pointed out that wage differences do not constitute an obstacle to integration. The latter may only be accomplished gradually in order to enable the necessary adjustments to be made. Large-scale migration from overpopulated areas would not appear to be desirable.

J. Viner, *The Customs Union Issue* (London 1950), discusses the consequences of a customs union and coins the terms 'trade creation' and 'trade diversion'. Purely theoretical: J. E. Meade, *The Theory of Customs Unions* (Amsterdam 1955), and J. Vanek, *General Equilibrium of International Discrimination: The Case of Customs Unions* (Cambridge, Mass. 1965); see also R. G. Lipsey, 'The Theory of Customs Unions: A General Survey', *EJ*, September 1960.

A thoroughgoing survey of the consequences of customs union is also given by T. Scitovsky, *Economic Theory and Western European Integration* (2nd ed., London 1962); H. O. Lundström, *Capital Movements and Economic Integration: A Study of the Role of International Long-Term Capital Movements in International Economic Integration with Particular Reference to Europe* (Leiden 1961), points to the fact that capital movements play a rather secondary role in integration.

For the operation of the international economic organizations see M. A. G. van Meerhaeghe, *International Economic Institutions*.

g. The balance of payments

See *Balance-of-Payments Manual* (3rd ed., New York 1961) for the balance-of-payments accounting system recommended by the IMF. See also Chapters 6 to 9 of M. J. Wasserman and R. M. Ware, *The Balance of Payments: History, Methodology, Theory* (New York 1965): almost half of this work is devoted to the history of the balance of payments.

D. G. Badger, 'The Balance of Payments: A Tool of Economic Analysis', *SP*, September 1951, examines the connection between the balance of payments and the national accounts, discussing the former's various constituent items, the method of financing a disequilibrium and the term 'fundamental' disequilibrium.

F. Machlup, 'Three Concepts of the Balance of Payments and the So-called Dollar Shortage', *EJ*, March 1950, points out that there are in fact three types of balance of payments – a market balance, or balance of unhampered demand for and supply of foreign currency; a programme balance, in which the expected or planned receipts and expenditure of foreign currency are recorded; and the *ex post* accounting balance of payments.

On the difference between the balance of payments and the record of foreign-exchange transactions: B. Hansen, *Foreign Exchange Credits and Exchange Reserves. A Contribution to the Theory of International Capital Movements* (Amsterdam 1961).

On the possible disequilibrating influence of forward exchange markets: P. Einzig, *A Dynamic Theory of Forward Exchange* (2nd ed., London 1967); see also E. Sohmen, *The Theory of Forward Exchange* (Princeton 1966).

On all monetary aspects of international economic relations: L. B. Yeager, *International Monetary Relations: Theory, History and Policy* (New York 1966).

The comment about the 29 definitions emanates from W. L. Thorp, *Trade, Aid or What?* (Baltimore 1954).

12 External relations (continued)

The theory of international trade, at its best, can provide only presumptions, not demonstrations, as to the benefit or injury to be expected from a particular disturbance in foreign trade ...

Jacob Viner

In addition to the aspects of international trade dealt with in the previous chapter, the emphasis in this chapter will be placed on the other monetary aspects, i.e. international liquidity, theories relating to exchange rates and ways of avoiding balance-of-payments difficulties.

1 International liquidity and monetary reserves

By international liquidity is meant the means available to the authorities for covering a balance-of-payments deficit. Part of these means are clearly demonstrable and quantifiable, namely monetary reserves (official stocks of gold and convertible currencies, the IMF gold tranche, and other amounts which are automatically disposable, e.g. under arrangements between central banks); others are not measurable. (It is not known beforehand how much can be borrowed on another country's money market, or the extent to which and the period for which foreign countries will wish to maintain a stock of certain currencies.)

International monetary reserves thus comprise world stocks of gold and convertible currencies and the facilities for receiving such currencies (on acceptable terms).

Currencies which can only be used on a bilateral basis and thus do not play any important part in international trade are not classed as international monetary reserves. This also applies to gold employed as cover for domestic currency reserves in Belgium, the Netherlands and Switzerland. Convertible currencies must form part of the foreign-exchange reserves of another country and be regarded as international reserves (i.e. sterling in the United Kingdom and dollars in the United States do not fall within this category).

To determine whether international reserves are sufficiently large, or the extent to which they must be expanded, is not easy. At first sight it would appear that they should follow the trend of the value of world imports. This, however, overlooks the effect of capital movements. Thus at the end of 1968 international reserves accounted for 33 per cent of world imports, which is more than in 1913 (21 per cent) but less than in 1928 (42 per cent) or 1937–8 (100 per cent). The explanation of this last situation lies in the fact that preparations for war had an adverse influence on trade relations. F. Machlup asserts that 'there is no "need" for any particular sum of monetary reserves in the world'. He does, however, feel that such an annual growth is required that restrictive measures in the fields of foreign trade and capital movements can be avoided.

The components of international reserves are gold, convertible currencies and the IMF 'gold tranche'. About 50 per cent (against 85 per cent in 1913) of the monetary reserves consist of gold (Table 39).

TABLE 39: Monetary reserves,[a] at the end of 1968 ($'000m.)

	Total[b]	United States	United Kingdom	Industrial Europe	Other developed countries	Less-developed countries
Gold	39·2	11·9	1·5	17·6	4·8	3·5
Foreign exchange	29·0	—	0·9	8·1	8·0	12·0
Reserve position in IMF	7·2	2·6	—	2·2	1·8	0·6
Special drawing rights	3·3	0·9	0·3	0·8	0·5	0·7
Total	78·6	15·4	2·7	28·7	15·1	16·8

[a] Excluding communist countries. The gold stock of the USSR has been estimated at $2,000 to 7,000 million
[b] Total does not always tally on account of rounding-off
Source: IMF, Annual Report 1969 (Washington 1969), p. 63

a. Gold

About a quarter of world gold reserves is owned by the United States; in 1949 the figure was as high as 70 per cent. Leaving aside theoretical objections, the United States has little inclination to raise the price at which gold is accepted as payment for its exports. This price – $35 per fine ounce – has remained unchanged since 1934. Moreover, the United States' own production of gold is of little consequence (approximately 4 per cent of the total output of the non-communist countries). Again, an increase in the price would only benefit a few large gold producers, principally South Africa (which accounts for roughly 70 per cent of the non-communist world's production) and the USSR. Elsewhere, the gold price has only been changed to the extent that the parity of the country's own currency in terms of the dollar has been altered. Despite the constant price and increased costs, output has been above its prewar peak ($1,264 million in 1940) since 1962. This has been possible through the rationalization of production, the subsidization of marginal mines and the fact that gold is in many cases a by-product.

World gold reserves are also experiencing the influence of the fluctuations in the volume of western goods being purchased by the USSR (whose annual gold production has been estimated as $200 million) with gold, along with the fluctuations in hoarding and in industrial requirements (Table 40).

TABLE 40: Gold; marketed stocks and distribution by use on the world market, 1966–8 ($m. estimated at $35 a fine ounce).

	1966	1967	1968
Production	1,440	1,410	1,421
Sales by the USSR	—	15	11
Purchases by China (Mainland)	−75	−20	−43
Total new quantity supplied	1,365	1,405	1,390
Change in countries' monetary gold stock[a]	−950	−1,400	−580
IMF gold transactions[b]	783	30	−394
BIS[b] and EMF[b] gold transactions	121	−209	263
Total added to official monetary gold stock	−45	−1,580	−710
Residual: supplies absorbed by industry, arts, and private hoarding	1,410	2,985	2,100

[a] Excluding communist countries
[b] Minus sign denotes net outflow of gold from the IMF, the Bank for International Settlements (BIS) and the European Monetary Fund (EMF)
Note: Totals do not always tally on account of rounding-off
Source: IMF, Annual Report 1969 (Washington 1969), p. 129

Since the IMF countries' currencies are expressed in gold and gold is used in international transactions, confidence in these currencies is conditional upon the certainty of a fixed gold price. In order to prevent substantial deviations from the official price, the 'Gold Pool' was set up in October 1961 by the central banks of Belgium, West Germany, France, the United Kingdom, Italy, the Netherlands, Switzerland and the Federal Reserve Bank of New York. The immediate cause of this move was the speculation which in the autumn of 1960 had hoisted the quotation on the London market to $40. With the aid of the United States, the price was brought back to its previous level by gold selling. The Bank of England was appointed operating agent. It was responsible for the sale of gold from a 50 per cent US-subscribed pool and secured the necessary coordination in purchases by the member countries.

Buying of gold was particularly heavy after the devaluation of the pound on 18 November 1967 (mainly through the sale of dollars). In 1967 and early 1968 this speculation led to intervention by the Gold Pool countries to the tune of about $3,000 million. On 17 March 1968 the countries actively engaged in the management of the Gold Pool (from June 1967 France took no further part in such transactions and in November 1967 it was excluded from the negotiations and discussions) decided:

1. to use official gold reserves for transfers between monetary authorities only, and consequently to cease supplying gold markets (such as London) – which meant the end of the Gold Pool;

2. to buy no more gold on international markets;

3. to sell no gold to monetary authorities to replace gold which the latter had sold on private markets.

As a result of the Washington decisions, there are now two gold prices (the 'two-tier' system), namely the official price of $35, at which the United States continues to buy and sell gold (in transactions with monetary authorities), and the free market price, which becomes the price applied on a commodity market. This has never exceeded $45. The Washington decisions presage a demonetization of gold. Since November 1969 a price below $35 dollars has often been quoted. Because a fall below $35 is also considered undesirable (see above), the IMF gave an undertaking on 23 December 1969 to purchase South Africa's current gold production at $35 over a period of five years, even if the free market price is lower. Gold stocks in existence at that date can also be gradually disposed of at the same price. South Africa may not, however, sell any gold to other monetary authorities.

b. Convertible currencies

Gold reserves are supplemented by convertible currencies, and in particular the dollar and the pound sterling. The United States and the United Kingdom have developed a wide-scale payments system of which many countries avail themselves. The latter are, moreover, always certain of obtaining the necessary resources on the large capital markets of the UK and USA. In contrast with the other convertible currencies, dollars and sterling, called the key currencies, are available in abundance (at the present time about $13,800 million and the equivalent of approximately $6,700 million respectively).

The key-currency reserves, however, are influenced by the balance-of-payments surpluses or deficits of the United States and the United Kingdom; the larger the deficit, say, on the United States balance of payments, the more claims arise on that country and the more monetary reserves increase. The United States balance-of-payments deficit is covered without any adjusting measures being necessary, because other countries maintain dollars in their reserves. If such a situation persists, the American currency becomes the subject of distrust and dollars are converted into gold so that monetary reserves once again contract. (In the United States, dollars do not form part of the reserves.)

Many states have in some way or other linked their currencies to the two key currencies. This is how the monetary areas originated. The most important of these are the sterling area and the dollar area.

1. The sterling area

In 1931 the countries which had close trading relations with the United Kingdom and preferred to have their currency stable to the pound rather than to gold followed the British authorities in devaluing. In this way, they avoided the uncertainty inherent in a floating pound (see Section 7). The countries concerned maintained their foreign-exchange reserves in London and where necessary applied the same exchange control. Thus the foreign-exchange standard came into being – an important currency now fulfilling the function of gold as an international standard. (Before 1914, the gold standard was actually a sterling-exchange standard.)

The sterling bloc – the term 'sterling area' has only been used since 1940 – originally consisted of the Commonwealth countries (excluding Canada) and Portugal, which in 1933 were joined by the Scandinavian countries and in 1936 by Iran and Latvia. Argentina and

Japan could, though not in the technical sense, be considered members of the sterling bloc. In 1940, however, all non-Commonwealth countries severed their links with the pound.

The sterling area now consists of the Commonwealth countries (except Canada), Iceland, Ireland, Jordan, Kuwait, Libya, South and South West Africa, Southern Yemen, the British Protected States in the Persian Gulf and Western Samoa. About a third of world trade is settled in sterling. Just as happened subsequently with the dollar, the key-currency role was acquired through the pound's being a major international instrument of payment. The importance of the sterling area, like that of the pound as a key currency, has now declined considerably. This is partly due to the weakening of political and economic ties with the Commonwealth and to the United Kingdom's persistent economic difficulties. The sterling area countries have secured a greater degree of independence in the monetary field. Thus it is easier for them than before to accumulate a deficit with countries outside the sterling area. After the 14·3 per cent devaluation of the pound in 1967, which involved the sterling area countries in losses, confidence diminished still further. In order to dissuade the countries concerned from disposing of their sterling balances, three-year agreements were signed by the Bank of England and the sterling area countries in July and August 1968, taking effect from 25 September 1968, by the terms of which

a. the United Kingdom gave these countries an exchange rate guaranteed in respect of that part of their official sterling reserves which exceeded 10 per cent of their total monetary reserves;

b. these countries undertook to maintain a specific proportion of their currency reserves in sterling.

These agreements (which the United Kingdom had to conclude before receiving credit facilities totalling $2,000 million from other countries) have served temporarily to strengthen the sterling area but really amount to its dismantlement. Moreover, they do not obviate the possibility of confidence in the pound declining still further among other countries (which are not members of the sterling area).

2. *The dollar area*
In the dollar area, there are still fewer formal ties. The countries of this area normally demand payment, and maintain the bulk of their

401

reserves, in dollars. Since their currencies are interconvertible, there is no exchange control among these countries.

The dollar area consists of the United States, Liberia, Panama (where the dollar is a freely circulating medium), the Philippines and most Latin American states (excluding Argentina, Brazil, Chile and Cuba).

Private domestic holdings of gold by residents have been prohibited in the United States since 1934 (external holdings by residents since 1961).

c. Other components

Any member of the IMF may at any time demand (or draw) unconditionally up to a quarter of its contribution to the Fund. Since every quota normally consists as to a quarter of gold (and as to the rest of the domestic currency), the drawing right is equal to the 'gold tranche' but the tranche may change as a result of IMF transactions in the currency concerned. It is equal to the quota less Fund holdings of this currency. If, for instance, Britain purchases dollars equivalent to its gold tranche from the IMF (with pounds), it no longer has an unconditional drawing right (unless other countries have bought pounds simultaneously).

There are also conditional drawing rights – above the gold tranche – (these are only granted on certain conditions, which may be related to the economic policy of the country applying for additional drawing rights) and special drawing rights. Neither type is shown in Table 39. Special drawing rights ($3,400 million on 1 January 1970 and a further $3,000 million on 1 January 1971 and 1972) can be taken up by either direct transfer (application by the drawing member to a particular country) or indirect transfer (application to the Fund, which itself designates a country where the special drawing rights have to be used). Special drawing rights amount to international money creation since on the average only 30 per cent has to be repaid.

Since 1958, international liquidity has been influenced by the Eurodollar or Eurocurrency market. This market consists of banks not operating in the United States which lend and borrow dollars on a short-term basis. (Where the transactions relate to a period of more than five years, the market is called the Eurobond market.) If a Frenchman has a dollar balance with an American bank, he may make it temporarily available to a British bank (or to a subsidiary of an American bank) – for a higher remuneration, of course, than he receives in the United States. The bank can use this amount to grant loans. Such operations are in fact arbitrage transactions. Their volume is continually expanding (being at the present time about $37,500 million in the case of Eurodollars and about $24,000 million in the case of Eurobonds).

2 Exchange rates under the gold standard

a. Theory

Under the gold standard system, the currency unit is exchangeable for a fixed quantity of gold. The central bank buys and sells gold in unlimited amounts at a fixed price. International gold movements are unrestricted and there is full convertibility.

Among the countries on the gold standard, exchange rates are shown by the ratios between the weights of the various monetary units in gold. Rate fluctuations are of necessity within narrow limits, one reason being that external payments can be made by deliveries not only of foreign currency but also of gold. These limits are determined by the 'gold points'; the gold-export point is reached when the rate is so high that it is more advantageous to send gold abroad than to purchase foreign currency, and the gold-import point when the rate falls so low that it is more profitable to import gold than to receive foreign currency. The margin between import and export points corresponds to the difference between the gold purchase and selling prices applied by the central bank (provided there is no longer any gold coin in circulation) and transport costs (consignment, packaging, insurance).

According to the classical authors, the balance-of-payments equilibrium (of the autonomous items) was effected by the gold standard in the following way. If there is a deficit, gold has to be shipped abroad. Thus the total money quantity decreases (either coin or bank notes which have been used to purchase gold), as a result of which, by the quantity theory, a fall in prices takes place which in turn stimulates exports. In the gold-receiving countries, converse phenomena occur, so that exports are restrained by the rise in prices. In this way, the balance of payments is restored to equilibrium.

b. Practice

The gold bullion standard was in almost universal application before the First World War (1870–1914) and, owing to propitious

403

circumstances (relatively peaceful international situation, London's role as international financial centre), appeared to give a certain degree of satisfaction.

In 1914 the obligation for central banks to give gold in exchange for paper money was abolished; in countries where they were still in circulation, gold coins were replaced by banknotes. Despite this increase in the central bank's gold reserves, coverage diminished owing to the appreciable expansion in the quantity of money.

To remedy the gold scarcity, the Genoa Monetary Conference in 1922 recommended the adoption of the gold exchange standard. When most countries one after another returned to the gold standard, they allowed coverage to be effected wholly or partially by means of gold currencies. In 1928 the gold standard was restored everywhere except in Spain and the Soviet Union, but many countries had only slender gold reserves and owed their balance-of-payments equilibrium solely to the influx of foreign capital. The 1929 crisis and the subsequent depression thus had catastrophic consequences.

Up to 1929, the flow of money from Europe to the United States, especially French debt repayments, had been compensated by a flow in the opposite direction aimed mainly at investment in Germany. In this way, it was possible for Germany to make reparation payments to France. When, as a result of the crisis and depression, these investments came to a halt (after the crash of the Austrian Kreditanstalt Bank, American investors lost confidence and withdrew their money from Europe), Germany was no longer able to fulfil commitments to France. The latter invoked this circumstance to suspend payments to the United States.

Other countries, which found their income falling owing to the decline in raw material prices and could no longer repay their debts to the United States, were forced to leave the gold standard (Argentina and New Zealand in 1929–30, the other South American states in 1930–1).

The United Kingdom's situation too became precarious, chiefly because it had been making long-term loans to Germany and receiving short-term credit from the United States. Furthermore, the export position had been unsatisfactory since 1926 on account of the stabilization of the pound at its prewar level. On 21 September 1931 the United Kingdom abandoned the gold standard. In 1933 the United States followed suit, not so much because of pressure on the balance of payments as in order to put an end to the adverse internal economic situation. In June 1934 the dollar was officially devalued 59 per cent.

After these devaluations, the price level in countries which had clung to the gold standard was too high; thus it came about that the belga (Belgium's currency unit from 1926 to 1946) devalued in March 1935 and the Swiss franc in September 1936, followed by the French franc (October 1936). The Dutch guilder became a floating currency (see Section 7) in September 1936 and only stabilized (see Section 6) in March 1940 (18 per cent devaluation).

The link between gold and the quantity of money became much looser, with the latter consisting increasingly of fiduciary money. To put it another way, gold exports did not necessarily bring about a drop in the quantity of money. The central banks therefore considered it expedient, far more so than in pre-1914 days, to take upon themselves the responsibility for reducing the quantity of money, e.g. by discount or open-market policy (Chapter 13.4b).

Appraisal

1. The classical authors accept the validity of the quantity theory. Fluctuations in the quantity of money, however, do not necessarily exert an influence on prices. Heavy gold imports into the United States during the years 1919 to 1924, for instance, did not cause prices to rise.

2. A drop in prices stimulates exports only if the latter are not offset by an intensification of protectionist measures. During a depression the downward movement of prices does not usually yield much in the way of results. The influence of price changes on imports and exports must not be overestimated.

3. Moreover, a fall in prices is difficult to accomplish, as wages are not very flexible. On the other hand, it may be the cause of a reversal in the business cycle.

4. The automatic restoration of the balance-of-payments equilibrium as propounded by the classical authors appears to be possible only in the first phase of the gold standard (only coin in circulation). Thereafter an appropriate monetary policy is needed. In other words, the central bank must observe the rules of the game.

3 The modern theory of balance-of-payments equilibrium

The classical theory was built up on purely deductive lines; whether it accorded with the facts was not verified. That the gold standard was not abandoned earlier must be ascribed to other factors in the balance-of-payments equilibrium.

The modern theory relates restoration of equilibrium more closely to the fluctuations in employment and the national income.

a. Current transactions

Let us examine, for instance, the influence of increased exports on the national income.

A rise in exports (and the resultant income of the factors of production) leads to heavier demand for domestic, but also for foreign, consumer goods. The intensification of activity in various industries similarly brings about an expansion of imports. The increase in exports is thus offset by an increase in imports. The greater the marginal propensity to import, the sooner equilibrium is restored. Whether it will be restored completely is by no means certain. The marginal propensity to save is also of importance, and account must be taken of the repercussions abroad. The changes in domestic incomes have an influence on other countries' national income, imports and exports: increased imports and exports cause an expansion of exports or imports abroad, which in turn have an effect on the foreign trade of the country concerned.

In addition, foreign currencies are generally converted into the domestic currency, which has the effect of increasing internal liquidity; demand expands further and contributes to increasing imports.

Restoration of the balance of payments may, however, be assisted in some measure by price fluctuations. While as a general rule these are of less significance as long as a state of full employment has not been attained, they exercise a preponderant influence during a boom period (all factors are at work), when a further expansion in real incomes is impossible. The elimination of an export surplus is then largely attributable to price increases. (In the case of an import surplus there may be income fluctuations but the adaptation process can be stimulated by induced price decreases.)

An unduly marked rise in prices causes an excessive shrinkage of exports and produces a deficit. Even so, the balance-of-payments equilibrium need not be disturbed, as a parallel drop in imports cannot be ruled out, in which case a slackening in economic activity and widespread unemployment are probable. That is to say, an

406

exchange rate at which a balance-of-payments equilibrium exists is not necessarily the desirable or optimum rate (e.g. in the United Kingdom from 1926 to 1931; Belgium from 1931 to 1935). In other words, balance-of-payments equilibrium and full employment exist simultaneously only with a specific price level in relation to other countries.

b. Capital movements

How far does the modern theory hold good for capital transfers? A distinction has to be made between short- and long-term movements.

The latter comprise unilateral transfers, such as reparation payments after the 1870 and 1914–18 wars, private and government loans and direct investment from country to country. Income changes occur, the extent of which differs in every state. The effects of capital transfers are determined in particular by the volume of payments, the elasticity of demand for exports from the debtor country and the period within which payment needs to be made. Generalizations on this subject are impossible. The circumstances in which such transfers take place sometimes vary a great deal (a case in point being the reparations mentioned above), so no general rules can be formulated concerning the degree to which the terms of trade are influenced.

In the normal course, various factors operate to restore equilibrium. Thus a loan contracted abroad in order to facilitate investment will probably be spent abroad forthwith for the import of capital goods. The remainder, which in the borrowing country is converted into the national currency and brings about an increase in the national income, leads in turn to an expansion in import demand.

Short-term transfers, e.g. in the form of bank deposits, usually leave domestic income unchanged, being intended in most cases to iron out temporary minor disturbances of the balance-of-payments equilibrium. They do not, as the classical theory asserts, fulfil a causal function.

While speculative capital movements (hot or flight money) also exert no influence on the national income (as long as they are not used, for instance, to make investments in the country of destination), they may accentuate a disequilibrium in the balance of payments.

Appraisal

The theory outlined above, according to which income fluctuations (multiplier) account for the restoration of equilibrium, applies only when there is not full employment (constant prices). It is based on the assumptions that the marginal propensities to save and to import remain constant and that it is always possible to finance deficits, which in point of fact is not so. It further postulates that exports result from current production (and not from stocks). In the less-developed countries, import requirements are becoming so heavy (demonstration effect) that the theory cannot be applied to these areas. Finally, price movements are of more significance in countries whose national income is largely conditioned by external economic relations.

Like the classical doctrine, this theory is based on an automatically operating mechanism, but the balance of payments is not necessarily brought into equilibrium in the modern theory. Instead of price fluctuations, it is mainly variations in the level of employment and the national income that perform a regulatory function.

But every country aims at least at maintaining stability in the national income, employment and prices and therefore endeavours to counteract such oscillations. It does not acquiesce in an equilibrium rate of exchange which has large-scale unemployment as its concomitant. Such a policy contributes to the uncertainty surrounding an automatic correction of the balance of payments.

If fluctuations in the national income and prices are to be avoided, there remain the following instruments for ensuring equilibrium in the balance of payments:

a. devaluation, revaluation or floating exchange rates (by means of which the domestic price level is kept constant and the country adapts itself to conditions of competition on international markets);

b. exchange control.

These possibilities are examined below.

4 Propagation of cyclical fluctuations

Since $E - M$, or the balance on current account, is equal to $S - I$ (Chapter 2.3c), it is clear that a deficit on this account arises when planned investment is greater than planned saving. Such overspending is in many countries the result of large-scale industrialization plans. A surplus of saving, on the other hand, gives a favourable balance.

The cause of the favourable or unfavourable balance may also, however, lie abroad. As has been seen, a change in a country's imports or exports soon has its effects on the external trade or economic activity of its partner countries. A particularly marked influence is exerted by countries such as the United States, whose imports and exports account for a substantial proportion of world trade. Capital movements also have deflationary or inflationary repercussions.

Increased demand by a certain country is frequently the result of the inflation prevailing in that country; there is more money available, not a little of which is used for purchases of foreign goods because the level of domestic prices shows a rising tendency. Other countries' exports will (at fixed exchange rates) increase; if this situation persists, the expansive influence exerted on the quantity of money causes an inflationary spiral, and it is said that inflation has been imported. The prices of foreign products will, of course, go up in these other countries too.

Countermeasures can be taken, but they are not without their disadvantages. For instance, a deflationary policy cannot be applied, owing to the rigidity of prices and wages. Limitation of demand for foreign goods can be achieved by a devaluation, but this, apart from its inherent drawbacks (see Section 6) frequently elicits reprisals.

Even if a country is afflicted with an inflationary situation, inflation can still be imported if the tendency is stronger in another country or countries. Deflation too can be imported, but this does not happen so often, since a policy of full employment is pursued everywhere.

International trade thus benefits by a policy of monetary equilibrium among the world's major trading nations. If this equilibrium is disturbed, the countries concerned themselves have to take the necessary measures to restore it and thus avoid reaction from other countries. In international organizations, indeed, pressure for such measures is frequently exerted by the members; they actually help the country concerned in its efforts at stabilization, in particular by refraining from retaliatory measures (to the extent that their promptings are duly acted upon in such fields as monetary policy) and by providing financial aid.

In other words, it is no longer a matter of indifference what economic policy, and more particularly what monetary policy, is pursued in the major countries.

5 The theory of purchasing-power parity

If a particular commodity costs £48 in the United Kingdom and DM

480 in West Germany, it is said to have a purchasing-power parity of £1 per DM 10. Such a parity can be ascertained for a large number of articles, and from this an overall or binary purchasing-power parity can be derived. Since consumer habits vary from country to country, the calculation should be made in two ways, i.e. weighted on the basis of the domestic and on the basis of the foreign pattern of consumption.

The theory of purchasing-power parity, which was formulated by G. Cassel after 1918, states that the exchange rate or external value of a currency is determined by the domestic value or purchasing-power parity of the foreign currencies concerned. This appears logical, as in normal circumstances demand for a foreign currency is based on that currency's internal purchasing power. Thus foreign currencies' external purchasing power must accord with their internal purchasing power. If DM 80 has the same purchasing power as £10, the rate of exchange should be £1 = DM 8.

In point of fact, the exchange rate between two countries is not invariably consonant with the purchasing-power parity or the ratio between the number of monetary units which have the same purchasing power in these two countries (Table 41).

TABLE 41: Comparison of the purchasing-power parities of industrial workers in the EEC countries (1963–6)

Currency unit	Parities (in Belgian francs)				Official exchange rates (IMF)
	1963	1964	1965	1966	
DM 1	11·7	11·8	11·9	12·0	12·5
FF 1	9·7	9·7	10·0	10·1	10·2
Lire 100	7·95	7·70	7·70	7·80	8·0
f 1	15·2	14·7	14·8	14·5	13·8
L. fr. 1	1·00	1·01	1·02	1·02	1·0

Source: Statistical Office of the European Communities, *General Statistical Bulletin,* No 10, 1967, p. 16

On the basis of the official exchange rates, European prices are not so high as American. Thus the purchasing power of one dollar in 1950 and 1955 was B.frs. 37 and B.frs. 37·6 respectively, as compared with the official exchange rate of $1 = B.frs. 50.2. The real national product in the European countries is therefore higher than would appear from a conversion of the various national products into the dollar at official exchange rates.

The differences just quoted are traceable mainly to the fact that many goods (fresh milk, fresh fish, certain fruits) and services (transport, hairdressing) experience no competition from abroad.

Even prices of raw materials traded on world markets are not the same everywhere on account of transport costs and customs duties (cf. Table 1). Thus high-tariff countries usually have a higher price level than low-tariff countries.

Consequently, in the comparative version of the purchasing-power-parity theory, changes in purchasing power are analysed in relation to a specific reference period. If, compared with this period, prices in one country have risen more steeply than prices in another country, exports are slowed down more and imports are given a more powerful stimulus. The resultant disequilibrium in the balance of payments causes a decrease in the value of the currency, the extent of which is determined by that of the relative changes in the domestic price levels of the countries concerned:

present exchange rate = exchange rate in reference period × $\dfrac{\text{domestic-price index}}{\text{foreign country's price index}}$.

If prices have risen by 300 per cent in A and by 500 per cent in B compared with the reference year, then on the foreign-currency market in A the exchange rate against B should fall from 100 to $(300 \div 500) \times 100$ or 60 per cent.

Cassel sought in particular to demonstrate that inflation, which in some countries has assumed serious proportions after the First World War must be viewed as the cause of rising exchange rates.

Appraisal

   a. It is difficult to find a reference period which is marked by a genuine equilibrium of exchange rates. We ought really to go back to pre-1914 days, but in the meantime every country's economic structure has changed.

   b. Which indices should be used? Prices of many world-market products, e.g. commodities, show only slight differences on national markets, with the result that the corresponding index numbers prove to be of little use.

More reliance is therefore to be placed on domestic-price indices (retail prices, wages, cost of living). If the cost-of-living index has risen more in one country than in another and at the same time wages have increased, the adverse effects of these movements are experienced by costs and selling prices.

The ratio between the various groups of domestic prices is consequently of prime importance, especially in sectors of industry competing on export markets.

c. The price level is not always the decisive factor in the volume of imports and exports. A change in demand for certain commodities, such as may follow inventions (e.g. sodium nitrate and artificial fertilizer), may cause a disturbance of the balance-of-payments equilibrium without any alteration of the purchasing-power parity. Modifications of customs tariffs frequently have similar consequences.

The purchasing-power parity relates to only a part of the balance of payments. Capital movements are not taken into consideration (e.g. imports of securities); when capital flows from country *A* to country *B*, an appreciation in the value of *B*'s currency may occur without any change in country *B*'s monetary policy.

Cassel has, indeed, himself pointed out that, apart from the purchasing-power parity, a great many other factors exercise an influence on exchange rates.

d. Many countries' currencies are indeed linked to that of another, economically strong country (Section 1). In such cases the exchange rate does not hinge on the purchasing-power parity, but the purchasing power of one currency is conditioned by that of another currency and the exchange rate between them.

Other theories are offered in explanation of the level of exchange rates (e.g. the balance-of-payments theory: which holds that the balance of payments determines the level of the exchange rate and also causes changes in domestic prices; there is assumed to be a causal instead of a functional connection between the balance of payments and the rate of exchange); but such theories only indicate the direction in which exchange rates move. The purchasing-power-parity theory can furnish concrete data on such changes. Despite the foregoing objections and its limited applicability, this doctrine has in many cases (especially in a period of marked inflation) proved its worth.

6 Devaluation

When a reduction in the value of a currency is effected by law, this is called devaluation. In other words, it is a legal reduction of the value

412

of the currency in terms of the standard coin (gold) or of other currencies: an existing depreciation is consolidated. In the case of free or floating exchange rates (see Section 7) the lowering or raising of the value in terms of other currencies is better expressed by 'depreciation' and 'appreciation'. While inflation may take a country unawares, so to speak, devaluation calls for a government decision. It becomes imperative in order to maintain competitive power on export markets.

Devaluation changes *ipso facto* exchange rates, unless a simultaneous, equally heavy devaluation is carried out abroad.

If, after a long period of currency depreciation with continual fluctuations in value, a constant ratio of the monetary unit to gold or to other currencies is laid down, this is called stabilization.

Devaluation usually brings about a rise in the domestic price level (unless paralleled by a deflationary policy); imports become dearer and the probable increase in exports serves to accentuate the inflationary tendency. This argument only holds good to the extent that there are no restrictions on exchange of goods. A country which has an overrated currency and has introduced import restrictions and monetary control usually has higher prices than other countries. Thus after the devaluation, through which the restrictive measures are discontinued, a fall in prices may occur.

If the rise is not kept within limits, the advantages of devaluation soon evaporate and, what is more, a second devaluation may be necessary. On top of all this, devaluation has an adverse effect on some items in the balance of payments (e.g. redemption of loans, except where expressed in the national currency).

Revaluation is the opposite of devaluation, i.e. an official raising of the value of the monetary unit in terms of the standard coin or other currencies (e.g. the 17 per cent revaluation of the Swedish krona in 1946, the 5 per cent revaluation of the German and Dutch currencies at the beginning of March 1961 and the 8·5 per cent revaluation of the German mark at the end of October 1969).

Membership of the IMF means that the exchange rates declared to this institution may only be altered with its approval. Consent is given where the balance of payments concerned shows a fundamental disequilibrium. This term, as has been said, is not defined. The Fund raises no objection to an alteration of not more than 10 per cent in relation to the initial parity. A second 10 per cent adjustment can be opposed by the IMF within three days; in the event of more far-reaching parity changes, it may ask for more time to consider the matter.

In order to ascertain the effects of a devaluation it is necessary, in the view of some writers, to examine the elasticity of internal demand for imports and of external demand for the country's exports (the 'elasticities approach'); according to others, it is the influence upon the national expenditure which must be studied (the 'absorption approach').

a. Elasticities

The importance of the coefficients of elasticity is brought out in the 'Marshall-Lerner condition', named after A. Marshall (see Appendix 9) and A. P. Lerner.

A devaluation – e.g. of the dollar by n (n always being assumed to be expressed in per cent here) – influences import and export prices and values. (Hereinafter the exchange rate is assumed to be quoted with a fixed internal value: see Chapter 11.7.)

1. Export prices

If prior to devaluation $\$1 = £P_S$ (P_S being the exchange rate) and therefore $£1 = \$1/P_S$, thereafter $£1 = \$(1 - n)/P_S$, since prices in terms of the foreign currency (provided prices in the domestic currency remain constant) fall by n (cf. Table 42) to a level $1 - n$ of the previous level, which in per cent is $100(1 - n)$.

2. Import prices

Assuming unchanged prices in the foreign currency, import prices in the domestic currency rise. Previously $\$1 = £P_S$; now $\$1 = £P_S/(1 - n)$. In order to accord the same number of currency units therefore, former prices have to be multiplied by $\dfrac{1}{1 - n}$ or divided by $1 - n$. In relation to the previous level, prices climb to $1/(1 - n)$, which represents an increase of $\dfrac{1}{1 - n} - 1$ or $\dfrac{n}{1 - n}$ (in per cent $\dfrac{100n}{1 - n}$). In the event of a devaluation of, for instance, 10 per cent, the rise amounts to 0·11 or 11·1 per cent when the price is equal to unity. If the rate of devaluation is 50 the exchange rate rises by 100 per cent.

3. *The value of exports*

Since the elasticity of external demand for a country's exports (which from the standpoint of other countries correspond to imports)

$$e_{E'} = \frac{dE'/E'}{n},$$

dE' or the expansion in the quantity exported is equal to $E'e_{E'}n$ (the devaluation rate is the change in the price; cf. the elasticity formula). The total quantity exported can now be represented by

$$E' + E'e_{E'}n = E'(1 + e_{E'}n)$$

and its value (in foreign currency) by

$$E'(1 + e_{E'}n)(1 - n)P_E$$

in which P_E represents the average former export price (expressed in foreign currency).

The increase in the value of exports is now obtained as follows:

$$E'(1 + e_{E'}n)(1 - n)P_E - E'P_E = P_E[E'(1 + e_{E'}n)(1 - n) - E']$$
$$= P_E[E'e_{E'}n(1 - n) - E'n].$$

4. *The value of imports*

As the elasticity of import demand is

$$e_{M'} = -\frac{dM'/M'}{n/(1-n)},$$

the diminution of the volume of imports is

$$dM' = -\frac{M'e_{M'}n}{1-n}.$$

Provided prices in the foreign currency (P_M) remain stable, their value is equal to

$$\frac{M'e_{M'}nP_M}{1-n}.$$

5. *The balance of payments*

For the balance of payments to be favourably influenced, the increase in the value of exports must be greater than the decrease in the value of imports; in other words, $dE > dM$:

$$P_E \left[E' e_{E'} n (1-n) - E'n \right] - \left(-\frac{M' e_{M'} n P_M}{1-n} \right) > 0$$

or after being divided by n

$$P_E \left[E' e_{E'} (1-n) - E' \right] + \frac{M' e_{M'} P_M}{1-n} > 0.$$

For a low rate of devaluation, $1-n$ is roughly equal to unity, so that:

$$E' P_E (e_{E'} - 1) + M' P_M e_{M'} > 0.$$

In the case of a slight deficit, $M' P_M$ is more or less equal to $E' P_E$, so that, after division

$$e_{E'} - 1 + e_{M'} > 0$$

or:

$$e_{E'} + e_{M'} > 1.$$

Devaluation in a country A thus has beneficial effects for that country if the sum of the elasticity of external demand for exports of country A and the elasticity of internal demand (by country A) for imports is greater than unity.

TABLE 42: Effects of a devaluation by n,[a] on which the Marshall-Lerner condition is based

Export prices (a) in domestic currency	stability
(b) in foreign currency	decrease by n to level $(1-n)$
Import prices (a) in foreign currency	stability
(b) in domestic currency	rise of $n/(1-n)$ to level $1/(1-n)$
Expansion in quantity exported	$E' e_E' n$
Decline in quantity imported	$\dfrac{M' e_M' n}{1-n}$
Increase in value of exports (in foreign currency)	$P_E \left[E' e_E' n (1-n) - E'n \right]$ (1)
Decrease in value of imports (in foreign currency)	$\dfrac{M' e_M' n P_M}{1-n}$ (2)
Condition for improvement in balance of payments (in foreign currency) (1) − (2) > 0	$e_E' + e_M' > 1$

[a] n is expressed in per cent

416

Appraisal

The Marshall-Lerner condition (which proceeds on the assumption of an insignificant deficit, a limited rate of devaluation and constant prices at home and abroad) applies to the extent that the country's industry can produce enough to cope with the increased foreign and home demand; in other words, the elasticity-of-supply coefficients must be sufficiently large.

In point of fact, the Marshall-Lerner condition is of minor significance (as has already been pointed out, there is usually a tendency for the level of domestic prices to rise) because knowledge of coefficients of elasticity leaves something to be desired. Research on the subject suggests that the relevant figures are low and therefore that devaluation is not an effective method. These estimates, however, have met with a good deal of criticism. Generalizations, moreover, are dangerous, on account of differences in the volume and structure of external trade. Demand for raw materials, for example, is less elastic than that for finished products. Furthermore, coefficients of elasticity vary with cyclical conditions.

Lastly, the condition takes no account of income effects: an increase in exports, for example, produces additional foreign-currency income, which in turn enables imports to be stepped up (see Section 3).

b. National expenditure

A balance-of-payments surplus or deficit can also be defined as the difference between the national income and domestic expenditure (consumption and investment). S. Alexander therefore considers that the elimination of a balance-of-payments deficit means that income must rise to a greater extent than expenditure.

A devaluation is of little help in this respect. Through the 'idle resources effect', the unused factors of production may result in higher exports and additional employment. If, however, the sum of marginal propensities to consume and to invest is greater than unity, the additional expenditure is higher than the additional income and the devaluation has an adverse effect on the balance of payments. S. Alexander allows for this possibility and also believes that the terms-of-trade effect will be detrimental because the elasticity of internal demand (for imported goods) is lower than that of external demand.

Where there is full employment, the necessary mobility of the

417

factors of production must involve a fall in consumption and/or investment. This must come about through an advance of prices. In the normal course devaluation results in a higher price level and a decline in the real value of cash reserves. In order to maintain the level of these reserves, expenditure has to be reduced. Such a reduction is also induced by the 'money illusion', although adverse effects on saving are not to be ruled out.

In conditions of full employment, the influence of a devaluation is as a rule slight and it is better to act on investment and consumption by means of monetary and credit measures. Restriction of imports, too, may yield better results than a devaluation. In the event of widespread unemployment, on the other hand, an internal expansion is required and a devaluation yields better results.

Appraisal

The 'elasticities approach' regards the balance of payments too much as an independent datum and, moreover, can only be used in the event of cost or price disparities. The 'absorption approach', on the other hand, stresses the monetary character of a balance-of-payments deficit and its relation to the functioning of the entire economy.

Just as the champions of the 'elasticities approach' are criticized for neglecting income effects, the charge levelled at the 'absorption approach' is that it ignores price effects. F. Machlup maintains also that too little attention is devoted to the repercussions of a devaluation on other countries' 'absorption'. Although the 'absorption approach' seems in practice to be the most suitable for analytical purposes, propensities to consume and to invest, like coefficients of elasticity, cannot be accurately calculated. Hence it is that 'devaluation analysis . . . has still somewhat further to go before it can be an absolute guide to policy makers' (M. O. Clement).

7 Floating exchange rates

After the First World War, some countries instead of devaluing straight away, allowed the exchange rate to be determined by the free play of supply and demand. They had adopted a floating currency; gold was no longer the basis of the monetary system, and the central bank was no longer obliged to maintain a specific cover ratio or to exchange bank notes for precious metals or gold currencies (paper standard).

A well-known example is that of the French franc, whose exchange rate was determined by supply and demand, without the intervention of the Banque de France, from March 1919. Up to 1921 the external value of the franc followed a steady downward trend (import surplus), after which the rate improved through an easing of the balance of payments due to the fall in prices of raw materials. In 1922 depreciation set in afresh, mainly as a result of capital exports – which had been made precisely because a further decline in value was feared (flight capital). Imports also increased, money being converted into goods. When in 1926 the French franc stabilized, the rate of devaluation applied was in fact too high. This was also what happened upon the stabilization of the belga in the same year. The reverse occurred with the pound in 1925.

When after 1931 several monetary units became floating currencies (the pound and the Swedish krona from September 1931 to 1939, the dollar from April 1933 to January 1934, the guilder from September 1936 to April 1940, the French franc from July 1937 to May 1938), equalization funds were set up by the authorities in an endeavour to stabilize the rates at the desired levels. (The equalization funds were also given the task of checking the effects of capital flights on the domestic money supply: open-market policy – see Chapter 13.4b.) The facility of exchangeability of paper for gold was retained, but at a constantly fluctuating rate.

In practice, it has proved far from easy to maintain exchange rates at the optimum levels, especially when substantial capital movements have taken place. Only minor fluctuations can be counteracted; otherwise the funds' resources soon run dry. The exchange fund prevents a fall in the rates by purchasing foreign currencies, and a rise by offering them, a rise and a fall respectively in Britain.

In 1932 the United Kingdom set up the first fund of this kind – the Exchange Equalization Account, which initially contained £150 million and subsequently £550 million of Treasury Certificates. Between 1932 and 1937, the Fund purchased gold and foreign currencies in order to keep the rate of the pound down and to facilitate exports. From May 1938, on the other hand, it had to counter the effects of capital exports by selling gold and foreign currencies.

From 3 April 1935 to 31 March 1936, there was an exchange-equalization fund in Belgium, but it did not have to intervene on the market as the exchange rate proved to have been judiciously selected. When in 1936 the guilder went off the gold standard, an equalization fund was established in the Netherlands too. The floating guilder also appreciated in the early stages as a consequence of the inflow of capital, but from 1938, as in the United Kingdom, flights of capital restarted.

Appraisal

a. The floating-exchange-rate system is not beneficial to trade owing to the uncertainties surrounding the rate. Coverage by forward purchase of the required foreign currency is certainly feasible, but the cost is sometimes so high that it is more advantageous to bear the risk itself.

As the free exchange rate is in most cases adopted because the currency reserves are exhausted and withdrawal from the gold standard in such circumstances causes a depreciation in the value of the currency, it is usually viewed with suspicion. Psychological factors may have a dangerous cumulative effect. The 'depreciation scramble' in the 1930s did nobody any good: in 1936, exchange parities were roughly the same as in 1930.

In somewhat exceptional circumstances, an appreciation is not beyond the bounds of possibility (Sweden in 1914–18). From 1950 to 1962, a floating rate was successfully maintained in Canada thanks to the continuous inflow of capital, especially from the United States. Similar circumstances were behind the decision to allow the Canadian dollar to float freely once again from 1 June 1970.

In 1935, Belgium had no hesitation in fixing the rate of devaluation (28 per cent) rather than let the currency go free, although up to 1936 fluctuations within certain limits, which corresponded to depreciation rates of 25 to 30 per cent, were possible. In 1969 the German mark was allowed to float for a few weeks (from 29 September to 27 October) before being revalued by 8·5 per cent, but this was due solely to internal political circumstances.

b. Like a devaluation, a depreciation, which in most cases results from the unrestricted fluctuation of a currency, does not necessarily promote exports.

c. Similarly, a floating exchange rate means that factors of production in industries which work for the home market need to be directed to export industries (or *vice versa*, but this is less usual). Such shifts do little to help increase productivity, and they also involve a great deal of expense. They are accompanied by frictional unemployment.

420

d. There is no pressure on domestic prices, but exchange rates are constantly adjusted to requirements. Since in this way a deflationary policy can be avoided, most of the countries which allowed their currencies to fluctuate emerged from the depression more quickly than those on the gold standard. Where a balance-of-payments deficit is due to overspending, a floating currency will not remedy the situation any more than a devaluation.

During recent years, numerous proposals have been made for a more flexible operation of the system of fixed exchange rates (which nevertheless provides for adjustments: the IMF's 'adjustable peg') – for instance, by means of exchange rates which are regularly and automatically adapted, possibly as a function of the changes in the monetary reserves ('crawling peg'), or by increasing the permitted deviations from the official exchange rates – not by 1 per cent but by 2 or even 5 per cent ('wider band').

8 Exchange control

If a country's gold and foreign-exchange reserve, which must be sufficient to make good a temporary deficit in the balance of payments, becomes exhausted, and no external credits are made available, measures of some kind need to be taken. As has been seen, devaluation or 'freeing' of the currency is not always a solution, especially as part of the balance of payments is sometimes adversely affected. Other methods of restraining imports (customs duties) or promoting exports (subsidies) are not invariably effective or propitious. If a stringent deflationary policy is to be avoided, there may be nothing for it but to clamp down on payments; i.e. the authorities assume responsibility for the balance-of-payments equilibrium. Convertibility is only partial. Quantitative restrictions or quotas are inevitably accompanied by exchange control.

This last is usually prompted by movements of capital. Thus in 1931, Germany had to resort to such measures. The authorities initially issued foreign currency to importers on the basis of their purchases abroad prior to the introduction of exchange control. When the foreign-exchange reserve dried up in 1934, the non-discrimination principle was thrown overboard: no longer were all persons and all enterprises treated on the same footing. Meanwhile, the volume of imports had become excessive, but the required amount

421

was not released at once. It is true that countries affected took reprisals, but for the most part they were in a weaker position.

Finally, clearing (or compensation) agreements were concluded with each individual state, under which settlement was not as a general rule made in foreign currency. Whereas it had previously been possible to cover a deficit with one country by means of a surplus on the balance of payments with another (multilateralism), this was no longer the case since the clearing agreements were bilateral; efforts under this system are directed to bringing a country-to-country equilibrium in the balance of payments.

In order to avoid substantial capital movements (especially to the United States) all countries were obliged to resort to exchange control from 1939. Before that, many of them had already introduced varying degrees of control over certain payments.

After 1945 it proved necessary to maintain exchange control in Western Europe owing to the large-scale import requirements and the disorganization of the various economies. A network of bilateral payment agreements was set up. In contrast with the clearing agreements, any excess amounts were settled in foreign currencies although a reciprocal credit to the extent of a specific sum (swing credit) was made available.

Estimates of trade movements incorporated in payments agreements were wide of the mark, so that some countries soon had a permanent import surplus. As a result, they were obliged, after first paying out gold or dollars, to enact more rigorous import restrictions.

Only during the 1950s did it become possible gradually to restore convertibility and free trade. In several western countries (e.g. France and the Netherlands), capital transfers are still subject to prior authorization.

In the USSR, imports and exports are determined entirely by the authorities, within the framework of the various plans. Trade with non-communist (and even with other communist) countries is conducted on the basis of world prices (corrected for cyclical and speculative movements). These prices, however, are not the same in trade with all countries. East-West trade relations are hampered because the USSR aims at stability; it can guarantee firm sales to other countries, but the latter cannot reciprocate (imports in the western world not being determined by the government).

Between the communist countries of Eastern Europe non-trade transactions such as tourism and other services are generally kept on separate accounts. Transfer to the general (trade) accounts takes place with the aid of an agreed exchange rate which normally varies from one category of transaction to another.

Appraisal
a. Exchange control, with its concomitant policy of quantitive restrictions, soon brings about the desired equilibrium in the balance of payments. However, it generates many technical difficulties; for instance, strict supervision over goods easily convertible into foreign currencies (diamonds) is necessary.

b. Exchange control causes a shrivelling up of international trade, especially where bilateral arrangements which are inconsistent with the international division of labour predominate. Monopolistic conditions and greater differences between foreign and domestic prices are also among its consequences (unless quotas are continuously adjusted to circumstances).

c. Reprisals are to be expected, unless the countries concerned accept the inevitability of such restrictive measures. Indeed, many countries were obliged to introduce exchange control; in countries with a centrally planned economy, and in certain less-developed countries, however, exchange control is a permanent instrument of economic policy.

d. The fixing of import priorities is quite a difficult task. It requires a clear insight into the further development of the national economy; planning of economic activity becomes imperative. While pride of place is accorded to imports of primary commodities and capital goods, consumer goods too have to be included in order to secure concessions from partner countries.

9 Multiple exchange rates

In the 1930s Germany supplemented its quota measures with a system of multiple exchange rates. Some thirty types of mark were created, and there was a different exchange rate for each class of transaction. The chief aim was to boost exports. One of the factors determining these rates was the extent to which the various countries were economically dependent on Germany.

Subsequently many Latin American states also employed multiple exchange rates, mainly in order to ensure the servicing of the external debt at a favourable exchange rate.

In point of fact, multiple exchange rates amount to a system of levies and subsidies, with the accompanying distortion effects on production and consumption.

In the case of multiple rates for imports, the hardest-hit countries are those producing less essential goods, while multiple export rates, by giving an artificial stimulus to exports, harm all countries.

So far as the less-developed countries are concerned, some economists prefer multiple exchange rates to quantitative restrictions (for one thing, they involve less administrative favouritism), although they do not have such a thoroughgoing and rapid effect on the foreign-exchange reserves. For their action to be really satisfactory, foreign currency reserves must be adequate and the national economy relatively stable.

10 Bibliography

See the introductory works referred to in Section 8 of the previous chapter.

a. International monetary reserves
Some theoretical ideas on the subject are expounded by F. Machlup, 'The Need for Monetary Reserves', *Banca Nazionale del Lavoro Quarterly Review*, September 1966. See also *International Reserves and Liquidity: A Study by the Staff of the International Monetary Fund* (Washington 1958).

J. O. N. Perkins, *The Sterling Area, the Commonwealth and World Economic Growth* (2nd ed., Cambridge 1970) – on the sterling area's trade and balance of payments; H. G. Aubrey, *The Dollar in World Affairs: An Essay in International Financial Policy* (New York 1964): urges 'a broader burden-sharing' among the richer countries.

b. Theories on balance-of-payments equilibrium
See also Chapter 11.8g.

J. E. Meade, *The Theory of International Economic Policy*, Vol. 1: *The Balance of Payments*, with a *Mathematical Supplement* (London 1951), is especially based on the price mechanism and therefore assumes high coefficients of elasticity.

S. Alexander, 'Effects of a Devaluation on a Trade Balance', *SP*, April 1952, on the other hand, lays the emphasis on the income effects (see also (*e*) below).

A lucid survey of possible adjustments in the event of a balance-of-payments disequilibrium is given by F. Machlup, 'Real Adjustment, Compensatory Corrections and Foreign Financing of Imbalances in International Payments', in *Trade, Growth, and the Balance of Payments* (ed. R. E. Caves, H. G. Johnson and P. B. Kenen, Chicago 1965).

On the evidence of considerable statistical material, O. Morgenstern, *International Financial Transactions and Business Cycles* (Princeton 1953), questions the foregoing explanation of the exchange-rate mechanism under the gold standard, stating that exchange rates have frequently deviated not a little from the gold points. See also the booklet by R. Triffin, *The Evolution of the International Monetary System: Historical Reappraisal and Future Perspectives* (Princeton 1964).

c. Capital movements
The thoroughgoing analysis by C. Iversen, *Aspects of the Theory of International Capital Movements* (Copenhagen 1935), remains a standard work, dealing first with the causes and effects of capital movements and subsequently with their mechanism (theories, facts and findings).

On capital flights, see *Capital Movements during the Inter-war Period* (United Nations, Lake Success 1949); A. Bloomfield, *Capital Imports and the American Balances of Payments 1934–39: A Study in Abnormal International Capital Transfers* (Chicago 1950), Chapter 9 of which contains a survey of the transfer theory; *id., Speculative and Flight Movements of Capital in Postwar International Finance* (Princeton 1954).

See finally *Capital Movements: Proceedings of a Conference held by the International Economic Association* (ed. J. H. Adler, New York 1967).

d. The theory of purchasing-power parity
This is expounded in G. Cassel, *Money and Foreign Exchange after 1914* (New York 1922).

M. Gilbert and I. B. Kravis, *An International Comparison of National Products and the Purchasing Power of Currencies: A Study of the United States, the United Kingdom, France, Germany and Italy* (OEEC, Paris 1954), compute the purchasing-power parities between the countries concerned in 1950. It is supplemented by M. Gilbert (and

425

associates), *Comparative National Products and Price Levels: A Study of Western Europe and the United States* (OEEC, Paris 1958), which gives figures (eight European countries) for 1955.

The ECSC and the EEC have carried out calculations for the purposes of a comparison of workers' real incomes; see the last relevant study: 'Consumer Purchasing Power Parities' (1963 survey), *General Statistical Bulletin*, European Communities, 1967, No. 10.

See the most recent study by J. M. Holmes, 'The Purchasing-Power-Parity Theory: in Defence of Gustav Cassel as a Modern Theorist', *JPE*, October 1967.

e. Devaluation

See the works of J. E. Meade and S. Alexander mentioned under (a).

For a detailed discussion of the effects of devaluation: E. Küng, *Zahlungsbilanzpolitik* (Zürich 1959), Part 4.

M. Michaely shows that devaluation causes a deterioration of the terms of trade (the elasticity of demand for imports is smaller than that of external demand): *Concentration in International Trade* (Amsterdam 1962); C. F. D. Alejandro, 'A Note on the Impact of Devaluation and the Redistribution Effect', *JPE*, December 1963, points to the shifts in income distribution to the benefit of producers.

In connection with the Marshall-Lerner condition, see in particular C. P. Kindleberger, Appendix D of the work cited in Chapter 11.8 (*International Economics*); E. Schneider, *Money, Income and Employment* (London 1968).

The basis of the condition is found in A. Marshall, *Money, Credit and Commerce* (London 1923) and A. P. Lerner, *The Economics of Control: Principles of Welfare Economics* (New York 1944).

For criticism of Alexander's 'absorption approach', see F. Machlup, 'Relative Prices and Aggregate Spending in the Analysis of Devaluation', *AER*, June 1955; *id.*, 'The Terms of Trade Effects of Devaluation upon Real Income and the Balance of Trade', *Ky*, 1956, No 4.

For a comparison of the 'elasticities' and 'absorption' approaches, see M. O. Clement, R. L. Pfister and K. J. Rothwell, *Theoretical Issues in International Economics* (Boston 1967), Chapter 7.

f. Floating exchange rates

Advocates of free exchange-rate determination include J. E. Meade, *The Theory of International Economic Policy*, Part 1; M. Friedman,

Essays in Positive Economics (Chicago 1953); E. Sohmen, *Flexible Exchange Rates: Theory and Controversy* (rev. ed., Chicago 1969).

On the nineteenth century: L. B. Yeager, 'Fluctuating Exchange Rates in the Nineteenth Century: The Experiences of Austria and Russia', in *Monetary Problems of the International Economy* (ed. R. A. Mundell and A. K. Swoboda, Chicago 1969). See also S. C. Tsiang, 'Fluctuating Exchange Rates in Countries with Relatively Stable Economies: Some European Experience after the First World War', *SP*, October 1959. General reflections on the interwar period are found in *International Currency Experience: Lessons of the Interwar Period* (League of Nations, Geneva 1944), which concludes in favour of the necessity of fixed exchange rates, adequate gold and foreign-exchange reserves and a certain degree of coordination in the most important countries' monetary policy (major contribution by R. Nurkse). On Canada, see P. Wonnacott, *The Canadian Dollar 1948–58* (Toronto 1960).

g. Quantitative restrictions and discrimination

On the pre- and postwar forms of such restrictions (and attempts to put an end to them), see respectively *Quantitative Business Controls: Their Causes and Their Nature* (League of Nations, Geneva 1943) and *Restrictive Business Practices* (GATT, Geneva, May 1959), the latter work being by J. L'Huillier.

For a favourable criticism of the German prewar experiment, see F. Child, *The Theory and Practice of Exchange Control in Germany: A Study of Monopolistic Exploitation in International Markets* (The Hague 1958).

For a brief systematic survey of the various discriminatory practices, see H. Ellis, 'Exchange Control and Discrimination', *AER*, December 1947. See also J. Faaland, *Essays on the Theory of Trade Discrimination* (Bergen 1964) (especially essay No. 3). Exchange restrictions in the various countries are summarized each year in the IMF's *Annual Report on Exchange Restrictions*.

G. Patterson, *Discrimination in International Trade: The Policy Issues 1945–1965* (Princeton 1966), discusses discrimination for balance-of-payments reasons, in temporary and permanent regional arrangements and organizations, and as a tool for protection and to facilitate economic development.

h. Multiple exchange rates

After examining the effects of this exchange-rate system, E. M. Bernstein, in 'Some Economic Aspects of Multiple Exchange Rates', *SP*, September 1950, expresses the opinion that the IMF must take action against them.

E. Schlesinger, in *Multiple Exchange Rates and Economic Development* (Princeton 1952), studies multiple exchange rates in relation to economic development (in the light of the Latin American countries' experience). He prefers them to quantitative restrictions.

A theoretical study: J. Bhagwati, *The Theory and Practice of Commercial Policy: Departure from Unified Exchange Rates* (Princeton 1968).

13 Government

We must not be dogmatic in choosing our ground; for we are not concerned with dogma, with being right, but with achieving our aim – a society that is as happy as possible.

J. Tinbergen

After first considering the aims of economic policy, we go on to the main forms this policy can take (see the definition in Chapter 1.1f), supplementing what has already been said in previous chapters.

Although the activities of households and firms can contribute to the attainment of policy targets, economic policy is here regarded as being a matter for government alone.

Economic policy need not necessarily imply government action: the authorities may feel that they further some of their objectives best by a passive attitude (*laissez-faire*). The active type of policy is sometimes termed interventionism.

1 Policy targets

It is generally accepted that economic science should not concern itself with setting targets. It should take them as given. The theory of economic policy, then, is teleological or finalist: it merely indicates how ends should be achieved, taking no sides in the matter. All wants have the same value once they make a claim on available resources. Economics is therefore neutral in this respect, as are physics and chemistry (though this view is not accepted in the USSR).

The most common targets *in fact* set by economic policy are summarized below.

a. Increasing the *per capita* national product, which involves combating cyclical fluctuations and making optimum use of the factors of production. It should be noted at this point that the elimination of business cycle fluctuations is easy in planned economies, where saving and investment are determined by the authorities.

429

In a country with full employment it is difficult to increase the number of hours worked: employing more women, working longer hours and raising the retirement age are all solutions that meet with all kinds of objections and resistance. Vocational training offers more opportunities.

Capital formation and technological advance are important factors. Too little investment effort will prejudice the future satisfaction of wants. Excessive capital formation is detrimental to present consumption but benefits future consumption. An extreme policy was conducted by the USSR (Chapter 10.5*a*): by keeping down the consumption of an entire generation, the Soviet authorities were able to push ahead with industrialization at a faster rate.

If the satisfaction of material wants is felt to be adequate already, a diminution of working hours is often preferred to further effort to increase satisfaction.

b. Equitable distribution of the national income, which means achieving full employment, provided the attendant level of income and distribution of income are satisfactory.

If we assume that money means more to people with low incomes than to those with high incomes, then a more even distribution will produce greater overall utility. There are, however, limits: over-taxation of profits and high incomes inhibits output because the factors of production do not consider themselves well enough remunerated to justify additional effort.

Opinions are divided on the optimum distribution of income; economic theory cannot supply accurate information about this since interpersonal utility comparisons are impossible. What is in fact done is to proceed from an existing situation and examine to what extent and in what way changes are needed. The position in other countries is one of the factors taken into account here. Rates of taxation, government transfers, subsidies for the production of certain goods, the setting of maximum prices and minimum wages are among the most common policy instruments.

c. In point of fact, it is difficult to segregate these two objectives: heavy unemployment or unbalanced distribution have repercussions on demand, and hence on supply. Even so, economic expansion does not necessarily bring about better distribution. Full employment does not guarantee economic expansion either: '. . . full employment can and has been known to coexist with inefficiency and stagnation' (E. Domar).

These major aims are usually supplemented by secondary ones, including the protection of specific industries and the maintenance of gold and foreign-currency reserves. These secondary aims are invariably comprised in the major objectives – economic expansion and equitable distribution of national income.

The maintenance of monetary equilibrium, for example, is important in any economic policy. Otherwise, it is not only more difficult to introduce structural changes (because of lack of confidence), but the second aim of economic policy (equitable distribution of national income) is jeopardized at the same time (as a result of inflation).

It goes without saying that monetary equilibrium must be realized without incurring a deficit on the balance of payments. The inflationary influence of investment and government spending is often offset by the deflationary effect of a balance-of-payments deficit, but a deficit cannot be allowed to persist.

Welfare theory

Even if they accept that it is no part of the economist's task to state the aims of economic policy, the practitioners of welfare theory maintain that it is his job to decide which economic system will yield maximum utility or maximum welfare.

Adam Smith held that this would result from the free exchange of production factors; by seeking profits each individual helps to maximize the common good (by the working of the 'invisible hand'). Later, V. Pareto proved this mathematically, but starting from not very realistic hypotheses (e.g. perfect competition, a stationary economy and a given income distribution, no social wants). Under perfect competition, there is no point in changing the distribution of goods: the prices of goods vary with their marginal utilities (or marginal substitution rates), factor prices with their marginal productivity. A change of income would impair at least the satisfaction of one consumer or the output of one producer.

Owing to the unreal assumptions of the welfare economists, we have little to gain from their directives. Thus the Pareto theorem is only valid for a given income distribution. As it cannot be proved that a certain distribution is better than another, welfare theory assumes that government will establish a scale of social preferences which is supposed to aggregate the preferences of the whole com-

431

munity. But this assumption disregards social wants and the view that some wants should be discouraged (duty is put on alcohol) and others encouraged (subsidies are given for cultural facilities).

2 Planning

Gouverner, c'est prévoir. In order to manage their affairs efficiently, governments, households and firms all need to work out a plan of action.

By economic planning we mean the properly considered drafting of a body of measures that the government intends to introduce in order to achieve predetermined aims. This plan will contain quantitative targets relating to the whole economy. It does not necessarily imply more government intervention: if it is limited to certain strategic factors, the state may be called upon to play a smaller part than it did before the plan was implemented.

We differentiate between imperative and indicative plans. In the first the government issues binding directives; in the second it simply indicates the lines the private sector should follow in reaching its decisions. Imperative plans are drawn up in the USSR and the Eastern European countries and also in some of the less-developed countries (but see Chapter 10.7*e*). Indicative planning includes the forecasting of economic activity and designation of the means to be employed by the authorities in trying to induce the private sector to take certain steps. Planning is a technique which can be used both in collectivist and in capitalist economies.

In Chapter 5 we have already discussed planning in the USSR and in Chapter 10 the difficulty of planning in less-developed countries. It is not surprising that the unrealistic plans which are usually drawn up cannot be carried out. In fact, it often happens that no effort is even made to carry them out. An expert from the World Bank has written: 'While most countries with development plans have not succeeded in carrying them out, some countries without national development plans or national planning agencies have been developing rapidly' (A. Waterston). Even where a country is able to frame a fairly general plan (and this is usually impossible because the necessary statistics are not available), well-prepared individual projects for executing the plan are generally lacking.

Indicative planning is being tried in some western countries – or at least they are trying to give that impression. The governments concerned (e.g. in Belgium and the Netherlands) generally worry very little about the activities of the planning board.

The Netherlands has played a major part in improving planning techniques: the Centraal Planbureau was set up in 1947, the year before the Commissariat Général du Plan was established in France. In Belgium a limited Bureau de Programmation was set up towards the end of 1959.

The Centraal Planbureau concentrated for many years on short-term planning and forecasting, quite unlike the French Commissariat Général du Plan, which has been more interested in medium-and long-term planning.

Short-term planning implies that the government takes action especially before (and during) a crisis and that it must act in good time if a depression is to be avoided. If the business cycle has already turned down, then the volume of, say, public works needed to stimulate recovery will be greater again. Public works must be planned ahead. Efficient research and documentation departments are essential. Here again, extensive and readily available statistical material is required. It is also important that there should be effective coordination between the various government departments.

The efficacy of action taken by the authorities is partly determined by the extent to which the country has to rely on international trade. Countries which are highly dependent on foreign demand find it more difficult to attain their economic policy targets.

We have said that the drafting of plans should be 'properly considered'. By this we mean that use should be made of modern technical aids such as national accounts, input-output tables and econometric models.

The repercussions of government action on other economic units are directly shown in the national accounts; input-output tables can be used to trace its impact on the various industries; and economic models are being utilized more and more. Let us now consider these last two techniques.

a. Input-output analysis
On the basis of the input-output table and technological coefficients, input-output analysis was developed. The output X_i of industry i is equal to the sum of final demand $D^*_{\lambda i}$ and intermediate demand (of the other industries). The sales of industry i to industry j equal the

purchases of j from i, i.e. the input of j multiplied by the technological coefficient o_{ij} (which indicates what value of goods produced in i is needed to produce the value of one unit of money in j). The total intermediate demand in industry i is represented by the summation

$$\sum_{j=1}^{n} o_{ij}X_j.$$

Hence:

$$X_i = D^*_{\lambda i} + \sum_{j=1}^{n} o_{ij}X_j \qquad (1)$$

or

$$D^*_{\lambda i} = X_i - \sum_{j=1}^{n} o_{ij}X_j.$$

So in Table 4 of Chapter 2:

$$D^*_{\lambda 3} = X_3 - (0{\cdot}146X_1 + 0{\cdot}071X_2 + 0{\cdot}206X_3 + 0{\cdot}071X_4).$$

Instead of trying to find $D^*_{\lambda i}$ we can also determine the total outputs X_i if all D^*_{λ}s are given. If we write an equation of type (1) for the n industries, we obtain a set of n equations with n unknowns (provided the D^*_{λ}s are known). This has, except in special cases of inconsistency, only one solution:

$$X_1 = D^*_{\lambda 1} + \sum_{j=1}^{n} o_{1j}X_j$$

$$X_2 = D^*_{\lambda 2} + \sum_{j=1}^{n} o_{2j}X_j$$

$$\cdot \qquad \cdot \qquad \cdot$$
$$\cdot \qquad \cdot \qquad \cdot$$
$$\cdot \qquad \cdot \qquad \cdot$$

$$X_n = D^*_{\lambda n} + \sum_{j=1}^{n} o_{nj}X_j.$$

The values found for the n outputs will be linear functions of the n final demands, since not a single D^*_{λ} appears as coefficient of an X.

434

We may therefore write:

$$X_i = \sum_{j=1}^{n} z_{ij} D_{\lambda j}^*$$

in which the z coefficients are functions of the o coefficients.

Appraisal

This enables us to check what are the direct and indirect repercussions of an increase in final demand (resulting from government action, for instance) on the various industries.

Application of this method of economic forecasting depends, among other things, on two bold assumptions – that output is proportional to the inputs, and that the technological coefficients remain the same. No account is taken, then, of technological progress or of the influence of changes in factor prices. It is also assumed that the industries are not running at full capacity; otherwise an additional input would not lead to an increase in output.

b. Econometric models

The purpose of a model is to give a quantitative explanation of the behaviour of economic variables by means of equations showing the connection between the economic data concerned. These equations are of different kinds and relate to:

1. a necessary equality (definitions: $X_{\alpha m} = C + S_\alpha$);
2. a technical relationship (e.g. the production function);
3. an institutional relationship (e.g. between profits and profit taxes);
4. the behaviour of economic units (e.g. the consumption function).

Unlike the first of these, the last three express a stochastic (probable) relationship.

We differentiate between exogenous and endogenous data. The first are regarded as changing independently of the economic system or as being operated by the authorities.

Example 11

$$C_h = C_z + c_\mu (X_{\alpha m} - T) \tag{1}$$
$$M = M_z + M_\mu X_{\alpha m} \tag{2}$$

435

$$T = t X_{\alpha m} \tag{3}$$

$$X_{\alpha m} = C_h + I_{\alpha e} + G_o + E - M \tag{4}$$

Substitution of (3) in (1) and (2) in (4) gives:

$$X_{\alpha m} = C_z + c_\mu(X_{\alpha m} - t X_{\alpha m}) + I_{\alpha e} + G_o + E - M_z - m_\mu X_{\alpha m}$$
$$(1 - c_\mu + c_\mu t + m_\mu) X_{\alpha m} = C_z + I_{\alpha e} + G_o + E - M_z$$

$$X_{\alpha m} = \frac{I_{\alpha e} + G_o + E}{1 - c_\mu (1 - t) + m_\mu} + \frac{C_z - M_z}{1 - c_\mu (1 - t) + m_\mu} \tag{5}$$

If c_μ, m_μ, C_z, M_z, E and $I_{\alpha e}$ are known, the impact on the national product of a change in G_o and t (caused by economic policy) can be established.

In fact, not much can be done with equation (5) since c_μ and m_μ are only known approximately and do not remain constant. The relationship between many economic data is valid for a limited period only. Some coefficients are almost impossible to calculate. The practical utility of the models is slight, but they offer a more systematic view of possibilities in economic policy.

3 Fiscal policy

When they levy taxes or float loans, governments are not only raising funds to cover their expenditures: they are at the same time seeking to realize certain of their economic policy objectives. Through its fiscal policy, a government exercises control over both its income and its expenditure, which gives it greater freedom of action than the ordinary household. H. Dalton, with some exaggeration, has said: 'Broadly speaking, while an individual's income determines the amount of his possible expenditure, a public authority's expenditure determines the amount of its necessary income.'

a. The consequences of changes in taxation
Taxes withdraw purchasing power from households and enterprises for the benefit of government. Further consequences depend on how the funds collected are spent. If we already know how tax revenue is to be expended (and other circumstances remain unchanged), then we can ascertain the influence of any change in the rate of tax or the degree of progression (where the rate increases with the income).

436

1. Direct taxes

An increase in direct taxation reduces income, with the result that saving and/or consumption decreases. Consumption is normally maintained, so it is saving that is affected. But consumption will go down first if we believe that our savings are not enough to see us through unforeseen circumstances. The size of our income is the determining factor. A fall in saving may cause investment to decline; investment, especially in the long run, is determined by the volume of saving. A tax reduction usually has a stimulating effect.

As the authorities' tax receipts are spent mainly on the lower income groups, who mostly buy consumer goods, an increase in direct taxes or in the degree of progression not only results in a more even distribution of income but also benefits the consumer-goods industries in the main. Any decline in consumption by the higher income groups, which is rather unlikely (although manufacturers of luxury goods sometimes feel the repercussions), will often be more than offset by the increased consumption of the rest of the community.

When the degree of progression is appreciable, this may have a detrimental effect on workers' efforts, though some are nevertheless encouraged to work more – as far as this is possible – so as to have the same take-home pay (this also applies in the longer term: workers are less inclined to retire). Tax evasion is likely to increase too.

In considering increases in profits tax we must differentiate between distributed and undistributed profits. Increasing the tax on distributed profits diminishes shareholders' expenditure on consumption or investment and encourages firms to plough back their profits. Investment may be held back, on the other hand, if the tax on undistributed profits is raised (self-financing is discouraged).

Wealth taxes generally have a bad effect on capital formation unless the rate is so low that the tax can easily be paid out of income.

The incidence of corporate income tax or profits tax is probably passed on to the consumer to some extent, especially in the longer term. The entrepreneur tries to set his prices in such a way that they yield a certain net profit. If this is not possible, capital will feel less attracted to the relatively higher-taxed industries; unwarranted business expenses may be incurred too.

Automatic adjustment of the scale of taxation to changes in prices and incomes lessens resistance to inflation.

2. Indirect taxes

Firms try to pass on indirect taxes to their customers. How far they succeed depends, among other things, on the elasticity of demand. In favourable circumstances for the firm the selling price goes up by the same amount as the indirect tax (if profits are calculated as a percentage of cost price, the rise is greater). The resulting price increase influences demand for other goods.

As numerous factors have to be taken into account in ascertaining the extent to which taxes are passed on, it is again difficult to make generally valid statements.

The difference between direct and indirect taxes is losing much of its importance since both are usually the occasion of increases in cost price. These are generally thought to be lower, however, in the case of direct taxes, which are based on profits alone.

b. The public debt

Government borrowing has a deflationary effect if money is attracted which would otherwise have been spent and the government reserves part of the proceeds; it has an inflationary effect if money is dishoarded and the proceeds are spent by the government. Inflationary side-effects (greater velocity of circulation) are possible. Borrowing abroad is inflationary when it does not correspond to a balance of payments deficit and the government spends the money received.

A governmental loan has a detrimental effect if demand from the private sector remains unsatisfied and investment is discouraged. This is usually what happens in boom years. In other words, before floating a loan the government should weigh up the economic situation; during a depression it is usually better to issue loans than to raise new taxes (so as to avoid cutting back consumption). Yet, public investment can be considered to have priority over private investment.

The influence of debt repayment depends on how the sums paid back are used. Either an internal or external loan represents a transfer of income. There are drawbacks to an external loan, partly because of its impact upon the balance of payments. External bonds can, however, be bought by residents.

c. The types of fiscal policy

1. The aim of fiscal policy used to be to keep the budget in balance at all times, if necessary by increasing rates of taxation during the

438

depression and lowering them in boom years. In this way business cycles were emphasized: during the depression, purchasing power was reduced just when it should have been increased.

2. Consequently, it is now felt that taxes should preferably be low during a depression and high during boom years. However, this is achieved automatically – even without changing the rates: a drop in national income results in a decrease in tax revenue, a rise in national income in an increase in tax revenue. Only a few taxes (land tax) are insensitive to the business cycle.

Owing to the stabilizing effect of taxation it is usually recommended that rates be left unchanged; this also makes it easier for industry to draw up its production programmes.

If the stability of tax rates conflicts with the policy of full employment, they should be lowered in times of depression and raised during the boom. However, it is difficult to ascertain when the changeover from one phase to the other takes place. Measures are usually taken too late to be effective, especially as the approval of parliament is required for many taxes. Hence also the difficulties of a system of cyclical budgeting, in which budget surpluses accrued during boom periods are used to finance government expenditure during years when the national income is lower. Moreover, whenever surpluses are made, they are immediately claimed to finance 'urgent' expenditure. As a matter of fact, deficits are the general rule. A budget-equalization fund was set up in Belgium in 1959 (to cover a deficit with future surpluses) but had already been abandoned by 1961. In some countries, such as Sweden and Switzerland, a system of this kind has been introduced for the business sector: firms are allowed to lay up tax-free reserves to be invested at a later date – the time and terms being decided by the government; if this is not done then the taxes must be paid.

C. Goedhart points out that fiscal policy, if it is used as an instrument of counter-cyclical policy, can only be assured of a reasonable amount of success if it is supported by and coordinated with other policy instruments – the central bank's monetary policy in particular, but also general policy on prices and incomes. Referring to monetary policy and fiscal policy, J. R. Schlesinger considers 'that neither of these instruments is necessarily either immediately or precisely effective. ... But both instruments have their role to play; neither can be disregarded'.

3. When the authorities cover additional expenditure by raising additional income, this appears at first sight to be neutral on the monetary plan. In fact, the taxpayers will not cut down their consumption as much as those who benefit from the additional expenditure will step up theirs. This has an inflationary impact (the balanced budget multiplier or the Haavelmo effect). In the opposite case we have a deflationary effect.

4. Depending on the phase of the business cycle, a change in the tax structure or in the rates of certain taxes can be used to stimulate or inhibit consumption or investment.

By means of a relative increase in certain taxes, national income can be distributed more equitably (income redistribution by transfer payments).

Tax measures are sometimes employed by the authorities to encourage geographical deconcentration – in order to promote the economic development of specified areas, for instance (as in the United Kingdom and France since the Second World War).

5. In order to prevent the burden of taxation from growing constantly, government expenditure should not fluctuate at more than the same rate as national income. More particularly, J. Zijlstra holds that the sum of increases in expenditure and changes in taxation should equal the underlying growth of real national income and the progression factor included in tax rates. With rising income and progressive taxation, government resources expand. If the effect of progression is to be counteracted, the rates must be regularly adjusted.

If the estimated increase in national income is, say, 4 per cent, taxes will presumably go up by 4 per cent too, but progression may make this a 6 per cent increase. With an estimated national income of £20,000 million government expenditure – in order to satisfy the 'Zijlstra norm' – should not exceed £1,200 million (unless taxes are lowered; if taxes decrease by £200 million, for instance, the 'permitted expenditure falls to £1,000 million).

This norm is not easy to apply, because parliament and pressure groups are always insisting on higher government spending. This policy is non-cyclical in character, but its advocates point out that the fluctuations of the business cycle can be mitigated by other means, including monetary instruments (apart from the difficulty, referred to above, of pursuing a counter-cyclical fiscal policy).

d. Central bank credit

Since temporary disequilibria between revenue and expenditure may occur in the course of a year, provision is made in most countries whereby the central government can borrow from the central bank.

In order to prevent unsound financing of government requirements, limits are usually imposed on these operations – in Belgium 16,500 million francs (adjusted every three years on the basis of the ordinary public revenue), in West Germany DM 6,000 million for the federal government and about DM 2,000 million for the *Länder*, in France 3,500 million francs; in Italy there is no absolute limit (14 per cent of the current budget expenditure), and in the United States the ceiling is $1,000 million. In the Netherlands a maximum of *f* 150 million can be borrowed without interest, but the Nederlandshe Bank is free to provide the Treasury with other forms of credit.

4 Monetary policy

The aim of monetary policy is to control the quantity of money, especially that portion which is in the banks. As this can also be achieved by fiscal policy, there is a close relation between the two. M. Friedman considers the increase in the quantity of money too important a matter to be left to the monetary authorities. He advocates an automatic annual increase of 2 per cent.

The responsibility for monetary policy normally lies with the central bank. In France it is assisted by the Conseil National du Crédit and the Commission de Contrôle des Banques, in the Netherlands by the Bankraad, in the United Kingdom by the Treasury. In Belgium there is some degree of decentralization: the Fonds des Rentes, the Institut de Réescompte et de Garantie and the Commission Bancaire each have special powers. In Italy, however, the Banca d'Italia receives directives from the Comitato Interministeriale per il Credito e il Risparmio. In the United States the Board of Governors of the Federal Reserve System is assisted by the Federal Open Market Committee.

The most important instruments of monetary policy are bank rate, open-market operations, the cash reserves that banks are required to hold, and direct banking controls.

a. Bank rate policy

Bank rate is the official rate of interest at which the central bank

441

rediscounts bills offered by the commercial banks (see Chapter 3.7*b*).
The central bank also fixes the rates of discount for other operations:
these usually keep in step with changes in the rate for bills.

Normally, a change in bank rate affects the discount rate of the
commercial banks and also – though this is sometimes delayed – the
interest rate. It may also attract foreign capital, which will help to
eliminate any deficit in the balance of payments.

Increases in bank rate have very little effect if the banks hold
sufficient liquid assets (so that rediscounting is not required) or
foreigners lack confidence in the country's economy (and capital is
not attracted). That is why there are official rules on the matter
in many countries. Even where this is not the case, as in Belgium
and the Netherlands, the banks are accustomed to taking the wishes
of the central bank into account and of following the lead of Bank
rate.

1. *The effects of an increase in interest rates*

a. Even though an increase in the rate of interest is often aimed at as
a way of limiting investment, the hoped-for result is by no means
guaranteed – as when entrepreneurs are expecting further price
increases, for instance (Chapter 6.2).

b. When a cutback in investment has in fact been achieved, sound
investment is generally the kind to suffer most, speculative investment
the least. Consequently, qualitative or selective controls are often
preferred.

c. The repercussions on the quantity of money are usually slight
(Chapter 8.6). Bank liquidity is not necessarily converted into bonds
or short-term paper (a policy of credit restriction is sometimes
hampered by simultaneous support for the price of government
bonds). Nor is it certain that there will be a decline in consumer
credit. Everything depends on what is expected in the future.

d. The most substantial effect seems to be psychological: some
entrepreneurs become more worried about their liquidity, while others
hesitate about the future trend of business.

e. If the interest rate is subsequently lowered, many firms, especially the smaller ones, can be in trouble (because they have to keep
on paying a high rate of interest, while their competitors have meanwhile managed to borrow at lower rates).

f. Government indebtedness increases; the price of bonds previously issued at lower interest rates drops.

2. *The effects of a reduction in interest rates*

a. Even though the reduction does not necessarily stimulate investment, it does lower the cost.

b. The Treasury benefits from the easing of the burden of debt. Compulsory conversion of former loans extends the benefit to all government debt.

c. Unearned incomes diminish, but there is a shift in the distribution of wealth (because of an increase in the price of shares and of bonds previously issued on more favourable terms).

d. Again, psychological factors may come into play: the authorities can use this as a means of indicating that credit restrictions are not really necessary.

A policy of reducing interest rates does not always succeed. If rates are set too low, then capital flows more readily to the private sector and abroad. Profit restrictions, dividend and foreign-exchange controls are required. And the public will show a greater preference for liquid assets if it feels that interest rates are unlikely to remain low. This leads to the sale of bonds, whereupon prices fall and interest goes up. If the authorities keep supporting prices the risk of inflation arises.

3. *Conclusion*

Since changes in bank rate and interest rates have such slight repercussions, it is often suggested that they be left unaltered – preferably at a low level in view of the cost of investment. Continuous changes hamper firms' long-term planning. Manipulation of bank rate and interest rates is an uncertain way to stimulate the economy.

A cheap-money policy is facilitated in most countries because the government has become the major buyer on the market for loanable funds. If international capital movements are free, this policy becomes difficult to pursue: should interest rates in a neighbouring country be high, there will be a capital outflow to that country. The looser the exchange controls, the greater account must be taken of international circumstances.

A policy of keeping interest rates low will also be obstructed if the government's cash position is poor: the authorities will not be able to wait until rates have settled down at the desired level.

As long as savings are sufficient, a dear-money policy will not be essential. An increase in interest rates can be defended when the economy is overheated and consumption and investment threaten to exceed available resources.

b. Open-market policy

Open-market operations are the dealings in government securities, generally by the central bank, for policy purposes. In Belgium the Fonds des Rentes was created for this purpose (though it takes decisions in conjunction with the Banque Nationale).

In the United States and the United Kingdom, open-market operations are the most important stabilizing weapon in monetary policy. In the United States, open-market operations are conducted through the Federal Reserve Bank's Open Market Committee. In the United Kingdom, this is done by a firm of discount brokers (the 'Special Buyer') for operations in Treasury Bills or by a firm of stockbrokers (the 'Government Broker') for operations in 'gilt-edged' securities (those carrying the least amount of risk). Both firms' activities are determined by the instructions of the Bank of England.

In EEC countries this policy is less common than in the United States and the United Kingdom. It is only in West Germany and the Netherlands that systematic open-market policy is pursued in order to affect the liquidity of the commercial banks. Generally, transactions are only carried out in the money market (though the Belgian Fonds des Rentes may also enter the capital market).

Open-market policy can be supported by other transactions. Italy and the Netherlands, for instance, have issued long-term loans, not to finance budget expenditure but to influence the quantity of money. The West German and Italian central banks, moreover, have concluded forward currency contracts with the banks, which affected the banks' foreign investment (the exchange rate cover encourages the banks to invest more of their liquid assets abroad). In this context we must also refer to central bank lendings to the Treasury (see Section 3d above).

c. Cash-reserve requirements

Direct intervention in the banks' liquidity position consists in obliging them to keep a portion of their deposits in the central bank or maintain part of their holdings in Treasury bills.

During the Second World War the banks invested most of their funds in Treasury bills because of the limited opportunities for lending to the business sector. After the war these short-term claims confronted the Treasury with the risk of having to make sudden and large-scale repayments. Given the size of the banks' liquid resources, a substantial expansion of credit was also likely, with all the risks that involved.

All countries have tried to restrict the conversion of this floating government debt into money. In the United States, the United Kingdom and the Netherlands funding operations have been used for this purpose. In France and Belgium the banks were obliged to hold a minimum amount of government securities, but in this way variations in bank deposits affected the Treasury.

To prevent this, Belgium gradually changed over to a system whereby, as in the Netherlands and West Germany, the banks are required to hold deposits with the central bank. The cash-reserve percentage, introduced at the beginning of 1962, is fixed by the Commission Bancaire on a proposal from the Banque Nationale. The statutory reserve requirement can be as high as 20 per cent for demand deposits and time deposits at up to a month, 7 per cent for time deposits at more than a month. It has been applied only hesitantly (1 per cent from 1 July 1964 to 15 July 1965) because of Treasury difficulties (a high percentage would have cut short the supply of credit to the government).

In 1954 gentlemen's agreements were concluded in the Netherlands concerning credit ceilings, liquidity ratios and the maintenance of interest-free cash reserves with the Nederlandse Bank (up to 15 per cent of the deposits held by the credit institutions). In October 1963 a new agreement was entered into, prescribing a supplementary cash reserve on the basis of credits granted.

In West Germany the maximum requirement is 30 per cent for demand deposits, 20 per cent for time deposits and 10 per cent for savings. The Deutsche Bundesbank imposes different requirements, depending on the size and location of the credit institution and the origin of the deposits (residents or non-residents). As in the Netherlands (but not Belgium or France), the deposits earn no interest.

d. Direct controls on banking

The government can also impose direct controls (e.g. supervision of security issues, restrictions on credit to the private sector), but this, like the other forms of monetary policy, is successful only in boom periods.

5 Price policy

Direct and/or indirect methods may be used to act upon the general price level or the price of a certain product.

a. Direct intervention

A system of general price fixing by the government and an accompanying system of rationing (including a wages and dividend freeze, rent control, control on investment) yields results only if the appropriate departments have extensive and accurate information at their disposal concerning output in the different industries. They must also be aided by efficient supervisory agencies. Here again it is difficult to avoid the consequences of repressed inflation (black market). Usually the government introduces general price control at the beginning of a period of scarcity: all prices are fixed at the level of an earlier period (making price ratios more 'normal' and less arbitrary). If necessary, the production of some goods can be encouraged by allowing a slight price increase.

Various forms of economic policy have direct repercussions on production costs and prices – for example, wages policy and social-security policy. Social-security contributions limit the consumption of the working population for the benefit of people who no longer participate in the production process.

Exchange-rate policy is also a form of price policy. Freedom of action with regard to exchange rates is limited by IMF rules, among other things.

Almost all Western European governments have extensive powers over prices, but in general they are now applied for a limited number of commodities only. The French government has the widest powers in this respect and has made good use of them at times. As in other countries (including Belgium), proposed increases in the price of a number of commodities must be notified before being applied so that the minister concerned can act if he sees fit.

Depending on whether they want to stimulate or inhibit the consumption of certain commodities, the authorities can make prices rise or fall by levying taxes or paying out subsidies. The consumer, then, is not the sole determinant of what is produced; even though his freedom of choice remains, he is no longer sovereign. The government can also start the production of goods and services which are not desired by the individual (social goods and services). In the

446

USSR government intervention in this field is much more extensive than in western countries; prices are regularly changed by manipulation of indirect taxes (on turnover), which generally represent a high percentage of the cost price.

We shall now stop to examine some of the means of influencing the price of a product.

1. *Price ceilings*

Direct government intervention in the determination of prices is usually aimed at protecting the consumer of the commodities in question – usually basic necessities – against a price rise. It may also be designed to safeguard the interests of producers (e.g. farmers); falling rather than rising prices will then be the object of preventive action.

The price increases that the government is concerned to prevent may be caused either by speculation or abuse of monopoly positions or by insufficient supply. If the latter is the reason for government action, however, price controls will not restore the balance between quantities supplied and demanded: rationing needs to be introduced.

Price ceilings to protect the consumer are unlikely to encourage producers, and production often declines, especially when the maximum price does not take production costs sufficiently into account. Even when it does, producers regard themselves as being at a disadvantage because of the effect of black market prices. The extent and efficacy of price control are of great importance.

2. *Subsidies*

It can also happen that a sharp increase in prices becomes necessary because the price of raw materials has gone up. When the increase mainly affects consumer goods and social complications threaten, the authorities can impose a price and compensate producers by means of subsidies.

Subsidies usually involve heavy budget expenditure and give a false picture of price ratios. The authorities should weigh these drawbacks against the benefits: in the case of a temporary price increase, subsidies are a suitable means of counteracting wage-price spirals and of maintaining social peace. If they manage to keep the cost-of-living index from going up too much, a compensatory increase in wages and additional government expenditure is avoided in countries where wages are linked to the cost of living.

447

3. *The regulation of supply and demand*

To protect producers (from, for instance, the effects of the Davenant-King 'law', Chapter 7.4c), the authorities sometimes cooperate in regulating or limiting supply. One method is to expand storage and low-interest credit facilities in the case of surplus production (as in the farm policy of the United States). Subsidies are granted to enable produce to be put to a less useful purpose or even to be destroyed. With an eye to future supply, further expansion of production is sometimes prohibited. Finally, demand at home and abroad can be stimulated by advertising – and foreign demand by dumping as well.

b. *Indirect intervention*

The government can exert indirect influence on the general price level by means of the various types of economic policy which affect the money quantity (e.g. tax and monetary policy).

Since the authorities have no power (or are unwilling) constantly to regulate market performance, they could influence it via market structure or market conduct if a certain correlation existed between structure and conduct, and market performance. As we have seen, only limited data are available on this.

It has sometimes been demanded of government that it should introduce pure competition. As if it were feasible to split up large concerns into smaller units and as if this would lead to better price performance! What we *can* expect of the government is that it should act to establish or restore effective competition. In all countries the major industries have monopolistic features. This calls for stricter control. The government should not stand idly by while firms take decisions (e.g. concerning investment at home or abroad) which will be detrimental to the country's whole economy.

6 Incomes policy

The aim of incomes policy is to try to influence the distribution of the national income and the level of income of the various sections of the community. The general level of income is important as regards competitiveness, investment policy and price policy. Wages policy is the most important form of incomes policy. The cooperation of the workers will, however, not be obtained if profits are not included as well.

a. *The consequences of a wage increase*

Starting from the assumption that a wage increase throughout industry has not been preceded by comparable measures in other countries and that there is no parallel increase in production per worker, we can investigate the consequences of such a wage increase.

1. Workers' incomes and their (monetary) demand for consumer goods increase (provided the reduced income of those who may have become unemployed does not have a compensatory effect). As entrepreneurs generally calculate their (excess) profits as a percentage of the (increased) cost price (as far as competitive circumstances permit), their (monetary) demand also increases.

Since the increase in production costs usually results in a rise in prices (which is neither general nor proportional and does not occur immediately either), physical demand often remains constant. It may even fall because of the progression of taxes. Much will depend on the state of the economy. This applies to demand from firms as well.

2. Owing to the increase in domestic prices, demand from abroad usually diminishes and imports may go up. This is especially harmful if the country is highly dependent on foreign trade.

3. A decline or increase in demand at home and abroad will lead respectively to a decline or increase in production. A slackening of activity will not necessarily be immediately accompanied by a reduction in employment.

Production *per capita* and overall production usually run in parallel: a drop in production is generally accompanied by a decrease in production *per capita*, and a rise in one coincides with an increase in the other (partly through utilization of reserve capacity, but for boom conditions see Chapter 9.8*b*).

4. In addition to these repercussions, which mainly come out in the short run, there are long-run effects, *viz.* a tendency towards greater rationalization and mechanization, which may prevent prices rising as described above.

b. Types of wages policy
1. First of all, wages can be adjusted to movements in prices. The latter may be caused by changes in the price of raw materials and need not necessarily be related to the effects of wage changes. The experience of recent decades has been that wage increases are not always the root cause of inflation. They have usually been designed to maintain purchasing power.

A policy of this type brings about no change in income distribution.

If prices rise and wages stay put, the wage earners' share in the national income will fall. When other income groups react to a wage increase and prices go up, the workers can claim this as a reason for demanding a further increase; this will be relatively easy in a period of full employment. An inflationary situation may result, however, with all its drawbacks. This can only be avoided if all income groups exercise a certain amount of discipline and cooperate in what we may call an incomes policy in the strict sense – 'a system of standards, maintained by the government, that applies to all persons in receipt of income, and by means of which pressure groups are held in check so that prices cannot rise' (J. Pen).

In a period of falling prices, wages should be kept down. Such a policy will meet with opposition from the trade unions; it will damage the social climate of industrial relations. Constant price reductions are not likely to stimulate economic recovery, for that matter. Cutting wages has not proved a successful means of emerging from a depression (as in the United States between 1929 and 1932).

In many countries, including Belgium, Denmark, Italy and France, most wages are linked to consumer prices, though this is true only of the major industries in the United Kingdom and the United States; wages in the German building industry were part-linked to prices in 1963. This is a means whereby the trade unions hope to maintain real incomes as they are. The employers are not always opposed to this, because it helps to keep the peace. A wage-price spiral can nevertheless be caused by a chance occurrence such as a poor harvest. The system also makes the economy less flexible. This can be remedied to a certain extent by not allowing adjustments to be made too rapidly (i.e. the percentage rise in prices that triggers off a wage rise should not be too low). Even in countries where this system does not exist (e.g. the Netherlands), wages and prices move along parallel lines.

2. These views were opposed by some economists and by the trade unions in the 1930s; they held that wages should be increased during a depression in order to stimulate demand. This standpoint is correct in principle. The proviso is that the country is not too dependent on foreign demand and that the effect of the wage increase is not neutralized by other factors (pessimistic expectations on the part of firms).

A policy of wage increases is also recommended in all circumstances as a means of redistributing national income. To ensure its success, corporate profits must be taken into account.

450

3. The stabilization of wages is sometimes recommended. Economic progress will then have to be expressed in a reduction of prices. Whether firms will reduce their prices spontaneously, especially in boom conditions, is doubtful. Keeping wages steady is a difficult task: piece rates would have to be lowered in many cases, and that would lead to social unrest.

4. For these reasons it is accepted that prices rather than wages must be kept constant. Two methods can be used. First, all the wages in a country or an industry can be increased by the percentage corresponding to the average increase in production per worker. Thus account can be taken of the regularly expressed demand for equal pay for equal work. This method benefits those firms in which production per worker has gone up most: they make the highest profits and spend a great deal on new investment.

A second method is to allow wages in each firm to vary with changes in production per worker in that firm.

Available data on the relation between wages and productivity are scarce and give us divergent results. As E. Lundberg complains: 'The tragic fact is . . . that we have very little empirical foundation of our generalizations about the complicated interdependence of wages, productivity, profits, level of employment, etc.' We should also remember how little meaning can be attached to the concept of productivity. In practice, therefore, it is difficult to apply the above principles.

5. Wages policy is sometimes designed to restore the balance of payments to equilibrium. When wages are held down, which may have a favourable influence on prices, exports are stimulated. Results are obtained mostly in countries whose foreign trade is extensive.

6. A reduction in the number of hours worked while wages are kept the same amounts to an increase in hourly wages, so this will entail some of the consequences mentioned above. Purchasing power does not increase, however. As this is usually a measure which is introduced simultaneously throughout the country, the effects vary from industry to industry (profit margins are not everywhere the same).

7 International economic policy

Trade policy and the various forms of integration have already been discussed (see Chapters 10.5, 11.3–5, and 12.8). The success of such attempts at integration depends on how far the member states succeed in preventing further distortion or, to put it another way, in attaining effective coordination of their economic policies.

This is evident as far as trade policy towards non-member countries is concerned: failing joint decisions, products from outside would not be able to be traded freely within the union. The other aspects of economic policy also call for prior consultation: all measures adopted by one member influence its partners.

Combating economic fluctuations must be a matter of joint concern. Price policy in one country, for example, can be obstructed by inflation in another.

Monetary policy gains in importance because quantitative restrictions between the members of the union may not be used to prevent balance-of-payments difficulties arising. The introduction of a single currency might clear away this problem. Such a step requires political unity, however, and that does not seem to be attainable as yet.

Coordination of interest-rate policies is also desirable with a view to liberalizing capital movements. However, unwanted movements may not be eliminated by coordination, since there is a tendency to invest in areas where industrial development has already been appreciable. Political and economic union in Italy, for instance, reinforced the supremacy of the north, and the difference in welfare between the northern and southern states of the United States has remained unchanged for decades. In other words, a completely liberal policy would further intensify the existing contrasts. This is why it is accepted that countries where capital is scarce restrict capital exports so as to promote expansion in less-developed areas at home.

As regards free movement of persons, the obstacles to labour mobility are difficult to surmount, but most governments have no wish to see their labour market disturbed by mass immigration from countries with a high rate of population growth.

Even in the case of integration between countries with almost the same economic and social structure, then, escape clauses appear to be essential, though they may be fewer and less far-reaching than in worldwide organizations. The countries concerned will accept no reduction in living standards and will put up with inconveniences only if they are inevitable and come about gradually.

Constant government supervision is needed to ensure that the benefits of integration are realized (maintenance of effective competition, restraint of economic power).

The efficient coordination of the economic policies of the member countries inevitably requires the establishment of supranational organs. Regular meetings of ministers can yield results, but they achieve nothing in cases of conflict where each party maintains its point of view and insists on its sovereignty.

Recognition of the principle of supranationality must eventually lead to the acceptance of political union.

8 Bibliography

Simple introduction: K. E. Boulding, *Principles of Economic Policy* (Englewood Cliffs, N. J. 1958); more extensive: H. Giersch, *Allgemeine Wirtschaftspolitik*, part 1: *Grundlagen* (Wiesbaden 1960).

See also the works on business cycles (Chapter 9), including J. A. Estey, *Business Cycles* (New York 1956), part 3; E. Despres, M. Milton, A. G. Hart, P. A. Samuelson, D. H. Wallace, 'The Problem of Economic Instability', *AER*, September 1950 – a synthesis for non-economists of the ways and means of combating economic fluctuations.

United Nations publications which recommend measures of economic policy: *National and International Measures for Full Employment* (New York, December 1949); *Measures for the Economic Development of Under-developed Countries* (New York, May 1951); *Measures for International Economic Stability* (New York 1951).

E. Küng, *Zahlungsbilanzpolitik* (Zürich 1959); in this monumental work the consequences of different forms of economic and balance-of-payments policy are clearly dealt with in a non-mathematical way.

C. Bresciani-Turroni, *Economic Policy for the Thinking Man* (London 1950), translated from the Italian (*Introduzione alla politica economica*), and W. Eucken, *Grundsätze der Wirtschaftspolitik* (ed. E. Eucken and K. P. Hensel, Tübingen 1952), a posthumous work; both these authors are members of the neoliberal school and engage in not very objective criticism of the centrally planned economy.

For actual cases: W. A. Jöhr and H. W. Singer, *The Role of the Economist as Official Advisor* (London 1955); in Sweden: E. Lundberg, *Business Cycles and Economic Policy* (London 1957); in the

EEC countries, Norway, the United Kingdom and the United States: *Economic Policy in Our Time*, Vols. 2 and 3 (Amsterdam 1964).

a. Policy targets

On the different views concerning full employment: *Problems on Unemployment and Inflation 1950 and 1951: Analysis of Replies by Governments to a United Nations Questionnaire* (UN, New York 1951): a few countries define full employment as a situation in which no more than a given percentage of the total labour force is unemployed (about 3 per cent in the United Kingdom and Belgium); in this connection: D. T. Jack, 'Full Employment in Retrospect', *EJ*, December 1952. The comment by E. Domar is drawn from his *Essays in the Theory of Economic Growth* (New York 1957).

For welfare theory, A. P. Lerner, *The Economics of Control* (New York 1944) – a non-mathematical consideration; P.A. Samuelson, *Foundations of Economic Analysis* (Cambridge, Mass. 1947), Chapter 8; I. M. D. Little, *A Critique of Welfare Economics* (Oxford 1950); J. de V. Graaff, *Theoretical Welfare Economics* (Cambridge 1957), points to its limited usefulness; E. J. Mishan, 'A Survey of Welfare Economics', *EJ*, June 1960. We have avoided the term welfare economics because it seems tautological.

b. Planning

J. Tinbergen, *Economic Policy: Principles and Design* (Amsterdam 1958), gives numerous examples of models; E. Beach, *Economic Models: An Exposition* (New York 1957), is more a survey of the most commonly used mathematical and statistical methods in economics, while J. Tinbergen and H. C. Bos, *Mathematical Models of Economic Growth* (New York 1962), is a textbook.

On indicative planning: B. Balassa, 'Planning in an Open Economy', *Ky*, 1966, No. 3, finds that planning is only necessary in public and semi-public sectors (agriculture, transport, energy); G. Denton, M. Forsyth and M. Maclennan, *Economic Planning and Policies in Britain, France and Germany* (London 1968); V. Lutz, *Central Planning for the Market Economy: An Analysis of the French Theory and Experience* (London 1969): an unfavourable appraisal of French planning.

On planning techniques in the Netherlands: *Scope and Methods of the Central Planning Bureau* (The Hague, August 1956); P. J.

Verdoorn, 'The Short-term Model of the Central planning Bureau and its forecasting Performance (1953–1963)' in *Construction and Practical Application of Macro-economic Models for Purposes of Economic Planning (Programming) and Policy Making* (UN New York 1967).

For the less-developed countries: *Programming Techniques for Economic Development: With Special Reference to Asia and the Far East* (Economic Commission for Asia and the Far East, Bangkok 1960); A. Waterston, *Development Planning: Lessons of Experience* (Baltimore 1965) – based on the experience of an IBRD official. A. W. Lewis, *Development Planning: The Essentials of Economic Policy* (London 1966) – likewise illustrated with numerous examples.

Planning and Markets: Modern Trends in Various Economic Systems (ed. J. T. Dunlop and N. P. Fedorenko, New York 1969) – the report of a conference held in 1966 on planning in western and eastern countries.

On planning in the USSR: *Economic Survey of Europe in 1962* (Economic Commission for Europe, Geneva 1965), Part 2; *Value and Plan: Economic Calculation and Organization in Eastern Europe* (ed. G. Grossman, Berkeley, Cal. 1960). More generally concerning the Soviet economy: H. Schwartz, *An Introduction to the Soviet Economy* (Columbus, Ohio, 1968); R. W. Campbell, *Soviet Economic Power: Its Organisation, Growth and Challenge* (Cambridge, Mass. 1960) with annotated bibliography; V. Katkoff, *Soviet Economy, 1940–1965* (Baltimore 1961); more theoretical: A. Nove, *The Soviet Economy: An Introduction* (London 1961). See also *Economic Trends in the Soviet Union* (ed. A. Bergson and S. Kuznets, Cambridge, Mass. 1963).

On China: A. Donnithorne, *China's Economic System* (London 1967).

c. Public finance
Good introductions are C. Goedhart, *Hoofdlijnen van de leer der openbare financiën* (2nd ed., Leiden 1967); R. A. Musgrave, *The Theory of Public Finance: A Study in Public Economy* (New York 1959). More difficult (and based on Swedish conditions): B. Hansen, *The Economic Theory of Fiscal Policy* (London 1958), translation of the Swedish edition of 1955. From the practical point of view: *Fiscal Policy for a Balanced Economy: Experience, Problems and Prospects* (OECD, Paris 1968), eight contributions.

Concerning the Haavelmo effect: T. Haavelmo, 'Multiplier Effects of a Balanced Budget', *Em*, October 1945.

On policy in respect of public works: J. M. Clark, *Economics of Planning Public Works* (Washington 1935); W. Drees Jr., *On the Level of Government Expenditure in the Netherlands after the War* (Leiden 1955): although government spending is inflexible, a certain amount of variation is yet possible.

On the 'Zÿlstra norm': J. Zÿlstra, *Möglichkeiten und Grenzen der Konjunkturpolitik* (Kieler Vorträge, Kiel 1962).

The quotation from H. Dalton is drawn from his *Principles of Public Finance* (4th ed., London 1954), that from J. R. Schlesinger from 'Monetary Policy and its Critics', *JPE*, December 1961.

d. Monetary policy

See, in addition to the above mentioned general works R. Goode and R. S. Thorn, 'Variable Reserve Requirements against Commercial Bank Deposits', *SP*, April 1959; discuss technique, importance, motives, drawbacks in respect of changing cash-reserve requirement.

For the operation of the British monetary system: *Committee on the Working of the Monetary System: Principal Memoranda of Evidence* (London 1960), 5 Vols. (the 'Radcliffe report', named after the chairman of the committee).

The Instruments of Monetary Policy in the Countries of the European Economic Community (EEC, Brussels, August 1962), gives a rather superficial analysis; see also *Eight European Central Banks* (London 1963).

A brief analysis of criticism in respect of the efficiency and consequences of monetary policy: J. R. Schlesinger, 'Monetary Policy and its Critics', *JPE*, December 1961; see also the concise study of M. W. Holtrop, *Monetary Policy in an Open Economy: Its Objectives, Instruments, Limitations and Dilemmas* (Princeton 1963), and R. A. Mundell, 'The Appropriate Use of Monetary and Fiscal Policy for Internal and External Stability', *SP*, March 1962.

The ideas of M. Friedman can be found in: *The Optimum Quantity of Money and Other Essays* (New York 1969).

e. Price policy

See the works mentioned in Chapter 9.14. Of the countless publications devoted to the combating of inflation, only a few can be mentioned: H. G. Moulton, *Can Inflation Be Controlled?* (London

1958), believes it would be possible if the increase in productivity were greater than that of wages; and two lectures: A. F. Burns, *Prosperity without Inflation* (New York 1957); J. E. Meade, *The Control of Inflation: An Inaugural Lecture* (Cambridge 1958).

An interesting publication of the Joint Economic Committee of the US Congress is *The Relationship of Prices to Economic Stability and Growth* (Washington 1958); it is composed of a *Compendium* (47 papers by experts), *Commentaries* (by 15 experts of employers' and employees' organizations) and *Hearings*.

The Problem of Rising Prices (OEEC, Paris, June 1961): a good report by experts, commissioned by the OEEC, on price increases from 1952 to 1960.

For a brief survey of the various instruments of price policy: M. A. G. van Meerhaeghe, *Price Theory and Price Policy* (London 1969), Chapter 3.

f. Wages policy
See the works mentioned in Chapter 8.

On the number of hours worked: *Hours of Work* (International Labour Office, Geneva 1958), which analyses the relevant regulations and gives a 30-page summing up of the consequences of a reduction of working hours.

See also C. Busch-Lüty, *Gesamtwirtschaftliche Lohnpolitik. Möglichkeiten und Grenzen, untersucht am Beispiel der Niederlande, Schwedens und Österreichs* (Basel 1964).

On incomes policy: H. A. Turner and H. Zoetewey, *Prices, Wages, and Incomes Policies* (Geneva 1966); A. Romanis, *Cost Inflation and Incomes Policy in Industrial Countries*, *SP*, March 1967.

On the links between wages and prices: E. M. Bernstein, 'Wage-Price Links in a Prolonged Inflation', *SP*, November 1958; B. Soffer, 'The Effects of Recent Long-term Wage Agreements on General Wage Level Movements', *QJE*, February 1959; see also the ECSC report (based on 1956–7 figures), published in 1962, concerning the different systems linking wages to production, performance and productivity.

Concluding Remarks

On a commis . . . l'erreur énorme de penser qu'être
scientifique, c'est être abstrait, alors qu'être
scientifique, c'est être vrai, c'est rendre un compte
exact et aussi général que possible de la réalité.
André Piettre

The following observations are not intended as a summing up of what we have said in the body of this textbook, nor as a full appraisal of the state of economic science. To do justice to any such intention we should require more than just a few pages. What we do think we ought to do, for the benefit of the student wishing to take his economics a step further, is to draw his attention to a few points worth noting – a few tendencies against which he should be on his guard.

1. We have deliberately endeavoured to define all our concepts as accurately as possible. We have tried not to introduce our own definitions, preferring to use those already current: there is enough confusion in economic discussion as it is because of the lack of terminological uniformity. And the variety of symbols used is another factor that does little to facilitate the reading of economic papers. This complaint is by no means new; it was already being uttered in the nineteenth century. More than thirty years ago R. Miry said that 'it would be hard to dream up a bigger muddle than the terminology we employ. In many cases we do not even understand each other because we assign the most varied meanings to one and the same word'. Ten years later J. S. Davis was warning us: 'If economics is to deserve recognition as a science, even in the modest sense of orderly arrangement of better knowledge, we need to do better in choosing and clarifying elementary concepts, standardizing terms, and becoming more explicit and consistent in our use of both'. Nothing has been done to improve the situation in the meantime. As a matter of fact, most economists would not think the matter important enough to warrant their attention.

2. Economic life is so complex and varied that the theory cannot take into account all the data available. It is obliged to simplify – to

458

assume, for instance, that many factors remain constant. The more we try to reduce it to a meaningful pattern, the less we succeed in truly reflecting the real world. Nevertheless, many economists are 'totally unconscious that their reasonings cannot, at one and the same time, be rigorous and yet capable of seizing all the essentials of reality' (G. L. S. Shackle). Hence H. G. Johnson's view that 'if economic theory is to be applied to problems of economic policy this can most usefully be done within the context of a particular problem occurring in a particular environment'. If we take simplification too far, he adds, theory can be more of a hindrance than a help. R. Triffin too, points out that a different type of economics 'disencumbered, . . . of all the limitations and taboos implied in the classical assumptions . . . will recognize the richness and variety of all concrete cases, and tackle each problem with due respect for its individual aspects'.

However much we may regret it, the fact remains that economics is of little empirical consequence. In a sense, economics is, to quote yet again the somewhat overstated view of Lord Keynes, 'a method rather than a doctrine, an apparatus of the mind, a technique of thinking'.

3. If the limited number of assumptions we make have no basis in reality, the theory will surely be useless. This is why we have repeatedly drawn attention in this book to any unreal hypotheses in the theories we have studied. Of course, we can maintain with P. A. Samuelson that 'the (empirical) unrealism of the theory "itself", or of its "assumptions", is quite irrelevant to its validity and worth', but then – we repeat – we must recognize that what we are engaged in is art for art's sake.

We might expect economists, then, to be aware of the importance of observing and analysing the real world. Alas, this is generally not the case. They select the hypotheses on which to base their theories and models according to whether they can be represented by a preferably highly complex mathematical formula or graph. They operate from purely deductive principles (thinking they can proceed as would a mathematician). Now mathematics can be a useful tool in stating economic problems, but today it is becoming an end in itself for some people – so much so that the 'non-mathematical practitioner [is] laboring under a dark suspicion (despite the history of economic thought) that nothing he does will be worth while' (M. Bronfenbrenner). Even more than in 1932, when J. Robinson made

459

the point, 'the subject matter of economics is neither more nor less than its own technique', and we agree with L. Robbins when he says that 'For all the proliferation of diagrams in recent literature, I doubt whether, analytically, we have advanced very far beyond Marshall's few lines of algebra; and I suspect that, in practical judgment and sense of proportion, we are often some way behind'.

4. In order not to discover 'old' theories again, a better knowledge of earlier authors is needed. Much too often in economics one comes triumphantly to conclusions which have already been formulated a long time ago. Ignorance (even among well-known authors) and language barriers are not always the only explanation; also more or less avowed plagiary often occurs. P. A. Sorokin mentions in this context 'amnesia' and the 'discoverer's complex'. 'The younger generation of sociologists and psychologists' – he writes – 'explicitly claims that nothing important has been discovered in their field during all the preceding centuries; . . . and that the real scientific era . . . began only in the last two or three decades with the publication of their own researches. . . .' Unfortunately, one can say the same about many contemporary economists.

5. Once we cease to take account of reality there is no end to the construction of models. E. J. Mishan has given us a witty but accurate description of this kind of sport, and we cannot resist the temptation to reproduce it in full – with the permission of the author.

To glance through the journals of the last ten or twenty years is to lose oneself in a carnival of possibility theorems. With so few empirical checks to speculative fervour the opportunities for economic science-fiction are practically boundless. One has only to outline the familiar routine of theory and counter-theory in economics to recognise, rather ruefully, the nature of the intellectual rake's progress involved. Thus, a well-known theory has it that, if we assume propositions A, B, and C, it can be shown that *if P then Q*, and *if R then S*. Some seminal mind now challenges this theory; to wit, if instead of B we assume B^*, and instead of C we assume C^*, we have the paradoxical result that *if P then S*, and *if R then Q*. It will not be long before it is pointed out that in the long run B^* tends to B and that C^* tends to C, at least if we make the reasonable assumption of E. A further contribution will reveal that if we introduce a new relationship, G, it no longer follows that *if P then Q*, and it will be concluded therefore that the original model had made the tacit assumption of non-G. This new contribution will therefore be regarded as a more general theory on the grounds that non-G is but the limiting case of G.

In the same spirit another paper will introduce a further relationship

H and conclude that all non-H models are special cases only. A controversy then begins about whether the proposition H is consistent with the A postulate: certainly it is not if we admit a fairly common assumption F. A new article now points out that the A postulate has been misunderstood; it has been misinterpreted as A'. In reply to this discovery, it will be insisted that A' is the proper interpretation. Generality of approach is promoted in a taxonomic paper that deduces the implications of A, of A', and of both A and A' together. Someone writing for *Econometrica* will then juxtapose all the possibilities in matrix notation: depending on the conditions assumed the key variables can move in any direction. Somewhere else a literary digest of the controversy will be given and a new approach indicated. And so, notwithstanding occasional perorations of the what-we-need-is-some-systematic-empirical-investigation sort, the game goes on without respite. Economics has become the thing that economists write about, and as such it has become the science of infinite conjecture.

6. We cannot expect of the economist that he should also be a sociologist, a historian, a psychologist, and so on. But he should have some sort of grounding in these disciplines or at least be prepared to carry out a number of investigations on an interdisciplinary basis. More coordination with related subjects is needed. K. Boulding has gone so far as to admit: 'I have been gradually coming under the conviction, disturbing for a professional theorist, that there is no such thing as economics – there is only social science applied to economic problems'.

Indeed, economic phenomena cannot be understood without some knowledge of the political and social circumstances in which they occur. As C. P Kindleberger has asserted, if the economist is not willing to study certain political and social conditions, on his own or together with representatives of other disciplines, he should give up the idea of explaining economic phenomena or even of giving advice on economic policy, except within very narrow limits.

7. It may be objected that the occasionally sharp criticism we have levelled against various concepts and theories in this book has been purely negative (since we have offered nothing as a substitute). This is to some extent true. However, it is no reason for continuing to uphold theories that are untenable. Furthermore, if we proceed from what has been said above we may doubt whether there *is* any substitute, whether a *general* economic theory is at all possible.

At any rate, the self-assurance that comes through in many

publications and statements by economists often seems to us misplaced. The layman is given the impression that economics is capable of solving all problems. Many economists simply will not admit that in many cases there just is no precise answer. What J. Tinbergen says in reference to the optimum savings function – 'It is characteristic of the underdeveloped state of our science that virtually nothing empirical is known about this generalization and that, as a consequence, nothing sensible can be said about the optimum level of savings at present' – holds good, as this book will have shown, not only for this concept. We do not deny that economic science has advanced over the last twenty or thirty years, but the advice given us by F. Simiand in 1937 still applies: 'What economic science should be working on at the moment is realizing how very little it knows. This is perhaps the step forward that would do it most good'.

The sources of our citations here are as follows: R. Miry, 'Vraagtekens en tekortkomingen', *Tijdschrift voor economie en sociologie*, October 1937; J. S. Davis, 'Whither Now?' in *Economic Research and the Development of Economic Science and Public Policy* (New York 1946); G. L. S. Shackle, in a book review in *EJ*, December 1967; H. G. Johnson, 'The Taxonomic Approach to Economic Policy', *EJ*, December 1951; R. Triffin, *Monopolistic Competition and General Equilibrium Theory* (Cambridge, Mass. 1940); J. M. Keynes, 'Introduction' to the *Cambridge Economic Handbooks*; P. A. Samuelson, during a discussion at a conference organized by the American Economic Association in 1962, *AER*, May 1963; M. Bronfenbrenner, 'A "Middlebrow" Introduction to Economic Methodology', in *The Structure of Economic Science* (ed. Krupp); J. Robinson, *Economics is a Serious Subject* (Cambridge 1932); L. Robbins, 'The Economist in the Twentieth Century', *Ec*, May 1949; P. A. Sorokin, *Fads and Foibles in Modern Sociology and Related Sciences* (Chicago 1956); E. J. Mishan, 'Britain, the Economist and the Six', *The Bankers' Magazine*, August 1962; K. E. Boulding, *A Reconstruction of Economics* (2nd ed., New York 1962); C. P. Kindleberger, 'Introduction' to M. Moret, *L'échange international* (Paris 1957); J. Tinbergen, 'Optimum Savings and Utility Maximization over Time', *Em*, April 1960; F. Simiand, in the article by R. Miry cited above.

Appendix

Appendix A

Economic Doctrines

The inclination of several of the recent opponents of economic science to sweep away what many generations have built up is not only intellectual presumption, but also incompatible with the normal progress of science.

P. Hennipman

A survey of economic doctrines, or of economic ideas, must not be confused with economic history, which relates to economic facts – in other words, history studied from the standpoint of economics. Although communication and knowledge of facts is sometimes indispensable for ideas to be understood – they interact upon each other – it is best not to mingle the two concepts. The history of economic ideas cannot easily be divorced from the history of ideas in general.

The present chapter is divided up according to major periods or schools, which in many cases overlap chronologically. Some authors have a place of their own. Each school forms both a continuation of and a reaction to the previous one.

1 Ancient times and the Middle Ages

The Greeks, who were first and foremost politicians, never thought in purely economic terms; and, their manual labour was done for them by slaves. Even so, dissertations on money and interest are to be found in the works of Plato (427–347 BC) and Aristotle (384–322 BC).

Nor did the Romans devote much attention to economic problems. Only the agrarian question was examined, from a technical standpoint, by one or two authors.

Although labour became more respectable during the Middle Ages and was no longer done by slaves, the Church condemned any unrestrained craving for wealth. The development of trade prompted the clergy, the intellectuals of the time, to deliver judgments on economic questions. In these they invariably adopted an ethical standpoint. Thomas Aquinas (1226–74) defined the position of the Church towards the economic problems of the day: interest was prohibited (time was God's and not marketable), whereas a compensation for the use of land was permissible. This was not regarded as exploitation but as a return for the natural properties of the soil made available. Later on, a moderate interest was allowed to be charged in respect of loans for non-consumption purposes which involved the lender in disadvantages (*damnum emergens*) or elimination of benefits (*lucrum cessans*). The price could only be a reward for the labour (*justum pretium*).

Also noteworthy for his monetary theory is Nicolas Oresme (1330–82). Unlike Aquinas, who viewed money as a medium of exchange, he considered its value to be determined by the metal from which it was manufactured. In addition, he was an advocate of bimetallism.

2 Mercantilism

The setting-up of nation states and the discovery of America (1492) had profound economic repercussions. The rationalist spirit gained more and more ground; profit-seeking assumed unusually large proportions. The formation of national armies made vast monetary demands on the sovereign rulers. The influence of the state increased at the expense of the authority of the Church.

a. Definition

The entire body of measures designed to make the state as powerful and as rich as possible was called the mercantilist system. The principal means employed to fulfil this aim were acquisition of a maximum amount of precious metals and the pursuance of an active population policy. Mercantilism – a name given by the physiocrats and adopted by Adam Smith – embodied the following tenets in particular.

1. States possessing gold and silver (e.g. Spain) endeavoured to keep such metals in their possession, exports being prohibited. Other countries exerted every effort to obtain gold and silver; if they had no mines to develop, they had to stimulate imports of precious metals. This could only be done if there was a favourable trade balance.

2. The achievement of a surplus on trade was deemed to necessitate protectionism (organization and protection of trade and industry). This mainly assumed a maritime and colonial form (trade using the nation's own ships).

3. As it was impossible for all nations to accomplish these aims, a spirit of hostility necessarily arose among them.

The mercantilists regarded interest as the price of money; they found that an increase in the quantity of money brought about a decline in interest rates. This view, which the classical authors contested, was later restored to favour by J. M. Keynes.

b. Forms

Mercantilism persisted as an economic system from about 1450 to 1750. Considering the length of this period and the number of countries with differing economic structures which conducted a mercantilist policy, it is not surprising that such a policy assumed a variety of forms, as described below.

1. Bullionism was a system which consisted in vigorous defence of stocks of precious metals, in particular by control over trade agreements and the prohibition of exports of such metals.

2. Industrialism (Colbertism) aimed at making the country rich by developing big 'manufactures'. The result, however, was a neglect of agriculture. Writers on the subject include Jean Antoine Bodin (1530–96), known for his naïve quantity theory (he came to the conclusion that the cause of the rise in prices at that time – they trebled between 1500 and 1550 – was traceable to the excessive quantity of gold and silver coin, and gave as an additional reason coin-clipping by monarchs); and Antoine de Montchrétien (1576–1621), in whose *Traité de l'économie politique* the designation 'political economy' was used for the first time in 1616. While Bodin and de Montchrétien were also alive to commercial interests, the orthodox champion of industrialism was Jean-Baptiste Colbert (1619–83).

3. Commercial mercantilism focused attention mainly on methods of achieving a favourable trade balance. It was marked by a less protectionist attitude. Among its advocates were Thomas Mun (1571–1641), who considered the ban on gold exports a mistake because goods bought with gold could be exported at a profit after processing, Sir William Petty (1623–87), Josiah Child (1639–90) and

467

Gregory King (1648–1712; cf. King's law). Richard Cantillon (1680–1734) was an economist with many ideas which put him ahead of his time.

Although the three tendencies described above were sometimes found simultaneously in one and the same country, in France it was mainly industrial, in the United Kingdom commercial, and in Germany and Spain metallic mercantilism that secured the most adherents. (In Germany it was also called Cameralism.)

4. According to John Law (1671–1729), money need not consist of coin, and paper money was even better. The term used for this concept is fiduciary mercantilism or neomercantilism.

Appraisal
1. The mercantilists had a one-sided view of wealth. The importance of money was overestimated. Even so, an increase in the quantity of money was necessary at that time in order to counteract barter, induced by the lack of currency.

2. International trade was not regarded as an exchange of goods, but as the means of acquiring the same good; hence the egoistic trade policy and the adverse consequences which it sometimes had. The bullionist policy followed by Spain was seen to be especially pernicious.

3. Numerous objections were subsequently raised to mercantilism. In the circumstances then prevailing, a great many measures were characterized by a high degree of realism. The anxiety concerning the demographic trend, for instance, was understandable after long-drawn-out wars had caused the population to drop considerably.

4. The economic problem was viewed in a national context – a transition from local to national economy.

3 Physiocracy

The physiocrats constituted a reaction to Colbertism and were therefore opposed to state intervention and to neglect of agriculture. They called themselves the *philosophes économistes* and during the years 1764–70 formed a sort of political party or sect. The leader of the school was François Quesnay (1694–1774), who studied medicine fairly late in life and became physician to Madame de Pompadour and Louis xv. He started publishing works on economic subjects when he was sixty years of age (notably two articles in the *Encyclopèdie*: 'Fermiers', 'Grains'). In 1758 he wrote his *Tableau économique* (*The Oeconomical Table* London 1766), which outlines physiocratic doctrine. Later on, he brought out a more extensive work entitled *Les maximes générales du gouvernement économique d'un royaume agricole*. Quesnay's chief followers may be said to be Victor Riquetti, Marquis de Mirabeau (1715–89), Pierre Samuel Dupont de Nemours (1739–1817) and Pierre Paul Mercier de la Rivière (1721–93). Anne Robert Turgot (1727–81) took a more independent stand.

Quesnay's underlying principle is that only agriculture should be considered productive since it alone serves to multiply products; industry confines itself to processing and trade to transport. Money is regarded simply as a medium of exchange.

Quesnay divides the active sector of the population into three classes – the producing class (farmers), the unproductive or sterile class (traders, manufacturers) and the proprietary class (landowners). These he contrasts with the employed, who – still according to Quesnay – form the passive section, which is only of importance from a consumption standpoint.

With the aid of *avances foncières* (investment made by the landowner to render the soil fit for cultivation, upon which his entitlement, and also that of his successors, to income is based – land development, road-building, enclosure), *avances primitives* (cattle, implements), and *avances annuelles* (seed, fertilizer), the *produit brut* (crop) is created (shown in Figure 62 as having a value of 5 million). Deduction of *nouvelles avances annuelles* (for the following year) and *subsistance* (combined value 2 million – arrow on the left in Figure 62) gives the *produit net*. The bulk of this is paid to the proprietary class (2 million) and the remainder is purchased from the sterile class (1 million). In addition, both classes must buy agricultural products (totalling 3 million), so that the producing class again has 5 million at its disposal and the cycle can restart. Taxes have to be charged solely on agriculture, the only productive activity, and to be paid by the landowners.

In the schematic representation of the system, we see the influence of Quesnay's medical studies, and more particularly of Harvey's theory on the blood circulation.

In order to stimulate agriculture, prices of agrarian products must be freely determined and, for example, any ban on exports is frowned upon. Absolute freedom is the best way to achieve prosperity.

Everyone must be able to seek his own interests without hindrance from the government; the individual's interests are at one with society's. Nevertheless, the state must be strong enough to safeguard freedom of action ('legal despotism' theory). If the natural laws cannot exercise their influence free from restrictions, society must be

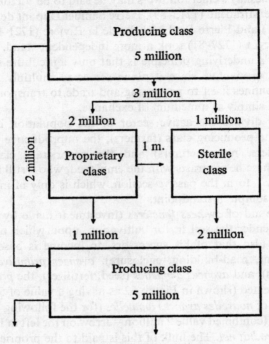

Figure 62: Quesnay's circular flow

changed in the desired manner (the natural order). Quesnay's disciples were outstanding in their insistence on the idea of the natural order, or the order willed by God.

Appraisal

a. As the production concept is erroneous – the physiocrats ignore the creative force of industry – the *tableau* too is inaccurate. Yet at that time there was a high regard for the *tableau*; the fact that the physiocrats 'always make their millions work out exactly has a heady effect on them and, like a great many mathematical economists of today, they do not see that in the final analysis all they discover is what they have put in themselves' (C. Gide and C. Rist). Ferdinando Galiani (1728–87) and Etienne Bonnot de Condillac (1714–80), the leading dissidents from the physiocratic school, were advocating a more accurate concept of value.

b. The physiocrats were the first to draw attention to the circular flow of goods and money. They also made clear the distribution of income among the various classes.

c. The physiocrats were the first economic school. Proceeding from specific principles, they developed a coherent theory; in addition, they brought the 'natural laws' concept to the forefront.

4 The classical school

The 'classical' authors rejected the idea that manufacturers belonged to the sterile class since industry is as much a productive branch of activity as agriculture. Labour was considered to be the basis of value. The concept of natural order, however, was adopted and developed further. Self-interest, the basis of human action, generates maximum performance (beneficial egoism). Initially, the inductive method was used – starting from the conditions in the United Kingdom at the time – but once the principles had been established the deductive method was followed.

a. Leading authors

The classical school, also called the liberal or orthodox school, is specifically British. Its chief personalities are Adam Smith, Thomas Malthus and David Ricardo.

1. A. Smith (1723–90) acquired fame – for a long time he was called the father of economics – with *An Inquiry into the Nature and Causes of the Wealth of Nations*, published in 1776. In this unsystematic and rambling work, he points to the great advantages of division of labour and expounds a theory of value based on labour. Smith is optimistic concerning the effect on output of economic liberalism (but less so as regards distribution). This optimism was not shared by Malthus and Ricardo.

2. T. Malthus (1766–1834) is known mainly for his theory of population. His *Essay on the Principle of Population* (published anonymously in 1798 and in an improved edition under his own name

in 1803) was written as a reaction to the argument propounded in 1793 by William Godwin (1756–1836) that mankind's misery is due to maldistribution of goods. Malthus maintained that pauperism was an inevitable phenomenon, caused by overpopulation.

The population increases, claims Malthus, by geometric progression (doubling in twenty-five years), whereas means of subsistence only increase by arithmetic progression. Malthus is thus opposed to the mercantilists' demographic policy. Unduly rapid growth of the population is what must first be arrested. If positive checks (wars, famines, plagues) do not work, preventive checks (moral restraint) must be applied. This theory, based partly on somewhat exceptional contemporary North American conditions (immigration), had some influence on the public assistance policy of the day. Malthus was very much in favour of the inductive method, in contrast with most classical authors.

Malthus does not agree with J. B. Say's *loi des débouchés* (see Chapter 9.2) on the impossibility of underconsumption (*Principles of political economy*, 1820). In this he was later supported by J. M. Keynes.

3. D. Ricardo (1772–1833) goes further in applying Smith's theory of value (*On the Principles of Political Economy and Taxation*, 1817). In particular, he makes a distinction between those goods which can and those which cannot be arbitrarily multiplied. His work is, however, heavy reading, highly abstract and unsystematically constructed.

Ricardo was particularly interested in distribution problems. His views on wage determination ('iron law of wages'), land-rent and international trade (comparative cost) commanded a great deal of influence.

Ricardo also formulated an early but naïve purchasing-power-parity theory (see Chapter 12.5). In addition, he was an advocate of the currency principle (*The High Price of Bullion*, 1810).

4. Various authors developed the classical doctrine – in France, Jean-Baptiste Say (1768–1832) and Frédéric Bastiat (1801–50), and in the United Kingdom, Nassau William Senior (1790–1864), who already called attention to the drawbacks of divergent definitions, and John Stuart Mill (1806–73). The last-named admitted (*Principles of Political Economy*, 1848) that distribution was not governed by economic laws and believed that government intervention – in the form of progressive taxation, for example – might be necessary.

Appraisal
The classical doctrine proceeds deductively. The laws derived from the egoistic behaviour of the *homo œconomicus* are considered too stringent. Although the theories of the liberal school are outmoded and inaccurate (the theory of value is incorrect, among other things), they are still considered 'classical' because of the way in which they were treated. The method of analyses employed – the mechanism of supply and demand – was later used as a model.

Under the influence of the classical authors, economics developed as an independent science.

b. Reactions
Criticism of the classical doctrine was soon forthcoming from various quarters.

1. According to Jean Charles de Sismondi (1773–1842), mechanization is the scourge of the working class. His criticism of the capitalist system made him a forerunner of socialism; his call for a return to a corporative society brought him closer to the romantic movement, which did not accept human egoism as a basis for economic science. The most prominent representatives of this movement were German Catholic authors (notably Adam Heinrich Müller, 1779–1829).

2. The adherents of the protectionist movement denied that the benefits of international trade were experienced by all nations. According to Friedrich List (1798–1846), the economic development process went through the following stages: (a) nomadism and (b) sedentariness, the latter being subdivided into the following phases: (i) agriculture; (ii) agriculture and manufacturing (iii) agriculture, manufacturing and trade.

The transition from phase (ii) to (iii) occurs when manufacturing (or agriculture) has developed sufficiently to produce at lower costs than those ruling in other countries. As long as this has not been achieved, protectionism is legitimate in order to promote the development of domestic agriculture and manufacturing. In List's view, the United Kingdom and France had already passed this phase, but Germany had not.

In point of fact, these phases are interwoven; trade sometimes exists before manufacturing. Different classifications were drawn up, mostly based on secondary factors (see Chapter 10.4).

In the United States, infant-industry protection found a champion in Henry Charles Carey (1793–1879).

3. The historical school, socialism and the Christian movement are enlarged upon in the following three sections.

5 The historical school

The historical school contested the universality of economic laws, which are limited by time and space. It exercised a particularly marked influence in the German-speaking area for about forty years (from 1843, when Roscher's *Grundriss zu Vorlesungen über die Staatswissenschaft nach geschichtlicher Methode* appeared).

The representatives of the historical school, Wilhelm Roscher (1817–94), Bruno Hildebrand (1812–78) and Karl Knies (1821–98), laid the emphasis, unlike Ricardo, for instance, on investigation of the facts. They viewed economic data in the overall context of political and social developments. On the model of F. List, Roscher (natural, labour and capital economies), and Hildebrand (exchange, money and credit economies) drew up development theories. K. Knies refuted these theories: he wanted economics reduced to a science of facts, in which every situation had a character of its own that must be described separately.

Knies was subsequently emulated by the members of what was called the 'young historical school', outstanding in which was Gustav von Schmoller (1838–1917). Among its other leading figures were Georg Knapp (1842–1926) and Karl Bücher (1847–1930).

Several of the young historical school's adherents advocated social reforms (including progressive income taxes, old age pensions and sickness insurance). In 1872 they founded the Verein für Sozial-politik at Eisenach, which had a considerable influence on social and political developments in Germany (especially the social legislation introduced by Bismark).

In their attempt to study economic problems in a wide framework, some writers later tended towards the ideas outlined above, notably Werner Sombart (1863–1941) and Max Weber (1864–1920).

Appraisal

The historical school had the merit of calling attention to the way in which economic phenomena are conditioned by history. The vast amount of material that they collected frequently proved unprofitable owing to lack of interpretation. Even so, pioneering work was accomplished in the determination of methods of calculation for macro-economic data (balance of payments, national income).

6 Socialism

In ancient times and the Middle Ages, we already find socialist arguments advanced, but no socialist doctrine proper. Only after the rise of mechanization and the resultant social abuses did a doctrine develop. In contrast with the liberals, socialists do not believe that individual efforts to secure a higher income bring prosperity to the entire population. What is needed is cooperation, which can only be achieved through fundamental equality of rights and opportunities. In the early stages, opinions differed as to how such equality was to be brought about.

Thus Robert Owen (1771–1858), Charles Fourier (1772–1837) and Louis Blanc (1811–82) hoped to establish the socialist society by setting up small communities in which property rights would be either abolished or severely restricted. Their frequently utopian projects were elaborated on more scientific lines by William Thompson (1785–1833), who together with Robert Owen laid the foundations of the cooperative movement, and Pierre Proudhon (1809–56).

On the other hand, Claude de Rouvroy, comte de Saint-Simon (1760–1825) and his pupils Barthélémy Enfantin (1796–1864), Saint-Amand Bazard (1791–1832) and Auguste Comte (1798–1857) advocated a centralized society in which the most important decisions would be taken under the guidance of men of science.

Louis-Auguste Blanqui (1805–81) must also be classed among the 'interventionists', but, in contrast with earlier authors who supported democratic ideas, he wanted to gain power by means of a *coup d'état* organized by a small group.

Developing the ideas expressed by Saint-Simon, a German land-owner, Karl Rodbertus-Jagetzow (1805–75), formulated the first economic theory of socialism. This doctrine only became widely known through the activity of Ferdinand Lassalle (1825–64), also a German, and by the writings of Karl Marx (1818–83), who, perhaps without being aware of it, adopted many of the ideas of Rodbertus as well as of Smith, Ricardo and William Thompson.

a. Karl Marx
Karl Marx's views are expounded mainly in two works – *The*

475

Communist Manifesto (1848) (London 1948) and *Das Kapital* (the first part of which appeared in 1867, the second and third parts being issued in 1885 and 1894 respectively by his friend Friedrich Engels) in English, *Capital: A Critique of Political Economy* (Chicago 1926).

On the basis of the classical theory of value, Marx demonstrated that profits and interest derived from non-remuneration of part of the work performed. Admittedly, the entrepreneurs pay the workers a daily wage that enables them to provide for their subsistence. The labour needed to produce the requisite goods is relatively modest (e.g. three hours), but in fact the workers do ten hours and more per day. The entrepreneur thus pays a wage that is commensurate with three hours' work, but for which ten hours are available. The difference in value, the 'surplus value', is used largely for the production of new capital goods through which the output per worker rises, production becomes more capital-intensive, unemployment arises (*die industrielle Reservearmee*) and consequently wages fall to the absolute vital minimum. Consumption thus does not expand to the same extent as output, which generates depressions increasing in intensity (*Krisentheorie*).

The smaller entrepreneurs, who do not possess the capital necessary to bring their production machinery into line with technological progress, are eliminated and join the ranks of the proletariat (*Proletarisierungstheorie*). This in turn has a detrimental effect on wages, so that misery becomes more pronounced (*Verelendungstheorie*). The disappearance of the smaller enterprises intensifies the concentration of all capital goods among a handful of capitalists (*Konzentrationstheorie*). Finally, the antithesis between the wealth of a few and the poverty of the vast majority of the population becomes unbearable and triggers off a revolution as the result of an acute economic depression (*Zusammenbruchstheorie*). This produces a classless society in which production is based on the satisfaction of wants and not on the profit motive.

Marx follows Hegelian dialectics. For instance, he says that thesis (the capitalist society, based on private ownership of capital goods) gives rise to antithesis (the proletariat, without the tools necessary for the work). From this contrast emerges synthesis, that is to say, the socialist society, in which the means of production belong to the community.

The exploitation of the workers was attacked by nearly all Marx's predecessors on the grounds of its injustice. Marx asserts that this is pointless, as the way in which each social class ensures its subsistence influences its views on such subjects as morality, religion and science; in other words, the economic structure determines the accompanying ideas (historical materialism). Each class thus has its own concepts of justice. The collectivist society is necessary, not for reasons of justice, but because capitalism, once it has fulfilled its 'historical' role (namely the accumulation of capital goods), is no longer in a position to ensure man's economic and consequently his cultural progress.

Appraisal

Marx is the father of scientific socialism. He anticipated important aspects of the development of capitalism (e.g. economic concentration). His explanation of these phenomena is, however, based on a faulty premise (the classical theory of value). Although Marx does not regard the appearance of great thinkers as necessarily being the consequence of a specific economic structure, he nevertheless believes in historical materialism. This is untenable, however, since there is an interrelation between 'being' and 'thinking'. The economy is not invariably the decisive factor. Marx's views are in line with the ideals of the *Aufklärung* and the positivist philosophy of the mid-nineteenth century.

b. Followers

Marx's followers tried to adapt his doctrine to changed circumstances. Karl Kautsky (1854–1938), in *Die Agrarfrage. Eine Übersicht über die Tendenzen der modernen Landwirtschaft und die Agrarpolitik der Sozialdemokratie* (Stuttgart 1899, 2nd ed., 1902), attempts to explain why concentration is a slower process in agriculture than in industry. Rudolf Hilferding (1877–1943), in *Das Finanzkapital. Eine Studie über die jüngste Entwicklung des Kapitalismus* (Vienna 1910; 3rd ed., Berlin 1947), studied the repercussions of trusts and restrictive agreements on the functioning of the capitalist economy. Rosa Luxemburg (1870–1919), in *Die Akkumulation des Kapitals. Ein Beitrag zur ökonomischen Erklärung des Imperialismus* (Berlin 1913; 2nd ed., 1921; trans. as *The Accumulation of Capital*, New York 1964), claims that the capitalist countries can only avoid depressions by exporting part of their production to less-developed countries (by making direct investment in those countries). The employment of cheap labour in these areas creates fresh surplus value. The moderate

Mikhail Tugan-Baranowsky (1865–1919) produced a noteworthy work on cyclical fluctuations in the United Kingdom (1894).

Lenin (whose real name was Vladimir Ilyitch Ulyanov; 1870–1924) was more a man of action. The regime which he established differed greatly from primitive communism, the chief upholder of which was Etienne Cabet (1788–1856), and which proclaimed that not only capital goods but also consumer goods were common property. In the USSR there is at present no question of communism in the original sense of the word. A collectivist system has been introduced, together with the dictatorship of the proletariat (the socialization process not having been accompanied by political and economic democracy). Such a dictatorship is necessary for a short period – according to Lenin – in order to eradicate the bourgeois mentality.

Among the later authors are Oskar Lange (1904–65), Maurice H. Dobb (b.1900) and Paul Baran (1910–1964). Together with P. M. Sweezy (b.1910), Baran wrote, among other works, *Monopoly Capital: An Essay on the American Economic and Social Order* (New York 1966). This draws attention to the fact that it is not competitive capitalism but 'monopoly capitalism' that must be the basis of analysis. A more pronounced tendency towards chronic depressions was predicted. This prediction had already been made by Fritz Sternberg (b.1895) in *The Coming Crisis* (1947). In *Der Imperialismus* (1926), he had challenged R. Luxemburg's theory.

c. Anarchism

Developing P. Proudhon's theories, Mikhail Bakunin (1814–76) and Pyotr Kropotkin (1842–1921) formulated the doctrine of anarchism. The aim of this system is to secure maximum freedom for the individual by abolishing all the causes of constraint (government authority, ecclesiastical institutions, employed labour). Production and the various tasks of the authorities (e.g. administration, maintenance, roads, education) should be assigned to various *ad hoc* associations, which would all work together and form federations for the more complex state functions. The means of production would belong mainly to these associations; individual producers (e.g. craftsmen) would continue to own their tools.

Anarchism exercised a marked influence on the trade-union movement at the end of the nineteenth century. The slogan 'the factory for the workers' formed the basic idea of anarchistic syndicalism, which, by strikes of a revolutionary character, aspired to force the employers to hand their businesses over to organized labour. This movement was particularly widespread in France, Italy and Spain.

d. Reformists

It was not long before a reformist trend set in, the adherents of which only accepted part of the Marxist doctrine. The leading representative of this school, Eduard Bernstein (1850–1932), in *Die Voraussetzungen des Sozialismus und die Aufgaben der Sozialdemokratie* (Stuttgart 1899, 3rd ed., 1921; English ed. *Evolutionary Socialism: A Critique and Affirmation,* London 1909), criticized several of Marx's principal standpoints (notably the surplus value, concentration and catastrophe theories) and urged development of the socialist movement by means of cooperatives, workers' associations and participation in parliamentary activity (e.g. for the purposes of social legislation).

In the Western European countries, opportunities for improving the lot of the workers were ample enough, by virtue of the existence of a parliamentary system and rapid economic progress, to induce most socialist leaders to adopt reformism.

In the United Kingdom, the need for gradual reforms was advocated by the members of the Fabian Society – Sidney Webb, later Baron Passfield (1859–1947), and his wife Beatrice (1858–1943), Bernard Shaw (1856–1950) and H. G. Wells (1866–1946); their counterparts in France and Belgium were Jean Jaurès (1859–1914) and Emile Vandervelde (1866–1938) respectively. In *Le Socialisme contre l'état* (1918), E. Vandervelde emphasized the necessity for training workers within socialist organizations so that they could later on assume control of the state and enterprises. To this end he also called for decentralization of government authority and development of a syndical, mutualistic, cooperative and cultural campaign.

Between the two world wars, attention was devoted, partly as a result of the socialist parties' being concerned in the government of some western countries, to the operation of a planned economy, the nationalization of the key industries and the application of social-security systems. The planned economy was championed as early as the thirties by a Belgian, Hendrik de Man (1885–1953), who, however, became better known for his psychological and sociological theory of socialism (*Au delà du marxisme,* 1927).

The liberal authors' criticisms of planning and collectivism have frequently been refuted. Socialism does not necessarily involve more state intervention and public enterprises. Personal initiative is not stifled in a socialist society, for there too are to be found many incentives, such as wage differentials. The notion that socialism endangers democratic freedom arises out of what has become a classic and sometimes deliberate confusion between socialism and the forms of government observed in the USSR. In the United States in particular the term 'socialism' is mostly used to denote communism. The confusion is heightened, incidentally, by the communist countries' habit of referring to themselves as the 'socialist camp'.

If collectivist measures are no longer considered an integral part of socialism, the dividing line between the latter and progressive neo-liberalism becomes, at least in theory, somewhat blurred. Thus the 'Frankfurt Declaration' (1951) issued by the Socialist International included the following passage. 'Socialism is an international movement which does not demand a rigid uniformity of approach . . . but socialists all strive for the same goal – a system of social justice, better living, freedom and world peace.' In this connection it is often pointed out that changes in communist, centrally-planned economies and the western capitalist market economies tend to reduce the differences between them.

7 The Christian movements

a. Catholicism

1. The leading advocate of paternalism was Frédéric Le Play (1806–82), who defended the small family enterprise in which the employer was virtually a father to his employees. Social legislation should restrain excessive concentration and its accompanying abuses.

2. Among the leading proponents of corporatism were Albert de Mun (1841–1914), René de la Tour du Pin (1834–1924) and Mgr. Wilhelm Emmanuel von Ketteler (1811–77) who considered the corporative organization of the Middle Ages an ideal to be aimed at. A similar standpoint was adopted by Heinrich Pesch, SJ (1854–1926), who was long regarded as the founder of Catholic economics; he was, however, against any corporatism imposed by the state such as that subsequently introduced in Germany and Italy. Here the prime mover was Othmar Spann (1878–1950), who asserted that a state-directed corporative organization must ensure that the value of goods was not fixed by fortuitous supply-and-demand conditions.

3. The first Christian democratic action was set on foot by Félicité Robert de Lamennais (1782–1854), who in 1830, together with Jean

Baptiste Lacordaire (1802–61) and Charles de Montalembert (1810–70), founded the review *L'Avenir*. After his – relatively moderate – views had been rejected by the pope (1832), he adopted a more revolutionary attitude. Also condemned by the Church was the *Le Sillon* movement, set up by Marc Sangnier (1873–1950), whose aim was to limit private ownership.

4. The Church's directives concerning social problems were embodied in the encyclicals *Rerum novarum* (15 May 1891), *Quadragesimo anno* (15 May 1931) and *Mater et magistra* (15 May 1961). In the first of these, Pope Leo XIII set out the duty of the Church, the State, the employer and the worker. Forty years later, Pius XI assessed the extent to which each of these had fulfilled his tasks, and found the employers in particular to be wanting in this respect. At the same time, the necessity for Christian love of one's neighbour was stressed. In 1961, John XXIII upheld the standpoint that means of production must be privately owned but admitted that in certain circumstances (excessively dominant positions) it is better to have them in the hands of the government; in addition, emphasis was laid on the useful function of cooperation in production.

b. Protestantism

Social protestantism arose in England about 1850 with the foundation of a society for promoting workers' organizations, under the impulse of two Anglican clergymen, Frederick Maurice and Charles Kingsley. This group of 'Christian socialists' (so called after their review *The Christian Socialist*), succeeded, mainly through legislative channels, in securing benefits for the workers. In the United States, the first association of 'Christian socialists' was established in 1889.

Appraisal

All these were in fact social rather than economic movements, aimed at a reconciliation between the various groups in society, not so much through the abolition of property as through the elimination of free market conditions. In most cases they linked up closely with the traditionalist, romantic tendencies.

8 The Austrian school and the Lausanne school

a. The Austrian school

The purely descriptive character of the historical school's work and the many weaknesses in the classical doctrine, as demonstrated by the socialist writers and in particular by Marx, created the need for an overhaul of economic theory.

In the van of this movement was Carl Menger (1840–1921), an Austrian. By contrast with the classicists, who regarded supply as the chief aspect of the theory of value, he laid the main stress on demand – human wants – and the use value, which found expression in his marginal utility theory of value (*Grundsätze der Volkswirtschaftslehre*, 1871; English trans. *Problems of Economics: First General Part*, Glencoe, Ill. 1950).

This theory was almost simultaneously expounded by William Stanley Jevons (1835–82), in his *Theory of Political Economy* (1871), and by Léon Walras (1834–1910), in his *Eléments d'économie politique pure* (1874; a second part being published in 1877; English trans. *Elements of Pure Economics: Or, the Theory of Social Wealth*, London 1954); the underlying ideas had already been advanced (but passed unnoticed) by Jules Dupuit (1804–66) in 1844 (*La mesure de l'utilité des travaux publics*) and Hermann Gossen in 1854 (1810–59; *Entwicklung der Gesetze des menschlichen Verkehrs und der daraus fliessenden Regeln für menschliches Handeln*). Johann Heinrich von Thünen (1783–1850) is also a forerunner of the Austrian or psychological school.

The deductive method found a new champion in Carl Menger (his *Untersuchungen über die Methode der Sozialwissenschaften und der politischen Oekonomie insbesondere* was published in 1883; English translation: *Problems of Economics and Sociology*, Urbana 1963); he is also known for his celebrated *Methodenstreit* with G. von Schmoller.

Menger deduced the value of capital goods (goods of the second order) from that of the commodities which could be produced with them. Friedrich von Wieser (1851–1926), who succeeded Menger in 1903 at the University of Vienna, developed this theory further. Another prominent representative of the Austrian school, Eugen von Böhm-Bawerk (1851–1914), formulated a theory of interest based on the fact that satisfaction of current wants was rated higher than that of future wants.

In the United States, the marginal utility theory of value was improved (the value of the factors of production is determined by their marginal productivity) and propagated by John Bates Clark (1847–1938).

APPENDIX

b. The Lausanne school

Léon Walras is known mainly for his studies of general economic equilibrium and for the way in which he tackles this problem, namely with mathematical aids. He was influenced by his father, Auguste Walras (1801–66), and Augustin Cournot (1801–77), who had already applied mathematics to economic problems before him. (J. von Thünen was also an adherent of the mathematical method.) Whereas Cournot mainly analysed monopolistic and oligopolistic price setting, Walras concentrated on the analysis of competitive pricing.

From 1870 to 1892 Walras held the chair of economics at the University of Lausanne. He was succeeded by one of his pupils, Vilfredo Pareto (1848–1923), who developed Walras's work, notably as regards general equilibrium. On the lines of the British economist Francis Edgeworth (1845–1926), he utilized indifference curves. He formulated what is known as the Pareto theorem (Chapter 13.1). Through Vilfredo Pareto's efforts, Lausanne became the centre of a 'school'. Its influence, however, remained confined mostly to Italy (Maffeo Pantaleoni, 1857–1924; Enrico Barone, 1859–1924).

Actually, there was no antithesis between the Austrian school and the Lausanne school, the difference consisting rather in the method employed.

Appraisal

The Austrian school gave economics a more modern aspect. Marginalism was the keynote of the later theories. The Lausanne school's mathematical method was later generally adopted. Econometric research thus acquired considerable importance. The impetus here was given by Ragnar Frisch (b.1895) and Jan Tinbergen (b.1903). The theory of general equilibrium also continued to be a focus of many studies, notably those by John R. Hicks (b.1904) and Paul A. Samuelson (b.1915).

9 Neoclassicism and the Swedish school

a. Neoclassicism

Alfred Marshall (1842–1924), Professor at the University of Cambridge, achieved a synthesis between the tenets of the classical and the psychological schools in his well-known *Principles of Economics* (1890). He contributed a great deal to the amplification of the instruments of economic analysis, developing the concepts of 'elasticity'

483

and 'external and internal economies', as well as underlining the distinction between the short and the long term.

Marshall is considered the founder of the neoclassical school, which dominated economic thinking up to 1936 (the date of Keynes's *General Theory*). Among his students was Arthur Pigou (1877–1959), who succeeded him at Cambridge. Sir Dennis Robertson (1890–1963) continued the tradition (Pigou's academic mantle falling upon him). Other neoclassical authors include: Frank William Taussig (1859–1940), Irving Fisher (1867–1947) and Austrian-born Gottfried (von) Haberler (b.1900).

b. The Swedish school
Knut Wicksell (1851–1926) performed the same work in Sweden as Marshall in Britain. He succeeded in presenting the Austrian school's doctrine mathematically and in integrating the theories on money and general equilibrium. It was he who brought the 'Swedish school' into being. His chief follower was Erik Lindahl (1891–1960), who, like Erik Lundberg (b.1895) and Gunnar Myrdal (b.1893), conducted dynamic analyses.

Gustav Cassel (1886–1944) linked up with Walras and is known for his purchasing-power-parity theory. His pupil Bertil Ohlin (b.1899) did pioneering work on the theory of international trade.

Appraisal
The neoclassical school mainly studied price and income determination from a microeconomic standpoint, with the result that no attention was paid to the study of cyclical fluctuations. In this field, the Swedish school achieved progress. Thus for a long time cyclical theory developed separately (the leading personalities here being Clément Juglar (1819–1905), Albert Aftalion (1874–1956) and Jean Lescure (1882–1947) in France and Wesley C. Mitchell (1874–1948) in the USA.)

10 Neoliberalism

The centrally planned economy and socialism were fiercely attacked by Ludwig von Mises (b.1881; *Bureaucracy*, 1944; *Human Action*, 1949), Friedrich August von Hayek (b.1899; *The Road to Serfdom*, 1944) and Louis Baudin (1887–1964; *L'aube d'un nouveau libéralisme*, 1953). In von Mises's view, it is impossible, if prices cannot develop freely, to adapt production to actual wants. Hayek is also opposed to any intervention in the field of prices because government measures clog the price mechanism to such an extent that further state intervention becomes necessary in order to restore the balance between quantities supplied and quantities demanded.

More moderate personalities are Walter Eucken (1891–1950), Walter Lippmann (b.1889; *The Good Society*, 1937) and Wilhelm Röpke (1899–1966; *Civitas humana*, 1944; *Internationale Ordnung*, 1945 and *Jenseits von Angebot und Nachfrage*, 1958). All these authors aim at the institution of a system of ordered competition (*Ordo-Liberalismus* in Germany) that would be largely in line with the classical authors' concept. Thus W. Röpke makes a distinction between appropriate and inappropriate forms of state intervention. Appropriate measures (e.g. antitrust laws) assist the operation of a free market economy, inappropriate measures disrupt it.

A well-known centre of liberal economics is the University of Chicago (among whose notables is Milton Friedman, b.1912).

Appraisal

Appraisal of neoliberalism is difficult because one finds not only extreme positions but also standpoints which do not differ a great deal from those of the moderate socialists. While a few authors disapprove of any kind of state intervention, most neoliberals accept a certain degree of social interventionism and a measure of social justice. In many cases, however, efforts are directed not so much to adjusting theory to facts as to bringing reality (by government measures) into line with liberal doctrine (cf. W. Röpke's appropriate measures).

11 Institutionalism

Institutionalism is an essentially American school. Its father was Thorstein Veblen (1857–1929), who did not himself employ the term 'institutionalism', but pointed out that 'institutions' or 'settled habits of thought common to the generality of men', notably 'usage, customs, canons of conduct, principles of right and propriety' (i.e. not profit-seeking alone) determine economic activity. Economic systems change with time; whereas technology constantly forges ahead, society usually lags behind in adjusting to technological progress. There is a dichotomy between 'industry' (technology) and 'business' (finance). The conflict of interests inevitably leads to a socialist or fascist society, depending on whether it is industry or business which gains the upper hand.

T. Veblen's followers – John R. C. Commons (1862–1945), Wesley C. Mitchell (1874–1948) and John M. Clark (b.1884), the son of John B. Clark – nevertheless took the view that in an improved form of capitalism cooperation between the various classes was possible.

Mitchell collected a great deal of data for studying the business cycle, and John M. Clark was quick to demonstrate that the market mechanism was no longer functioning satisfactorily and the American economy was being controlled by a small number of large-scale concerns. Prominent among the non-American institutionalists was an Englishman, John A. Hobson (1858–1940), who in many spheres was ahead of his time.

After the Second World War, the institutionalists drew attention to the fact that a minimum of indicative planning was necessary in the United States. In contrast with T. Veblen, they proceeded along operational lines. Among them are included Clarence E. Ayres (b.1891), who emphasized afresh that it was not the market that was responsible for the allocation of the factors of production, but the organizational structure of society, Gardiner C. Means (b.1896), Gerhard Colm (b.1897), Allan G. Gruchy (b.1906) and Ben B. Seligman (b.1912). John Kenneth Galbraith (b.1908) may also be classed as an institutionalist.

Appraisal
Institutionalism sets out to ascertain how the economy works in practice, showing that economic activity cannot be accounted for by economic factors alone. This, indeed, is why its influence has remained limited: most economists view economic activity quite apart from other activities of a social character. In the United States, moreover, it is sufficient to advocate a certain degree of planning to arouse antipathy in some quarters *ipso facto*.

12 J. M. Keynes

The General Theory of Employment, Interest and Money (1936), by J. M. Keynes (1883–1946, from 1942 Lord Keynes of Tilton) brought about an important change in economic theory in several areas. Although no model of clarity – P. A. Samuelson calls it 'a badly written book, poorly organized; . . . arrogant, bad-tempered, polemical, and not overly-generous in its acknowledgements' – it immediaately had a marked influence. Samuelson, indeed, concludes the passage in question with the words: 'in short, it is the work of a genius'.

Keynes does not agree with Pigou that unemployment can be cushioned by reducing wages. He underlines the possible drawbacks of excessive saving. This was a point that had hitherto been overlooked. It had been held that interest would invariably restore the balance between saving and investment; this may, however, take some time. Such long-term reasoning was not accepted by Keynes ('in the long run we are all dead'); recessions and depressions have to be avoided.

Keynes stressed the danger of stagnation in the capitalist countries. He saw two ways of obviating such a situation – increasing consumption by better income distribution, and expanding public works.

A rise in income – through the creation of money or the granting of credit for instance – has varying repercussions on the national income and on the level of prices, depending on the degree of employment. The classical and neo-classical authors (Keynes lumps them together as 'classical') had not made this distinction and regarded the purchasing power of money as being determined by the quantity of money and the velocity of circulation.

Appraisal
Numerous ideas, closely related to the *General Theory*, had been developed earlier, notably by Richard F. Kahn (b.1905) on the multiplier and Sir Dennis Robertson and K. Wicksell concerning the relation between saving and investment. But Keynes built up a remarkable synthesis from which economic theory acquired its present-day form. As a result of the discussion provoked by the *General Theory*, more importance is now attached to macroeconomics, and economic statistics is flourishing.

Keynes also left his influence on political thought. Although not a socialist himself, he had a considerable influence on the socialist philosophy.

13 J. A. Schumpeter

Joseph Alois Schumpeter (1883–1950) deserves a place of his own, not only because he cannot be classed in any particular school, but also because of his penetrative thinking and the high level of his published works. He is accorded special mention in this chapter on economic doctrines by virtue of his *History of Economic Analysis.*

Like other well-known North American economists, he is of Austrian origin. From 1932 he was a professor at Harvard University. As far back as 1911 (*Theorie der wirtschaftlichen Entwicklung:'Eine Untersuchung über Unternehmergewinn, Kapital, Kredit, Zins und den Kunjunkturzyklus*; English translation: *The Theory of Economic Development: An Inquiry into Profits, Capital, Credit, Interest and the Business Cycle,* Cambridge, Mass. 1934), he made a noteworthy attempt to integrate business-cycle theory in to the general theory of economic development. This work evolved into his *Business Cycles* (1939), which deals predominantly with the role of the innovator. According to Schumpeter, cyclical fluctuations arise through the irregularity with which innovations occur and the adjustments which they entail. Depressions are an inevitable consequence of progress.

In 1942, his much-discussed *Capitalism, Socialism and Democracy* was published. He was unable to complete his most important work, the above-mentioned *History of Economic Analysis;* it was issued in 1954, after being edited by his wife, and is an excellent reference work.

Appraisal

Schumpeter did not make the same impact as Keynes. He did not establish any school. (His business cycle theory is, indeed, open to criticism.) He shows evidence of wide reading and extensive culture. Schumpeter employs both the theoretical and the historical approach, although preferring the latter.

At a time when technical virtuosity in economics carries too much weight and has engendered many writings bearing little relation to reality, Schumpeter's publications remind us that a good economist must view economics in a broad setting and have a working knowledge of other sciences, such as history and sociology.

14 Bibliography

In the compass of the present work, it may suffice to quote only those books which deal with the general pattern of economic thought.

Good introductory works are: E. Roll, *A History of Economic Thought* (4th ed., London 1949) is not so complete in respect of continental authors; E. Whittaker, *Schools and Streams of Economic Thought* (Chicago 1960); and, on the most recent schools, B. B. Seligman, *Main Currents in Modern Economics: Economic Thought since 1870* (New York 1962).

Also to be recommended C. Gide and C. Rist, *Histoire des doctrines économiques depuis les physiocrates jusqu'à nos jours* (7th ed., Paris 1947); English translation: (*History of Economic Doctrines*, London 1915), and R. Gonnard, *Histoire des doctrines économiques* (5th ed., Paris 1947): although both are out of date as regards the latest tendencies.

A thorough-going analysis is provided by J. A. Schumpeter, *History of Economic Analysis* (ed. E. B. Schumpeter, New York 1954); (see Section 13).

O. Spann, *Die Haupttheorien der Volkswirtschaftslehre auf lehrgeschichtlicher Grundlage* (24th edn., Leipzig 1936); English translation: (*Types of Economic Theory,* London 1930), can usefully be consulted for the German authors – 19th century in particular.

Despite the existence of a prolific literature, there is a lack of good works dealing succinctly with all aspects of socialism. With this reservation, see B. P. Beckwith, *The Economic Theory of a Socialist Economy* (Stanford, 1949); G. D. H. Cole, *Socialist Economics* (London 1950) is a simple introduction. P. M. Sweezy, *Socialism* (New York 1949), expounds a neo-communist standpoint. See also A. P. Lerner, *The Economics of Control* (New York 1944); P. J. D. Wiles, *The Political Economy of Communism* (Oxford 1964): – written from a non-communist angle (which does not deal with agriculture, banking, income distribution or international trade).

The quoted words of P. A. Samuelson are taken from his 'Lord Keynes and the "General Theory",' *Em*, July 1946.

Index of Authors

492

495

Index of Subjects

512